Social Security in a Developing World Context

Editors

Vijaya Kumar, S.

Council for Social Development, Hyderabad, India

Scott Fritzen,

National University of Singapore, Singapore

SERIALS PUBLICATIONS
New Delhi

First Published–2004

ISBN : 81-86771-49-2

Published by:

Head Office : **SERIALS PUBLICATIONS**
4, B.S.S. Hall, Khyber Pass Market,
Civil Lines, Delhi–110 054 (India)
Phone: 91-11-23245225
Fax: 91-11-23272135
E-mail: serials@satyam.net.in

Branch Office : 4830/24, Prahlad Street, Ansari Road,
Darya Ganj, New Delhi-110002 (India)

Printed at : R. K. Offset Process, Naveen Shahdara,

Printed In India

Contents

Acknowledgements

We greatly acknowledge the encouragement given by Prof. Mukul Asher, Social Policy, National University of Singapore; Mr. R.K.A. Subrahmanya, Secretary General of Social Security Association of India, Dr. K.S. Bhat, Regional Director of Council for Social Development, Hyderabad; Dr. S. Irudaya Rajan, Centre for Development Studies, Trivandrum. Mr. C.S. Reddy, Chief-Executive of CEASE Child Labour (ILO-IPEC) and Mr. B.K.M. Naidu, Focal Point, NHRD-India.

Our contributors took the pains to take time out of their busy schedule to write papers and have evinced considerable interest to bring this work. We owe a deep sense of gratitude to each one of them individually and all of them collectively.

We acknowledge the facilities offered by the Council for Social Development, Hyderabad where most of the editorial work has been carried out.

This task would not have succeeded without the sincere support of Mr. S.K. Jha, Managing Director of Serials Publications, New Delhi. We are thankful to him.

Vijaya Kumar S.
Scott Fritzen
Editors

List of Contributors

1. Mukul Asher, Professor in Public Policy Programme, National University of Singapore, SINGAPORE.
2. David Newman, Professor in Public Policy Programme, National University of Singapore, SINGAPORE.
3. Yansui Yang, Professor in Social Security Institute, Tsinghua University, Beijing, CHINA.
4. Wasan Karunarathne, Dept. of Economics, National University of Singapore, SINGAPORE
5. R.K.A. Subrahmanya, Secretary General, Social Security Association of India Bangalorem INDIA.
6. Scott Fritzen, Assistant Professor, Public Policy Programme, National University of Singapore, SINGAPORE.
7. Shalendra D. Sharma, Associate Professor of Political Economy, University of San Francisco, CA, USA.
8. S. Vijaya Kumar, Fellow, Council for Social Development, Hyderabad, INDIA.
9. Phoebe S. Liebig, Associate Professor of Gerontology and Public Administration University of Southern California, Los Angeles, USA.
10. M. Mahadeva, Associate Professor, Institute for Social and Economic Change, Nagarbhavi, Bangalore, INDIA.

11. M. Chakraborty, Faculty Member, National Informatics Centre Training Unit, Lal Bahadur Sastri National Academy of Administration, Mussoori, INDIA.
12. B. Meena Rao, Associate Professor, Dept. of Politics and Public Administration, Andhra University, Visakhapatnam, INDIA.
13. S. Uma Devi, Associate Professor, Centre for Criminal Justice, Andhra University, Visakhapatnam, INDIA.
14. R. M. Sarkar, Editor Man in India, Kolkata, INDIA.
15. G.C. Pande, Professor of Emeritus, Dept. of Economics, Kumaun University, Nainital, INDIA.
16. D.C. Pandey, Reader, Dept. of Geography, Kumaun University, Nainital, INDIA.
17. K.N. Selvaraj, Faculty Member, Dept. of Agricultural Economics, Centre for Agricultural and Rural Development Studies, Tamilnadu Agricultural University, Coimbatore, INDIA.

INTRODUCTION

Facing Constraints, Seizing Opportunities: Strengthening Social Security in Developing Countries

Scott Fritzen & Vijaya Kumar, S

"A decent provision for the poor is the true test of civilization"
(—Samuel Johnson 1770)

POVERTY AND INSECURITY IN A DEVELOPING COUNTRY CONTEXT

It has long been recognized that poverty is multidimensional phenomenon, encompassing not only lack of income but vulnerability and powerlessness as well (Chambers 1983). It is only more recently, however, that major multilateral banks have emphasized such interrelationships in their flagship publications. Indicative of this shift was the publication of the World Bank's world Development Report 2000-2001, *Attacking Poverty* (World Bank 2000). This report defined poverty in terms of limited economic opportunities (the mainstream approach), social and political disempowerment (related to the governance agenda that had emerged in the Bank over the 1990s - see Miller-Adams 1999), and insecurity. Importantly, it did so without prioritizing analytically any one of these aspects, something that

---

Assistant Professor, Public Policy at National University of Singapore.
Fellow, Council for Social Development, Hyderabad.

caused considerable controversy among more mainstream-oriented analysts, including in the popular press (*The Economist* magazine).

At its most basic, the 'insecurity-as-poverty" perspective begins from the recognition that every stage of human life is exposed to numerous risks and hazards. The poor and near-poor are least able to withstand shocks, which often send them tumbling into a vicious cycle of asset depletion and continued vulnerability. Breaking this cycle - strengthening the strategies by which the poor and near poor better attempt to negotiate these multiple shocks-becomes a key anti-poverty intervention.

Whatever the conceptual underpinnings of the poverty-insecurity linkage, there is little doubt that both poverty and insecurity are truly global phenomenon. Massively large numbers of citizens in the developing world live either under or just above internationally comparable poverty lines. While poverty rates that appear to be declining marginally as a percentage of the overall population in many, if not most countries (World Bank, 2001), certain countries particularly hard hit by economic restructuring have suffered from markedly higher poverty rates among their populations.

For many observers, the most dramatic aspect of world poverty is the way it exists against a backdrop of affluence. According to the United Nations, overall consumption of the richest fifth of the world's people is 16 times that of the poorest fifth. Nearly 1.3 billion people live on less than a dollar a day and close to 1 billion cannot meet their basic consumption requirements. The share in global income of the richest fifth of the world's people is 74 times that of the poorest fifth. The world GDP increased from 30 billion to 3 trillion in the past 50 years, but the share of the poor countries fell from 20 per cent to 10 per cent (UNDP 1999).

India has the single largest population of poor people in the world today. The UNDP's India Human Development Report (2000) points out that after 50 years of independence, one out of every three persons in India earns less than a dollar a day (even in purchasing power parity terms). Broaden the definition of poverty and its incidence rises much higher: malnourishment and lack of access to safe drinking water, for instance, affect as many as two-thirds of the population. By the year 2020, the absolute majority of the world's poor will reside in South Asia (Kananaikil, 2003).

Global economic integration, the most recent prescription for speeding up economic development, is creating new threats to human security in both rich and poor countries alike (UNDP 2002). Such 'globalization' has brought affluence to well-positioned countries with a positive policy environment, while others - including many landlocked countries - have struggled to participate in its purported benefits (World Bank 1997, 2002). Even countries that benefit from increased economic growth driven by economic integration face major social challenges in ensuring equitable economic and social outcomes. Economic integration brings both opportunities and dislocations - the "creative destruction" that sculpted touted - will severely test the administrative, fiscal and political capacities of the developing country governance systems. In 'successful' globalization, economic gains from economic integration will outweigh economic costs, and the standard economics text-book assumption is that therefore 'losers' in the process can be compensated. Yet that theoretical possibility will be a cold comfort to those affected negatively in countries in which the requisite institutional and political capacities enabling such redistribution are in short supply.

In short, the picture is one of short - term, often-acute downward fluctuations in living standards superimposed upon longer term, persistent deprivation associated with generally low standards of living (Burgess et al. 1999; World Bank 1986; Dreze and Sen 1989). Against the background of such issues, this book brings together analysis on a wide range of government interventions to improve social security in developing countries, with considerable attention paid to the Indian experience. In the rest of this introductory chapter, we first review types and modalities of state support for social protection. We then consider the existence of a "low income - low social protection" trap (Fritzen 2003), in which developing countries face serious difficulties expanding the coverage of formal social security programs to more than a minority of the population. After introducing each of the chapter contributions to this book, we close with reflections on the interlocking constraints that all attempts to substantially improve the coverage and quality of social protection in developing countries will have to overcome.

THE ROLE OF GOVERNMENT

Ensuring basic security is essential for developmental success, with the reasons for this falling into at least two categories. The first is pragmatic, with a political and economic variant. The long-term political sustainability of economic reforms depends on achieving a social compact: that economic growth is in the best interest of the population; this is, of course, particularly important in democratic contexts such as India, where populist-based political challenges to economic reforms are always possible. The second pragmatic consideration concerns the necessity of a 'human capital' based developmental path if mobility in the international division of labor is to be achieved. Such investments in human capital - with health, nutrition and educational components-will in themselves lessen vulnerability of households as they facilitate a labor-intensive employment generation strategy.

A second category focuses on human rights. Providing basic security for all is the fundamental characteristic of social justice. Basic security as suggested by ILO (2000), requires policies and institutions by which every one has access to health services, a decent level of education and basic needs of their existence, which would enable them to function to the best of their capabilities. According to the Universal Declaration of Human Rights social security is a basic human right and every citizen has right to survival, protection and development.

Who is "vulnerable," and what would such a social safety net entail? There are many ways to delineate vulnerable groups, generally designating those whose ability to participate in social and economic life is compromised to some extent. Social vulnerability might be broadly defined as the inability of an individual, for certain specified reasons, to exploit opportunities for their self-betterment. The term could also designate groups which, without support, would experience hardship going beyond what a "civilized society" would tolerate. In a narrow sense, safety nets can be defined as "those instruments aimed at mitigating possible adverse effects of reform measures on the poor" (Chu and Gupta 1998). This is an important part of the meaning of safety nets in developing countries undergoing economic reforms. More broadly, a crucial policy issue is how lives and livelihoods can be made more secure against adversity and deprivation. Attaining social security for vulnerable populations means in effect "the avoidance of poverty by social means" (Burgess and Stern 1999).

The 'social means' implied above is not restricted to government intervention. Safety nets have fallen into two categories for most developing countries: formal and informal. In the East Asian 'miracle' economies, safety nets were primarily family based; countries relied primarily on localized kinship networks and their own dynamic economic growth to serve in this capacity. Countries such as South Korea, Taiwan and Malaysia did not have extensive formal safety nets in place as their economies began their ascent. The broadest generalization is that as economies develop, they shift gradually to more formal systems (on which more below). As important as traditional safety nets are, assistance from kin and community is often insufficient to cope up with sweeping changes affecting a whole community or, indeed, an entire economy - so-called 'co-variant risk' - nor to more severe shocks to household income. Many have come to expect developing country governments to take on, as a fundamental and obligatory responsibility, the protection of vulnerable sections of the society; yet such governments are often ill equipped for the magnitude of this task, as we explore in the next section.

THE LOW INCOME-LOW FORMAL PROTECTION TRAP

There are two primary types of public-sector interventions designed to strengthen social security. The first is *promoting* the poor out of poverty, by enhancing general living standards and expanding basic human capabilities. Employment generation or education policies are a good example of promotion-oriented strategies.

The primary focus of this book is on the second means: policies that aim directly to reduce the vulnerability of the poor to shocks, i.e. *social protection*. These two aims may involve separate policy instruments, but in the long term, they are mutually reinforcing: "promoting the poor facilitates their protection, by both private and social means, while protecting the poor facilitates their longer-term promotion" (Ravallion, 1995, p. 296). It is thus important to see safety nets as an important part of a pro-poor strategy, not just as a separate measure to compensate the short-term losers in the process of economic reform in order to secure sociopolitical stability.

'Classic' forms of social protection involve social insurance, primarily for pensions and unemployment. Social insurance refers to the financing of benefits by compulsory contributions or pay-roll taxes, and differs from private insurance in that contributions need not fully cover benefits for certain groups - such as the elderly - who are considered too weak to purchase insurance in the marketplace. A further characteristic is that there may be an element of public subsidy; as such, there is an element of redistribution in any social insurance scheme. In theory, social insurance performs a preventive function whereby all present and formerly economically active persons build up entitlements to receive protection in the event of contingencies such as unemployment, sickness, maternity, old-age, invalidity and death.

Table 1 : Broad estimates of workers and the elderly enrolled in any formal social security programs, selected regions and Vietnam

OECD countries	90-100%
Eastern European transition economies	70-80%
Middle-income countries of South America	50-60%
Most of East Asia	Less than 30%
Sub-Saharan Africa and South Asia	Less than 10%

Source: Chu and Gupta, 1998

In developed countries, social security is generally promoted through social insurance public programs. Yet in developing countries, the most outstanding fact regarding social insurance is that coverage is typically limited to a minority of formal-sector workers (see table 1). Since "economic development is the major determinant of coverage rate," (James 1999) formal coverage will rise with income. How long, then, will substantial expansion of such programs take? Most of the countries, which have operating social insurance schemes, are well into the middle-income range. "As of 1998, only China, the Republic of Korea and Mongolia had some form of unemployment benefit scheme among Asian countries. Even in the Republic of Korea, where coverage has been expanded in response to the massive increase in retrenched workers, merely half of al employees are receiving coverage. Elsewhere coverage extends only to a minority of formal sector employees" (Drouin, 1999).

There are two basic reasons for this low coverage. First, it is almost always impossible for fiscal reasons for developing countries to provide universal coverage (one of the few recent attempts to do this - in Bolivia - was abandoned within three years). Second, the costs of enforcing collection from a stable group of workers are only sufficiently low in the formal sector - lowest of all for government employees. Indeed, an ILO review in the wake of the Asian financial crisis failed identifies any reliable mechanisms to extend coverage of social insurance (Drouin 1999).

Shifting to more formal systems is extremely difficult to accomplish for low-income countries, due to competing pressures in the budget (not least from other social sector components, such as on human capital formation), low administrative capacity and political economy constraints - to which we return later in this chapter.

OTHER POLICY OPTIONS FOR PROTECTING THE POOR

Expectations regarding the expansion of formal insurance schemes in developing countries must therefore remain modest in the medium-term. Yet other options for the promotion of social security beyond formal social insurance are available to developing countries. Program effectiveness will depend greatly on specific conditions, and some are more relevant than others to each country's developmental situation. The challenge is to design safety nets that are targeted to those in greatest need, and to do so cost-effectively and sustainably. Below three additional major types of instruments are introduced (Chu and Gupta 1998).

1. *Consumer subsidies:* Governments often subsidize the consumption of specific goods deemed to be important for securing welfare and security. Ideally, to reduce inefficiency, commodities to be subsidized would be those consumed only by the poor, but few goods fit this description. The stylized fact about consumer subsidies is that they should be limited in time and targeted so as to avoid excessive public expenditure.

One of the most widespread applications of consumer subsidies in developing countries lies in food stamps. Food stamps are meant to directly improve food security of the extreme poor, for whom expenditure on food constitutes typically constitutes over half of total expenditure. Three types of food-related subsidies programs are common: 1) A national food subsidy operates on the principle of subsidizing (small-scale) producers and consumers of basic commodities; such systems have typically been found to be very costly and to provide extremely limited benefits to the poor. (2) Rations with a public distribution system are typically more limited (a more general one failed in the former Soviet Union), but can be effective in providing, for instance, milk and preventive health care through schools. (3) Quantity food stamps, in which selected beneficiaries (which might vary regionally) are provided stamps which can be redeemed at local traders for basic consumption staples (rice etc.); the retailers then can be reimbursed in-kind (plus a handling charge), or in cash by the state.

A comparison of the recent experiences of the Philippines and Jamaica in attempting to put a floor under the consumption of food staples for the poor is revealing. The Philippine National Food Authority provides, from Government revenues, a subsidy for producing rice and corn at higher-than-market prices, and subsides to consumers by selling rice at lower than market price. In part because of its failure to target, a World bank study (Subbaro and Ahmed 1996) found the subsidy boosted the poor's total income by less than .8%, and thus that "eliminating this consumer subsidy will have a negligible effect on the poor's food consumption and nutrition, and entail considerable savings from government."

Jamaica serves as a contrast. It introduced its Food Stamp Program (FSP) in 1984 in order to mitigate the adverse short-run impacts of macro-economic stabilization measures. It was targeted to two main categories of people who were considered at nutritional risk: *i)* pregnant and lactating women and children under 5 years of age; and *ii)* the poor, elderly and handicapped. A different World Bank review (Ezemunari and Subbaro 1998) concluded that "in the absence of the FSP, the poverty gap in Jamaica would have been much higher" in its economic programs, and contributed directly towards a reduction in poverty, at acceptable overall cost. Thus a targeted approach proved more effective in this case. Clearly, the design of particular food stamp programs will have a profound impact on their effectiveness.

2. *Direct transfers to uninsured vulnerable social groups:* Perhaps the bulk of developing country social protection budgets falls into this category. International experience suggests that the extent to which such transfers actually assist in protecting the poor depends on four variables: *1)* administrative capacity; *2)* practical constraints and transaction costs; *3)* political will for means testing; and *4)* overall fiscal outlays. Delivery mechanisms can take place through government, or NGO's and other community groups. Mechanisms for means testing vary considerably: from computerized models which select recipient villages of households based on a fixed formula computing need; self-selection mechanisms (waiting in lines, or providing only in-kind transfers, so that in either case only those in substantial specific need will apply); to village elders identifying recipients (James 1999).

3. *Targeted employment creation on public works:* If formal mechanisms for unemployment insurance are unlikely to substantially assist the very poorest, particularly in rural areas, this current category offers a practical alternative. International experience with such programs highlights the need to make public works labor-intensive, flexibly organized and to keep pay low so that only the needy participate (i.e. so that the schemes are "self-targeting") (ILO 1999; Chu and Gupta 1998).

PROMOTING THE POOR: LINKAGES TO A GROWTH WITH EQUITY AGENDA

While the focus in this book is on *protecting* the poor, it is important to recognize connections between social protection and broader choices of economic strategy. A "growth with equity" agenda (Watkins 1997) for achieving positive social outcomes has been developed largely based on a particular reading of the experience of East Asian countries. It is widely known that successful East Asian economies such as South Korea and Taiwan have been able to combine comprehensive economic transformation with relative social equity, while many Latin American countries -Brazil and Mexico are the classic examples - have made far less social progress, despite substantial economic growth. Several studies (Watkins 1997; World Bank 1993) suggest the success of the "tigers" in this regard rests on three important factors: *i)* higher levels of *initial* equality and equal distribution of assets (in part due to major socioeconomic traumas, such as World War II, the Korean War etc.); *ii)* egalitarian, high-quality educational systems; and *iii)* a labor-intensive growth strategy which contributed to employment creation and growth in real wages. These three factors worked to Latin America's detriment. It has been plagued by continued economic and social inequalities which actually predate its period of rapid industrialization. Its income distribution has been skewed by an educational system and social expenditure biased heavily against basic services (e.g. favoring university education). And its import substitution industrial strategy was decidedly less successful in creating flexible labor markets with low unemployment and growing wages.

Four specific linkages between social protection and economic strategy might be identified. The first is to a targeted framework for *regional fiscal transfers* to reduce the interregional disparities within countries and to promote regional development. This linkage stems from recognition of the strong association between physical isolations and vulnerability, particularly where lack of access to markets acts prevents diversification of livelihood strategies. Policies targeted on regional development themselves function as a kind of safety net.

A second linkage is to basic social services. An important rationale for expanding coverage of basic services is to replace 'negative' coping mechanisms households are forced to adopt when facing sudden livelihood shocks-such as withdrawing children from school or not getting treated for illness-with formal protection that does not force them to draw down their precious human and financial capital. Health and basic education can be among the most neglected issues in the social security policies of many developing countries (Caldwell 1986).

Third, governance capacities vitally influence the attainment of social protection. One example of a governance capacity that in many contexts needs to be strengthened is the promotion of civil society's contribution to social security. Informal transfers and mutual assistance are far more important coping mechanisms than access to formal assistance in many countries. Clearing the way for a more proactive contribution of civil society to welfare provision may be one of the most effective means available to cash-strapped developing country governments to strengthen household resilience to shocks.

A final linkage between social protection and economic policy is to sustainable poverty reduction. Whether and to what extent poverty reduction is sustainable in a country is an important question, particularly given that so many households even in 'successful' poverty reducing countries such as China and Vietnam tend to be precariously balanced just above the poverty line. While economic growth is not the *only* answer by which such gains may be consolidated, it is arguably a *necessary* one.

The last point deserves some elaboration. The relationships between growth, inequality and poverty reduction have generated an enormous literature over the years (Srinivasan [2001] and Bruno and others [1997] provide an overview). While interpretive emphasis may differ, a number of analysts and institutions previously holding quite contrary positions have in recent years embraced certain key general propositions, including the following (Fritzen 2002):

Table 2 : Relationship between growth and poverty reduction for selected countries

	Poverty reduction : Low or negative	High
High	Botswana (1980-92) Brazil (1965-80) Mexico (1965-92)	Korea, Rep, Of (1965-92) Malaysia (1965-92) Mauritius (1965-92) Indonesia (1978-84) Taiwan (1950-1980) Vietnam (1993-1998)
Low	Costa Rica (1980-92) Sri Lanka (1965-92) Zimbabwe (1965-92) Sub-Saharan Africa (1965-92) Bangladesh (1965-92) India (1965-92) Vietnam (1970-80s)	possibl Cuba (1960-70) no others?

Source: Taylor and others, 1997, p. 443

1. *Necessary relationship between growth and poverty reduction:* Even typical critics of orthodox development theory increasingly acknowledge the critical role of growth in reducing poverty sustainably, particularly in very low-income countries. In the absence of growth, few government interventions can sustainably reduce poverty, and radical measures to affect income distribution generate huge inefficiencies and lack political feasibility (see Table 2).

2. *Need for high-quality' growth to maximize poverty reduction:* While the impact of growth on poverty reduction is almost always positive, the speed and depth of the impact varies significantly. A range of policy measures is available to governments to improve the impact of any given level of economic growth on poverty reduction.

3. *No necessary relationship between growths with inequality:* Contrary to earlier theories going back to Kuznets (1959), several studies (reviewed by Srinivasan, 2001) suggest that there is no *necessary* connection between rapid growth and inequality generation. Country experience varies dramatically; in a study of 44 countries over the period 1981-92, inequality was found to slightly rise with greater rates of economic growth in about half of the countries, and in half it actually fell (Bruno and others, 1997). One must therefore look at the specific propelling forces behind the growth-inequality relationship in any given case.

OVERVIEW OF THE CHAPTERS

We now introduce the rich case study material found throughout the rest of this book. **Mukul Asher & David Newman** discuss China's attempt as a transition economy to introduce market mechanisms while having to deal with a variety of other problems such as social security reform, a rapidly ageing population, high unemployment and the ever-present prospect of industrial-based social unrest. Social security reform has been viewed as central to the reform effort since the existing, but largely insolvent, enterprise based pension system frustrates the country's efforts to rationalize its state owned enterprises. While China has adopted the World Bank's "three pillar model" of social pool, individual accounts, and supplementary pensions, the challenge for China is to implement this system by decentralizing control over social security policy by implementing a national scheme to replace the existing decentralized enterprise system. To do this, China needs to develop a professional capability able to assess alternatives and design a sustainable pension system. Their chapter reviews China's current pension scheme, its efforts to implement the three-pillar model, and assesses the challenges China will face going forward.

Yansui Yang focusses on how China has brought radical reform to the social security systems in order to give better quality of life to its population. Considering the huge agrarian population in countryside, importance has been to this sector in social security policy. This chapter highlights different social security programs for self-employed in cities, working group and for those in countryside.

Waszana Karunarathne provides an assessment of the formal social security arrangements in Sri Lanka. Mainly it focuses on analyzing the existing formal social security arrangements in the country, as well as future reform directions. Social welfare provision in Sri Lanka goes back to the earliest days of Sri Lanka as a British colony. Current social legislation, which is still based on the original form of British policies, comprises Defined Contributory (DC) and Defined Benefit (DB) plans. Public sector social security arrangements comprise Public Sector Pension Scheme (PSPS), Public Sector Provident Fund (PSPF), and newly introduced Contributory Pension Fund (CPF). The private sector social security schemes consist of three major schemes: Employees' Provident Fund (EPF), Employees' Trust Fund (ETF) and the Approved Private Provident Funds (APPFs). Employees in the unorganized sector are also covered by few voluntary schemes, but the size and the coverage of them are limited.

A number of economic as well as social factors including population and individual ageing has put a considerable pressure on the current arrangements. Therefore, the provision of social security arrangements has become an acute problem in Sri Lanka. As a result, there is an urgent need for reforms towards a sustainable system. It is in the above context that this paper analyses the current arrangement with a view suggesting possible reforms. Social safety nets are considered as the best sources to address the social security problems of unemployed and this system is prevalent in industrialized countries says Subrahmanya. Some of the developing countries are also having unemployment insurance schemes; however, here is no such system in India where the problems exists. This paper examines the feasibility and possibility of introducing such schemes in India.

Scott Fritzen returns to the low income - low formal protection noted earlier in this introduction, exploring it through the case of Vietnam. Despite over a decade of rapid economic growth and poverty reduction, approximately 40% of Vietnam's population is below or just above the poverty line and is highly vulnerable to community - wide and household - specific shocks. Yet Vietnam's social protection budget has largely financed formal entitlement programs that are failing to deliver substantial reductions in vulnerability for this broad spectrum of the rural population. His chapter outlines the state of social protection in Vietnam and presents an agenda for improving effective coverage rates. It also asseses the political and bureaucratic feasibility of social protection reforms in other developing countries.

While discussing the social security schemes for informal workers, especially in Indian context, it is suggested that welfare funds are the best alternative model for social security schemes. At present in India there are six welfare funds operated by the Central Government and several State Governments are having their own welfare funds. Kerala State, for example, has as many as 16 different categories of welfare funds. Among the Central Government operated welfare fund Beedi workers welfare fund is having wider network but it has its own constraints in terms of coverage and benefits. **Vijaya Kumar** in his paper discusses the existing structure of Beedi workers welfare fund and its shortfalls and finally suggests a model in which an effective coverage with need based benefits could be possible.

Shalendra D. Sharma argues that although, poverty reduction remains India's most compelling challenge, there is broad consensus that poverty levels have fallen in the past decade. The official estimates, based on data in the quinquennial 50th (1993-94) and 55th (1999-2000) National Sample Round (NSS) round, claim that poverty rates fell from 36% of the population in 1993/1994 to 26% by the end of the 2000. However, there is little agreement as to the magnitude or the reasons for the decline. Critics argue that the methodology used to calculate the monthly per capita total consumer expenditure or the consumption levels in the 55th round are not comparable and therefore provide misleading data on poverty levels. This paper shows that although the "poverty debate" in India is not new, the current debate has tremendous implications for policy. Since data and policy are closely linked, only when there is general agreement on the questions of measurement, data, and methodology can policy makers carefully think about the kinds of information needed to better monitor and alleviate human suffering and poverty.

Phoebe S. Liebig in her article examines economic security in old age for vulnerable populations (eg. women, rural workers, lower class / caste), with an emphasis on the structure of retirement systems and the life course perspective. Cumulative advantage or disadvantage over the lifespan is a key issue; the gap between the privileged and the disadvantaged grows in old age. Economic security in old age centers on providing basic protections against income losses in retirement, assuring the stability of retirement income systems, and maintaining a fair and acceptable balance of costs and benefits across many subgroups of the elderly. Population aging and economic development affect the structure of retirement income systems in both industrialized and developing nations.

In a discussion of these systems, examples are drawn from developed countries in the West, primarily the United States, and developing nations in Asia, especially China and India. All are facing the challenge of providing an adequate standard of living for elders. Concerns about provident funds, self-funded systems and social insurance are raised for their impact on the economic security of vulnerable populations. In keeping with the life course perspective and to avoid substantial numbers of poor older women, retired agricultural and other very low-income workers in the future, particular attention must be paid to employment - care giving patterns of women and to the need for social insurance programs (eg. disability, unemployment) that enable younger persons to avoid poverty.

M. Mahadeva points out that Employs State Insurance Scheme being one of the self-sustaining social security measures in India, the joint administration of the same has limited the success. ESI authorities have successfully mobilized the resources in the form of contributions both by the employers and employees of factories / establishment. Infrastructure created under the program (ESI hospitals, dispensaries, beds in other hospitals) needs also to fulfill the intended objectives of the scheme. However, state governments as administrative partners have failed to deliver the medical services to the satisfaction of ESI employees. Inadequate medicine care / services have given rise to employees' resentment. This chapter examines the performance of ESI and casts light on the growing resentments surrounding its implementation. Despite covering a large number of employers-employees, still over one-tenth of them continue to be deprived of ESI benefits. There are indications that medical inadequacies have led to an under-utilization of medical services, even as a higher scale of contributions has led to revenue surplus. The chapter concludes with some policy options.

Public Distribution system in India is one of the popular social security mechanisms that covers larger sections of the population. **Chakraborty highlights** the objective of the existing Public Distribution System which acquired prominence in India during the second world war. By PDS is meant a system in which the whole or a part is controlled by public authorities on behalf of general public for their well-being. Its social objective of enhancing the developmental and welfare impact of commercial activity. Public distribution is resorted to only in the periods of shortage. The PDS aims to provide fair distribution and self-sufficiency in good grains to the public. This system works as an instrument for efficient management of consumer goods for maintaining stable price conditions.

Of all the social security programs, housing is one of the important schemes. **M. Mahadeva** points out that out of the two principal inputs, finance plays a very crucial role in housing development. Its adequate supply causes housing surplus or deprivation respectively. Therefore if any country is serious about arresting housing poverty or deprivation, substantial flow of funds for the same is an important pre-condition. Under the context of a successful experience in housing, the purpose of Mahadeva's chapter is to draw a few lessons for the Indian situation in which case resource crunch has aggravated the housing problem.

Involving private financial institutions, mortgage loan insurance, rental and ownership subsidies and lower interest and down-payment have not only brought about substantial investment but also increased the housing stock both in the ownership as well as rental segments. Interestingly, financial facilitation and incentives have prompted the market to produce housing surplus. Since the national housing and habitat policy is intend to create a conducive environment to various players in the market to alleviate housing deprivation, the Canadian experience of market-supported housing success could be one direction for the Indian context. The chapter also offers a few policy options for financial facilitation for housing development.

Women's empowerment is another issues that has figured in most social security and social development programs. In this context **Meena Rao and Uma Devi** point out that social development can be achieved only if women got equal share and opportunity to participate in all spheres of development. Considering this, from different quarters of the world gender analysts have focused attention for providing access to facilities and means, and eliminating discrimination on the basis of sex. In the direction of emancipating the women several movements have been taken place in different countries. These authors' contribution is to examine the outputs of such movements and to critically evaluate India's national strategies in this context.

Life is need-oriented. In the proper maintenance of life in relation to any human community there are relevant basic needs that are required to be satisfied properly for the fuller satisfaction of the people. Thus, at the time of taking any effective measure for development in relation to any human community special stress must always be laid on the nature and extent of the felt needs of the people concerned. Any sort of disrespect, knowingly or unknowingly, to the traditional values regarding these needs would spoil the whole endeavor even if it is implemented with due sincerity and seriousness, writes **Sarkar** in his piece. The thinking and working patterns of human communities are processed by cultural traditions conditioned by deep-rooted philosophic principles of the people concerned. Tradition is culture-specific, molded and patterned according to the life-philosophy of the people. In order to understand a human community in its proper perspective it is essential to analyze the social system concerned in the background of the traditional features that have been influencing the social sentiments through the ages.

Pande and Pandey argues that the development of congenial environs for an equitable social growth is the cornerstone of social sustainability. It demands open opportunities of development as well as the engineered empowerment of the weaker social components. In the Indian social scene, the socio-economic status and the relative pace of cultural growth of scheduled caste and scheduled tribe population as also of the so-called backward communities are by far eminently lagging as compared to more elite social wings. This is mainly caused by the impact of the age-old discriminatory social traditions. The interlocked system of socio-economic and cultural stratification establishes the fact that lagging caste groups follow mostly the less remunerative and less prestigious occupations that demand less education and formally acquired skills.

In the recent five decades after Independence it is marked that education and opening of opportunities for the lagging social wings under democratic order of society have led to a noticeable intergeneration occupational change among these wings. The tribal communities in some cases were on the verge of extinction mainly due to a dearth of social sustainability for them in a highly competitive and progressive society. The lagging social wings are the worst victims of environmental deterioration. A policy of social sustainability has to ensure sustainability of resources as well as the sustainability of the people with the changing conditions of habitat, social setting and the technological development. The cultural frame, institutions and habits change with education, occupation and the command on income. Empowerment strengthens social equity and ensures social sustainability in a long run. The changes occurring fast in Indian social scene suggest that social sustainability is well attainable by an interventionist approach and is not a myth.

K.N. Selvaraj says that there are discernible trends in the incidence of rural poverty in India; the absolute numbers of people in poverty have grown in part due to the overall growth in the rural population. Output per head has virtually stagnated, and there is a clear evidence of an inverse relationship between rural poverty and agricultural performance. After allowance is made for the changes in the incidence of rural poverty associated with other variables, a definite negative relationship is noted between the incidence of rural poverty and agricultural growth in India. The results clearly reveal that government expenditure policies are important determinants of the performance of the agricultural sector and the growth of agriculture can be further augmented through adequate investment from public finance. Further, it is evident that instability in government expenditure has a detrimental effect on agricultural production growth.

SUMMARY: CROSS-CUTTING CONSTRAINTS ON OVERCOMING THE TRAP

The need for strengthening social protection is acute in developing countries. Greater incidence and severity of deprivation, a low degree of development of formal social-security systems, limited or inappropriate coverage of public support, resource constraints, low levels of institutional development for social-security provision, and the relative powerlessness of the poor and vulnerable are all factors which combine to make the problems of social security in developing countries both important and difficult (Burgess et al. 1999).

Although the contributors to this volume are not working from one analytical perspective, some elements of a common strategy for reform may be discerned. The overarching theme is to move from a situation in which safety net coverage essentially is not functioning to put a consumption floor under vulnerable groups, to one in which the state effectively leverages the contribution of both civil society and itself provides substantial assistance for the most vulnerable groups. Limited government assistance should be as focused as possible onto groups facing the greatest immediate needs, combined with the increasing presence and effectiveness of non-state welfare provision.

The formidable challenge facing developing country governments in trying to reach this vision is how to boost effective coverage and better targeting, to get the biggest effect for its limited fund availability. The only realistic way of doing this is through a combination of the following: *i)* **shifting expenditure** towards programs with the greatest impact on poor and vulnerable populations as well as towards regions and communities in greatest need; *ii)*

targeting coverage within broadly vulnerable groups onto sub-groups most in need; *iii)* **boosting administrative capacity** at both central and local government levels to do this; and *iv)* **encouraging non-State involvement** in welfare and social service provision.

Yet we have also seen that attempts to rapidly expand formal safety net coverage through cash transfers typically founder in low-income countries, which must look to alternative mechanisms to boost social protection. Differences in the level, coverage, and effectiveness of state provision of social security partly reflect the acute constraints found in developing countries (Ahmad et al 1999). These constraints fall into three categories.

The first is fiscal capacity. Social protection programs based on direct cash transfers and/or consumer subsidies are typically prohibitively expensive for developing country governments faced with competing priorities. The second is administrative capacity. The targeting called for above requires substantial administrative capacity - capacity that is lowest in precisely those communities and regions within a country that may need social assistance the most. The implementation of any nation-wide social program will likely be marked by highly differential performance by different local governments. Boosting the capacity and efficiency of safety nets where these are undergoing the greatest stresses will demand effective forms of decentralized decision-making combined with an activist role for upper levels of government in setting overall policy direction, enforcing minimum standards and providing technical assistance.

Superseding both of the constraints above is a third category: political economy. What practical incentives exist for both politicians and administrators, both at central and local government levels, to devote resources to social protection programs? How - through what specific mechanisms - can they be made more accountable for the achievement of positive social outcomes? The poor - and *particularly* the most vulnerable elements of the poor most in need of social protection - almost by definition have limited standing in society and in political life generally.

There is no global answer to this question. The major international development agencies are betting on democratization

(UNDP 2000xx) and on the shoring up of accountability relationships between the end-users, service providers and local authorities (World Bank 2004) as potential templates for an effective response to the political economy challenge. The analysis of most contributors to this volume would suggest that localized strategies for improving such incentives can be found given moderately facilitative governance and policy environments, but that progress is likely to be incremental. Their findings highlight the necessity for reformers seeking to strengthen social protection arrangements in developing country settings to carefully consider and work through the fiscal, administrative and political constraints on better outcomes in practice.

References

Bruno, M., Ravallion M. & Squire, L., 1998. Equity and growth in developing countries: Old and new perspectives on the policy issues. In Tanzi, V. & Chu, K.-Y. (Eds.) *Income distribution and high-quality growth* (pp. 117-146). Cambridge: The MIT Press.

Caldwell, J.C 1986, "Routes to Low Mortality in Poor Countries", Population and Development Review, 12.

Chambers, R. 1983 *Rural Development: Putting the last First.* Addisson-Wesley, New York.

Chu, K. and S. Gupta 1998. "Economic reforms, social safety nets, and the budget in transition economies," in Chu, K. and S. Gupta (eds.) *Social safety nets: Issues and recent experiences.* International Monetary Fund, Washington, D.C.

Dreze, J and Sen, A.K, 1989, "Hunger and Public Action" Oxford : Clarendon Press.

Drouin, A. 1999. Unemployment, social protection and crises: A perspective from the International Labour Organization. Asia Recovery Information Center, The World Bank and Asian Development Bank. Downloaded from www.aric.adb.org <http://www.aric.adb.org>, November 22, 1999.

Ehtisham Ahmad et all (ed), 1999, "Social Security in Developing Countires", New Delhi : Oxford University Press.

Fritzen, S. 2002. "Growth, poverty and the future of poverty reduction in Vietnam," *Asian Journal of Economics*, 13(2002): pp. 635-657.

ILO, 2000, "In Focus Program on Socio-economic Security", Geneva : ILO.

James, E. 1999. "Coverage under old age security programs and protection for the uninsured-What are the issues?" The World Bank, mimeo.

Jose Kananaikil, 2003. "Caring for the Exploited" in Lal, A.K (edt) Social Exclusion: Essays in Honour of Dr. Bindeshwar Pathak, New Delhi: Concept publications.

Kuznets, S. 1959, *Six lectures on economic growth.* Glencoe: Free Press.

Miller-Adams, M. 1999, *The World Bank: New agendas in a changing world* , New York: Oxford University Press.

Ravaillion, M. 1995, "Household vulnerability to aggregate shocks: Differing fortunes of the poor in Bangladesh and Indonesia." in K. Basu, P. Pattanaik & K. Suzumura (eds.), *Choice, welfare and development*, Clarendon Press, Oxford.

Robin Burgess and Nicholas Stern, 1999, "Social Security in Developing Countries : What, Why, Who, and How? In Ehtisham Ahmad et all (ed) Social Security in Developing Countries, New Delhi : Oxford University Press.

Srinivasen, T.N. 2001. Growth and poverty alleviation: Lessons from development experience. ADB Institute Working Paper No. 17.

Taylor, L., Mehrotra, S., & Delamonica, E. 1999. The links between economic growth, poverty reduction, and social development: Theory and policy. In Mhrotra, S., & Jolly, R. (Eds.). *Development with a human face: Experiences in social achievement and economic growth* (pp. 435-468). Oxford: Clarendon Press.

UNDP, 2000, India Human Development Report 2000, New Delhi: Oxford Press

Watkins, K. 1998. Economic growth with equity: Lessons from East Asia. Oxford: Oxfam GB.

World Bank, 1986, "Poverty and Hunger: Issues and Options for Food Security in Developing Countries, Washington, DC: World Bank.

World Bank, 1997, "World Development Report" Washington, D.C: World Bank.

World Bank 2001b. Attacking poverty: World development report 2000/2001. New York: Oxford University Press.

World Bank 2002a. Globalization, growth, and poverty: Building an inclusive world economy. New York: Oxford University Press and World Bank.

World Bank 1997, World Development Report 1997, New York: Oxford University Press.

World Bank 1993. The East Asian miracle: economic growth and public policy. New York: Oxford University Press.

World Bank 2004, World Development Report 2004, New York : Oxford University Press.

1

The Challenge of Social Security Reform in Transition Economies : The Case of China

Mukul Asher and
*David Newman**

I. INTRODUCTION

Since Deng Xiaoping announced his open door policy in 1978, China's economic progress has been nothing less than spectacular. In constant 1995. U.S. dollars, real per capita income in China increased from $168 in 1980 to $727 in 2000 (OECD 2001). "In 1978 it was estimated that nearly 60% of the population was living on less than US$1 a day, while in 1995 this had been reduced to just 22% of the population (Armstrong 1999). Thus, government policy over this period lifted several hundred million Chinese out of poverty.

While we recognize the successes, there is the need to be balanced when appraising China's economic progress. First, while the averages suggest impressive growth, there have been real

* *Authors are in Public Policy Programme, National University of Singapore, Singapore. (contact email: mappasher@nus. edu.sg & dnewmanl2 @hotmail. com)*

regional inequalities in growth rates in China and many regions remain woefully poor. Second, urban-rural income differences are very high and 70% of China's working population is still employed in agriculture. Oxford Analytica reports that China's gini coefficient increased from 0.33 in 1980 to 0.45 in 2001 and that the bottom sixty percent of the population has a smaller share of total income in 2001 then they did twenty years ago while the top quintile increased its share of total income by 15% since 1980 *(Asia Pacific Daily Brief,* June 25, 2002). Third, China retains many vestiges of its centrally planned pre-reform economy. One remnant is the inefficient and bloated State Owned Enterprises (SOEs), which while declining, still account for 28% of output, 44% of urban employment, and 70% of government revenue *(The Economist,* September 28, 2000).

Fourth, China is rapidly ageing and unlike the developed countries, it is ageing while still relatively poor. It is estimated that there will be a sixty percent increase in those over the age of 60 in the next twenty years (Ding 2002), that by 2030 sixteen percent of China's then 1.5 billion population will be over 65 (McKinsey 2002) and "by 2050, the ratio of workers to pensioners will decline to about 3 to 1 from 10 to 1 in 1995" (www.worldbank.org/html/extdr/extme/ampr–007.htm). It is not only the absolute number of elderly but the pace of population change which is important. The proportion of people in China over the age of 60 doubled from 10% to 20% in just 27 years (Clark 2002). While not the fastest country in the region to double, among the fast ageing countries, it is the poorest. Finally, because of rapid development, the elderly cohort is likely to have a higher percentage of poor than other cohorts. China will also experience individual ageing as reflected in higher life expectancies. This along with a shift from communicable to non-communicable conditions (such as heart attacks, depression, strokes, and cancer) and the rapid introduction of more expensive medical technology is also likely to significantly increase China's national health care expenditures.

Against this backdrop of economic change, China is in the midst of an effort to reform its social security system and its social safety net.[1] China has embarked on a unique transition attempting to recentralize control over the social security system; China previously centralized the social welfare system after the Communist revolution in the late 1940s and adopted a decentralized enterprise system during the Cultural Revolution in the 1960s. The current reform efforts are viewed as critical since the national pension fund deficit doubled between 1999 and 2000 and now totals more than 30 billion yuan,[2] and provincial and city schemes are facing insolvency.[3] While one may take some solace in the fact that the rulers in Beijing appear to understand the links between the social security system and enterprise reform, corruption, unemployment and civil unrest, it is these linkages which make reform so difficult to address. After briefly discussing social security reform generally and then reviewing the Chinese social security system, this paper will examine the difficulties China faces in structuring its reform efforts.

II. AN AGENDA FOR REFORM

There are five core functions which any social security organization must perform (Ross 2000). These are: reliable collection of contributions, taxes and other receipts, including any loan payments; payment of benefits for each of the schemes in a timely and correct way; securing financial management and productive investment of provident and pension fund assets; maintaining an effective communication network, including development of accurate data and record keeping mechanisms to support collection, payment and financial activities; and production of financial statements and reports that are tied to providing effective and reliable governance, fiduciary responsibility, transparency, and accountability.

---

1. *For a good review of the theoretical issues surrounding social insurance, see Gent (2001).*
2. *As of July 1, 2002, the exchange rate was 8.27 yuan to one U.S. dollar.*
3. *It is not uncommon for local governments to manage retirement pools. The State Council decreed in 1991 that retirement pools be managed at the provincial level. This issue highlights the difficulties the central government has in reforming a disaggregated pension system. Zhoa and Xu (2002) report that by 2001 only five provinces were complying with the decree. They further note that a by-product of the reform decree was that local governments no longer had an incentive to enforce pension collections since they no longer benefited by having access to the funds.*

At the macro systemic level, a well designed social security system should be broad based, actuarially sound and sustainable, provide reasonable levels of post-retirement income (as determined by a considered evaluation of alternative and trade-offs within the society) coupled with a *safety-net* for the elderly poor. Clearly, all of this has to be done within the context of macroeconomic requirements and constraints including economic efficiency, incentives to work and to save, fiscal flexibility and international competitiveness. Effective reform needs to be directed toward better organizational efforts and the broader system design issues.

III. THE CHINESE SOCIAL SECURITY SYSTEM

China's pension *system* consists of at least three distinct arrangements. Each arrangement is in a degree of flux, with regional and local variations, as the central government tries to unify the system taking into account regional differences. It is estimated that about 200 million workers out of a total of 700 million workers in 1998 were nominally covered by a pension (Wu, et al. 2000), covering 28.6% of workers.

Like many developing or traditional societies, China relies on the family to provide old age support for the vast majority of its population. This segment of the population, generally employed either in agricultural production or the informal sector, is outside of any formal system. With longer life expectancies, lower birth rates and urbanization, the burden on children is increasing and raises concerns about the adequacy of traditional care. In China, the adoption of the one child policy, at the limit, suggests a high dependency ratio for traditional care of two married working children taking care of four retired parents—a very heavy burden.

Pensions for rural farmers were introduced in China only in 1991.[4] This scheme is financed by voluntary personal contributions

4. *Under the Communist system, a "portion of the income generated by communes and collective enterprises in farming communities were set aside as public reserve funds, public welfare funds and management expenses to be retained and allocated by the communes and collectives themselves. The system of five guarantees households' (households guaranteed food, clothing, medical care, housing and funeral expenses) in farming villages provided the rural household with social security" (Taipei Times* April 10, 2002).

supplemented by a collective subsidy and individuals must contribute for ten years to be eligible. Of the five hundred million rural workers, only 61 million were covered under the rural pension scheme with each having an average balance of US$311. In China, many of the rural poor are too poor to be expected to contribute to their retirement savings. Moreover, any accumulated balances are likely to be used to offset personal and natural calamities over life, rather than being particularly earmarked for old age.

The second arrangement is the pension and social security system that emerged from the turmoil of the Cultural Revolution to address the needs of workers in state-owned enterprises and urban workers.[5] Prior to the Cultural Revolution, workers were covered under the Labour Insurance Fund (Zhu 2002). Under the enterprise based social security system a worker was provided with lifetime protection covering income, housing, health insurance, pensions. The retirement age was 60 for men and 55 for women, with exceptions for women engaged in physical labor (age 50 after 15 years of service) and 60 for women engaged in agriculture (Ding 2002). These distinctions were carried over to the design of pension schemes with further differences based on the nature of firm ownership resulting in a very complicated system. There are additional differences depending on whether the pensioner retired before the recent reforms or worked following the reforms.

In recent years many listed state-owned companies, encouraged by their Ministries at the time of listing, divided themselves into two entities at the time of the listing. One entity, essentially a shell, generally retained the marginal assets and the pension obligation to retirees. The valuable assets were transferred to a new entity. The shell company in turn received shares in the new and more valuable entity but often these were not liquid. Receipt of these pensions is dependent on the future viability of the listed entities. The design of

---

5. *Civil servants and the military are covered under a different scheme. Currently civil servants are covered by a non-contributory scheme providing 80-90% of their last drawn salary. In addition, they are provided with health insurance. Government salaries have gone up in recent years and there is some expectation that retirement benefits will be adjusted downward*

the scheme recognized that pensions were not portable and benefits were tied to the employer. Moreover, the scheme made it difficult to restructure SOEs because unnecessary workers were retained since the social safety net was tied to employment. Most state owned businesses have not listed and retain the obligation to pay current and future pensions. Some companies have as many retirees as workers and such high dependency ratios in turn raise the issue of financial sustainability.

In 1997, the government embraced the "three-pillar" World Bank model involving a social pool, individual accounts, and supplementary pensions (Wu, et al. 2000).[6] The three pillar model seeks to unify the state enterprise and private sectors. This system is designed to try to solve several problems including: portability and a high dependency ratio within the government system (Zhao and Xu 2002). Individuals participate in a national pension scheme involving employer and employee contributions. Most of the money paid into the individual pension accounts does not go into independently managed investment funds, but is used to meet existing commitments. While these are referred to as "individual accounts", this term refers more to portability rather than balances—it is purely notional with administered rates of return. The government set rate of return is lower than that offered on government bonds *(The Economist,* June 13, 2002).[7] Zhao and Xu (2002,400) highlight that these efforts to develop a unified system addressed the high dependency ratios found in the state owned enterprises by incorporating young private sector new hires into the scheme.

6. *It would be a mistake to assume that the central government in China is a monolithic entity with an ability to effectively permeate society with policies designed in Beijing. As Zhu (2002) reports, China does not have a national social security law and policy has been made by State Council decisions on a "piecemeal" and "ad hoc" basis with provincial governments left to formulate detailed rules in accordance with local circumstances.*
7. *In Liaoning, a northeastern, highly urban, Chinese province, an experiment in individual, fully funded, accounts was started in 2001. The contribution rate is 8 percent. Unfortunately by year end, contributions were delinquent and the central government was compelled to kick in US$120 million. State-owned enterprises reported that they simply did not have the funds to make contributions.*

With some regional variation, contributions under the first pillar, into the social pool, are supposed to be funded by a 20% of payroll payment by the employer. Employees are supposed to contribute 8% of salary to their individual account. Collectively, these two pillars with a contribution rate of 28% of payroll are supposed to give a wage replacement rate of 56% (www.britishembassy.org.cn/english/about_china/business/sr_pen.shtml). Although this new system is technically in place, in practice the system does not exist. Loss making and technically bankrupt SOEs are unable to contribute to the Pillar 1 pool informing authorities that they did not have the funds to make contributions. The authorities have raided the individual pillar 2 accounts to top up the pillar 1 social pool. In addition, the central authorities have had to make on and off-budget supplementary top-ups. The shortfall, US$4.3 billion in 2000 *(South China Morning Post* June 25, 2001) and estimated to be cumulatively as large as US$231 billion over the next 25 years, is being made up by the Ministry of Finance and is viewed by them as manageable.[8]

Benefits to retirees with fifteen years of service consist of two parts. The first part is 20 percent of the average regional wage paid in the preceding year. The second part is an amount equal to 1 / 120th of the individuals' notional account balance. Since part of the benefit was tied to current lagged wages, there is some protection against inflation. However, from an actuarial perspective, the scheme initially does not appear to be sustainable since the obligation to pay is for life while the individual's contributions self-extinguish in ten years leaving an unfunded liability.[9] Part of the shortfall is made up

---

8. *The picture with respect to current and soon to be retired workers may require more management than the Ministry of Finance believes. Protests by laid off state-factory employees and retirees have been growing as state enterprises fall increasingly behind on the payment of both unemployment and retirement benefits. In some cases, retirees have not received pension benefits for over three years. Demonstrations have even reached the capital, Beijing, where retirees from the Beijing Automobile Works factory blocked traffic this year protesting non-payment of pensions.*
9. *Wang, Xu, Wang and Zhai (2001) conducted a sophisticated fifty year simulation of the current system and also concluded that the current system is not sustainable. Other simulations such as (Zhao and Xu 2002) may be overly optimistic about real rates of return on investments in individual accounts and should perhaps be used with caution when making policy*

from a pool consisting of employer contributions to workers who died prior to collecting ten years of benefits. Employee contributions are inheritable if the retiree dies before collecting ten years of benefits.

To fund the government's obligations under the social pool, the plan, until very recently, was to accelerate the *privatization* and listing of state-owned enterprises and earmark 10% of the proceeds from these initial public offerings to fund national pension obligations.[10] In addition, Beijing planned to sell off the shares it owned in companies that have already listed *(Asian Wall Street Journal,* January 30, 2001). This scheme, it was estimated, could provide between US$40 and US$100 billion. The share sale was envisioned to free SOEs from pension obligations, introduce the discipline of the market to state-owned enterprises by weaning them from state bank loans,[11] and aid in the reform of the financial sector by expanding investment options.

On June 24, 2002, the government announced that it was backing away from the share sale scheme as the proposal and the threat of a large increase in the number of shares available, had depressed local share prices by 30 percent. The backtracking on this reform effort highlights China's difficulties. Stock markets are still relatively new and the government still views one of its roles as buttressing share prices. The authorities also are fearful of alienating middle class investors who must be courted, both politically and

10. *The word privatization is a misnomer since as of 1998, the government retained a majority stake in all of the companies listed on the Hong Kong stock exchange (Dixon and Newman 1998).*

11. *The situation has been described as a vicious circle (OECD 2002) in which the banks are forced to lend money to state-owned enterprises. The state-owned enterprises are inefficient but are pressed to retain workers in order to avoid social unrest thus avoiding the very reform that would potentially make them more efficient. The government retains its equity control of the SOE's to ensure that they do not lay off workers and the SOE's are rewarded with new loans regardless of their financial situation. Moreover, by removing commercial considerations from a variety of decisions, reform of corporate and banking governance is deferred to a later date. While reform efforts are underway (FRBSF 2002), we are skeptical of their likely success in the short to medium term.*

economically, over the long run to purchase future share offerings in state owned enterprises.[12] The uncertainty of government policy spooked investors who had come to expect that one only made money in the stock market. When the government announced the change in policy, both the Shanghai and Shenzhen stock exchange indices jumped more than 9% in one day.

Press reports the following day read: "Economists [had] regarded the construction of a social welfare network, led by the creation of a funded pensions system, as perhaps the most crucial of China's reform tasks" and "Without it, state companies are restrained by fears of social instability from making the mass redundancies they need to" *(The Financial* Times, June 25, 2002, p17). The belief was that the need for political stability surrounding a leadership change later in the year required a change in policy. Under the third pillar, China recognizes the need to introduce what are called in China, *supplementary pensions,* involving voluntary tax-advantaged retirement savings accounts. There has been some work undertaken on the legal and regulatory structures, which would be appropriate for supplementary pensions, but as of early 2002 the authorities have taken no firm decisions.[13] As part of the effort to respond to regional variations and to respond to the need to experiment at the regional level, the Asian Development Bank in 2002 awarded two technical assistance contracts to international consultants to assist Liaoning Province develop an information system to administer individual accounts, collect contributions and manage payments.

---

12. *Almost every listed Chinese company traces its roots as a state-owned enterprise.*
13. *China 's financial problems have been characterized as "colossal" (The Economist* June 13, 2002) *and the financial services infrastructure, regulatory framework, and products necessary to support the third pillar of tax advantaged personal savings is lacking. First, the banks require recapitalization and a change in investment underwriting to commercial standards. Second, the insurance industry is relatively immature beyond life and casualty insurance products. Third, domestic investment alternatives are limited to deposits, government bonds, a property market with boom/bust cycles, and an equities market based on shares in government dominated companies.*

The state enterprise pension system covered about 18 percent of the labor force in 1999 (see Table 1) and about 41.3 percent of the urban labor force (Zhao and Xu 2002). While close to one-third of the 113 million people working in state enterprises at the peak of employment in 1995 have been retrenched *(The Economist,* June 13, 2002), estimates are that a further 40 million state enterprise employees may lose their jobs in the next several years following China's accession to the World Trade Organization. In addition, the government has embarked on an effort to reform the civil service and has announced plans to cut the public sector by 50 percent although the extent of real cuts is uncertain. We might view these coverage rates as potentially a high-water mark for years to come since the public enterprise and civil service sectors (with high rates of coverage) are likely to shrink over the next several years (with more cuts likely from public enterprises than the civil service) and these very same *covered employees,* if they are fortunate to find employment are likely to find employment in non-covered sectors of the economy. Table 1 also suggests that the system is not sustainable as there are very high replacement rates relative to contributions. Current retirees may face a reduction in current benefits and future retirees will likely have to contribute more and receive less.

Table 1 : China's Pension System Compared to Selected Regions in the World

Region	Participation as share of labour force %	Contributions as ratio to wages (%) Pensions	All social insurance	Average income replacement ratio (%)	Average pension as per cent of GDP per capita	Pension spending as per cent of GDP
China (1999)	18[a]	25[b]	30[c]	77[b]	99[b]	3
OECD	90	19	34	38	54	10
Range	79-98	6-35	14-57	25-49	23-98	5-15
Asia and Pacific	26	14	17	NA	NA	1
Range	3-73	3-40	4-46	NA	NA	0-3

Source : OECD 2002 (Table 8).

Notes : a The regular urban pension system and that for civil servants.

b The regular urban pension system. NB. employee contribution rates increased every year 1997-2001.

c Approximate national average.

Thus, China's social security reform, which is still underway and uncertain, is designed in part to relieve state enterprises from pension responsibility as commercial considerations predominate. This objective however is being balanced against the concerns of the policymakers regarding social unrest.

IV. ASSESSMENT

Section 2 of this paper outlined a reform agenda using Ross's (2000) five core functions that a social security organization must perform and adding three systemic level functions linking a social security system to the broader political economy of a country. We begin with the macro-functions first.

Regardless of whether one is addressing pension and social security issues narrowly or considering the broad society as a whole, effective governance in China is a challenge and as such we have purposely limited our discussion to two salient points. First, China must firmly establish the rule of law with respect to the sanctity of savings such that individuals believe that setting aside funds for old age is a rational act. Imbedded in this is a need to develop good regulations including a fiduciary duty for trustees, investment managers, employers in which they are held to a high standard of responsibility for the funds placed in their care, and a system of enforceable rights. Second, policymakers need to understand and appreciate that in order to prod individuals into saving for the long-term individuals need to have some minimum degree of certainty regarding future policy. China has repeatedly announced a policy only to backtrack at a later date. For example, as noted above, China's decision to backtrack on listing state owned enterprises earlier this year. Basically, long term savers require a minimum degree of certainty, not absolute, that the money set aside for their future will be there when they need it.

A social security system should be broad based, actuarially sound and sustainable. As noted, historically the social security system in China covered civil servants and employees of state owned enterprises. While about forty percent of urban workers (80 million workers out of a total of 200 million urban workers) participated in a pension system in 2000, the vast majority of the rural population and most town and village enterprise workers were outside any scheme. China recognizes the need to expand coverage although SOEs in financial distress often find it difficult to subscribe to the new pension system and many other companies do not make contributions. Zhao and Xu (2002) note that the state council mandated all state owned and urban enterprise employees be covered under the pension system by June 1999, but that the participation rate among this group was only 63.4 in 2000, up from 50.4 percent in 1998. While there are prospects for significantly improving the participation rate further, one should not dismiss the two year, twenty-five percent improvement already achieved.

Further expansion of the base, improving compliance, and reducing evasion are all steps toward making the system actuarially sound and sustainable. These changes, however, need to be coupled with a reduction in the target replacement rate (to be provided by the first and second pillar), from 77% (table 1) to something in the mid 50% range. In addition, China will need to raise its retirement age and eliminate the distinctions based on sex, location and nature of work.[14]

China has historically sought to achieve high replacement rates for urban workers while ignoring the needs of others. Historically, replacement rates for urban workers and civil servants were an average of 77 percent (table 1) and as noted above, the British Embassy estimates that if the first and second pillar systems are actually implemented as designed, they should offer a combined replacement rate of 56% which is both reasonable and consistent with world averages.

---

14. *There are actually two components to the retirement age: the age that one works until and the age that one can begin to draw retirement benefits (Clark 2002). A gap between retirement and drawing benefits is not necessarily a problem as early 'formal" retirement, often at age 55, is often viewed as a benefit and the delay in taking benefits allows further accumulation of invested returns. In China, many older workers are likely to be "retired" from the formal sector well before they are aged 53. Some are likely to find employment in the informal sector where they are not likely to be covered by the pension scheme. In order to achieve the target replacement rates, integrating the informal sector becomes important.*

At a very basic level, a social security system must be able to reliably and accurately collect contributions, credit the amounts, and any accumulated gains, to the contributor (this is true regardless of whether individual accounts are maintained or a worker is simply credited with participation in a scheme) and then make payment of benefits in a correct and timely manner. While good governance plays a role in these functions at the macro level, these basic administrative functions must be performed at the organizational level for a system to be effective. The Asian Wall Street Journal reports that it is "typical" for employers, even state owned companies, to avoid pension contributions by listing employees as "loaned" from another entity rather than as being employed (June 29, 2002). Since employees do not receive benefit contribution statements, they only become aware of the situation when they are laid off and find out that they are not entitled to either unemployment or pension benefits. A genuine individual account based system should ensure that each member has access to his or her own account details on a regular basis.

Under the current system, employers are not able to make pension payments to retirees because the funds are simply not there because pension obligations under the pay-as-you-go system require that the payor, in the case of China, state-owned enterprises, actually has the financial wherewithal to make the payments. Since more than half of all state-owned enterprises are money-losing, and on average the entire sector loses money, the funds are not there to make the payments. An analyst at the National Academy of Sciences in China estimates that lay-offs from SOEs will average 10 million per year over the next several years *(Business Week* April 8, 2002) further taxing their ability to make profits or pension benefits.

Before China actually adopts a supplementary pension scheme, the third pillar, management and investment of assets will not be a major issue. However, individual supplementary savings accounts will introduce a whole host of additional problems in China. China has a small equities market dominated by state linked companies with the government often maintaining majority control of shares. The regulatory regime under which financial and capital markets operate remains weak, although it is improving, and these markets continue to be viewed by many more as legitimate gambling or speculation than a vehicle for long term savings and investment. In this context, there will need to be a significant change in the mind-set of savers that long term saving and investment in domestic equities is reasonably prudent for generating long term returns that can be used for retirement. Similarly, investment related products such as annuities need to be developed by insurance companies to offer longevity protection. China's entry into WTO, and provision for Sino-foreign joint ventures should accelerate these offerings.

Accurate data, record keeping, and effective communication, is a massive undertaking in China's case given the number of individuals covered. While most of these tasks could effectively be performed within the workplace under the old state enterprise system, new approaches need to be developed if workers have nominally portable accounts and the record keeper is independent of employment. Regulations, applicable to all three pillars, will be needed governing the frequency and nature of disclosure, a challenge and appeals process needs to be developed when errors are alleged, and fiduciary responsibility needs to be legislated covering every entity having possession of retirement funds.

V. CONCLUSION

Our discussion is meant to suggest that there is a realization among policymakers in China of the need to improve the performance of the social security system.[15] While some may say that China is "muddling through", muddling through is what can be expected given the enormity of the problem and the interconnectedness of social security reform to state enterprise reform, reforming the banking sector, economic growth, employment, and social peace. In addition, social security reform in any country needs to deal with the reliance of current retirees, the expectations of near-term retirees, and the current and future needs of younger workers. As such, incremental change is far easier than radical reform.

---

15. *While we have focused on the provision of pensions, the social safety net requirements are much broader as the economy changes from centrally planned to more market oriented and includes unemployment, health care protection, and disaster relief programmes. Zhu (2002) summarizes recent developments in China that relate to unemployment insurance and healthcare provision.*

As we have quoted in this paper, "the creation of a funded pensions system is perhaps the most crucial of China's reform tasks". China is ageing fast, it is urbanizing rapidly, its economic institutions are in flux and as a consequence the traditional social safety net provided by the state, the enterprise and the family is being swept aside. With a massive unfunded future pension liability, China must maintain very high growth rates and to avoid social unrest, which will undermine high growth, it must be able to absorb millions of new workers a year.

Again, the economic challenges do not sit in isolation. To develop a viable second and third pillar, China needs pension regulations and a legal structure that will allow individuals to save with confidence knowing that the funds will be managed as promised and be returned when due. So many more institutions are required to develop an effective third pillar, such as legal standards, mature equity markets, appropriate financial products, a population of investors reasonable educated about financial and retirement matters, and effective regulation. In the case of China, these tasks are so daunting that it would not be unreasonable to delay implementation of this pillar until the prerequisite institutions are in place. As Rodrik (2000) has argued, while there is consensus that institutions matter, there is ample room for being humble concerning the practical knowledge required to develop appropriate institutions from the existing ones.

Finally, while we recognize that social security reform is inherently a political process and as such each country will undertake those activities which are consistent with its domestic political economy, the reform efforts need to strive for greater professionalism and results need to be benchmarked against best international practice. This task is particularly difficult in the Chinese context because unlike other transition economies, China's reform efforts are targeted at recentralizing its social security system and removing the basic functions from state owned enterprises. Thus, there is a critical need for the state to develop a professional capability to fine tune the development of national policy, to ensure correct implementation of policy and to assess successes and failures.

REFERENCES

Armstrong, Jill. 1999. "Towards an East Asian Social Protection Strategy." Washington, D.C.: Human Development Unit, East Asia and Pacific Region, World Bank.

Clark, Robert. 2002. "Ageing Populations and Income Security: The Challenges in East Asia." In *Public Policy in Asia: Implications for Business and Government.* eds. Mukul Asher, David Newman and Thomas P. Snyder. Westport: Quorum Books.

Ding, Yuan-Zhu. 2002. "Current Pension and Its Reform in Transition China", Prepared for the International Symposium on Asian Pension, Tokyo, February 1-2, Mimeo.

Dixon, J. and D. Newman. 1998. *Entering the Chinese Market: Risks and Discounted Returns.* Westport, CT: Quorum Publishers.

FRBSF (Federal Reserve Bank of San Francisco) 2002. "Reforming China's Banking System" *FRBSF Economic Letter.* May 31, 2002.

Gent, David. 2001. "Social Insurance: Theoretical Background" in *Social Protection in Asia and the Pacific.* ed. Isabel Ortiz. Manila, Asian Development Bank.

International Securities Institute. 1998. *A Capital Guide to Marketing Unit Trusts and Mutual Funds in Asia.* Hong Kong: International Securities Institute.

OECD (Organization for Economic Cooperation and Development). 2002. *China in the World Economy: The Domestic Policy Challenges (Synthesis Report).* Paris: OECD.

Rodrik, Dani. (2000). "Institutions for High-Quality Growth: What They Are and How To Acquire Them", Working Paper 7540, Cambridge: National Bureau of Economic Research.

Wang, Y., D. Xu, Z. Wang, and F. Zhai. 2001. *"Implicit Pension Debt, Transition Cost, Options, and Impact of China's Pension Reform: A Computable General Analysis"*

Economic Policy and Poverty Reduction Division, Policy Research Working Paper 2555.

Wu,X., Wei, *Y* Zhenghuai, L. Fu, A. and A. Chow 2000. "The Demography of Aging in China and its Implications for Old Age Pension" www.actuaries.ca/ meetings/aging/Chow.pdf.

Zhao, Yaohui and Jianguo Xu. 2002. "China's Urban Pension System: Reforms and Problems" *Cato Journal* 21(3).

Zhu,Yukun. 2002. "Recent Developments in China's Social Security Reforms" International Social Security Association, Regional Office for Asia and the Pacific, Manila. Mimeo.

2

Social Security for Non-coverage Population in China

*Yansui Yang**

I. SOCIAL INSURANCE FOR PRIVATE SECTORS AND SELF-EMPLOYED IN CITIES

1.1 Overview of the Participants of Employed from Private Sectors and Self-employed

Since the middle of 1980s, China government launched the reform of social insurance system aiming to integrate separate social insurance schemes, "enterprise insurance", into a unified social pooling system out side of enterprise. In initiai stage, only parts of state owner enterprises and collective enterprises participated in the reform of social insurance system. After 10 years, a great change had taken place, especially for old age old-age pension.

Related to the information on old age old-age pension system, more than 87.38 million workers from cities and towns are covered by the scheme in 1995, which account for 76.9% of grass workers and another 1/4 of workers are excluded from coverage. The categories of participants as following: reaching to 95.8% in SOEs, 46.5% in collective economies, and less than 10% in non-SOEs

* *Professor, Social Security Institute, Tsinghua University, Beijing, China.*

(covering only 2.4 million workers among 29.4 million workers), such as private firms and foreign companies. *An Inform of the State Council on Deep Old-age pension reform for Enterprises Employees* was issued in 1995, which provided an extending target of old age old-age pension scheme to cover all workers from various kind of economic units in cities and towns, including self-employed, until the end of 2000. According to the information of the State Council, the former Labour Ministry of China made and issued an executive plan of "basic old age old-age pension scheme coverage" in May, 1995, extending the coverage of old-age pension scheme to all enterprises, private firms and their employees, also including self-employed and professionals in cities and towns.

Since the middle of 1990s, the trend of employment is that employed number has been increasing in non-state owner enterprises and collective enterprises as well as decreasing from state owner enterprises and collective enterprises under economic structure transferring. Employed in state owner enterprises has been reduced from 112.61 million in 1995 to 81.02 million in 2000, and in collective economies from 31.47 million to 14.99 million; on the contrary, employed in private economies has increased from 4.85 million in 1995 to 12.68 million in 2000; and self-employed has increased from 15.6 million to 21.36 million.

However, old-age pension scheme covered employed in private firms and self-employed only 3.475 million, which accounted for 10% of all employed there. In 2000, employed in foreign companies were 6.42 million, but covered by old-age pension only 4.89 million, which accounted for 76.2% of all employed there. That is to say, the coming target of extending will be in the areas of private economies and self-employed.

Small economies and self-employed are called informal sector with the natures as:

- small size, most of them are private owners;
- informal employment relationship based on contract, labour frequency movement;
- income in non stability;
- flexible working rules on time and part-time job, such as hour-job, season-job.

The features mentioned above cause some difficulties to cover the employed in those sectors into old-age pension scheme.

1.2 Reasons for Low Participation from Private Sectors and Self-employed

It faces a series of barriers to cover employed in informal sectors (small and private firms, self-employed) into old age old-age pension scheme:

(1) The lack of understanding on social insurance. China has a long time under planned economic system; employed in informal sector is a new social phenomenon occurring after China reform economic system and open door and has been increased since 1990s. Most of the employed are young age so that they don't think of saving for old age in priority and aren't conscious of having social insurance rights.

(2) Non-stable job and income is the main problem for the employed in non formal sector to participant to contribute for social insurance fund and account based on an periodic contribution (monthly), fixed income basis and contribution rate.

(3) Current contribution rate is relatively high. The high contribution rate (employer) in formal sector is around 20% of payroll in enterprises due to a high dependency rate between young generation and old generation in coming years in China; more and more redundancy and retirees come from state owner enterprises and collective enterprises. Forenamed contribution rate may be too high for the employed in informal sectors, especially for employed in small firms and with low income, so that they don't accept the contribution rate.

(4) Under a labour market of buyers in priority in China, normally the employed from the informal sector choke with silent fury if their employer makes no contribution for their old age and health care because the immediate priority needs on them is to keep the job and income. Redundancy in China labour market is relative austere because:

- more than 6 million employed have lost their job in state owner enterprises;
- more than 6 million are unemployed;
- 20 million redundancy in state owner enterprises is waiting to be recallocated;
- 12 million new labourers are waiting for a job every year; and
- 130-150 million redundancy arises from agriculture sector.

1.3 Approaches to Extend Coverage

(1) Legal education. Related social insurance rights and obligations on private employers have been laid down into related regulations. On one hand, it is necessary to let the employed there understand their rights/interests and obligations; on the other hand, it is necessary to press the employers to implement their obligations of contribution in law.

(2) Set up flexible rules and measures to coincide with their needs on contribution rate or administration. Initial policies and rules on the new social insurance scheme were made based on the circumstances in state owned enterprise with high dependency rate and heavy liabilities, which caused a relative high contribution rate. Unlike the situation mentioned above, old age old-age pension to informal sector is a very new matter. So high contribution rate, 20% of payroll, should make a sudden pressure and negative influence to informal sectors, so that they try to escape social insurance contribution. Also when they understand that the heavy liability in social pooling fund arises from former state owner enterprises, it is a certain complaint to share the liability of old-age pension for state owned enterprises. Therefore, Government of China ought to make different contribution rates to different sectors and try to make a "low contribution rate for entrance" of non-state owned sector, especially for very small firms. For instance, the contribution rate for state owned enterprises is made based on the old-age pension replacement around 60% of average wage in local. It is possibly based on the old-age pension replacement around 17% of average income in local to make the contribution

rate for non state owner enterprises. Of course, this is just a transferring measure the trend in future is that a unified contribution rate should be realized for public sectors and non public sectors, but the contribution rate for public sectors should be decreased gradually and for non-public sectors should be increased gradually.

(3) On the other hand, according to the case of instable job and income at informal sector, especially for self-employed, it is necessary to set up a unified number system of social insurance to keep the contribution data of the insured whether they are employed or unemployed, and to collect their contribution based on the average income in the cities.

II. SOCIAL SECURITY FOR THE WEAK GROUPS

2.1 Social Security of Poverty Population in cities - Minimum Living Guarantee

2.1.1 Reasons and Dimensions of Cities in Poverty

Before 1980s, the Chinese government had focused attention to poor population in the countryside, but, since 1990s poverty phenomena have arisen in cities more and more, which have become an extrusive problem influencing social and economic development. Therefore a new social allowance scheme was issued and practised, namely "Minimum Living Guarantee in Cities", which is an important portion of social security system in China.

Since 1990's, increasing poverty in cities has caused redundancy in the SOEs due to the juvenility of unemployment insurance. A lot of unemployed people couldn't receive social allowance or only receive too low benefit, so that they became the poverty group.

In the middle of 1990s, a deep SOEs reform policy was presented as " reducing employment for increasing efficiency" so that a lot of employees were dismissed. By the statistic data from the MOLSS from 1997 to the end of 2000, totaling 21 million employees were of their job in the SOEs. In the end of 2000, totaling 6.572 million employed lost their job and 93.5% of them entered into the Re-employment Service Center. But, only 97.3% of redundancy received a living on the minimum living guarantee in the Reemployment Service Center. In fact, a number of unemployed were not in the statistic data due to various reasons.

On the other hand, the registered unemployment number was between 5.5 million to 6 million during 1997 - 2000, 5.95 million at the end of 2000, but only 1.9 million unemployed received unemployment insurance benefit. Two facts must been paid attention to, that:

- a large number employees have been in job and no any payment within the enterprises, but they are not in the statistic data of the Re-employment Service Center and also not in the statistic of unemployed in the Social Insurance agency. What happened to them?
- Some retirees' old-age pension benefits were later-paid or defaulted;
- Residents in cities are facing new risks on housing, children, education, medical cost and inflation;
- Since 1990s, a rising gap between different groups, such as high income and low income, eastern and western areas, which cause a number of poverty.

Finally, according an assessment by an expert in 1997, existing population of 15 million in poverty in the country was composed of the employees who were off job without payment (Xia Gang), unemployed, retirees under default and their families and beneficiaries qualified social assistance.

2.1.2 System of Minimum Living Guarantee in Cities

In China, the system of minimum living guarantee in the urban area was found in 1950s, which is kept at low payment and limited coverage.

Since 1993, the Chinese government have launched a reform of social assistance in order to set up of scheme of minimum living guarantee in cities, which has been extended broadly covering 668 cities and 1638 towns of the county where governmental locus is until Sep. 1999.

The *Regulations on Minimum Living Guarantee in the Urban Area* was enacted by the State Council in 1999, providing that :

- *"the residents, who have non-agricultural registered permanent residence, and their family members in cities have the right to apply social assistance from the local governments when their income is under the defined minimum level."*
- *"the residents in cities, who are disabled, haven't stable income for living on, haven't supporter, have the right to receive full-benefit social assistance;*
- *the residents and their family members in cities, who have a number of income sources, but not enough, have the right to receive a supplement benefit, which equals the proportion under minimum living guarantee in cities.*

Until the end of 2000, the existing population of 4.026 million received the benefit from the system of minimum living guarantee in cities. The benefit level per beneficiary is about RMB 140-300 yuan monthly and average income per person (including dependants) is at RMB 87/per person monthly in the country. Annual expenditure of minimum living guarantee in cities was RMB 2.71 billion yuan from the national fiscal.

2.1.3 Problems arising from the System of Minimum Living Guarantee in Cities

(1) Coverage and shortfall.

For coverage of minimum living guarantee in cities, beneficiaries realized that only population of 0.849 million in 1996 and 4.026 million in 2000 accounted for 1/4 of poor population 15 million.

(2) Some obstacles come from traditional ideology and thinking.

Although a new definition was laid down into the *Regulations on Minimum Living Guarantee in the Urban Area* that all residents have the right to apply the social benefit when they are in need forenamed, the traditional ideology and thinking from the officials of government civil affairs departments is that only those who aredisabled or are under or over labour age, have the right to apply social assistance. In fact, most of unemployed are between 18-59 years old who are always neglected from this social assistance system.

(3) Financing burden rate among regions is not in reason and fairness.

Generally financing resource of minimum living guarantee is from the cities government and district government. In fact, financing between two levels of governments is not in reason and fairness, also without any support of transfer payment from the central government and provincial government. The rate on share of finance expenditure between cities government and district government is different at 7:3, 5:5 or 3:7. Financing burden among regions is imbalanced due to different economic circumstances.

(4) Part of beneficiaries are still in poverty.

Those existing beneficiaries living on the minimum living guarantee are still facing social risks on children's education and medical cost, as the benefit is too low to meet the needs.

2.1.4 Proposals on Policies to Improve the System of Minimum Living Guarantee in Cities

(1) Defining the standards of minimum living guarantee in reason and fairness.

The goal will be achieved by the following activities to :

- set up unified adjusting mechanism according to inflation index and other elements to guarantee the real value of minimum living guarantee;
- set up unified social security norm, for instance a comprehensive reference index on per capita of GDP, average commercial expenditure of per residence and so on;
- based on the norms mentioned above, the specific and current level of minimum living guarantee will be decided by the local government according to the local circumstances.

(2) Financing burden from all levels of governments.

The principle should be that :

- main burden takes place from cities' government;
- low burden takes place from district government;
- partial financing must share from central and provincial government.

(3) Strengthening administration and service at grass roots level.

The system of minimum living guarantee in reason and fairness linked with the specific situation of residence's employment, income, family structure in cities. This is why it needs to strengthen administration and service at grass roots level for learning exact data and norm.

(4) Completing the system of minimum living guarantee in comprehensive structure.

The demand of social assistance for poor family is not only a minimum living guarantee, but also the needs on minimum living guarantee. Therefore, it is necessary to complete the system of minimum living guarantee in comprehensive structure including children education, housing, medical cost etc. Maybe it is sound way to set up two benefits, one of which is a flat-rate payment, and the other is the special benefit for the special needs.

2.2 Social Security for Special Poverty Group Social Assistance System

Special poverty group in China refers to elders, orphans and the handicapped. Social assistance system supports them on minimum living guarantee and employment promotion. *The Law on Protection of Elder's Rights and Interests of China, The Regulations on Five Kind of Protection in the Countryside* and *The Law on the Protection of Handicapped' Rights and Interests of China* was enacted and force in the country. A number of social welfare establishments have been set up using for the integration social service to elders and orphans, such as the baby forms and the elder welfare institutes. Until the end of 2000, existing social welfare institutes 40 thousand and supporting poverty population 0.854 million. On the other hand, setting up social welfare enterprises more than 40 thousand and employed handicapped 0.85 million.

The challenges to the system of social assistance can be focused on the following two aspects :

- existing social welfare establishments and staff is impossible to meet the needs due to the lack of sustaining financing support. In China, population 012 billion are more than 60 years old and 3-4 million of them need social assistance, but until the end of 2000, only population 0.854 million of them were adapted really. Aside, among handicapped 60 million, 20 million of them gave labour capacities, but only 15% of them are employed in a normal way and 0.85 million of them are employed under social welfare economies.

- Governance and administration in China like many developing countries has been disappointing due to a broad rang of problems, which is obstacle to improve the social assistance system.

The main improvement measure can be focused on the following two aspects :

- To create multi-ways to finance for the supporting of social assistance system, special government's finance; it needs to set up a balance rate between social assistance finance increasing and governmental fiscal income increasing; to issue encouraging taxation policy on society, enterprises and individual's contribution to social assistance system.
- To strengthen socialization's and marketable administration and service of social assistance, empowering social medi-organizations (NGO) to provide the service in efficiency and quality.

III. SOCIAL SECURITY FOR COUNTRYSIDE

Based on historic reasons, in China there exists a dual economic structure between cities and countryside, which causes a gap of social security level between two areas. Of course, the advantage is for cities, not for the countryside. Most countrymen are supported by their family mainly when they are facing social risk and poverty.

China is developing from agricultural economy into modern economic society, but it is impossible to realise the goal without a complete social security system. Also, a complete social security system is impossible to be realised without social security system for countryside due to nearly 80% of the population living there.

To improve the social security for countryside, the main tasks are focused on old age old-age pension and medical care, especially a protection for employees in township enterprises.

3.1 Old-age pension for Countryside

3.1.1 Risks to Family Old-age Guarantee

Great changes have taken place in China's economic structure, which causes a serious challenge to traditional family guarantee structure on old age and medical cost, for instance :

(1) Ageing population exists in countryside due to birding control policy. Current family structure is composed of 1 young couple, 2 parents couples and 4 grand parents couples.

(2) More and more young Labourers have moved and entered the cities and town labor market and most of them would like to be use to the social insurance system of cities and wouldn't like to go back home town in future, which cause the challenges on old-age pension' of countryside. That is to say, an urgent demand for countryside is to set up propriety old-age pension in countryside of China as soon as possible.

3.1.2 Establishment, Development and Stagnation of Social Old-age Pension System in Countryside

The Ministry of Civil Affairs of China launched a series good experience on social security in countryside since 1986. then, based on the results from preceding experiences, the *Interim Plan on Social Old-age pension System at County level of Countryside* was issued by the Ministry in 1992. The plan provides the basic principles to set up social old-age pension system at the county level as following :

- social old-age pension linked with family guarantee;
- individual and mutually fund in priority and government supporting by policy;
- all kinds of employed (workers, farmers and business man) in countryside will be covered by an integrative social old-age pension plan.

By the plan forenamed, the model of social old-age pension at county level of countryside is an individual saving account.

- individual saving account for per beneficiary and contributed by the individual and related collective economic unit;

- capital in the individual account belongs to the beneficiary;
- full funding;
- old-age pension benefit will be paid according to DC principle, which will be decided on all accumulation in the account.

Until the end of 1999, the social old-age pension was spread covering 2102 counties within 30 provinces. 64.6 million population in the rural insured on social old-age pension and elders 0.8977 million received old-age pension benefit from the system. Rolling fund reached RMB 18.418 billion yuan.

Since 1998, the plan execution has been moved from the Ministiy of Civil Affairs to new Ministry of Labour and Social Security; at the same time, a series of argument has exists between the different departments of government in China such as

- it is good to continue family guarantee model in countryside avoiding a heavy financing burden to government so early due to a lot of poverty families in countryside;
- it is possible to add finance burden to countrymen;
- a rising gap between high income families and low income families in the countryside, which causes some of them is possible to buy commercial life and health insurance products;
- may be the benefit is too low to meet the needs;
- it is possible the governance and administration were not appointed, even the fund was embezzled, and so on.

In 1999, the *Decision on Neatening Insurance Trade* was issued by the State Council of China, which covered the plan of social old-age pension for the countryside. The main point-view in the decision presented that the social and economic conditions in China were not possible to provide and administrate social old-age pension to so large number of population in countryside. Therefore, the decision required that the old-age pension plan execution was stopped from that time and if the condition in possible, may transfer the social old-age pension into commercial life insurance products. The big problem is how to neaten preceding work and to compensation for beneficiary's interests.

Another good model arisen from Guangdong province, it is called "Old-age pension for Birding Control Family". The main policy is transferring the allowance to register family for complain birding control policy by local government, RMB 1000 yuan for per family, to buying commercial life annuity products. Based on the model, a suggestion on "Social security benefits for birding control family" has been laid down into the *Economic and Social Development of China for 10th Five Years Plan* in 2001.

3.1.3 Signification of Social Old-age pension Scheme for Countryside

Looking over in 2001, the report presents that *Plan on Social Old-age pension System at County* is practiced well in the economic developed countryside, that is to say, if making rational improvement on the plan mentioned above, it is possible to develop the social old-age pension for the residents in the countryside. Signification of reestablishment social old-age pension system in the rural area are as following :

(1) It is good to promote the national population strategy of bird control, that is changing the traditional ideology of "more sons better to old age" and family guarantee model through the social old-age pension plan.

(2) It is better to farmer and their family reducing the relying on the land as well as to go to multi-running and citifying.

(3) It is good to encourage farmers, to saving for old age as well as reduce non-rational commercial action, such as build extravagance family tomb.

(4) It is sound to promote labor rational movement between urban and countryside.

3.1.4 Policy Proposals on Old-age Security for Countryside of China

(1) We deem that the policy and plan of social old-age pension for countryside preceding is a useful design in china, which ought to be insisted and executed, also to keeping a stable policy is a pre-condition to spread the social old-age pension in countryside, in order to avoid the worries of countrymen,

such as altering policy, altering principals and impossible to encash and so on due to disappoint experience in the past.

(2) Enacting regulations and law to define the rights and obligations and laid down the plan into the *Social Security Law of China,* which is on-making work.

(3) Insisting on voluntary principle and flexible scheme coincides with countrymen's willing and contribution capacities. It must avoid the compulsion policy of "only one choice" and provide multi-choices to countrymen and decided by themselves in voluntary, such as: commercial life insurance products, social old. age pension.

(4) Setting up individual saving account for each participant linked with limited subsidy from collective economies; individual account must be easy to transfer between different provinces, to contract-out, to inherit and to link with other social insurance schemes, in order to move in the labour market. Supplementary contribution from the collective economic units is good way to encourage countrymen participate in the scheme actively, but **it** must equal a flat-rate for every one without any privilege to any person.

(5) On the one hand, regulating the fund management under a prudential supervision system and guarantee the fund's real value; on the other hand, investing the fund into financing market for good return; also mandate the fund to the professional fund company to invest in the capital market under a contract.

(6) Setting up an independent social insurance system (including old-age pension) for township enterprises (section 3.3).

3.2 Medical Care for Countryside

3.2.1 Establishment, Development and Stagnation of Collaboration Medical Care Scheme for Countryside

In the early days of new China, a medical care net was set up gradually in the countryside, which was composed of three levels, namely county hospitals, town small hospitals and community cliniques. This net provided necessary and limited medical service.

On the other hand, as security model, collaboration medical care scheme was created and spread in the countryside very popular to support the medical service net there, which was financed by the individuals(very low contribution) linked with collaboration economics(very limited subsidy) for a mutual-fund and was administrated under the medical care net. Until 1976, 90% of all population in the countryside participated in the collaboration medical care scheme instead of former family guarantee. This issue was rooted coinciding with the specific circumstance of countryside in China therefore spreading rapidly and created a long life of countrymen, average years old has been from 35 to 68 in 1981.

The collaboration medical care for countrymen had been in stagnation since 1980s, due to the transfer of countryside economic structure and fadeaway of collective economics so that the participants of collaboration medical scheme was reduced gradually from 90% to 5% of all countrymen in 1986. The former medical care net had been stopped and closed gradually and some of them were transferred to private business. In fact, most countrymen come back the risk of health and have to face the heavy medical cost.

Since 1990s, Chinese government launched a programme again to improve the collaboration medical scheme for countryside, which was laid down into a series of policies during that time. Besides, other models had been practiced in some regions. But, it has had to face a challenge under new economic circumstance. In 1998. the investigation report II on health service in the country by the Health Ministry of China showed that 12.56% of countryside were insured under different medical care models including the collaboration medical scheme covered 6.5% of all countrymen. 87.44% of them were financed by individual or family for medical cost (44.13% of all residents in the urban areas). However a relative high collaboration medical care system coverage (22.1%) exists in the economic developed areas such as Shanghai cities, Zhejiang province, Shandong province etc.. On the contrary, the coverage is less than 3% in the economic poor areas (form-8).

3.2.2 *Reasons for Stagnation of Collaboration Medical Scheme for Countryside*

Reasons for stagnation of collaboration medical Scheme for countryside can be presented concerning a broad aspects:

(1) Decreasing collective economics of countryside is the main element. The former collective economic organization was called *People's Public Community,* which is not only a collective production organization but also had multi-administrative and social functions. People's public community was a necessary pillar to support the collaboration medical scheme. Since the reform of economic structure in countryside, each family has become a contractor of infield and organized agriculture production by individual instead of collaboration activities. Therefore the collaboration medical scheme had only been insisted in those economic developed areas such as that in Sunan in Jiangsu provinces.

(2) Countrymen are not satisfied with the administration of the system, such as no equal and regulating benefit payment to every one, but some managers and their family members always be in priority, so that they would like to keep far from the system. A questionnaire by the Health Ministry of China in 1997 covering families 2960 in the countryside showed that 1/3(families 897) of them didn't care the collaboration medical scheme.

(3) Countrymen are not satisfied with the governance of the system due to the living standards and needs rising up more and more in the last 20 years so that the demands on medical care cost rising up also. They complain too low benefit to meet the needs of medical cost as well as they have to face too much qualifying conditions, this situation causes a negative influence to countrymen's willing choice.

3.2.3 Problems arisen from Collaboration Medical Scheme for Countryside

(1) The medical cost has been rising up rapidly so that most countrymen are finding it impossible to bear. Due to collaboration medical care service net had disappeared and some medical services have been provided by market way. During 1990s to 1999, person average income from RMB 686.31 yuan has been increased to RMB 2210.34 yuan, which was increased for 2 times. But, per seeing doctor cost and

treatment in hospital cost had been increased from RMB 10.9 yuan, 473.3 yuan to 79 yuan, 2891 yuan, which is accounted for 6.2 times and 5.1 times. Therefore 4% of them have no money to go to see doctor when they ill in 1985, 7% in 1993; and 13.4% of them have no money to go to hospital in 1985, 24.5% in 1993. This rate forenamed arisen in the poverty areas, such as that of mountain areas will be much more at 89%. A report of looking over selected areas during 1985 to 1993 shows that the agricultural labor productivity went down due to leaving on ills. Within 2 weeks, leaving on ill 5-4 and 2-4 at 69% and 86% went up 6-8 and 3-2 at 128.2% and 130.7%.

(2) Shortfall financing from government. In 1998, governmental gross expenditure on health service expenses was RMB 58.72 billion yuan, which was used to that in the countryside just RMB 9.25 billion yuan accounting for 15.9% of the governmental gross expenditure. Shortfall financing from government cause two problems:
- medical service at countryside provides in much shortfall;
- medical service at countryside goes to market service.

Besides, governmental financing budget to the health institutes at county level was account for 1/3 of real cost and expenditure, so that the medical service charge is main financing resource to support grass root health institutes. It causes no money to support the prevention of disease so that some epidemics spreading again there.

3.2.4 Proposals on Setting up a Medical Scheme for Countryside

In China, there had been a gap between cities and countryside on whatever governmental medical care expenditure or health resource's allocation; of course, residents in cities had been cared in priority. People's good health must be a precondition to realise modernization in the country. In the new century, China government should pay more attention to improve the health service and medical care for countryside. The main tasks can be focused on the followings :

(1) Increasing financing support to improve health service basic establishment, to- train medical service staff for quality medical service;

(2) Strengthening common prevention of various epidemics and public health service, which is value work of low cost and high interest. These works preceding are the liability of government with financing and staff.

(3) Developing and completing the collaboration medical scheme. The main tasks are :

- a sustainable financing resource by the local and grass root governments, which is necessary support to re-setting up the collaboration medical care scheme and an incentive to encourage countrymen to participate in;
- strengthening governance and administration for the scheme in order to put an end to defalcation; to supervise the fund management in open, equity and justness avoiding inequity phenomenon concerning contribution and benefits arisen between managers and mass.
- Regulating medical service action, controlling medicine price, defining a rate of compensation and creasing the account balance between expenditure and income.

(4) Trying to find and set up multi-form medical care scheme to meet the needs in accordance with the specific circumstance in local. Until 1998, 12.56% of countryside were insured under different medical care models including the collaboration medical scheme covered 6.5% (about population 50 million) of all countrymen. A flexible developing strategy can be designed as following :

- in the economic developed areas, it is possible to link the collaboration medical scheme with social medical scheme of cities without the gap;
- in the mid-income areas, it is possible to improve the collaboration medical scheme in high pooling level or to transfer the collaboration medical scheme into another, namely collaboration health insurance scheme for hospital cost or seeing doctor cost;
- in the poor areas, the current task is to provide social medical assistance avoiding some families to go back to poverty due to medical cost.

3.3 Social Security System for Township Economics

Township economics is comprehensive concept integrating all kind of countrymen's business, which has been developing rapidly after economic structure reform since 1978. Until the end of 2000, existing township enterprises were 20.84 million and employed 128.2 million is account for 25.7% of the gross population in the countryside. Township economics has become an important proportion of national economy accounting for 1/3 of GDP. The employed in Township economics is near the number of employed in cities.

3.3.1 Adscription of Township Economy's Social Security

Township economies has two features: on the one hand, it is an enterprise with the function of production, sale etc under market risk; on the other hand, it composed of farmers from local, most of them are in possession of land. Employed in township enterprise may live on their infield when they are facing social risks.

The features from township enterprises mentioned above are different to define social security model for them so that a multi-pillars structure are practised in the countryside in the last years, such as :

- most employed in township enterprises insured social security system;
- partial large size township enterprises set up retirement scheme by themselves likes that in the urban areas (retirement benefit is a replacement rate of individual former wage);
- social pooling old-age pension fund is set up in some economically developed areas;
- small township enterprises bought commercial life insurance for their employees;
- a limited number of employed in township enterprises have been covered by the formal social basic old-age pension scheme.

The specific situation presents that it is confused to define which kind of schemes are using to the residents in the countryside, social basic old-age pension or commercial model and collaboration model, due to township economy being a large transferring area between cities and countryside in developing China.

3.3.2 An Independent and Transitional Social Security Scheme for Countryside

On the one hand, employed in township enterprises are different with agriculture residents who have to face a series of social risks such as unemployment, occupational injury & disease and sick etc.; therefore they need the social security familiar with that for cities employed. On the other hand, employed in township enterprises are still closed to their infield, no historic burden to young township enterprises on social security liability, therefore the administrative model and benefit level of social security for them are not necessary to follow the model in cities. Before the reform of registered permanent residence system in China, a wise strategy is to set up an independent social insurance for township enterprises, which can be linked with that of cities.

(1) Keeping some differences between township enterprises employed, old-age pension scheme and the social old-age pension scheme for countryside due to the former are organized and the later are not. It is the essential characteristic as contribution of insurance scheme from the employee (individual) or employer (enterprises). Only township enterprise is possible to contribute for their employee and residents have to contribution by themselves totally.

(2) The essential characteristic of the township enterprises decides that its social insurance system is impossible belonging to that system in cities.

- Township enterprises are composed of countrymen. Normal it is small size and density labourers, which is as main field to increase employment (provide more jobs) under macro-economic policy. Therefore the policy option of township enterprise's social insurance system must be controlled in low labour cost (low contribution) to coincide with the employer's financing capacities and feeling there, otherwise, the final result will be contrary.

- Contribution and benefit for the employed in township enterprises may be lower than that in cities, because employed in township enterprises who has infield to live on when they are old-age.
- Social insurance system of township enterprise is just in beginning with a minimum level and giving up gradually. On the contrary, a heavy historic burden of liability for high level payment arisen from the social insurance system in cities, so it is necessary to avoid a unfair social policy option, namely transferring the historic liability of that in cities to township enterprise.
- The gap in broad between cities and countryside in China will disappear gradually accompanying the process of citilisation. For a long-term plan, the social insurance system of township enterprise is just a transitional social phenomenon in special economic developing period of China. Finally it will be integrated into the unified system of social insurance in the urban areas.

3.3.3 Initial Proposals on Social Insurance system for Township Enterprise

(1) What kind of schemes will be set up.

- Occupational injury and disease insurance scheme must be urgent and in priority for the protection of employee's health and safety at working place due to relative poor administration and high occupational accident rate currently;
- secondly, social old-age pension scheme contributed by the employees and employer together;
- thirdly, medical insurance scheme at enterprises level, which may be controlled at low cost;
- Finally, unemployment benefit to those who sold their own infield.

(2) Basic policies of seffing up the social insurance system of township enterprises.

- Administrative structure. An administrative agency will be set up within of the Labour and Social Security Bureau to governance and control the matters of the social insurance system of township enterprises;

- For occupational injury and disease insurance scheme will be contributed by the employer only and insurance benefit level must equals to that for the sufferers in the urban areas;

(3) Old-age pension scheme. Old-age pension scheme is managed by individual account model for per employee and financed by the employer and employee, each side 50%; contribution rate may be decided based on 60% pension replacement rate; contribution of the employer can be put into the production cost. And the individual saving account will be very easy to transfer, such as :

- When the insured employee is leaving the enterprise and returning agriculture labour, his (her) saving account may be transferred into another kind of scheme, namely social old-age pension in the countryside;
- When he (she) becomes a city resident, his (her) saving account may be transferred into another kind of scheme, namely old-age pension of township enterprises.

(4) Medical care scheme. For the badly ill, sets up a low level pooling fund, which is financed by the employer & employee, and 2/3 from the former, 1 / 3 from the later.

(5) Unemployment insurance. Linking with the reform in field in China, it is necessary to compensate those who sold the run right of contracting infield (including the employed in township enterprises), then ask them saving the compensative into the unemployment fund, in order to cover their risk when they are unemployed since it is impossible to go back their infield.

(6) Qualifying conditions. An economic assessment of all township enterprises will be necessary before setting up the social insurance scheme in township enterprises, due to existing a big economic gap among them. For those of running well, it is possible to prescribe them (the both of employer and employee) on legal obligation to contribute

for the social insurance scheme of township enterprises, and for those of running not well, it is possible to prescribe them (the both of employer and employee) to participate in the social insurance scheme of township enterprises voluntarily.

Abbreviations and Key words

The Labour and Social Security Ministry of China (MOLSS)

State Owner Enterprises (SOEs)

Badly illness pooling scheme

System of Minimum Living Guarantee in Cities

Social Old-age pension Scheme for Countryside

Collaboration Medical Care for Countryside

Social Insurance Scheme of Township Enterprises

*****

Appendix

1. The national population and structure (ten thousands)

Years	Gross population	According to sex		According to town		According to the age		
		Male	Female	Cities	Country side	0-14	15-64	65 and above
1990	114333	58904	55429	30919	84142			
1991	115823	59466	56357	30543	85280			
1992	117171	59811	57360	32372	84799			
1993	118617	60472	58045	33351	85166			
1994	119850	61246	58604	34301	85549			
1995	121121	61808	59313	35174	85947			
1996	122389	62200	60189	35950	86439			
1997	123626	63131	60495	36989	86637			
1998	124810	63629	61181	37942	86868			
1999	125909	64189	61720	38892	87017			
2000	126583	65355	61228	45844	80717	28979	88793	8811

2. Employed population in the towns (ten thousands)

Years	1990	1995	1996	1997	1998	1999	2000
1. Employed population	63909	67947	68850	69600	69957	70586	711 50
Employed Urban	16616	19093	19815	20207	20678	21014	21274
#SOEs	10346	11261	11244	11044	9058	8572	8102
Collecive Economies	3459	3147	3016	2883	1963	1712	1499
Share-hold Co-operation					136	144	155
Co-operation Corporate	96	53	49	43	48	46	42
Share-hold Corporate		317	363	468	410	420	457
Private company	57	485	620	750	973	1053	1268
Economies from Hong	4	272	265	281	294	306	310

Kong, Taiwan and Macao							
Foreign economies	62	241	275	300	293	306	332
Self-employed	614	1560	1709	1919	2259	2414	2136
Employed in rural	47293	48854	49035	49393	49279	49572	49876
#Township enterprises	9265	12862	13508	13050	12537	12704	12820
Private economies	113	471	551	600	737	969	1139
Self-employed	1491	3054	3308	3522	3855	3827	2934
2. Employees	14059	14908	14845	14668	12337	11773	11259
# enterprises							7507
Non-profit public institutes							2689.1
Organs							1061.6
#SOEs	10346	10955	10949	10766	8809	8336	7878
Collective economies inurban	3549	3076	2954	2817	1900	1652	1447
Others		877	941.7	1085.5	1627.6	1785.4	1934.5
Agricultural labourers employed in urban					913.8	928.8	
# State units					399.8	.390	
Collective units					239.6	226	
Others					273.7	312.8	

3. Private Enterprises and Self-employed In Cities and Countryside (1 999)

	Units (per)	Employed (ten thousand)
1. Both in urban and rural	33034345	82624624
# Private		2021 5478
Self-employed		62409146
2. Employed in Urban	1343321 2	34668671
# Private		10526269
Self-employed		24142402
3. Employed in rural		47955953
# Private		9689209
Self-employed		38266744

4. Employed who lost job within Cities Enterprises (person, 1999)

	Number	No. In center of re-employ-ment	Full received minimum living guarantee	Partial received minimum living guarantee	Non-received Minimum living guarantee
Employed lost job	9371765	7155462	5688764	894025	630480
#SOEs	6525157	6232677	5146362	690908	395407
Collective	2589115	829639	476100	183103	228243
Others	257493	90346	63502	20014	6830

5. Old-age pension Insured in Cities (ten thousand, %)

Years	1995	1996	1997	1998	1999	2000
Participants in law					11164.8	
Insured	8737.8	8758.4	8671	8475.8	9501.8	10448
Insured rate	76.9	78.4			85.1%	
Insured in enterprises	8737.8	8758.4	8671	8475.8	8566.3	9124.2
Insured in SOEs	7130.7	7044.9	6888.4	6647.2	6454.5	5136.7
Insured rate in SOEs		95.15				
Insured in collective enterprises in urban	1370.3	1455.5	1437.3	1370.3	1479.3	1467
Insured rate in collective enterprises in urban		51 .47				
Insured in others	236.8	258	354.3	458.3	721 .5	
#Insured in foreign* Hongkong* Taiwan * Macoa * enterprises			214.7	244.5	303.9	489
Insured in others		27.5				
Insured in law, but not		2414				
The rate insured in law, but not		21 .6%				
Insured in organs and non-profit public institutes					642.6	956
Insured in others					203.8	367.8

6. Minimum living guarantee in Cities and Countryside

Years	1996	1997	1998	1999	2000
Beneficiary in urban (ten thousand)	84.9	87.9	184.1	265.9	402.6
Expenditure (MM yuan)					27.23
Beneficiary in rural (ten thousand)				265.7	300.2
Expenditure (MM yuan)				8.3	7.34

7. Social Old-age Pension Scheme in Countryside (1999)

Insured (ten thousand)	6460.8
Beneficiaries(ten thousand)	30.1
Income in the year (ten thousand yuan)	240771
Expenditure in the year (ten thousand yuan)	65419
Rolling saving fund (ten thousand yuan)	1841795

8.the Coverage of All Kind of Medical Care in Countryside (%)

Years	1993	1998
Collective Co-operation	9.8%	6.5%
# Countryside I	28.7	22.21
Countryside II	9.1	3.24
Countryside III	0.7	1.62
Countryside IV	1.0	1.83
Free public medical care		1.16
Labour insurance medical care		0.71
Medical insurance		1.41
Pooling medical care fund		0.05
Medical care in charge		87.44
Others		2.73

9. Employed in Township Enterprises

Years	1997	1998	1999	2000
Enterprises (ten thousand)	907.5	2004	2070	2084
Employed (ten thousand)	13050	125337	12704	12820

3

Social Security Arrangements in Sri Lanka: An Assessment

Wasana Karunarathne

1. INTRODUCTION

Income insecurity in old age has become an acute problem in Sri Lanka. Given the demographic trends exhibiting individual and population ageing due to a mix of increasing longevity and declining fertility, time is of the essence in making a beginning towards reforms. Other than demographic concerns there are few other factors that challenge the existing social security system in Sri Lanka. First, the gradual collapse of the traditional old age support mechanism, mainly due to economic and social changes associated with industrialization, urbanization, migration and increase in female labour force participation, has necessitated increasing role for the formal social security arrangements. Secondly, macro-economic and micro-economic impacts of the formal social security arrangements, particularly of Pay-As-You-Go (PAYG) system have also come under increasing scrutiny in recent years. Third, pension reforms have become essential for fiscal consolidation and fiscal flexibility, and for deeper economic reforms relating to financial, capital and labour markets.

The social welfare provision in Sri Lanka goes back to the earliest days of Sri Lanka as a British colony. The current social legislation, which is still based on the original form of British policies, comprised Defined Contributory (DC) and Defined Benefit (DB) plans. Retirement saving is mandatory for the formal sector employees and the employees in the unorganized sector, which is defined as the self-employed including traders, farmers, fishermen and unpaid family workers, are covered by voluntary systems. In Sri Lanka unorganized sector is relatively large and represent more than one third of the labour force. Of the total employed labour force of 6.5 million in 2002, 13.2 percent was in the public sector, 45.1 percent was in the organized private sector and 2.9 percent was reported as employers (the Central Bank of Sri Lank, 2003). Thus, the bulk (38.8 percent of the labour force) in the unorganized sector does not have a proper security system in their old age. Inspite of the limited scope and size, the dualistic nature of the social security arrangements in Sri Lanka represents another crucial problem, which should be mitigated. This feature has caused labour market distortions creating a wide disparity between public and private sector workers.

Rest of the paper is organized as follows. Section 2 discusses the structure of the current social security arrangements. Private sector pension schemes are discussed in section 2.. Section 2.2 analyses the pension schemes in the public sector. Section 2.3 summarizes voluntary schemes for organized sector employees. An assessment of the existing system and reform directions are discussed followed by the concluding remarks.

2. STRUCTURE OF THE CURRENT SOCIAL SECURITY ARRANGEMENT

Chart 1 summarizes the formal social security system in Sri Lanka. While the private sector employees primarily rely on mandatory savings schemes, which are of the defined contribution (DC) type; public sector employees are covered by Defined Benefit (DB) schemes and have been linked with the Widows and Orphans (W&OP) schemes that cover the dependents of the members. Initially, the government employees were covered by Pay-As-You-Go type non-contributory Public Service Pension Scheme (PSPS) and by the contributory Public Service Provident Fund (PSPF), which was mandate for non-permanent public sector employees. As a result of continuous pressure on social security reforms from many national and international organizations, including the World Bank and IMF, the government recently introduced a new contributory pension scheme for the new entrants to the public service. The Contributory Pension Fund (EPF), Employees' Trust Fund (ETF) and the Approved Private Provident Funds (APPF) are the schemes for private and semi government sector employees.

While the coverage for the formal sector is significantly high as it covered under the mandatory pension systems, the current pension systems have not yet sufficiently penetrated the unorganized sector. During last couple of years few voluntary pension plans for unorganized sector (Farmers Pension and Social Security Scheme, Fishermen's Pension and Social Security Benefit Scheme, Pension and Social Security Benefit Scheme for the Self-Employed) were introduced, but the coverage and the size of these funds are limited.

The formal retirement system in Sri Lanka is financed by three methods: general tax revenues, contributions from members or from a combination of the both general tax revenues and contributions. The public sector pension scheme is totally an unfunded system which is financed by the general tax revenues. In contrast, all the provident funds are contributory and fully funded. On the other hand widows and orphans schemes are partially funded schemes that receive contributions from both the government as well as from the employees.

2.1 SOCIAL SECURITY ARRANGEMENT IN THE PRIVATE SECTOR

Private sector social security arrangements in Sri Lanka consist of three major schemes; Employees' Trust Fund (ETF) and the Approved Private Provident Funds (APPFs). The Mercantile Sector Provident Society (MSPS), established in 1940 was the first provident fund in Sri Lanka. The rules of the MSPS were revised in 1978 and encompassed with the EPF, the largest social security fund in Sri Lanka.

Employees' Provident Fund (EPF)

The Employees Provident Fund is established in 1958 with the objective of providing superannuation benefits to employees of the private sector and government corporations. EPF, the largest single fund in term of its asset size and membership is administered by the Monetary Board of the Central Bank of Sri Lanka on behalf of the Department of Labour. The board is also responsible for management and investment of the balances.

There is no wage ceiling to contribute to the fund. The total contribution rate is 20% of gross wages; 12% from the employer and 8% from the employee. The benefits are paid as a lump sum upon attaining the retirement age of 55 years. This sum represents cumulative net contributions (gross contributions less any pre-retirement withdrawals) and the rate of return credited to the individual accounts. Table 1 and Table 2 summarize main characteristic of the EPF for the 1990-2002 period, on the basis of which the following observations may be made.

Coverage: Contributions to the EPF is mandatory for all the private sector organizations and government corporations regardless the nature and size of the organization. In 2002, the EPF had 1.98 million contributions (slightly more than a quarter of the labour force) contributing Rs. 18.93 billion (1.19 percent of GDP). The membership of the EPF however has exceeded labour force since 1994 as a result of a large number of document accounts, as members are not allowed to transfer their accounts when changing jobs. Thus, contributors to members' ratio have been declining (in 2002, only about 1 in 5 members were contributors) creating administrative burden of the EPF. The coverage of the EPF scheme has expanded over time with the increased formal sector employment. The number of employers has increased from about 28,000 in 1990 to about 47,400 in 2002.

Contributions: As a result of moderate economic growth, expanding employment, rising wages and contribution rates, contributions to the EPF have increased in absolute terms over the past two decade. In 2002, the total contributions were Rs. 18.93 billion as compared to 0.74 billion in 1980 and 3.9 billion in 1990. However, compared to other countries (5.5 in Malsysia, 10.4 in Singapore), in Sri Lanka, EPF contributions as a percentage of Gross Domestic Product (GDP) and Gross National Product (GNS) are quite low and stagnant. In 2002, the ratio of contributions to GDP was only 1.19 and of contributions to GNS was 6.06 percent.

Members' Balance: The average balance per members in quite low at Rs. 31,653. While 40.5 percent of the member accounts have a balance below Rs. 2,500,87.5 percent have a balance below Rs. 50,000, which is even lower than the country's per capita income of Rs. 83,382 (in 2002). It is obvious that the inactive member accounts can have a low balance in their accounts, but the average balance per contributor is also low at Rs. 148, 503 in 2002. The average amount withdrawn at retirement in 2002 was Rs. 91,493 equivalent to 1.1 times the per capita income. This suggests inadequate retirement balances for most the members.

Pre-retirement Withdrawals: In 1988, EPF act was amended in order to facilitate pre-retirement withdraws for the members in the form of housing loans. According to the amendment, active members are eligible to obtain housing loans up to 75% of their member balances from the approved lending institutions. In the year 2002, the EPF has approved 19,502 loan applications adding Rs. 2.67 billion, to the total sum of Rs. 10 billion during the period of 1988 to 2002. If a member fails to pay due installments, the short payment will be paid from the debtor's EPF balance with huge penal rated on evasions.

Investment performance: The EPF is the major primary market investor in Sri Lankan bond market as its funds are mandated to invest largely in government debt instruments (In 2002, EPF owned 59 percent of the government's rupee loans and 31 percent of the treasury bonds). This indicates that the investment function is not undertaken to obtain an effective diversification of the portfolio and this has resulted to low rate of returns on member balances. The bond market is relatively undeveloped, with only a few players, low turnover and low returns on long-term investment portfolios. EPF also participated in secondary market operations of government securities and equities.

In 2002, 97.5 percent of EPF's total investment of Rs. 262.56 billion was invested in government securities (65 percent in rupee loans), while Rs. 1.22 billion was invested in equities. EPF has earned a gross rate of return of 19.27 percent by operations in equity market while the rate of returns from investments in government securities was 14 percent.

Rate of Return: Rate of return on EPF is mainly linked to the interest rates applicable for those government papers and it is determined after ascertaining the net income of the fund (gross income minus expensed incurred and the income tax paid). Interest rates on government papers are comparatively low compared with the other investment instruments and these rates are not indexed to the high inflation. EPF is also required to build up prudential reserves before declaring interest on member balances. Therefore the rate of return on member balance remains very low. The average annual compound growth rate (AACGR)5 for the real rate of return on investments of EPF was -o.29 in the period of 1961-2002 and it was 1.44 in the period of 1988-026. Negative and low positive returns obviously do not permit the power of compound interest to be harnessed for retirement benefits. The potential provided by the mandatory savings scheme to benefit from the power of compound interest is thus not realized, and neither has been the opportunity to enhance efficiency of the saving-investment process.

EPF is considered as the largest corporate taxpayer of the government. This is an unusual treatment, as in most countries; provident funds are exempted from income taxation. The fund is subjected to a 10 percent tax on its gross income. In 2002, it was liable to pay a sum of Rs. 3.32 billion income taxes contributing 14.49 percent of the corporate tax (Rs. 22.90 billion) revenue of the government.

Employees' Trust Fund (ETF)

The Employees' Trust Fund, a DC plan set up in 1981, is administered by the ETF Board and supervised by the Ministry of labor and Vocational Training. It covers the employees of private sector enterprises, government establishments, corporations, and universities. The contribution rate is 3 percent of gross earnings, and is payable by the employer. Unlike the EPF, ETF allows its members to withdraw accumulated balanced upon changing employment.

Other then the benefits paid at retirement ETF provides variety of other benefits to members. These non-retirement schemes include Automatic Life Insurance Scheme, Permanent Disability Insurance Scheme, Financial Assistance Scheme for Heart Surgeries, Financial

Grants for the Children who pass the Year Five Scholarship Examination, and Viyana Housing Loan Scheme. Similar to EPF'S housing loan scheme, ETF, with the assistance of National Development Bank (NDB Housing) introduced a Housing Loan scheme for the ETF members since June, 2002. The eligibility criterion is maintaining a minimum of five year continuous member ship with the ETF Board (ETFB) through the employer. Under this scheme members can obtain loans up to one million Sri Lankan Rupees by pledging their member accounts. However, approval of the loans is subjected to Bank's assessments of employees' ability to repayments.

According to Table 3, the ETF had 2.4 million member accounts and 1.8 million contributors in 2002. There were 39.112 employers contribution to the fund. In the same year ETF had total contributions of approximately Rs. 3.46 billion. It paid claims worth of Rs. 2.5 billion and other benefits worth of Rs. 0.21 billions. Its accumulated balances as of December 2002 were Rs. 38.98 billion.

Unlike the EPF, the ETF regulations permit domestic equity investments. However, for the last few years ETF has also been shrinking its investment horizon from diversified portfolios to bulk government investments given the volatility and the uncertainty prevailing in the equity markets in the country. In 2000 , around 77 percent of the ETF's total investment were in government securities while the percentage increased to 82.7 at the end of 2002. In 1996, nearly 20 percent of ETF'S investments were in shares and debentures but the share in 2002 was only 4.7. ETF is also liable to pay an income tax of 10%.

The AACGR of real rate of returns on its investment was 0.48 for the 1982-2002 period, and 0.22 for 1989-2002 period. The corresponding figures were 0.57 for and 0.33 for the 1982-99 and 1989-99 periods respectively. The reduction of accommodated growth of the average real interest rates in mainly due to reduction in rates of returns. Low real rate of returns once again reflects poorly on investment policies and performance.

Approved Private Provident Funds (APPF)

Under the EPF act, Commissioner of Labour has the power of

approving private provident funds for specific firms to cover its own employees. APPFs are closed funds managed by the Board of Custodians. While both employers and employees make contributions for these schemes, the rate varies from firm to firm. Some APPFs contribute to a total of 25 percent (15 percent by employer and 10 percent by employee) However, there is a requirement that the rate of contribution cannot be lower than the one required by the EPF.

By the end of 2002, there were around 200 APPFs with 165,000 members and about Rs. 79.7 billion (5 percent of GDP) assets (Central Bank of Sri Lanka, 2003; p 259). The Mercantile Sector Provident Fund (MSPF), which covers the firms belonging to the Ceylon Chamber of Commerce, is one of the major funds among them (Ranan-Eliya et al, 1998).

APPFs are considered as more flexible that the EPF scheme. Unlike the situation with the EPF, APPFs have greater freedom in investment management. They can therefore seek market opportunities for higher returns. The provision to withdraw balances as a lump sum when a member leaves the establishment, even if it is not due to retirement, is however not conducive financial security in old age. Details of investment performance of the APPFs are not available. There is no centralized agency which supervises them and keeps records.

2.2 Social Security Arrangement in the Public Sector

Originally, the public sector pension system was consisted of mandatory schemes: Public Service Pension Scheme (PSPS) and Public Service Provident Fund (PSPF). Widows and Orphans Pension Scheme, Widowers and Orphans Pension Scheme and Teachers, Widows and Orphans Pension Scheme are the three other schemes those cover the close defendants of the public sector employees. In addition to the mandatory schemes, there are three government administered voluntary pension schemes to cover the informal sector employees: Farmers' Pension Scheme, Fishermen's Pension Scheme, and Pension Scheme for the self-employed.

Pension payments under the PSPS currently account for 9.5% (in 2002) of recurrent expenditure of the government and is expected to grow steadily, especially given the adverse demographic trends in the country. As demographics dictate that the future working population will decrease, it would place a greater burden on future generations which will create severe intergenerational conflicts. PSPS, which covers the bulk of the government employees is a defined benefit type unfunded scheme thus there is an explicit obligation the government is responsible to be met. But it would be very difficult to meet this obligation as the government debt is already at an astronomically high level of 105.3% if GDP (2002).

Thus, the non-contributory public pension scheme is not sustainable and would have dampened fiscal consolidation efforts in the future specially given the adverse demographic trends in the country. In the light of these issues the PAYG type PSPS was replaced in January 2003 by a contributory pension scheme; Contributory Pension Fund (CPF) applicable to all new recruits to the public service.

Contributory Pension Scheme (CPF)

The CPF, a contributory but defined benefit type social security scheme, replaced the PSPS from January 2003. It will cover the employees recruited to the public service or provincial public service on permanent basis. Nevertheless, the casual and temporary staff will continue to contribute to the PSPF, which is also contributory but defined contributory type. While the head of the department of pensions is charged with the administration of the fund, the Monetary Board of the Central Bank is vested with the management of the member accounts and investments.

The contribution rate for the eligible employees will be as same as for EPF members (8 percent by the employee and 12 percent by the government or provincial government), while retires are entitled to a monthly pension according to the period of service. Further, an employee, who is entitled to a monthly pension according to the period of service. Further, an employee, who is entitled to a monthly pension will also receive a gratuity equal to twenty four months of the monthly pension payable. A member who has contributed to the fund for thirty years or more will receive a monthly salary of seventy percent of his last drawn salary, whereas when the service is less than thirty years of service one percent for each six months period will be deducted.

Public Service Pension Scheme (PSPS)

PSPS, a Defined Benefit (DB) mandatory scheme set up in 1901 is an funded scheme, which is financed from the government budget. It covers public sector employees including civil servants, armed served, provincial and local government employees, government teachers and judicial officers. The scheme absorbed the teachers of non-government schools and the local government employees in 1970 and 1987 respectively.

The public service employees are also mandatorily covered for survivor and disability benefits. These contributory schemes currently cover the dependents of all government employees who are eligible for pensions, and they are entitled to the full amount of the pension of the deceased pensioners. The mandatory contributions vary between 4 and 7 percent of the basic salary, depending on the salary scale.

Pension payments are calculated to the last drawn salary and the replacement rate (85-90 percent) depends on the salary grading and the Year Of Service (YOS). In addition, a lump sum of two years of last drawn salary is payable upon the retirement.

For the last couple of decades the on-going civil war has considerably contributed to increase the number of armed-forces pensioners. Further, number of retirees increased immediately as a result of the special public retirement circular 44/90. Table 4 and 5 show the sharp increase in number of pensioners and the pension expenditure. According to table 5, Pensions expenditure has grown four times from Rs. 8.10 billion in 1992 to Rs. 31.12 billion in 2002 and the growth rate is comparatively high compared with the GDP growth (however the ratio of pension expenditure to GDP is relatively constant). The average growth rate of the pension expenditure during last decade was 12.65 percent, while the average economic growth was only 5 percent. In 2002, the government expenditure on pensions as a percentage of current expenditure was 9.42, equivalent to 1.96 percent of GDP. The escalating trends and fiscal impact of the public sector pension schemes (along with rigid wage bill in the pubic sector) has led the Central Bank to warn about the medium term fiscal sustainability unless strong measures are taken to tackle these expenditures (Central Bank of Sri Lanka, 2002 P.1).

The Public sector pension scheme in Sri Lanka is relatively generous when viewed in terms of replacement rate, protection against longevity risks and survivors' benefits. However, the average salary in the public sector is low as compared with the private sector. Low salary obviously result in low monthly pension payments although the replacement rate is reasonably high. Char 2 shows that 38.1 percent of the civil service pensioners receives monthly pension between Rs. 2001-4000 and around 50.1 receives monthly pension between Rs. 4001-6000 (per capita GDP in 2001 is Rs. 75,133). Among the other pensioners (including Teachers, Armed forces, W & OP pensioners) 54.3 percent receive monthly pension payments between Rs. 2001-4000 and 38.8 percent receive pension between 4001-6,000 However, as the pension payment is not indexed to wages or inflation but has been adjusted on an ad hoc basis the replacement rate in real terms has been low. There have been only five pension adjustments in the last fifteen years and these adjustments were only motivated by short term political goals and not solely based on economic considerations. In 2000, around 45 percent of the beneficiaries received monthly pension below Rs. 4,000 (US$ 41), 91 percent of them earned below Rs. 6000 (US $62) and only about 0.01 percent had monthly pension between Rs. 10,000-20,000.

In Sri Lanka, the minimum retirement age of government service is 55 years (mandatory retirement age is 60). This low retirement age allows employees to join the private sectors after retiring from the public service wild collecting their monthly pension installments from the government.

Public Service Provident Fund (PSPF)

The Public Sector Provident Fund (PSPF), first established in 1942 under the act number 18 of 1942, is a mandatory scheme, which covers government employees, who are not eligible for the pension scheme. Unlike PSPS, this scheme requires contributions from both employees and employers. It is therefore fully funded by these contribution. The benefits are form of lump sum payment on the retirement and the contribution rates are 12% from the government and 8% from employee on the gross salary. This scheme is governed under the Ministry of Public administration and Home Affairs.

The governance structure comprises a board of management, chaired by the Director of Pension including three public servants and a member representative.

The PSPF is considered as a transit point for government employees who are looking to join the PSPS (for an example, temporary staff until they are entitled to pension scheme after getting permanent positions). A member in this scheme can stop contributions and claim what he is entitled, when he join the PSPS. By 1999, there were 1,65,455 member accounts with 59,021 contributors contributing 420 million rupees.

PSPF invests only in government papers. Therefore as the case with EPF, the rate of return on its portfolio investment is low. In 1999, its nominal rate or return was 12.02 percent and this is a 15 percent decrease when compare the peak of 14.22 percent in 1995. AACGR of the nominal rate of returns of the PSPF was 8.2 during 1960-99 8.2 percent (-0.14 in real terms) and 15.25 during 1989-99 (1.7 in real terms)

Schemes for Dependents of Government Employees

The public service employees are mandatorily covered for survivor and disability benefits. These contributory schemes currently cover the dependants12 of all government employees who are eligible for pensions, and they are entitled to full pension of the deceased pensioners. Unlike PSPS, W & O.P is contributory; the contributions are made of employees' mandatory contribution of 4-7 percent on their basic salary, depending on the salary scale. Before 1997, the scheme was maintained as a separate fund, but not it has been absorbed in to general revenues. Thus, though contributory, it creates fiscal burden.

The first scheme called Widows' and Orphans' (W & OP) Pension fund was introduced in 1898 under the ordinance of No 1 of 1898 and Widows' and Orphans' Pension Scheme was introduced under the ordinance no 13 of 1906. In 1951, the scheme was extended to teachers and in 1983; the Widowers' and Orphans' pension scheme was introduced.

In 2001, contributions amounted to Rs. 4.75 billion (0.3 percent of GDP); and 103,528 dependents received survivors' benefits under these schemes. The dependency ratio13 of this scheme can be expected to increase in the future because of individual ageing. The current contribution rates many therefore prove to be inadequate.

2.3 ARRANGEMENT FOR UNORGANIZED SECTOR

Bulk of the labour force participated in the unorganized sector. The effort to provide a better social security for these workers has been few and fragmentary. This category, whose incomes are very low and subjects to wide fluctuations, consists of small farmers, fisherman, construction and manufacturing workers and retail traders.

Farmers' and Fisheries' Pension Scheme

Recently government has introduced three mandatory pension schemes for self employed in order to provide a better security in their disabled age. Under these arrangements, the first scheme: Farmers' pension scheme was introduced in 1987 under the Agricultural and Agrarian Insurance Board (AAIB). The prime objective of this scheme is to provide financial assistance to farmers to conduct their livelihood providing an old age pension to members after the age 60 and to provide group insurance over death and disability in the age group 18 to 60 (Gunatilake, 1992). Under the farmers' and fishermen's pension schemes members are required to contribute around Rs. 65 to Rs. 345 once every three months. Benefits, ranging from Rs. 1,000 to Rs. 4,167, are paid after the retirement age of 60 according to the age of involvement to the scheme. Under this scheme, other benefits; such as permanent or partial disability benefits and survivor benefits are also paid.

Since its establishment, nearly 6,70,000 farmers have obtained membership in the Farmers' Pension Scheme and around 17,000 are receiving pension payments (Daily news, 13 January 2003). AABI currently spends over RS. 15 million monthly to pay pensions to a large number of farmers. Later, the farmers' pension scheme was extended its benefits to the fisheries community. Currently 48,000 fishermen have obtained membership under this pension scheme, while 460 are receiving pensions.

Pension And social security benefit scheme for self-employed

The social security board was established in 1996 under the Ministry of Social Services under the terms of the Social Security

Board Act No. 17 of 1996 to implement a pension and social security benefit scheme for self-employed and informal sectors employees other than those in fisheries and agricultural sectors. Self-employed persons in the age group of 18-59 years are eligible to enrol themselves as members. Similar to farmers' and fishers' pension scheme, benefits are paid as a monthly pension and partial and members are also eligible for partial or total disability gratuity, and death gratuity. The Act (and amendment to the original Act in 1999) has introduced three schedules (A, C and D) for contributions and benefits (Gazette, Government of Sri Lanka 1996, 1999). The amount of contribution and the benefits are different from one schedule to another. For a contributor, who joins the scheme under Schedule A at an age of 18 years are required to pay a quarterly instalment of Rs. 50 (186 installments) and will entitle to a monthly pension of Rs. 2,500 at retirement. Under the Schedule C, a person, who join at the same rate but contribute a monthly payment of Rs 100 (504 instillments) will be entitled to a monthly pension of Rs. 5,000. While according to the Schedule D, a contributor should pay Rs. 155 of monthly instalment (totally 504 installments) to receive a monthly payment of Rs. 8,000. Further, the Act has given permission to pay the total contribution as lump sum. Again the monthly pension entitlement is different according to the schedule and the age of joining the scheme.

Nearly 60,000 self-employed had registered themselves for membership in the Pension and Social Security Benefit Scheme of the Social Security Board of the Ministry of Social Welfare by the end of 2001.

2.4 AN ASSESSMENT OF THE EXISTING SYSTEM

Sri Lanka has a well-established social security system to provide income security for the elderly. However, after examining existing retirement income arrangements, De Mel concludes that they lack coherence and planning in the design, management and in methods of financing that have been adopted (De Mel P. 48). Thus, there are several impressive reason that the current person arrangement require urgent reforms. These reforms however, should be taken carefully considering the overall consequence of such reforms.

In recognition of the hazards of the unfunded public pension scheme, introduction of CPF is a big step. A mandatory funded pension scheme can provide substantial social security for its members if the fund collects and receive adequate level of contributions relative to salary and a respectable level of real returns on the investment of the accumulated contributions (Shah, 1997). Publicly mandated defined benefit pension funds can be found around the world including in Japan, Korea and United States. However, most of these funds are partially funded and there is no evidence of a fully funded defined benefit plan (Iglesias et al, 2000). Iglesias et al also find that the performance of publicly managed pension funds in the countries that have low governance rating is considerable poor that in the countries which have better governments. Being a defined benefit pension scheme, CPF will definitely face lots of challenges in the future. As benefits are defined, the government is always responsible for the investment risk. Looking at the poor investment strategies that the EPF has followed for last couple of decades, earning higher returns for CPF's investments will be much more challenging.

In recent years, Sri Lanka has experienced persistently large budget deficits. The cost of the PAYG, Public Service Pension Scheme has been a significant contributor or the deficit. Although implementation of the new pension scheme eases the growing budgetary pressure, financing the transition cost will be big challenge. Size of he transition cost varies with the level of the benefits, retirement age, and replacement rates act. Given that adverse side of all those factors; i.e. Higher and generous benefit and replacement level and early retirement age of 55, funding the transition cost will be another burden that can result increasing general taxes, reducing government investments and to increase government budget deficits.

The overview of the current social security arrangements reveals that there can be a dichotomy in the labour market due to the dualistic nature of the current social security system. Firstly, it was criticized as being a deterrent to labour market mobility between sectors (World Bank, 2000; De Mel, 2000; Rannan-Eliya et al, 1996). One has to retire out of the public service to be eligible to government pensions, for examples a public sector employee cannot conceive making a move to the private sector at say age 50 since he or she loose all pension benefits, this severely inhibits labour market mobility. Secondly, the private sector employees are covered under Defined Contribution (DC) fully funded scheme, without any protection against longevity and inflation risks, while the civil servants are privileged for generous pension benefits, though they do not contribute for their pensions but are protected against not only longevity risk but also receive survivos' benefits. These features adversely impact on the labour market mobility between the two sectors as benefits are heavily skewed towards the public sector.

Retirement income system in Sri Lanka is heavily biased towards the wage employees (Wijewardena, 1999). Thus, the informal sector employees including self-employed, which contains 41.1 percent of the labour force of not have a proper income security in their old age. The entire process of EPF, including the registration lies with the Employers, and do not have any contact with the beneficiaries. As a result, beneficiaries become aware of failures of their employers only at the time of retirement. Further, because of this process, it has been also recognized that there is an evasion of registering with Provident Funds, for both EPF and ETF. Employers have obvious reasons for evasion of registration; thus, employees in many small-scale firms have missed the chance of getting in income security. There is a need to empower the employees and the members of various schemes.

The funded DC system has not been able to realize full potential, and a result the respective organization are hard pressed to justify their administrative records practices, and investment policies and performance. Even after 50 years of operations, the Provident Fund scheme has not been able to institute genuine individual accounts, relying instead on employers' registration thus have major challenges in compliance and in lowering administration costs.

The Monetary Board of the Central Bank of Sri Lanka responsible for investment of the EPF balances is also assigned the task of managing government debt. These two roles are conflicting because the fiduciary responsibilities require maximizing returns to the members, while its debt management role requires it to finance government debt in the cheapest possible manner.

It is also evident that there is no regulatory or other agency which ensures that all the different elements of formal social security systems are supervised with a view to enhancing effectiveness of each component, and ensuring that the elements from a coherent whole. Thus it is necessary to consider an independent provident and pension funds authority with the mission to fill the above gaps. This would end the conflicts of interest noted above. Such an authority should also be entrusted with regulating and supervising tax-advantage voluntary savings schemes; and pension products of life insurance companies.

The level of financial protection provided by provident funds is quite uncertain since its benefits are form of a lump sum rather than annuities. In addition, though the replacement rate is higher public sector employees, it has also been estimated that the replacement rate14 provided by EPF is much lower than the desirable level for the lower income countries. In spite of the high contribution rates, the accumulated balances of EPF members are low due to pre-retirement withdrawals (mostly done by lower income workers) and low rate of returns on accumulated balances. Thus, pre-retirement withdrawals from provident fund balanced have further increased the longevity risk after retirement. Given the increase in individual ageing, considerably low member balances at retirement can hardly be called as a proper income security during their old age. Therefore it is essential to control pre-retirement withdrawals.

Tax arrangement for mandatory saving schemes are rather unsatisfactory. (Despite of low rate of returns earned investing in government securities; EPF is subjected to a 10 percent tax on its gross income). Taxation on retirement savings is important due to many reasons. Most importantly, taxes on pension fund assets could significantly reduce the actual funds available for consumption during retirement and could significantly affect viability and effectiveness of financial products for retirement. Secondly, different tax treatments for different financial institutions and products in to which retirement saving are channeled to impact on efficient allocation of savings and credit in the economy. The tax treatment of income from pre-retirement investment schemes could also impact on allocation of savings to various uses. Finally, taxes can directly and indirectly affect the incentives for individuals retirement saving. There are three flows; contributions, Income accruing from investment of accumulated funds of taxation or withdrawal at the time of Retirement whether in the form of an Annuity or a lump sum; of a DC pension plan (Asher, 2001).

Provident fund balances are nearly wholly invested in government debt instruments. There is thus little effective diversification of even the largest provident funds. Main argument of EPF for not diversifying its portfolio is that the high risk of investing in some asset classes mainly in equities. However, financial theory suggests that when the investment horizon is long, potential risks of equities will decrease and the respective returns will increase. Risk can also be reduced by diversification among less (or uncorrelated) correlated assets. Thus, EPF neglects the benefits of investment diversification, Particularly as most of the bonds are government bonds with administered interest rates.

There is a case for pension regulator on the grounds of financial solvency, fiduciary responsibility, professionalization of management. But investment regulations beyond prudential requirements are not justified in financial theory (Bodie, 1990; Shah, 1995; Valdes-Prieto,1999). Several studies have Shawn that the long-term returns of pension funds in many countries, which have restrictions on asset allocation, are relatively low. Chile and Peru in 1997 (Shah, 1997); Malaysia in 2000 (Asher, 2001); US (Thaler, 1994), India (Asher, 2002) are few examples. They argue that the potential losses due to restrictions on investments are very high as they have created profound biases against competition, efficiency and specialization.

Although, the EPF began diversifying its portfolio since last couple of years, poor corporate governance, political motivation, and lack of good quality assets due to poor and uncertain capital and financial market conditions in the country has complicated and reduced alternative portfolio investment capacities. Thus, provision of adequate real rate of returns for investments is a major challenge.

Gradual de-linking of the private and the public sector provident funds from budgetary financing will be an essential step in moving to professional investment policies and performance (De Mel, 2000;

The World Bank, 2000). Positive signals in ending long standing internal conflict in Sri Lanka provides a good opportunity for steps in this direction. India has formally accepted the need for such de-linking but the results have so far been very limited. Efficiency with which the mandatory savings are translated into investments is of crucial importance. If a provident fund invests totally in government securities it become similar to a PAYG system in its effects, as it is serviced by future generations from taxes. Therefore, effective investment diversification across asset classes and across sectors is essential for any provident fund investment portfolio (Asher, 2000). For this task, however, financial and capital market reforms are essential, but can not be expected to achieve neither easily nor quickly due to current economic performances in the country.

ETF also does not reveal a successful investment history. Given its current practices, which are different from the original goals, the ETF is essentially duplicating the EPF.

2.5 Concluding Remarks

The brief overview of the social security system of Sri Lanka provided in this paper strongly suggests that each of the elements or components of the social security system is in need of carefully planned reforms to bring it to the international benchmark concerning governance and sustainability.

The largest ccmponent, the EPF, suffers from serious administration and compliance problems; its investment guidelines do not permit effect investment diversification among asset classes, products, and internationally. It also has high-retirement withdrawals. The measures to empower members are also inadequate.

There is also duplication of functions between the ETF and the EPF. Their consolidation should therefore receive urgent consideration. The avenue of exemption from the ETF for large firms, who can provide at least the same level of benefits at the EPF, can be expanded to provide additional point of comparison with the EPF and the ETF.

The EPF authorities may also wish to consider a phased withdrawal of accumulated balances (e.g. by requiring a fixed deposit to be made of a minimum sum, above which lump sum withdrawals may still be permitted)15.

While Sri Lanka has relatively good social and economic indicators and social security system compare to most of the low-income countries, the above suggest that reforms are urgently needed. Political commitment to such reforms and greater literacy among public and policy makes will remain crucial elements in addressing the challenges of social security reforms in Sri Lanka.

References

1. Abeykoon. A. T. P. L., 1996. Demographic Implications of Healthcare in Sri Lanka, *Asia pacific Population Journal,* Vol. 1, No. 2, pp. 47-58.
2. Aeher M. G. 2002. "Reforming India's Mandatory Savings Schemes and Civil Service Pensions Arrangements", Paper presented at symposium on problem and prospects of pension reforms in India, National Insurance Academy, Pune, India, February 20-21, 2002
3. Asher M.G. 2001. Pension Reform, Capital Markets, and corporate governance in Malaysia, *Journal of Financial Regulation and Compliance,* Vol. 9 (1), pp. 30-38.
4. Asher, M.G. and Karunarathne, W., 2001. "Social Security Arrangements m Singapore: An Assessment, a Discussion Paper, International Seminar on Pensions, Institute of Economic Research, Hitotsubashi University, Tokyo, Japan.
5. Asher, M.&, 2000. "An Assessment of Social Security Arrangements in Malaysia" A paper for the volume edited by I. R. Rajan, Center for Development Studies, Trivendrum.
6. Bodie., Z. 1990. "Managing Pension and Retirement Assets: An International Perspective", *Journal of Financial Services Research*, 4. pp. 419-460.
7. Central Bank Of Sri Lanka, Annual reports, Various years, Colombo Sri Lanka.
8. Cooper, G. and Brooks, P. (1999) "Pension Fund Management Fundamentals", A paper presented at the Asian Development Bank Pension Funds reform Workshop, Singapore, November 9-13, 1999.
9. Daily News, Online edition of Daily News, http://www. dailynews.1k
10. De Mel, N.C. 2000. "Designing Retirement—Income—Security Arrangements : Theory Issues and Applications to Sri Lanka", Human Resources Development Series No. 3, Institute of Policy Studies, Colombo,

Sri Lanka

11. Department of Census and Statistics of Sri Lanka, Official Web-site, http://www.lanka.net/etf.
12. De Silva, W.I., 1994. "How Serious is Ageing in Sri Lanka and What Can Be Done about It", *Asia-Pacific Population Journal*, 9, 1, pp. 19-37.
13. De Silva, W. I. 1997. Population Projections for Sri Lanka : 1991-2041, Human resources Development Series No. 2. Institute of Policy Studies, Sri Lanka.
14. Government of Sri Lanka. 1996. Gazette Extraordinary of the Democratic Socialist Republic of Sri Lanka.
15. Government of Sri Lanka, 1999. Gazette Extraordinary of the Democratic Socialist Republic of Sri Lanka. Part I, Section (I).
16. Gunatilake, G., 1992. "Social Security in Sri Lanka : A Country Case Study", ed. by Getubi& L.P. and Schmidt S., *Rethinking Social Security : Reaching Out to the Poor*, Asian and Pacific Development Center, Kula Lumpur, Malaysia
17. Iglesias, A and Palacios R. J. 2000. "Managing Public Pension Reserves, Part 1: evidence from the international experience", SP discussion paper, No. 3, The World Bank.
18. Karunarathue, W. and Goswani, R., 2002. "Reforming formal social security systems in India and Sri Lanka". *International Social Security Review*, 55(4), pp. 89-106.
19. Ranan-Eliya. R.P., De Mel, N., Ramachandran. E. and Senagama, D., 1998. Ageing and Pensions Study, Final Report, Institute of Policy Studies, Colombo, Sri Lanka.
20. Rannan-Eliya, R.P. 1999. "Economic Impacts of Demographic Ageing : with Special Emphasis on Sri Lanka and Old-age Income Security, Institute of Policy Studies of Sri Lanka, Health Policy Programme, Colombo, Sri Lanka.
21. Shah, H., 1997. "Toward Better Regulation of Private Pension Funds", working paper 1791, The World Bank. Washington D.C.
22. Thaler, I. and Williamson, J.P. 1994. College and University Endowment Funds: Why not 100% Equities?, *Journal of Portfolio Management*, Vol. 21(1) Fall Issue, pp 27-38.
23. The World Bank, 1994. "Averting the old age crisis : policies to protect the old and promote growth", New York : Oxford University Press.

24. The World Bank. 1996. "Sri Lanka — In The Year 2000: An Agenda for Action", World Development Sources, New York : Oxford University Press.

25. The World Bank, 2000. "Review of Superannuation Benefit Programs in Sri Lanka", Report, No. 20468-CE, Finance and PSD Sector Unit, South Asia Region.

26. Wijewardene, W. A. 1999. Social Security Systems For The Elderly In Sri Lanka, 'Ageing Population And Social Security Systems, a conference conducted by the Central Bank of Sri Lanka and the World Bank in 27-28 May 1999, Colombo, Sri Lanka.

Table 1: Main Characteristics of EPF, 1992-2002

Year	1992	1993	1994	1995	1996	1997	1998	1999	2000	20001	2002
Coverage											
Members(a) ('000)	5,485	5,825	6,173	6,506	6,876	7,285	7,716	8,109	8,577	8,996	9,308
Contributors(b)(thousands)	1,406	1,490	1,538	1,553	1,549	1,699	1,790	1,783	1,913	1,913	1,984
contributors as % of members	25.64	25.58	2492	23.87	22.53	23.32	23.20	21.99	22.30	21.27	21.31
Labour Force ('000)	5,808	6,032	6,079	6,106	6,242	6,266	6,634	6,646	6,730	6,731	7,121
contributors as % of labour Force	24.21	24.70	25.30	25.43	24.82	27.11	26.98	26.83	28.42	28.42	27.86
Number of Employers	31,275	33,018	34,033	34,853	35,487	36,531	39,345	42,782	45,232	46,875	47,400
Contributions and Members' Balances											
Contribution (Rs. Bn)	5.29	6.61	7.41	815	9.30	10.85	12.04	13.68	16.85	17.74	18.93
Gross National Savings (GNS) (Rs. Bn)	76.28	101.10	110.83	129.97	145.67	191.30	237.97	260.34	269.99	273.45	312.29
Contributions as % of GNS	6.94	6.54	6.68	6.27	6.39	5.67	5.06	5.25	6.24	6.49	6.06
Gross Domestic product(GDP)(Rs.Bn) (d)	425	500	579	668	768	890	1,015	1,111	1255	1400	1585
Contributions as % of GDP	1.24	1.32	1.28	1.22	1.21	1.22	1.19	1.23	1.34	1.27	1.19
Total member balances (Rs. Bn)	58.09	70.85	85.39	102.33	122.33	144.09	167.47	193.85	222.93	256.29	294.63
As % of GDP	13.66	14.18	14.75	15.32	15.93	16.19	16.51	17.45	17.76	18.31	18.59
Average balance per member	10,591	12,163	13,832	15,728	17,791	19,779	21,704	23,905	25,992	28,489	31,653
Average balance per contributor	41,302	47,547	55,508	65,889	78,961	84,810	93,559	108,719	116,536	133,973	148,503
Returns											
No. of Benefit payments	49,864	51,289	49,986	52,258	56,536	60,909	68,928	76,418	95,157	93.008	91,493
Amount paid (Rs. Mn)	2,265	2,377	2,630	2,886	3,512	4,775	6,402	7,691	10,802	11,194	12,553
Interest Rates on investments(%)	11.5	11.5	13.5	12.75	12.75	12.75	12.25	11.5	11.5	11.5	12.1

Annual average inflation (%)	11.39	11.74	8.45	7.67	15.94	9.6	9.4	4.7	6.2	14.2	9.6
Real Interest Rates (%)(e)	0.11	– 0.24	5.05	508	– 3.19	3.15	2.85	6.80	5.30	– 2.70	2.50
Allocation of investments											
Value of Portfolio by end of the year											
(Rs. Bn)	54.83	66.53	81.05	96.90	115.60	137.30	161.00	185.96	215.79	246.88	262.56
Investments in govt papers											
(% of portfolio)	99.80	99.00	98.60	98.40	97.60	98.20	98.00	97.50	97.40	97.90	97.5
Ownership of domestic debt(%) c	30.77	30.72	31.89	32.83	31.75	34.78	34.03	33.41	31.29	30.03	29.91

Exchange Rate (as at August, 2002): US $ I = Rs.97

(a) Members refer to any individual who has contributed to the fund even once in the working like.

(b) Contributors refer to active contributors at the given time period.

(c) Government borrowing from EPF as a percentage of domestic debt.

Table 2: Contributory, DC Pension Schemes: Coverage and Contributions in Different Countries

COUNTRY	to Labour Force (%)	Contributors to members (%)	Contributors as%ofGDP	Coutributions as % of GNS	Contributions Balance as % of GOP	Members' Balances (US $)	AVG Members'
MALAYSIA (EPF)	2001	53.2	49.5	5.5	16.9	57.3	4,953
S1NGAPORE (CPF)	2002	60.3	50.1	10.4	24.6	61.92	19,479
SRI LANKA (EPF)	2002	27.9	21.3	1.2	6.1	18.6	326

Source: Central Bank of Sri Lanka; EPF Sri Lanka; Bank Negara Malaysia. Singapore Department of Statistics: CPF Board Singapore

Table 3: Main Features of 1990-1999

Year	Member Accounts (Mn)	Active Accounts (Mn)	Contributing Employers - (Number)	Contributions (Rs. Mn)	Claims Paid (b) (Rs Mn)	Other Benefits Paid (Rs Mn)	Total Member (c) Balance	Investments of the Fund (Rs Mn)
1990	n.a.	n.a.	23,909	682	294	13.55	4,858	4,465
1991	n.a.	n.a.	24,268	808	412	20.77	5,961	5,485
1992	n.a.	na.	24,506	967	504	22.27	7,293	6,664
1993	n.a.	n.a.	25,193	1,183	494	18.77	9,320	8,481
1994	1.6	na.	26,017	1,467	508	25.85	11,757	10,950
1995	1.7	n.a.	26,823	1,503	628	48.59	14,182	13,228
1996	2.2	1.7	27,280	1,720	804	48.06	16,921	15,785
1997	22	1.7	26,427	1,983	936	64.90	17,853	18,698
1998	3.1	1.5	25,860	2,270	1,215	80.94	22,734	21,940
1999	2.2	1.7	29,344	2,665	1,422	127.82	25,557	25,243
2000	2.4	1.8	35,281	2,928	1,487	100.00	29,620	29,221
2001	2.4	1.7	32,180	3,310	1,649	55.00	33,148	33,840
2002[a]	2.4	1.8	39,112	3,545	210.00	210.00	39,998	38,985

(a) Provincial.
(b) Claims paid under termination of employment, Permanent incapacity, or death of a member.
(c) Benefits paid for Automatic Insurance Scheme, total and permanent disability scheme, financial assistance for heart surgeries
Source : Employees' Trust Fund Board

Table 4: Pensions Exnditure 1992-2002

	1992	1993	1994	1995	1996	1997	1998	1999	2000	2001	2002[a]
Pension Expenditure (Rs. Bn)	8.10	10.52	12.83	14.55	15.47	17.92	19.47	19.06	21.60	26.49	31.12
Percentage Increase in Pension Expenditure	– 8.27	29.88	21.96	13.41	6.32	15.84	8.65	– 2.11	13.33	22.64	17.48
Budget Deficit Before Grants (Rs. Bn)	34.04	43.32	60.72	67.22	72.38	90.06	93.14	83.25	124.54	152.22	141.10
Pension exp. as a % of Gov. Budget Deficit	23.80	24.28	21.13	21.65	21.37	19.90	20.90	22.89	17.34	17.40	22.06
Cunent Expenditure (Rs. Bn)	89.64	102.28	127.08	154.16	175.15	184.75	199.65	207.22	254.28	300.41	330.27
Pension Exp. as a % of Total Current Expenditure	9.04	10.29	10.10	9.44	8.83	9.70	9.75	9.20	8.49	8.82	9.42
GDP (BN)	425.28	499.57	579.08	667.77	768.13	890.27	1018.00	1106.00	1258.00	1400.00	1585.00
BudgetDeficit as a % of GDP	8.00	8.67	10.49	10.07	9.42	10.12	9.15	7.53	9.90	10.87	8.90
Pension Expenditure as a Percentage of GDP	1.90	2.11	2.22	2.18	2.01	2.01	1.91	1.72	1.72	1.89	1.96

a. Provincial

Source : Central Bank of Sri Lanka

Table 5 : Coverage of Public Sector Pension Schemes 1993-2002

	1993	1994	1995	1996	1997	1998	1999	2000	2001	2002
Number of Pensioners ('000)	293.71	303.99	310.85	332.82	342.34	346.36	358.22	363.78	371.72	393.30
Percentage increase in number of pensioners	3.01	3.50	2.26	7.07	2.86	1.17	3.42	1.55	2.18	5.81
Government Employment a ('000)	680	699.86	737.5	752.19	762.08	790.49	822.12	856.67	863.29	825.99
Employed labour force ('000)	5,201	5,281	5,357	5,537	5,608	6,005	6,136	6,310	6,236	6,467
Percentage of employed labour force covered by PSPS	13.07	13.25	13.77	13.58	13.59	13.16	13.40	13.58	13.84	12.77
Labour force ('000)	6,032	6,073	6,106	6,242	6,266	6,660	6,673	6,827	6,773	7,121
Percentage oflabour force covered by PSPS	11.27	11.52	12.08	12.05	12.16	11.87	12.32	12.55	12.75	11.60

(a) **Includes both permanent and non permanent employees of the central and local government and provincial councils.**

Source : Department of Pensions and The Central Bank of Sri Lanka.

Chart 1: Structure of the Existing Social Security System in Sri Lanka

- Wage Employees
  - Public Sector
    - DC Schemes
      - PSPF
    - DB Schemes
      - PSPS
      - CPF
      - Widows/widowers
      - Teachers/Orphans
      - Schemes
  - Private Sector (DC Schemes)
    - EPE
    - ETF
    - APPFs
- Self-Employed
  - * Farmer's Pension Scheme
  - * Fishermen's Pension Scheme
  - * Pension Scheme for the Self Employed

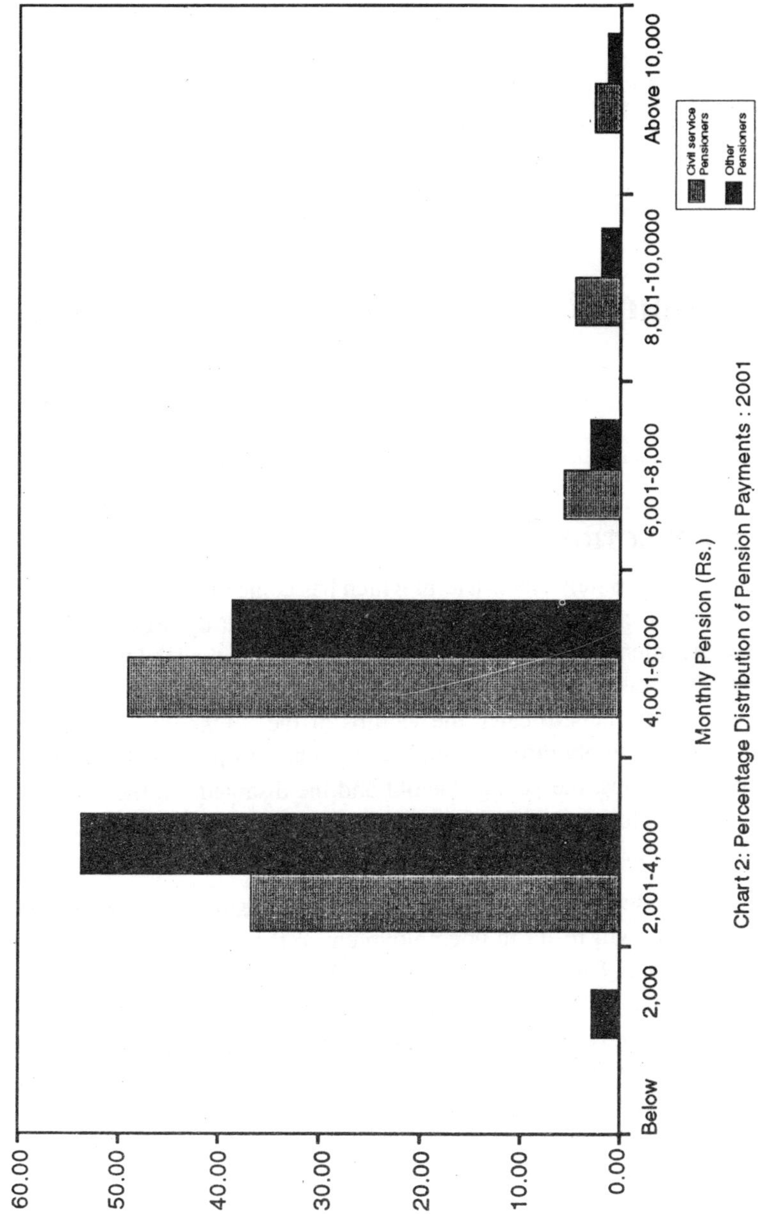

Chart 2: Percentage Distribution of Pension Payments : 2001

4

Labour Reform and Social Safety Net

R.K.A. Subrahmanya*

INTRODUCTION

Social Safety Net is a term which has come into vogue recently to mean social assistance, a form of social security. Social safety nets are intended for a dual purpose. According to the UNDP Human Development Report 1993, every country needs to establish effective social safety nets to catch the victims of the competitive struggle-such as the temporarily unemployed — and to protect the lowest income groups, the young, the old and the disabled.. In the context of labour reforms, social safety net is required for catching the victims of the competitive struggle.

It is well known that labour reforms leading to structural adjustment will result in unemployment in the short term if not in' the long run. There is at present no scheme to protect the workers against such involuntary unemployment and that is coming in the way of any movement towards labour reforms This was recognized as soon as the new economic policy was introduced in 1991 but there has been no progress in that direction. In this connection what Prem Shanker Jha, a columnist, wrote in November 1991 is highly relevant. I quote:

* *Secretary General, Social Security Association of India, Bangalore, India.*

"The obstacles to an exit policy, whether for sick enterprises or inefficient or redundant workers are the same: in a country with an already alarming level of unemployment, where will the retrenched worker or government employee go? How long will he take to find another job? And what will happen to him and his family if he does not? Small wonder then that trade unions stop at nothing to prevent retrenchment and political leaders eternally shy away from closing the 225,000 sick units that litter the industrial landscape. This is not politics but simple humanity.

"The solution to the problem must therefore also be a human one. It lies in the creation of a comprehensive system of unemployment insurance. The scheme must first cover the entire organised sector of industry and government and, when its managers have acquired sufficient experience , be extended to cover the self employed the unorganised sector. The proposal is by no means new. At the annual meeting of the Federation of Indian Chambers of Commerce and Industry, in 1990, the outgoing President urged the V.P.Singh Government to consider setting up an unemployment insurance scheme to which employers and employees would contribute one percent of their gross salaries. The proposal has also been made to the present Government (P.V.Narasimha Rao Government) and is believed to be under consideration."

Such a scheme is long overdue. Despite every effort of the Government and the trade unions to make retrenchment as difficult as possible, between 25,000 and 40,000 workers do get laid off every year. Officials in the Labour. Ministry estimate that upto twice that many get retrenched illegally because their employers simply close down their enterprises and disappear. Lastly, large number of temporary workers are retrenched without the employers having to go through the elaborate formalities of sacking permanent workers. It is true that most of the workers who are laid off do manage to get other work But the harsh fact is that under the present supposedly benign system, no one bothers to find out what happens to them when their severance benefits are exhausted.

A steady stream of reports in the daily papers of mass suicides by entire families suggests, however, that very few among them are left with no choice but death. The despair of many others who are not driven to the point of suicide and therefore do not impinge upon the consciousness of the elite, can easily be imagined. Thus, in a society where the safety net provided by the joint family system is beginning to break down under the pressures of urbanisation and destitution, the creation of a social security system cannot be postponed.

The then Union Finance Minister, Dr. Man Mohan Singh had also accepted the need for developing credible instruments of social security for the workers in the unorganised sector as well as the workers who may be affected by technical change. Inaugurating the Social Security Association of India on Dec 31 1991 , he stated , inter alia:

"The need for social security is an established reality in all civilised societies to day.

> "A caring society, and any civilised society must aspire to be a caring society, cannot leave those who suffer from these misfortunes to suffer in silence. Society has a responsibility to its unfortunate members to come to their assistance.

"Technical change is a fact of life. We cannot survive in a world in which knowledge is growing at such a fast pace without making conscious efforts to absorb assimilate and adapt this knowledge for improving our living standards. But the process of technical change howsoever beneficial it might be, is also disruptive. When you introduce new technologies it hurts who are using techniques of an earlier vintage. There is the problem or the fear of unemployment, loss of jobs. This cannot be wished away. If we want our society to accept the need for technical change then we need to credible instruments of social security to ensure that the process of technical change will not impose undue burden on the working classes. We must work towards a society which would be a caring society, a society which would ensure that if technical change is essential for the country as a whole, then the costs of technical change and the costs of adjustment would not be borne exclusively but the working class and that those who have the least capacity to bear those costs are not asked to bear them."

Dr Man Mohan Singh, when he was the finance Minister, gave solemn assurances that the economic reforms would not be carried out on the back of the working classes. But economic reforms are being carried out and workers are being thrown out of employment and people affected by globalisation are dying in large numbers by committing suicide. Weavers in Andhra Pradesh, cotton growers in Maharashtra, maize producers in Karnataka coconut oil producers in Kerala and even rice producers in the Punjab are reported to have committed suicide not being able to bear the burden of life. But no social security measure has been introduced to protect them.

In the wake of the announcement of the new economic policy the Social Security Association organised a seminar on Social Security in the context of the New Industrial Policy. It was inaugurated by the then Dy Chairman of the Planning Commission, Mr. Pranab Mukherjee. The seminar recommended the introduction of an Unemployment Insurance Scheme. With the help of Sri S.K.Jain who had just retired from the office of Deputy Director General of the ILO the Association worked out an outline of the scheme and submitted it to government. A delegation of the Association met the Finance Minister and presented the scheme. He gave a patient hearing to the delegation and promised to have the matter examined. Subsequently, the Ministry of Industry appointed an official committee to go into it. The committee too recommended the introduction of an unemployment insurance scheme. In the meantime the major organisations of employers FICCI and ASSOCHAM also submitted memoranda to Government suggesting the introduction of an unemployment insurance scheme so as to enable them to carry out structural adjustment.

In a paper prepared by FICCI for a workshop on "Exit Policy for Sick Industrial Units" the existing arrangements for retrenchment of workers were described and it was stated that " so far what has ruled out the formulation of an exit policy is the total absence of social. security net to take care of the retrenched workers. Therefore a social security net broadly on the lines of an insurance policy should be devised at the earliest." "A formal system of providing unemployment benefit should be evolved instead of the existing system where by individual companies have provided such benefits on a case to case basis.. The unemployment benefit may be provided under the umbrella of a specific Act introduced for this purpose. The paper also set out the details of a scheme.

The Associated Chamber of Commerce and Industry in a paper on Deregulation Imperatives had indicated the need for introducing a " privately run industry specific contributory insurance scheme for risks of unemployment"

No action has been taken on these recommendations. What is intriguing is why the Government is dragging its feet when even the premier organisations of the employers who normally oppose any scheme adding to their costs have themselves initiated proposals for introducing a scheme.

I must however point out that unemployment insurance schemes are not as common as other branches of social security. Social security unemployment benefit schemes are to be found mainly in industrialised countries. Very few developing countries have such schemes. Unemployment benefit schemes have recently been set up in certain transition countries and in middle income countries like the Republic of Korea. It is therefore understandable that the Government is cautious in embarking on such untried ventures. There seems however to be no reason to be apprehensive about introducing an unemployment insurance scheme. I would therefore like to take a few minutes to explain the concept and the experience of other comparable countries in that regard.

There are different types of unemployment, viz.,

(i) Persons who have just entered the job market and have not found a job yet.

(ii) Persons who are in seasonal employment for part of the year and remain unemployed for the remaining short periods.

(iii) Persons who are employed on very low income and need to supplement the same.

(iv) Persons who are thrown out of employment due to retrenchment or closure of establishments.

(v) Persons who have lost jobs due to nationwide or global recession.

Unemployment insurance is concerned mainly with the last category of persons

The best way to tackle unemployment is to provide alternative employment. If that is not possible the unemployed may be given assistance for their subsistence either through an unemployment insurance scheme or through a social assistance programme whereby the unemployed may be given relief directly by way of an allowance.

"The first protection against unemployment is a solid policy towards full employment consisting of macro economic policies at the national and international levels; sectoral regional and local policies; and labour market and training policies. Nevertheless, there is an increasing need for specific unemployment protection policies given that full employment policies are either not in place or take time to come to fruition and that short term crises may lead to unacceptable levels of unemployment hardship" (World Labour Report 2000).

DEFINITION OF UNEMPLOYMENT BENEFIT

Unemployment benefit is paid to those individuals who, through no fault of their own, have become unemployed and who, as a result, have lost the earning on which they and their families depended. The principle underlying this scheme is that if a person for no fault of his is deprived of an income consisting of his earning from employment he has a right to expect income support at least for the necessities of life while he remains available for work. This benefit is usually paid for a relatively short period under the assumption that he will find alternative employment within that period.

This benefit is usually financed by contributions from employers and the employees but sometimes, the government may also share in the cost in the form of either regular contributions or a subsidy. According to "Social Security throughout the World" a biennial publication of the US Government, "unemployment insurance contributions often are shared equally between employers and the employees; alternatively, the entire contribution maybe made by the employer . However Government subsidies may be quite large amounting in some cases to as much as two thirds of the programmes expenditures. Means tested unemployment assistance programmes are financed entirely by government, with no contribution by the employers or the employees."

POSITION IN ASIA AND THE PACIFIC

"Fifteen (out of 49) countries in the region provide for unemployment benefits but they are mostly the former USSR republics and the developed countries of Australia, Japan, Hong Kong and New Zealand. In Thailand this benefit is provided for under the 1990 Social Security Act but implementation is still pending. In a number of countries such as Bangladesh, India, Iraq Philippines Solomon Islands and Turkey, the Labour Laws require employers to pay severance or dismissal indemnity to their separated employees" (ISSA 1990).

POSITION IN CHINA

China has an unemployment insurance scheme which covers workers in state run enterprises and some collective enterprises. It is a contributory scheme for which workers contribute at the rate of 1% and the employers at 2%. Local governments subsidise the scheme to the extent necessary. The rate of benefit is determined by the local authorities at a level higher than local public assistance benefit but lower than local minimum wage. The benefit is payable for 12 months if the period of coverage is less than 5 years and for 18 months if the period of coverage is more than 5 yeas but less than 10 years and for 2 years if the period of coverage is ten or more years.

The Government of China has introduced a three tiered programme for dealing with the problem of unemployment.

(a) The unemployed persons may report themselves to reemployment centres for retraining and for reemployment.

(b) If they are unable to get alternative jobs, they will be put on unemployment subsidy.

(c) After two years they will be handed over to the third line of urban poverty alleviation programme.

Nearly 10 million persons were covered by the State Unemployment Scheme at the end of 1999. In 1997, 878,836 persons were under the poverty alleviation programme (Yang, Zhengua 2000).

POSITION IN KOREA

The Republic of Korea has introduced an employer financed unemployment allowance which took effect in July 1995. The scheme is financed by a contribution equal to 0.6 per cent of total pay roll shared equally between employers and workers. The Act fixed 1.5 per cent as the maximum total contribution that could be levied for all components of the employment insurance system (which also icludes a large number of labour market policy measures, such as training). From March 1998, Parliament revised this maximum upwards to 3% of payroll. The unemployment benefit is 50 per cent of the workers' earnings during the month prior to dismissal. In March 1998 the minimum benefit was raised to 70 per cent of the minimum wage. As the minimum wage is about 25 per cent of non average earnings the minimum unemployment benefit is equivalent to just under 18 per cent of average earnings The duration of unemployment benefit is calculated on age at dismissal and length of the period insured. As an incentive to job seeking, an early reemployment allowance is payable to unemployed workers who find a new job within half the period for which they entitled to unemployment benefit. The coverage of the scheme was initially limited to employees in firms with 30 or more workers. It is now applicable to establishment employing five or more persons (World Labour Report 2000).

POSITION IN BRAZIL

Brazil has an Unemployment Insurance Scheme which is wholly financed by the Government. The rate of benefit is 50% of average earnings in the last 3 months of employment up to 3 times the minimum wage. Minimum benefit would be equal to minimum wage. The benefit is payable after 60 days waiting period for a period of 4 months in any 16 months period.

POSITION IN ARGENTINA

In Argentina rate of contributions is 1% for insured persons and 1.5% for employers. Rate of benefit is 60 % of the highest wage the worker received in the 6 months before the date of unemployment. Duration of the benefit ranges from 4 to 12 months depending on the length of coverage between 12 an 36 months.

POSITION IN INDIA

There is no unemployment insurance scheme in India. Industrial Disputes Act provides that a worker who is retrenched should be paid compensation at the rate of 15 days wages for every completed year of continuous service in addition to gratuity. It is said to be a form of unemployment benefit meant to help the workers who are thrown out of employment to maintain themselves until they are able to secure alternative jobs. But it is more akin to a terminal benefit than 'an unemployment benefit. Even this benefit is usually not paid in cases where industrial establishments are closed down due to financial stringency.

In 1967, the Government of India drew up a pilot scheme of unemployment insurance to cover workers in coal mining industry who were members of the Coal Mines Provident Fund. An expert of the ILO was invited to examine the scheme and to make suggestions for improving it in the light of experience in countries in which such schemes were in operation. The expert found it feasible and had made certain suggestions for improving it.

In 1969, the National Commission on Labour expressed the view that a long term solution to the problem of retrenchment lies in adopting a scheme of unemployment insurance for all employed persons. The Commission observed," While provisions relating to retrenchment and lay off compensation afford some relief and act as a deterrent to hasty retrenchment, certain unsatisfactory features have come to light in the course of their working. A permanent remedy may be in the form of unemployment benefit. The Central Employers' Organisations have suggested in their evidence that since the existing provisions relating to lay offs and retrenchment are adequate, there is no justification for grant of additional financial compensation against the job security hazard resulting from temporary unemployment. On the other hand, the general feeling among workers' organisations is that we must move towards an all inclusive scheme covering all recognised contingencies including unemployment . We feel that the present arrangement by which lay off and retrenchment compensation is required to be borne by the employer at a time when he is already in difficulties, whatever the reasons, works somewhat harshly on him but even more harshly on the workers who are on many occasions deprived of the benefits provided under the Act. On the other hand, if its incidence is distributed over the whole industry it might under certain conditions imply subsidising of inefficient management. With due safeguards against such contingency the long term solution lies in adopting a scheme of unemployment insurance for all employed persons.

Subsequently, the question of introducing an unemployment insurance has been coming up often and several proposals have been submitted to Government of India.

DESIRABILITY OF INTRODUCING AN UNEMPLOYMENT INSURANCE SCHEME

The World Labour Report has pointed out that the recent Asian financial crisis has established that unemployment insurance schemes could play a substantial role in coping with the unacceptable levels of hardships caused by rapidly escalating unemployment. Had unemployment insurance coverage been sufficiently extensive in the countries affected by the crisis then a majority of job losers would have been eligible for unemployment benefits.

FEASIBILTY OF INTRODUCING A SCHEME

The Report has further pointed out that a recent feasibility study carried out by the ILO for Thailand estimated that the required contribution rates for a scheme that could pay benefits for a period of six months at a level equal to 50 per cent of previous earnings would be 2.5 per cent of payroll in the first year of operation but would fall steadily to 0.6 per cent by the seventh year. This rate allows for the accumulation of a reserve equivalent to one year's expenditure on benefits.

SALIENT ASPECTS OF AN UNEMPLOYMENT INSURANCE SCHEME

An unemployment insurance scheme would be a social insurance scheme. A social insurance scheme transfers the uncertainty of the risk from an individual or individual employer to the community and the transfer enhances the welfare of the community as a whole. It is a form of social security, an organsied and systematic form of protection against a defined risk, whereby contributions are pooled in a fund from which benefit is paid to those experiencing the risk at any time. Contribution income and benefit expenditure are rationally related, solvency is protected and objectivity in paying the benefits ensures that those receiving it are not blamed for having been affected by circumstances which they could not control.

For the most part, contingencies covered by social security systems are associated with demographic phenomena, such as fertility, marriage, morbidity and mortality. Although these contingencies can to some extent be conditioned by economic factors, the main contingencies such as oldage disability etc. can be predicted to an acceptable degree by the application of actuarial techniques. In this respect unemployment is different. It is a contingency which in effect is imposed upon workers, at best by local employers at the local level and at worst by national recessions which can affect virtually all sectors of labour or single out specific industries affected by a fall in demand for their products or by inability to supply them. This in turn might mean singling out specific areas in which those industries are the predominant employers of labour. The impact can be sudden. Moreover, technological structural and economic changes are inevitable and will cause some unemployment in market economies In the result the unemployment contingency being essentially economic in origin is not easily predictible.

The almost inevitable response of unemployment benefit schemes , in order to preserve their viability, is to define the contingency under which payments have to be made in precise terms to be explicit and often restrictive about coverages and to attach to the provisions of benefit a variety of controlling and other conditions of which duration — the maximum period during which the benefit can be paid — is currently one of the most important.

Payment of unemployment benefit Would normally be subject to the conditions that the insured person is capable of and available for work, and that he has registered himself in an employment exchange and that he complies with such other requirements as may be prescribed.

Under a compulsory social insurance scheme the right to receive the benefit will be subject to a period of qualifying service or payment of contributions for a specified period.

The right to receive the benefit may be limited to a prescribed period. According to Convention no. 44 of the ILO it may be limited to 156 days per year but it should not be less than 78 working days per year.

The usual rates of unemployment benefit are approximately 50 to 60 per cent of previous earnings.

GROUP INSURANCE SCHEME

The Union Finance Minister in his recent budget speech for 2001-02 announced that he proposed to introduce a new scheme of groups insurance, viz., Ashraya Bima Yojana to extend cover to workers affected by liberalisation of the economy. The policy will provide compensation of up to 30 per cent of last drawn annual pay for a period of one year to workers who lose jobs. It is proposed that the policy will initially cover all employees drawing a salary up to Rs.10,000 per month. The four Government owned general insurance companies will administer this policy on a no profit no loss basis and will announce full details including premium rates of the proposed policy by the end of June 2001.

I am not aware if the details of the scheme have been announced yet. There was a discussion on the subject at a meeting of insurance companies which was organised by IRDA recently when the representative of the association of Government owned insurance companies explained that it would be a scheme for which workers will only contribute, and the rate of contribution would be about 5%.

The proposal of the Government is unusual and unprecedented. No country in the world has an unemployment insurance scheme for which contributions are made exclusively by workers only at such a high rate as 5 %.

In the course of discussion with the insurance companies mentioned earlier the representative of the Employees Provident Fund Organsation stated that that organisation had proposed to introduce an unemployment insurance scheme for which the rate of contribution would be 1.80% of salary or 2.20 % depending on the period for which the benefit is to be paid. Prescription of a high rate of contribution by workers only is the surest way to kill the proposal at its very birth.

The correct rate of contributions and the rates and period of benefit will have to be determined actually. To begin with however the rates may be fixed on ad hoc basis based on the experience of other comparable countries. In this connection the following facts may be relevant :

PROPOSALS OF STUDY GROUP ON SOCIAL SECURITY

Having regard to these facts the Study Group on Social Security of the National Commission has proposed the introduction of an unemployment insurance scheme conforming to the pattern envisaged in the Convention of the ILO brief particulars of which are as follows :

The scheme should be financed by a tripartite contribution to be determined actuarily. To begin with however, the rates of contribution may be fixed at 0.5 per cent to be contributed by the employees , 1.5% by the employers and the deficit if any being met by the Central Government from the NRF.

The rate of benefit should be 50 per cent of last pay/wages drawn.

The benefit should be payable for a period of one year or till reemployment whichever is shorter.

It should preferably be implemented through the EPFO and be applicable to all establishments and employees to which the EPF Act is currently applicable and may be extended to in the near future with no wags ceiling for coverage but with a ceiling of Rs.10,000 for contributions and benefits.

There was a national consultation on the various proposals formulated by the Study Group to which the organisations of employers and workers had been invited. There was no comment on the proposal concerning unemployment insurance scheme It is therefore assumed that it is acceptable to all.

PENSION SCHEME

I should however mention that there are two ways in which income security may be ensured to retrenched employees; one is by way of an unemployment benefit and the other by way of a pension scheme.

If a person is retrenched at an advance age when the prospects of his finding alternative employment would be dim, he may be deemed to be retired and paid a pension.

In India, there is no unemployment benefit scheme but there is a pension scheme. Under the Employees Pension Scheme, a person will normally be entitled to a pension on attaining the age of 58. But there is provision for payment of pension at age 50 or more at a discounted rate. If a person is retrenched between the ages of 50 and 60 he will get a pension but at a reduced rate. If the pension scheme is dovetailed with an unemployment insurance scheme the reduction in the rate of pension may be made good from the unemployment insurance scheme. If a person is retrenched before the age of 50 he will not be entitled to any pension and therefore he will have to be paid an unemployment benefit.

TRAINING AND RETRAINING

An unemployment insurance scheme is meant to provide to help a worker to tide over a short period of unemployment when he is switching over from one job to another. In these days of changing pattern of economic and social relations and fast rate of scientific and technological development it may not be easy for a retrenched worker to find new job unless he undergoes fresh training in new trades and newer techniques of work. An unemployment insurance scheme may therefore make the right to receive a benefit conditional upon the attendance at a course of vocational or other instructions. More importantly , arrangement should be made to provide training or retraining to such workers. The National Renewal Fund was established with this as one of the objectives. The performance of the Fund in this area has not been encouraging and needs to be improved. Separately additional or alternative arrangements may also be thought of.

In this connection, I would like to recall that the Employees Relations Conferences held recently in Bangalore had recommended the establishment of a Skill Development Fund for improving the skill of our workers. The NRF could be transformed into a Fund of that kind or a separate fund may be created. It is however necessary that adequate steps are taken to protect persons against unemployment and loss of income due to lack of demand for their skills.

OTHER MEASURES

Under the ESI Scheme the medical benefit provided under the scheme will be discontinued after a person ceases to be in an insurable employment. Although the Scheme now provides for continuation of the benefit to persons after retirement from service on payment of a nominal contribution, it is doubtful whether retrenched workers will also be entitled to that benefit. It needs to be extended to them.

Similarly if an employee has been provided with residential accomodation by the employer, he will have to vacate it on termination of his service. When this happens, his children will have to leave the neighbourhood schools where they are studying. It will be necessary to allow, them to retain the accomodation for a reasonable period to enable them to relocate themselves conveniently.

RELEVANCE OF THE SCHEME FOR THE UNORGANISED SECTOR

An unemployment insurance scheme has to be distinguished from a scheme under which some assistance may be given to a person who has never been employed and is searching for a job in the form of unemployment relief or assistance which some of our State governments pay to the educated unemployed registered in the employment exchange.

An Unemployment Insurance Scheme requires regular contribution, mainly by the employer and if necessary, by the employee as well as the government In cases where employment is casual, temporary, seasonal or otherwise irregular, it would not be practicable to collect such contributions. It may not therefore be feasible to introduce an unemployment insurance scheme for the unorganised sector. There seems to be no case where such persons have been covered under an unemployment insurance scheme. In such cases the only way to provide protection against unemployment is to provide them employment under a Public Works Programme.

The Report further says : "Employment provided under an EIP (Employment Intensive Programmes) can be organised so that workers can obtain an employment guarantee for a certain number of days per year. An employment guarantee may therefore be seen as a form of unemployment insurance in which employment security is provided and thereby income security. The guarantee is most extensive when employment is provided on demand of workers and a government meets that demand by organising the EIP".

India has had long experience in running employment guarantee, schemes. The Maharashtra Scheme has been acclaimed as the most successful scheme. The Study Group on Social Security of the National Commission on Labour has therefore proposed that an Employment Guarantee Scheme should be introduced at the national level failing which the unemployed persons should be paid an unemployment allowance.

The Government of India also seems to be thinking on those lines. Indeed the Union Minister for Rural Development recently announced that it was the ultimate objective of the government to introduce an Employment Guarantee Scheme in India the object of which would be to provide work to all those who ask for it or to pay them a subsistence allowance.

REFERENCE

1. ILO 2000, World Labour Report, Geneva ILO.
2. ISSA 2000, *"Overview of the Principal Social security trends in Asia and the Pacific"*, Geneva ISSA.
3. Jiang Zhenhua 2000, *"Social Security Systems in China"*, Paper presented during the Asia. Sub-Regional Seminar on Social Security for the elderly. Organized by Social Security Association of India and ILO, New Delhi.
4. Yang Yansui 2000, *"Social Security Legislation in China"*, Paper presented during the Asia Sub-Regional Seminar on Social Security for the elderly. Organized by Social Security Association of India and ILO, New Delhi.

5

Strengthening Social Protection in Low Income Countries: The case of Vietnam

Scott Fritzen

1. INTRODUCTION

The challenge of protecting the poorest and most vulnerable members of society from economic and other shocks is shared by both developed and developing countries. Countries in which a substantial percentage of the population is poor have a particular need for effective social protection, as do countries rapidly undergoing socioeconomic transformations, such as urbanization and economic liberalization (Ortiz, 2001; Cook et. al, 2003).

Yet the means for poor countries to achieve effective protection are severely limited by both low public expenditure and low administrative capacity. In addition, social protection cannot be divorced from the broader set of economic and social policies affecting the rate and distribution of economic growth and human capital formation. The political economy of development in countries rapidly

* *Assistant Professor, Public Policy Program, National University of Singapore, 5 Arts Link, Level 6, Singapore 119260.*
Email : *fritzen amus edu sg; Phone: (65) 97776275; Fax (65) 687781020*

urbanizing and industrializing from low levels may also create difficulties in developing coalitions supporting pro-poor policies (Ramesh, 2000). As a result of such constraints, formal social security and protection programs typically cover only a small minority of those in need of assistance, and what limited assistance exists is poorly targeted.

How can this situation be changed? What practical options for effectively improving social protection in low income countries exist for national policy-makers and donors to consider? This paper adopts a case study approach to these questions, recognizing that answers must be country specific and that broader lessons for low income countries (sharing, as they do, key constraints) may be drawn. It explores the state of, and prospects for strengthening, social protection as a key component of social policy in Vietnam. The Vietnam case is interesting because in some ways it tests the outer limits of the possible for very low income countries: it enjoys a long-standing commitment to social development, generally strong social organization, and government coffers that have expanded rapidly as a consequence of its rapid economic growth over the past fifteen years.

This paper has four sections. The first presents some background on Vietnam and its reforms. The second assesses the state of social protection measures in Vietnam, arguing that the failings of the current system are being exacerbated in some cases by misguided policies, and by low implementation capacity in others. The third outlines an agenda for institutional and policy reform that might enable relatively rapid improvements in the situation over the medium term. The concluding section assesses the political feasibility of the proposed strategy, one that has implications for other low income countries.

2. BACKGROUND

For at least the past twenty-five years, Vietnam has been widely cited as a country with moderate levels of human development despite being very poor (NCSSH, 2001; Fritzen, 1997). Its per capita GDP in the early 1990s placed it below that of Bangladesh and India, and on par with the average for least developed countries. Yet several important social indicators, such as infant mortality, life expectancy and adult literacy, place Vietnam in the same company as considerably richer countries, such as Thailand, the Philippines and China (NCSSH, 2001). A high-level policy commitment to primary education and health care (as in other socialist countries such as China and Cuba), coupled with strong social organization, underpinned Vietnam's considerable pre-transition achievements (Fritzen, 2002; Word Bank et. al, 2001).

With the economy languishing under the constraints of state planning, the aftermath of decades of war and continued international isolation, Vietnam launched a comprehensive economic reform program in 1987 known as *doi moi* (renovation). Documented extensively elsewhere (Fforde and de Vylder, 1996), the reforms generated economic growth rates that have consistently placed Vietnam (with China) among the most rapidly growing economies in the world over the 1990s. The *doi moi* reforms were, economically speaking, a huge success.

Their impact on the social sectors, in contrast, have caused much debate (Nguyen, 1997; Fritzen, 1999). On the positive side, Vietnam has avoided precipitous decline in social indicators and coverage of services, quite in contrast to most transition countries. In fact, it has managed to expand coverage levels in almost all social service areas. Any set of economic reforms that generate the large-scale reductions in poverty seen in Vietnam-from 58% to 37% between 1992-98, according to a large scale living standards survey (GSO, 1999) - is bound to have generally positive impacts on most social indicators.

Yet *doi moi* introduced a broader set of institutional reforms that also badly disrupted the service delivery network, such as the disbandment of the agricultural cooperatives that had underpinned rural service delivery (Fritzen, 1999). Major changes in the way services are planned for, financed and implemented were often made *ad hoc* in the first years of the transition. Some fifteen years on, major reviews of the social sectors (UNICEF, 2000; World Bank et. al, 2001) outline an unfinished agenda of institutional and policy reform to cope with both old and new challenges. Indeed, some observers point to growing regional and socioeconomic inequalities, a 'crisis' of affordability of social services for the poor, and the generally poor quality of public services as evidence of a growing gap between reform needs and progress in the social sectors (Fritzen, 2002).

Nowhere is this disjunction greater than in the field of social protection. The tumultuous context of *doi moi* has generated much talk in government and the donor community concerning how to develop a reinforced social safety net during economic and other shocks to protect the most vulnerable in society (van de Walle, 1999). Yet long an important function of the old cooperatives, social protection assistance is at present extremely limited in wide stretches of the country. With many millions of households precariously clustered just above the poverty line, the lack of a functional safety net poses a serious social-and by extension political-risk (particularly since economic growth in recent years has decelerated). Serious organizational reform is likely to be necessary to revive the pace of poverty reduction and social development and perhaps even to avoid decline.

3. THE STATE OF SOCIAL PROTECTION IN VIETNAM

The Vietnamese government refers to vulnerability as "the inability of an individual...to exploit opportunities presented by society for their self-betterment" (Socialist Republic of Vietnam, 1998a, p. 9). In a narrow sense, safety nets can be defined as "measures adopted to mitigate short-term adverse effects of economic reforms on the poor" (Chu and Gupta, 1998, p. 64). This is an important part of the meaning of social protection in Vietnam, where concern over adverse, short-term impacts of continued economic reform play into ongoing debates over how quickly economic restructuring should proceed. More broadly, safety nets are linked to the quest for social security, understood as the reduction of vulnerability or poverty by social means (Howell, 2001).

Table 2 sums up available data on government safety net programs for a number of vulnerable groups. Though much information is sketchy, the basic conclusion is unmistakable: formal safety nets cover only a small portion of Vietnam's population; in fact, "only 2.2% of the population lives in households that have received a payment from any of the poverty programs" (World Bank et. al, 1999, p. 125). Where cash support is provided, it is very limited; even adding the additional 40% which community contributions form on average within safety net expenditure, overall expenditure constitutes on average only some 5% of household income for recipients (table 3).

Table 2 : Available data on safety net programmes, 1998

Beneficiaries	Estimated numbers	Programs to assist	% of social assistance budget spent on program	Coverage level
Unemployed	6.85%	Proposals exist to introduce to formal sector		
Sick		Health insurance		6 million have health insurance of which about 62.2% are mandatory, and 37.8% are voluntary, of which 3.4 mill. are students
		Exemptions		about 3 millions of the poor received formal exemptions**
Retired state employee	about 1.2 million	Social insurance	38%	11.2% of all households
War affected		Special transfers	40%	
Affected by disasters or crop losses	crop losses 2.9 mil disasters 1,400 (incl. deaths and wounded persons average per year	Contingency Fund for Natural Disasters and Pre-Harvest Starvation	73 bill. Vietnamese Dong Less than 5%	49% (of those affected by crop losses)

Table 2: (Contd...)

Poor (general)	15.7% (approximately 2 million households)	HEPR-related programs	20%	2.2% of overall population
Social subsidies group (also includes drug addicts and Prostitutes)		Social subsidies	1-4%	
Orphans displaced children	155,757 19,047			24% of target group benefited from social allowance regularly 11% of them are cared for in centers 39% of target group*
invalids including who can work and cannot work	1.3 million			
old people living by themselves	133.829			46% receive social benefits regularly*

*** Source :** Socialist Republic of Vietnam 1998a
 # Source : UNDP and MOLISA 1999a
**** Source :** World Bank et.al., 2001
$ Source : SRVN et.al., 2000

Coverage of social transfers is also generally not effectively targeted towards relatively poor groups. Social subsidies and the social insurance fund both benefit better-off households more than poor households. Various government and NGO poverty alleviation programs are somewhat better targeted: some 60% of government anti-poverty assistance received by households goes to the poorest 40% of households (World Bank et. al, 1999).

Why is coverage so low? One reason is that aggregate expenditure on the social sectors as a percentage of GDP is low in Vietnam. This is true in absolute terms and as a percentage of GDP (table 4). Cross-national expenditure data is unreliable for the social sectors, but what data do exist that the share of social expenditure to GDP rises-fact nearly doubles - from the poorest to the richest of the East and Southeast Asian developing countries. Despite greatly increased expenditure on the social sectors leading up to the period shown in table 4, Vietnam is still caught in a low GDP-low social spending trap.

Table 3. Incidence of social welfare income, 1998

Quintile	Income received from the following programs (Veitnamese Dong per annum per capita)*					Total receipts as % o household income
	social Insurance Fund	Social Subsidies	Poverty Allevia-tion Programe	NGO Assis-tance	Total Social Welcome Income	
Quintile 1 (poorest)	15,961	11,282	1,472	1,152	29,868	2.7
Quintile 2	42,020	15,597	2,415	554	60,586	3.7
Quintile 3	77,120	24,500	1,053	313	102,986	4.8
Quintile 4	153,840	23,535	869	298	178,542	6.1
Quintile 5 (richest)	207,654	21,776	659	443	230,532	3.8
Total	99,325	19,339	1,294	552	120,537	4.4
	(82.4%)	(16.0%)	(1.1%)	(0.5%)	(100%)	

Source: World Bank et. al (1999), based on VLSS-2 data p. 125

* Exchange rate: approximately 13,000 VND:US$1 in 1998.

Poor targeting of expenditure may be just as important as low aggregate expenditure. For many programs, there are no reliable means for monitoring eligibility for, and receipt of, entitlements. Many people within the target groups may not even *know* they are entitled to certain assistance by law. Definitions for target group eligibility (the handicapped, street-children etc.) may be unclear. In addition, the system of intergovernmental finance is failing to provide sufficient resources where they are needed the most, the poorest provinces. Since an estimated 43% of the outlays are financed from non-budget resources, including mandatory and voluntary contributions, social assistance programs in poorer localities, which may have a higher percentage of vulnerable populations, are under funded.

For these reasons, formal safety nets at present do not offer significant coverage or protection to reduce the vulnerability of rural populations, a point emphasized in table 2. These programs are not equipped to handle an acceleration in the numbers of vulnerable households in an economic downturn.

Table 3 : GDP and public expenditure on health and education in selected East Asian countries

	GDP per capita at PPP - 1998	Health and education expenditure share in GNP (1996-98)	Average health and education expenditure p.c (1996-98) at PPP
Cambodia	1286	3.5	45
Lao PDR	1726	3.3	57
Vietnam	1755	3.4	60
Indonesia	2439	2.0	49
China	3291	3.0	99
Philippines	3815	5.1	195
Thailand	5599	6.5	364
Malaysia	7963	6.2	494

Source: UNDP (2000)

If the poor cannot rely much on formal safety nets, informal, family- and neighborhood-based ones are in fact highly active (SRVN et. al, 1998). Largely as a result of these informal transfers, a major recent review found that the situation of some individuals and households classified as "vulnerable" is in many cases not dire relative to non-vulnerable households (SRVN et. al, 1998). Yet informal nets serve to exacerbate disparities in 'coverage' just as formal ones do. Remittances from overseas Vietnamese, estimated at an astonishing two billion dollars per year (x% of GDP), are highly unevenly distributed geographically. In a classic shortcoming of intra-community risk pooling, locally redistributed resources are obviously relatively lacking in poorer areas (Fritzen, 2000). There is an unavoidable role for more formal mechanisms of social protection as Vietnam deepens its economic reforms.

4. AN AGENDA FOR SOCIAL PROTECTION REFORM

Vietnam's challenge is that facing many developing countries. How can it effectively leverage the contribution of civil society and its own resources to provide meaningful assistance for the most vulnerable groups, given obvious resource and other constraints? Following the framework presented in section three, priority strategies can be divided into two main categories: directing support towards those who are already vulnerable, and strengthening risk-reducing mechanisms that help prevent households from falling into that trap to begin with. The following six measures fall evenly between those two categories.

1. Target vulnerable sub-groups with higher formal safety net coverage and support. Financing such increased support could be achieved by allocating new resources to the sector, though this option is limited by their already high percentage within the state budget. More feasible in Vietnam would be to hold the line on existing benefits which are not well-targeted onto the poor, while clarifying target group definitions to achieve greater transparency in benefit distribution (UNDP et. al, 1999).

2. Encourage non-State sector participation in welfare service provision. Given the predominance of informal transfers, the large role played by civil society in several other neighboring countries and budgetary limitations, probably the single most effective step the government could take is to create a facilitative environment for private transfers and civil society organizations to get involved in welfare provision. The conceptual basis for doing this in Vietnam is already widely acknowledged in the concept of socialization *(xa hoi hoa)*, in which the state shares responsibility with the communities and mass organizations for the financing and provision of social services (Marr, 1994). This concept needs extending to embrace the concept of civil society as well, since much welfare provision will take place through non-state groupings altogether (whereas mass organizations in the Vietnamese political tradition are still considered parts of the state apparatus). Involving civil society in welfare provision may eventually be seen as analogous to the active encouragement of the private sector in economic reform, which is being voiced by high-level political leaders in Vietnam at present.

While informal safety net assistance is currently being supplied by many community groups, family members and neighbors, there is also evidence of "community failure" or "family failure" as well - instances in which cultural norms of mutual assistance appear to be disregarded in practice (SRVN et. al, 1998). Mechanisms for local government to help motivate or leverage community involvement in protecting vulnerable groups may have a large impact in such a context, though concrete measures have yet to be identified. Tax or other incentives, or direct public subsidies for civil-society-based care-giving arrangements, might be considered for this role.

3. Create mechanisms to mitigate social costs of industrial reforms. Vietnam is preparing to deepen structural reforms to the economy. In the medium term, these will have a profound effect on generating employment in the modern sectors of the economy. There may be short-term costs, however, in terms of transitional unemployment, which the Government can help alleviate.

The there are two main policy levers available. The first is transitional assistance to unemployed formal-sector workers, including various employment relocation programs, vocational education and credit provision. The second is unemployment insurance. For both, the main beneficiaries of these programs are a relatively small group of workers in the formal sector. Compared with the rural poor, these groups tend to have more resources for dealing with vulnerability. To the extent possible, unemployment insurance programs should be funded by worker contributions and should minimize the level of government subsidies provided. The best unemployment insurance is greater job creation in the private sector. Changes in the labor law and enterprise law and their implementation, as well as continued macroeconomic and structural reforms, will be required for this (Webster 1999).

China's industrial reform experience has points of similarity and contrast with Vietnam. The biggest similarity lies in the combination of low formal coverage for safety nets with extended kinship-based (informal) networks. Yet China has a much higher percentage of workers who are still dependent on their enterprises for basic welfare and social services. As of 1992, over one hundred million workers-some 10% of the population-were employed in the state sector of specifically *urban* areas; these were areas that had enjoyed some formal safety net coverage prior to the reforms. Enterprises had provided such protections as guaranteed job security, housing, pension benefits, and social services such as day care and schools. Resistance to their removal served as a major brake on enterprise- and social welfare reform in China over the course of the decade.

The Chinese authorities introduced several social sector reforms in conjunction with industrial reforms. Unemployment insurance was introduced in 1986 and is administrated at the city and county-government level (not through enterprises themselves). Though limited to formal sector workers, the program has been evaluated as quite successful, providing coverage to 200,000 SOE workers in 1992, though this is quite small relative to total workforce in sector (Hu Zu Liu, 1998). The program suggests what Vietnam might accomplish given a significantly smaller population to cover. Vietnam's position is in fact more fortunate; it has a far smaller percentage of workers in these sectors, and thus can better target them for transitional assistance in a way that China may have greater difficulty doing.

4. Reduce community-wide vulnerabilities. The overall objective is to reinforce a safety net system that serves an insurance function for vulnerable communities and households. Some recent analysts (van de Walle 1999) have suggested that existing safety nets are failing to adequately shield households from *co-variate risk*, defined as risks that tend to strike neighboring households or communities simultaneously. Some type of independent contingency fund, funded in poorest provinces by central transfers and with decentralized decision-making for fund use within central guidelines, is essential to buffer poor communities. A contingency fund for natural disasters and "pre-harvest starvation" currently exists but is under funded and has poorly specified management mechanisms. Better disaster preparedness and support-through capacity building (including monitoring and evaluation capacity) for all concerned agencies, and better coordination with international agencies - are also vital to this aim (Nguyen and Dao, 2002).

5. Reduce household-level risks and vulnerabilities. An ambitious agenda for reducing household risks can be mapped out, whereby the primary limits are fund availability and administrative capacity. To address these constraints, each of the programs below should apply two principles widely emphasized in the international literature: i) resources should be targeted to poor areas; and ii) schemes should employ self-targeting-"whereby conditions are built into program design such that only the poor choose to participate" (World Bank et. al, 1999, p. 127)-wherever possible. Several options are available within this category.

The first is to expand work-based, self-targeted employment generation schemes, linked to public infrastructure creation. The increased availability of publicly provided employment on infrastructure projects (self-targeted to poor because of low daily wage rates) as a key element of regional development plans could have a significant impact on seasonal rural underemployment. At present a number of agencies and levels of government implement these schemes; scope exists for systematizing their contribution to safety net coverage.

The second possibility is to research and pilot food stamps program. Food stamps are a specific means of reducing both household and, at times, community vulnerabilities, and they have been employed successfully by a number of countries in the region (Howell, 2001). Stamps that can be used as payment for food items are issued to households falling into a specific target group, such as the 'hungry' category, or households with nutritionally deficient children; the regional distribution of stamps can similarly reflect the distribution of poverty or malnutrition. The main drawback associated with such schemes is the high administrative capacity associated with identifying eligible households, but capacity may be considered a comparative strength of Vietnam's administrative apparatus, at least outside mountainous areas.

A third measure is to explore mechanisms to increase household access to (non-subsidized) credit and savings facilities. In doing so it will be important to lessen emphasis on subsidized credit since it "limit(s) the overall reach of the programs and tend(s) to direct credit at more dynamic and better informed households" (ILO, 1999, p. 23). Accessible facilities for the poor to contribute savings are currently lacking in rural areas and could make a positive contribution to reducing vulnerability to shocks (Nguyen and Dao, 2002).

Agricultural and veterinary extension services in poorest areas have been widely piloted in Vietnam, but meaningful assistance to farmers is available in only a small number of better-off communities. This is particularly true in poor provinces with little budget to supplement central transfers for such programs (Fritzen, 2000). Redesigning these extension models to make them appropriate to upland-based household production strategies (including systems appropriate for poor households) is a special priority.

The prospects for actuarially sound voluntary health and social insurance have generated some debate. Some analysts (Nguyen, 1997) are optimistic that coverage can be expanded beyond the current minority (less than 10%) with access to some health insurance; others (UNICEF, 2000) feel coverage will expand too incrementally to play a major role in cushioning socioeconomic shocks over the medium term. The balance of evidence lies with the second group. Few, if any, countries have succeeded in quickly expanding such insurance coverage to a large rural population at Vietnam's level of socioeconomic development (Ramesh, 2000). Improving the current system of fee exemptions for basic services for the poor will be just as important as formal health insurance in this regard, but is subject to the constraint of high administrative capacity necessary for the identification and issuance of exemptions (World Bank et. al, 2001).

6. Boost administrative and fiscal capacity for safety nets. As noted earlier, the current low coverage of services is related both to low resource availability and to poor administrative capacity. Several steps need to be taken to improve such capacity. Improving information and planning systems is the first one. It is currently impossible to say with an acceptable degree of precision what percent of target groups are being covered by formal social assistance. Improved information systems will also assist in another approach: better program coordination and integration across related sub-programs, notoriously weak in Vietnam (van Arkadie, 1993).

Secondly, Vietnam should build on its incremental decentralization efforts to move towards more flexible, community-based implementation of at least a substantial component of funds allocated for safety nets (Fritzen, 1999 and 2000).

Finally, fiscal reforms should aim at mobilizing from better-off localities a higher share of local revenue for safety net programs, while concentrating central-level transfers onto relatively poor areas. Provinces at present devote on average only 1% of their budget to social protection interventions (ILO, 1999). Boosting this figure in better-off provinces, with better supplementation for the coffers of poorer provinces, is an important component of the approach.

6. ASSESSMENT: THE FEASIBILITY OF REFORM

Three points have dominated the discussion so far. First, as emphasized in the introduction to this volume, international experience as well as the literature suggests that countries shift gradually to more formal safety net systems in line with their economic development. Attempts to rapidly expand formal systems at low income levels will likely founder due to competing budget pressures and low administrative capacity.

Second, despite its historical achievements of its social sectors, Vietnam conforms to this general story. Despite being a low income country, one might have hoped that two factors - its ideological commitment to social development and large increases in real government expenditure enabled by a decade of growth - would have helped it escape from the 'low formal coverage' trap in safety nets.

This spending has not been well targeted. Households currently classified as "poor or hungry" *(ngheo doi)* and those in better-off rural and urban areas lifted just above the poverty line together comprise approximately 40% of the overall population. Much of the increased expenditure on safety nets has been spent on formal entitlement programs that are failing to deliver substantial reductions in vulnerability for this spectrum of the population.

Third, a number of more cost-effective and feasible investment modalities exist to more rapidly reduce vulnerability. These include reorienting expenditure towards programs with greater impact, boosting administrative capacity and encouraging non-state involvement in welfare and social service provision.

What is the feasibility of the reform agenda described above, both for Vietnam and other low income countries? While specific policies to improve social protection will differ across countries, four types of systemic capacities will be important to reform success. Vietnam's experience can help show how these may constrain reform adoption in a specific country context.

The first capacity is for fiscal reorientation. The reform agenda for Vietnam does not foresee significant increases in fiscal commitments to social protection programs, already moderate within an increasingly tight state budget. But the process of shifting expenditure away from politically influential groups (such as war veterans and civil service pensioners) towards subgroups that are by definition more socially invisible is a politically risky and painful one. This reform barrier is generic to other contexts, and underlies the slow progress seen to date in the so-called 20/20 initiative (whereby governments and donors pledged to devote at least 20% of their budgets to social programs) since the 1995 World Summit for Social Development in Copenhagen (UNDP et. al, 1999).

The second demand is for the state to open to greater civil society involvement in service provision. In Vietnam, the primary barrier to this is ideological. The dominant development discourse in Vietnam is still heavily slanted towards the state as ultimate service provider (Marr, 1994). Ideology will slow reform more in some regions and sectors than others. The role of religious organizations in remote areas, for instance, is highly sensitive, as the internationally reported unrest in the Central Highlands region in 2001 and 2002 proved. In urban areas, where the private sector and associational life are rapidly expanding, more diversification can be expected.

A third requirement for the agenda described above to be implemented concerns greater implementation capacity. The 'policy-implementation' gap is indeed wide in Vietnam's poorest areas, due to insufficient central resource transfers, the absence of any systematic policy of capacity building, and poor socioeconomic infrastructure (Fritzen, 2000). These are exactly the regions that have the greatest demands for enhanced social protection. Improvements to bureaucratic coordination at central and local levels - a classic problem in socialist polities (van Arkadie, 1993) - will be essential. Numerous initiatives are underway to improve the institutional environment for service delivery at local level, such as an incipient decentralization agenda (in theory improving incentives for service delivery) and a 'grassroots democratization' initiative (to increase transparency and enforcement of rules underlying minimum standards). Yet these reforms tend to be limited by existing governance arrangements that centralize power and depend on the Communist Party policing its own ranks (Fritzen, 2002). Decentralization reforms much in vogue world-wide as a solution to poor governance performance in fact tax administrative capacity in new ways that have been difficult for countries to handle.

Ultimately, prospects for social protection agenda above are linked to a fourth requirement, which involves a political calculus. Will political benefits outweigh potential political costs? In Vietnam, political benefits would potentially accrue to the national and local leadership, who by adopting the strategy would reaffirm commitment to broadly-based, equitable growth as a defining element of Vietnamese socialism. Costs figure in terms of bureaucratic opposition to reorientation and elite (urban-based) interests supporting a 'growth-fist' agenda. In Vietnam, the pattern of economic growth in recent years may be increasing regional and rural-urban inequalities in ways that make it politically more difficult to adopt a broadly based "growth with equity" agenda (Fritzen, 2002).

The constraints will need to be flushed out for each low income country context, and for sub-regions of larger countries as well. But the case of Vietnam suggests that political and bureaucratic barriers to social protection reform will be considerable.

REFERENCES

Chu, K. and S. Gupta (1998). "Economic reforms, social safety nets, and the budget in transition economies," in Chu, K. and S. Gupta (eds.) *Social safety nets: Issues and recent experiences.* International Monetary Fund, Washington, D.C.

Drouin, A. (1999). Unemployment, social protection and crises: A perspective from the International Labour Organization. Asia Recovery Information

Center, The World Bank and Asian Development Bank. Downloaded from www.aric.adb.org <http://www.aric.adb.org>, November 22, 1999.

Fforde, A. & S. de Vylder (1996). *From plan to market: The economic transition in Vietnam.* Westview Press, Boulder.

Fritzen, S. (1997). "Human development in transition: Policy orientations for expanding choice in Viet Nam." United Nations Development Program, Hanoi.

Fritzen, S. (1999). "Decentralization, disparities, and innovation in Vietnam's health sector," in Litvack, J., & Rondinelli, D. (eds.) *Market reform in Vietnam: Building institutions for development.* (pp. 71-94). Quorum Books, Westport. pp. 71-94.

Fritzen, S. (2000). Decentralization and local government performance: A comparative approach with application to social policy reform in Vietnam. Ph.D. dissertation. Princeton University.

Fritzen, S. (2002). "Growth, poverty and the future of poverty reduction in Vietnam," *Asian Journal of Economics*, 13(2002): pp. 635-657.

General Statistics Office [GSO] of the Socialist Republic of Viet Nam (1999). *Viet Nam Living Standards Survey 1997-98.* General Statistics Office, Hanoi.

Howell, F. (2001) "Social Assistance: Theoretical Background" in Ortiz, I. (ed) Social Protection in Asia and the Pacific. Manila: Asian Development Bank, Manila. pp. 257-306.

Hu, Z. (1998). "Social protection, labor market rigidity, and enterprise restructuring in China," K.Y. Chu and S. Gupta (eds), *Social safety nets: Issues and recent experiences.* International Monetary Fund, Washington, D.C.

International Labour Office [ILO] (1999). "Development, employment and social safety nets. Summary report of an SPPD Project on social safety nets for vulnerable groups in Viet Nam (VIE/98/039)." Hanoi, mimeo.

James, E. (1999). "Coverage under old age security programs and protection for the uninsured-What are the issues?" The World Bank, mimeo.

John, M. (2002). "Social protection in Southeast and East Asia - Towards a comprehensive picture," in Adam, E. (ed.) *Social protection in Southeast & East Asia.* Friedrich-Ebert-Stiftung, Bonn.

Marr D. (1994). "The Vietnam Communist Party and civil society." Paper presented at the Vietnam Update 1994 Conference: Doi Moi, the state and civil society, 10-11 November, Australian National University, Canberra.

National Center for Social Sciences and Humanities [NCSSH] (2001). *National human development report 2001: Doi moi and human development in Vietnam.* The Political Publishing House, Hanoi.

Nguyen Huu Dung & Dao Quang Vinh (2002). "Social protection in Vietnam," in Adam, E. (ed.) *Social protection in Southeast & East Asia.* Friedrich-Ebert-Stiftung, Bonn.

Nguyen Nguyet Nga (1997). Health sector development and economic reform in a transitional economy: Vietnam 1989-1997. Ph.D. dissertation. University of Manchester.

Ortiz, I. (2001). "Introduction" in Ortiz, I. (ed.) *Social Protection in Asia and the Pacific.* Asian Development Bank, Manila. pp. 41-58.

Ramesh, M. with M. G. Asher (2000). *Welfare capitalism in southeast Asia: Social security, health, and education policies.* Macmillan Press: Houndmills.

Ravaillion, M. (1995). "Household vulnerability to aggregate shocks: Differing fortunes of the poor in Bangladesh and Indonesia." in K. Basu, P. Pattanaik & K. Suzumura (eds.), *Choice, welfare and development*, Clarendon Press, Oxford.

Riedel, J., & W. Turley (1999). "The politics and economics of transition to an open market economy in Vietnam," Organization for Economic Co-operation and Development, Technical paper No. 152.

Socialist Republic of Vietnam [SRVN] and Donor Working Group on Public Expenditure Review (2000). "Managing public resources better: Public expenditure review 2000." World Bank, Hanoi.

Socialist Republic of Vietnam and ADUKI (1998). "Vulnerable groups in rural Vietnam: Situation and policy response." Nha Xuat Ban Chinh Tri, Hanoi.

United Nations Childrens Fund [UNICEF] (2000). *Children and Women: A Situation Analysis 2000.* UNICEF, Hanoi.

United Nations Development Program [UNDP] and Ministry of Labor, Invalids and Social Affairs [MOLISA], (1999). "Monitoring the 20/20 Initiative: An analysis of state and donor expenditures for basic social services in Vietnam." Hanoi.

United Nations Development Program (2000). *Human Development Report 2000.* New York: Oxford University Press.

Van Arkadie, B., (1993). "Managing the renewal process: the case of Vietnam," *Public Administration and Development*, **13**: 435-451.

Van de Walle, D. (1999). "Protecting the poor in an emerging market economy," in J. Litvack and D. Rondinelli (eds.). *Market reform in Vietnam: Building institutions for development.* Quorum Books, Westport.

Webster, L. (1999). "SME's in Vietnam: On the road to prosperity," Mekong Project Development Facility, Private Sector Discussion Paper No. 10.

World Bank and Donor Working Group (1999). "Vietnam: Attacking poverty," World Bank, Hanoi.

World Bank and Donor Working Group (2001). "Growing healthy: A review of Vietnam's health sector," Hanoi: World Bank.

6

Is India's Poverty Falling? The Debate Surrounding The 55th NSS Round

*Shalendra D. Sharma**

INTRODUCTION

Over the past fifty years the world's population has more than doubled—from 2.5 billion to 5.5 billion, and the global Gross Domestic Product (GDP) has increased sevenfold—from about $3 trillion to over $22 trillion. Yet, over one billion people, a fifth of humanity live in conditions of abject poverty. The World Bank's *World Development Report* 2000/2001: *Attacking Poverty,* defines poverty as an unacceptable deprivation in human wellbeing that can comprise both physiological and social deprivation. Physiological deprivation involves the non-fulfilment of basic material or biological needs, including inadequate nutrition, health, education, and shelter. A person can be considered poor if he or she is unable to secure the goods and services to meet these basic material needs.

Based on the international poverty line of US$ 1 per day, the number of people living on less than US$1 a day grew from 1.18 billion in 1987 to 1.20 billion in 1998— an increase of 20 million

* *Associate Professor of Political Economy University of San Francisco, San Francisco, CA, sharma@usfca. edu.*

people. The vast majority of the world's poor live in rural areas. For example, in the Philippines, the percentage of the poor living in rural areas is almost 75%. In India, Thailand and Pakistan it is approximately 80% and over 90% in Indonesia, Bangladesh, Cambodia and Laos. No doubt, rural poverty constitutes the most important development challenge facing many developing countries. Nowhere is this a greater challenge than in India. With over 1 billion inhabitants (in mid-1999), and a per capita income of US$300, India continues to have one of the highest incidence of poverty in the developing world and accounts for about one-fourth of the world's absolute poor. In fact, according to the 2000/2001 *World Development Report,* India has the largest concentration of poor people than any other country in the world[1]. In fact, the world's largest constitutional democracy also has the dubious distinction of being the largest single-country contributor to the poor of the world's poor.

POVERTY TRENDS IN INDIA: AN OVERVIEW

According to the estimates made by the Government of India's (GOI), Planning Commission Report of 1960-61, over 50% or approximately 211 million people were living below the poverty line in the sense they lacked the Rs. 15 per capita per month in the rural areas and Rs. 18 per capita per month in the urban areas to maintain minimum subsistence needs (GOI 1963). The Planning Commission Report for the early 1970's revealed that the percentage of people living in poverty had remained the same, but in absolute terms their numbers had increased to over 220 million (GOI 1972). In the mid-1970s, rural poverty line became based on a nutritional norm of 2,400 calories per day, and defined as the level of average per capita total expenditure at which this norm could be typically attained. The Planning Commission determined this line at Rs. 49 per capita monthly expenditure at October 1973–June 1974 all-India rural prices. For the urban area, the poverty line was computed at Rs. 57 per month reflecting a nutritional norm of 2,100 calories. Estimates by the Planning Commission for the year 1977-78 placed the proportion of the population below the poverty line in rural areas at 51% and in the urban areas at 38%. These estimates were based on a poverty line of Rs. 65 per capita per month (1977-78 prices) for rural areas corresponding to a minimum daily caloric requirement of 2,400 units per person, and Rs.

75 in urban areas corresponding to a calorie intake of 2100 units. Currently, roughly one-third of India's population is poor by the same standards as the early 1960s. Because of rapid population growth and modest rates of poverty reduction, the numbers of poor people have risen from 164 million in 1951 to roughly 312 million in 1993-94.[2]

DID POVERTY DECLINE IN THE 1980?

The Indian government's Planning Commission's 1983-84 Report (GOI 1985), and the World Bank study, *India: Poverty, Employment and Social Services* (1989a) made a startling claim on poverty trends for the 1980s. The reports contended that since the beginning of the 1980s there has been a "clear trend" towards "greater" income redistribution, and that the proportion of those living below the poverty line declined significantly—according to the Seventh Plan from 48.3% in 1978 to 37.1% in 1984. The Planning Commission's 1993 *Report of the Expert Group on Estimation of Proportion and Number of Poor* confirmed its 1983-84 findings claiming that by the early 1990s under 30% of Indian were living below the poverty line.

This official claim has not gone unchallenged resulting in heated debates and outpourings of published materials on the "poverty problem." Several of these analysts have criticized the Reports for its "exaggerated conclusions" arguing that the data have been based on the unprecedented assumption that incomes increased uniformly across all expenditure classes, and on the "untenable assertion" that all families enrolled in the major anti-poverty programs benefited sufficiently to cross the poverty line. Others have pointed out that since the poverty ratio fluctuates, the fact that the 1983-84 National Sample Survey (NSS) took place on an exceptionally good year for agricultural production largely explains the lower incidence of poverty. They add that while at any given time, poverty levels reflect the variability in individual incomes, and while the transient component may be large, there also exists a substantial core of the chronically poor that has not changed much over time. They point out that poverty alleviation remains India's major developmental challenge because the poverty problem has not been mitigated—despite efforts by some to wish the problem away (at least statistically). For example, Minhas (1991: 1673) notes:

The massive reduction in the incidence of poverty in 1987-88, as reported by the Planning Commission is again largely a consequence of the peculiar statistical artifacts used by the Commission. Just as it did with the 1983 NSS data, the Planning Commission has continued to indulge in mindless tinkering with the observed NSS size distribution of consumer expenditure for 1987-88 also. Appropriately computed incidence of poverty in 1987-88 comes to about 48.7 for rural and 37.8 per cent for urban India, rather than the artificially low estimate of 32.7 and 19.4 per cent reported to parliament by the Planning Commission.

It should also be noted that poverty estimates by the Planning Commission and the World Bank are based on requirements of minimum caloric intake only, to the exclusion of other then basic necessities of life such as clothing, shelter, access to safe drinking water, sanitation and health facilities. Clearly, in excluding these variables the official data grossly overstates the socalled "improvements"—its overall percentage "decline" in poverty levels not only reflects the changes associated with measurement techniques (changes in what is considered to be an acceptable minimum level of consumption), but also the normal fluctuations in poverty levels between a poor person to someone who is even poorer. Granted, while precise data on how much poverty is transient and how much is persistent is difficult togather as poverty levels vary over time, reflecting the variability in family employment and incomes, the fact that in India there exists a substantial core of chronic and persistent poverty is difficult to deny.

DID POVERTY DECLINE? ROUND TWO

Using three different measures of poverty—the head-count index (H), the poverty gap index (PG) and the squared poverty gap index (SPG), — in a attempt to capture alternative dimensions of poverty corresponding to its incidence, depth and severity, the National Sample Survey for 1993-94 reported that approximately 37.3% of the rural and 32.4% of the urban populations lived in poverty — which were virtually the same as the poverty rates reported in the previous quinquennial survey, the 43rd NSS round carried out in 1987-88. The Survey revealed a national average of 35% living in poverty, and sharp regional disparities in poverty levels. For example, in 1990-

91, less than 20% of the population of Punjab and Haryana were poor, compared with nearly 60% in Bihar. Also, in Bihar, the proportion of poor in the rural population was estimated to be 64%, in Uttar Pradesh 42%, while in the Punjab and Haryana 25% was classified as poor[3]. Adding further fuel to the fire — a World Bank study (Datt and Ravallion, 1995; 1996), reported that the Indian government's economic liberalization policies in the early 1990s led to sharp rises in the prices of key commodities such as rice, sugar, cotton and gasoline, hurting the poor and increasing the incidence of poverty from 36% to 41% of the population. A more comprehensive World Bank report, *India: Achievements and Challenges in Reducing Poverty* (1997), using the Planning Commission's poverty line (Rs. 49.09) and Rs. 56.64 at 1973-74 prices in rural and urban areas respectively), argued that the poverty ratio which declined from 39.23% in rural India and 36.60% in urban India in 1987-88 to 36.43 and 32.76% respectively in 1990-91, subsequently rose to 37.42% and 33.23% in 1991 and 43.47% and 33.73% in 1992.

The authorities found these findings quite shocking as there was a lot of expectation on the part of the Indian government that poverty levels would have declined sharply following the implementation of economic reforms. While some analysts pointed out that the findings were hardly surprising since reform experiences suggest that poverty generally rises in the initial years of reform, followed by a reversal in the later years, the critics of the reforms were not convince. Many gleefully concluded that the high economic growth rates fueled by economic liberalization was leaving the poor behind. Indeed, many felt that economic liberalization, in particular, the stabilization and structural and reform measures with its pro-market bias simply did not have the ability to generate improvements in the lives of the poor.

Yet, the critics also noted an anomaly. They conceded that despite the persistence of poverty, India's overall human development social indicators have improved. The average life expectancy at birth has increased from 49 years to the current 63 years.

The total fertility rate for India's large and growing population has been lowered from six children per woman to three since the 1960s. Similarly, since 1950, there was a dramatic reduction in infant mortality from 146 to the current average of 69 per 1,000 live births. The 1990s witnessed important achievements in literacy with enrolment of primary school-aged children rising from 68 percent in 1992/1993 to 82 per cent at the end of the decade. India today has 108 million children aged 6 to 10 attending primary school — the world's second largest education system after China.

However, the findings of the 55th Round of the NSS held in 1999-2000 concluded that there was no such anomaly. As the results started pouring in (beginning February 2001), the NSS declared that poverty had fallen sharply. At the all-India level there was a significant reduction in poverty of about 11% (from about 39% of the population to roughly 28%) during the second half of the 1990s. More specifically, the 55th Round claimed a net reduction in rural poverty of some 60 million people between 1993-94 and 1999-2000. In rural India, poverty was down to 27.1% while urban poverty fell by around 8% — from 32% to 24%. However, the critics were not convinced. What explains this? Some background is necessary here.

HAS POVERTY DECLINED IN THE 1990S? THE PROBLEMATIC NSS 55TH ROUND

In 1950, at the behest of Prime Minister Jawaharlal Nehru, the Indian government's Planning Commission created the National Sample Survey Organisation (NSSO) to track via the National Sample Survey (NSS), the performance of the Indian economy by collecting data from a random sample of the population. Over time, this project has compiled a time series of consumption data from 36 National Sample Surveys spanning 1951-99. This is one of the longest series of national household surveys suitable for tracking living conditions of the poor. In fact, India has one of the richest sources of data on household-level consumption expenditures across time of any country in the developing world.

Specifically, a NSS has been carried out every five years with a sample size of approximately 123,000 households. As a complement to these quinquennial "thick rounds", smaller "thin rounds" with a much smaller sample size have also been carried out on an annual basis. The thick rounds of the NSS collect household consumption expenditure data — focusing mainly on food and durable goods, but also including data on educational and medical expenditures. On the other hand, the thin rounds focus on non-consumption variables. However, the estimates from the thin samples are not officially accepted as representative surveys. Consequently, official poverty estimates are available only in five-year intervals, making it difficult to study their time series properties.

Yet, despite this limitation, the results of the NSS constitute the primary basis for national poverty estimates, and the comparisons between various rounds allow trends in poverty levels and income distribution to be monitored. Most researchers consider the surveys to be large enough to be considered representative at the urban and rural levels for most states, and to be reasonably comparable over time since the basic survey method has changed relatively little. Other data (on price indices and explanatory variables) are also available on a reasonably consistent basis. Although there were many data problems (some, but not all, of which could be fixed), they are modest by the standards of cross-country comparative studies. The NSS data provides a unique opportunity to study the link between living conditions of the poor and the key macroeconomic and sectoral variables which are thought to have important influences on progress in reducing poverty.

In an effort to be consistent over time, the NSSO has given special attention to the question of the appropriate recall period for various items and categories of expenditure. A certain amount of experimentation has taken place in the effort to identify the recall period that would yield the most accurate data on actual expenditures. Specifically, since the 1950s the NSS has used a 30-day recall period for consumption. However, in the thin samples of the 51th, 52th, 53rd, and 54th rounds, households were randomly divided and some given an experimental questionnaire with a 7 day recall period for some items (including foods) and either 30 day or 365 day recall for others, while others were given the traditional 30 day questionnaire for all items. The results from those rounds showed that the experimental questionnaire, and particularly the 7 day recall period for yielded higher reported rates of monthly purchases and, thereby, much lower rates of poverty than the traditional questionnaires. This effect was large enough to cut poverty rates in half when the experimental questionnaire was used in place of the traditional 30 day questionnaire.

However, after much discussion, the 55th round made a significant deviation from the earlier technique. The basic change was in terms of the reference period used in the questionnaire dealing with consumption. Specifically, all households were given both questionnaires, a procedure which invited them (or possibly the enumerators) to reconcile the rates of consumption over the two reporting periods. The question on consumption of clothing, footwear, education and institutional health were asked with a reference period of 365 days and that on food consumption for only a recall period of (alternately) 30 and 7 days. However, cognizant of the fact that a sudden switch would make it impossible to compare earlier rounds with the new ones, the NSS decided that in the 55th round people would be asked about their consumption in the previous 30 days and in the previous 7 days. To make the comparisons easy to understand, the answers were carefully recorded in two adjacent columns in the survey questionnaire.

The results were simply astonishing. During 1994-98, on a weekly recall basis, the proportion of people below the poverty line in India as a whole was 20.4% (in the rural areas it was 21.5% and in the urban areas, about 17.5%. It is assumed that 28% of population lives in the urban areas.). For the same period, but on a monthly recall basis, the proportion of people below the poverty line would have been about 40.5% (in the rural areas, about 39.5% of the people, on an average, would have been below the poverty line, and in the urban areas, this would have been about 33%, on an average.) Thus, the weekly recall basis shows the proportion of the poverty line to be lower by nearly 51%, compared to the proportion on a monthly recall basis. Put bluntly, according to the 55th round, India's poverty rate fell by 12.8% over 18 months - removing some 60 million persons from poverty. Clearly, in India when people are asked to recall their expenditure over the previous week, they tend to indicate a higher level of food expenditure than they would have had they been asked to recall their expenditure over the previous month. If this is the case, had India adopted the weekly basis on an international comparable basis, poverty would have been shown to be nearly 50% less. The NSS does not indicate why the weekly recall basis should show substantially lower consumer expenditure than the monthly recall basis. However, some hold the view that people simply multiply the weekly recall expenditure by four to derive the monthly expenditure and, hence, there would necessarily be an under-estimate of expenditure on a monthly basis.

THE DEBATE AND ATTEMPTS TOWARDS A RESOLUTION

The methodology and the data generated a great deal of controversy. Although the NSS correctly pointed that the weekly recall approach is the standard international practice (whereas in India, the monthly recall basis is adopted), and that the changes were supported by a cross-section of economists because the 7 day recall period for food consumption would give a better indication of actual consumption, the critics were not convinced. Some alleged that the two sets of questionnaires may have confused both respondents and enumerators thereby making the recall estimates not comparable with those of the earlier large sample studies (Sen 2000). Others claim that the NSS has deliberately changed the method of collecting data in the 55th round to hide the extent of the real poverty levels. Thus, the sharp poverty reduction in the 55th round is not real, but an artifact of measurement.

The critics do raise a valid point in India. In India, consumption data used to be collected by asking people how much they had consumed over the previous 30 days. This practice, which is at variance with that in most other parts of the world where people are asked about their consumption over the previous seven days, had been coming under criticism for some time now. As the late Pravin Visaria (former chairman of the National Sample Survey), used to constantly note, several studies in the 1990s showed that people have a notoriously poor memory. People's daily consumption computed from the 30-day question turns out to be close to 20% less than that computed from the 7-day question. Yet, there is a problem: If you use the 1999-2000 survey and check how much less the consumption of various goods turn out to be by the 30-day method as compared to the 7-day method, the answer to turns out to be a mere 2 or 3%, nowhere near the 20% suggested by Visaria. It is clear what had happened. When you ask people how much they have consumed in the last seven days and then follow up this question with what they consumed in the last 30 days, it is natural for people to do mental checks to make sure that the two answers are roughly consistent[4]. In other words, the answer to the 30-day question had been contaminated by the 7-day question, and the trouble is that we do not know the extent of the contamination.

How do you reconcile these seeming incomparable data sets? A number of attempts have already clarified some of the outstanding issues. For example, Angus Deaton (2003) has developed a procedure for adjusting poverty estimates from the 55th round to make them comparable with estimates from earlier large-sample rounds of the NSS. His method exploits the fact the although the questionnaire design was changed from most of the goods in the survey, data on some broad categories of expenditures (or consumption) were measured consistently (i.e. using the same recall period) across all rounds of the NSS, including the 55th round. In particular, a broad category of goods, including "fuel and light," "miscellaneous goods," "miscellaneous services," "non-institutional medical services," "rent", and "consumer cesses and taxes" were measured the same way across all rounds of the NSS. That is, data on these items has always been collected using the 30-day reporting period.[5]

Deaton estimates the corrected poverty levels for the 55th round based on two assumptions: first, the marginal distribution of the consistently measured goods is not affected by the change in survey design, and second, the distribution of total consumption conditioned on consumption of these goods does not change over time and can be inferred from the 50th rounds. Specifically, this means that for some goods, which people buy in "bulk" and only occasionally, such as fuel and light and some durable goods, all rounds of the NSS ask only a 30-day question. It turned out that these goods form a fairly substantial part, approximately 20% of a typical person's total consumption. Thus, by using data from uncontaminated samples, we can roughly estimate how the proportion of income that an average person spends on these select items varies as his/her income changes. According to Deaton, once you have estimated this relation, you can use it in reverse to make a guess about a person's income from data on the amount a person spends on these select items. So the best one can do now is to use the consumption data from the 55th round on these select items, to estimate incomes and, from that, to estimate the number of people with income below the poverty line. Deaton's method yields the following findings: Rural and urban poverty in 1999-2000 are 30.2% and 24.7%. While the decline in poverty is not as sharp as the government had claimed, it is significant, nevertheless.

Finally, K. Sundaram and Suresh Tendulkar's new empirical reasearch on poverty trends yields similar findings to Deaton's. They estimate that the poverty head-count ratio declined by over 8 percentage points between the 50th and 55th rounds of the NSS. The authors resolve the issue of comparability by using consumer expenditure data from the NSS 55th round Employment—Unemployment Survey (Schedule 10), augmented by data from the four rounds (the 51st to the 54th) of the Consumer Expenditure Survey (Schedule 1). Sundaram and Tendulkar's results indicate that the size distributions of consumer expenditure from the 55th round Consumer Expenditure Survey are comparable to those from the 50th round Consumer Expenditure Survey, subject to appropriate recalculation. The revised data provide clear evidence of a decline in poverty in the 1990s.

The fact that India's stubborn poverty statistic has been dented a little at last is encouraging. However, there is urgent need to further improve the official methodology used to measure poverty, including the approach used to calculate official poverty lines, price indices and measurement of household welfare. Nevertheless, poverty is not solely a matter of consumption and income deprivation. The poor are a heterogeneous group and poverty is comprised of a complex mix of economic and non-economic dimensions. Clearly, statistical information germane to poverty measurement should be enriched by the addition of non-traditional indicators.

NOTES

1. This roughly assumes a poverty line of daily consumption expenditure of (PPP adjusted) a dollar a day. Purchasing power parity (PPP) adjustment of the rupee-dollar exchange rate takes care of real purchasing power of a rupee, as against the nominal exchange rate. If one uses a nominal exchange rate of Rs. 40 to a dollar, then the non-PPP adjusted per capita income of India is roughly a dollar a day. This would make all Indians below an official poverty line of a dollar a day.
2. It is important to note that India's progress in fighting poverty is modest when compared with some of its Asian neighbours. Between 1970 and 1993, the proportion of Indonesia's population living in poverty dropped from 58% to 8%, an annual decline of nearly 10% - a greater decline in 20 years than India has been able to achieve in 50. Similarly, China

reduced the incidence absolute poverty from 270 million in 1978 to 65 million in 1996.

3. What accounts for the regional variations? Higher growth rates in agricultural output per acre, lower inflation, and higher growth in state developmental expenditures all led to more rapid reductions in absolute poverty in rural areas. Differences in initial human and physical resource development were also important factors. For details see Datt and Ravallion (1997).
4. There is also the view that as the last week of the month would necessarily involve economies, and people would remember the last week more clearly than the previous ones, the monthly recall process should necessarily be an underestimate. This cannot be upheld because the NSS investigations are on a continuous time basis. Anyway, the question, should the differences from the weekly and the monthly basis be so large remain.
5. Clearly, the first four are important items, and expenditures on the first three are reported by virtually all households. Non-institutional medical expenditures are also important on average, with a mean that is comparable in size to expenditures on miscellaneous goods or expenditures on miscellaneous services—although they are incurred by less than half of households over a 30-day period.

REFERENCES

Ahluwalia, Montek. 1978. "Rural Poverty and Agricultural Performance in India" *Journal of Development Studies* 14, vol. 3. April, pp. 289-324.

——,1986. "Rural Poverty, Agricultural Production, and Prices: A Re-examination" in J.W. Mellor and G.N. Desai, eds., *Agricultural Change and Rural Poverty.* Delhi: Oxford University Press.

Dandekar, V.M. 1988. "Agriculture, Employment and Poverty" in Robert Lucas and Gustav F. Papanek eds., *The Indian Economy: Recent Developments and Future Prospects.* Delhi: Oxford University Press.

Datt, Gurav and Martin Ravallion, 1995. *Why Did Poverty Increase Sharply after Indias Macroeconomic Stabilization.* Poverty and Human Resources Working Paper. Washington D.C.: The World Bank Policy Research Department.

——, 1996. *Macroeconomic Crises and Poverty Monitoring: The Case of India.* Policy Research Working Paper, no. 1685. Washington, D.C.: The World Bank.

——,1997. "Why have some Indian states done better than others at reducing rural poverty" World Bank Working Paper.

Deaton, Angus, 2003. "Adjusted Indian Poverty Estimates for 1999-2000" *Economic and Political Weekly,* January 25, pp. 322-326.

Eswaran, Mukesh and Ashok Kotwal. 1994. *Why Poverty Persists in India: An Analytical Framework for Understanding the Indian Economy.* New Delhi: Oxford University Press.

Gaiha, Raghav. 1989. "Poverty, Agricultural Production and Prices in Rural India" *Cambridge Journal of Economics.* No. 13, pp. 333-52.

Minhas, B.S., L.R., Jain and S.D. Tendulkar. 1991. "Declining Incidence of Poverty in the 1980s: Evidence Versus Artefacts" *Economic and Political Weekly.* Vol. xxvi, no. 27-28. July, pp. 1673-82.

Sen, Abhijit. 2000. "Estimates of Consumer Expenditure and its Distribution: Statistical Priorities after the NSS 55th Round" *Economic and Political Weekly,* December 16, pp. 499-518.

Sundaram, K and Suresh D Tendulkar. 2003. "Poverty has Declined in the 1990s: A Resolution of Comparability Problems in NSS Consumer Expenditure Data" *Economic and Political Weekly,* January 25, pp. 327-337.

World Bank. 1975. *The Assault on World Poverty.* Baltimore: John Hopkins University Press.

——,1984. *Situation and Prospects of the Indian Economy: A Medium Term Perspective.* World Bank: Washington, D.C.

——,1989. *World Development Report 1989.* New York: Oxford University Press.

——,1989a. *Country Studies: India—Poverty, Employment and Social Services.* World Bank: Washington: D.C.

——,1993. *The East Asian Miracle: Economic Growth and Public Policy.* New York: Oxford University Press.

——,1996. *World Development Report 1996.* New York: Oxford University Press.

——,1996a. *India: Five Years of Stabilization and Reform and the Challenges Ahead.* World Bank: Washington, D.C.

——,1997. *India: Achievements and Challenges in Reducing Poverty.* World Bank: Washington, D.C.

——,1999. *World Development Report 1998/99.* New York: Oxford University Press.

7

Welfare Boards

With special reference to Beedi Workers Welfare Fund

—*S. Vijaya Kumar*

INTRODUCTION

The fundamental characteristics of social justice is providing basic security for all. Basic security, as suggested by ILO, requires policies and institutions by which every one has access to health services, a decent level of education and the basic needs of their existence, which would enable them to function to the best of their capabilities. In this process of providing basic social security Indian government has formulated several obligatory measures in the form of policies such s constitutional provisions, retirement benefits, pensions and other welfare services.

Further and more particularly considering various forms of risks and vulnerabilities among the unorganized sector people, Government of India has focused attention on creating a welfare state. The fundamental characteristic of welfare state has to provide a minimum level of well-being for all its members, especially to the most vulnerable sections such as the young, the old, the unemployed and the sick. Further, it also has to guarantee minimum standards of income, nutrition and health for all as of human right. In his report Beveridge (1942) came out with this concept for the first time and suggested the need of health services and insurances are much essential issues under the social security program.

Giving due consideration to this, Indian constitution lays special stress on the goal of welfare state by directing the State to follow certain principles which are essential to secure a just social order and for the promotion of the welfare of the people. The directive principles are maimed at eradication of poverty, exploitation, inequality and injustice and thereby ensuring equal opportunities through decentralization of power, employment, social security and welfare to all sections of population.

In the process of providing social security measures welfare funds/boards came in to existence. These funds are being raised by levying a cess on the production sale or export of specified goods or by collecting contribution from various sources including employer as well as employee. Such funds have to be utilized for the well-being/welfare of the 89 per cent of the workers who are informal economy.

WELFARE BOARDS

In India several welfare funds are in operation and some of these are set up Central Government and some by the State Governments. Nutshell information on existing welfare funds are as follows.

Beedi workers welfare fund (1976); Building and other Construction workers welfare fund (1996); Cine workers welfare fund (1961); Iron ore Manginess ore and Chrome ore labour welfare fund (1961); Lime stone and Dolomite mines labour welfare fund (1972); Mica mines labour welfare fund (1946) are the welfare funds managed by the Central Government.

Besides some of the State Governments are also having their own welfare funds. Out of all States in India, Kerala is having maximum number of welfare funds and they are—Coir workers welfare scheme; Handloom workers welfare scheme; Motor transport welfare fund scheme; Auto rickshaw workers welfare fund scheme; Cashew workers welfare scheme; Toddy workers welfare fund scheme; Beedi and Cigar workers fund; Bamboo kattuvali Thazaha workers welfare fund; Kerala labour welfare fund; Tailoring workers welfare fund; Advocate clerks welfare fund; Construction workers welfare fund; Fishermen welfare fund; Khadi workers welfare fund; Abkari workers welfare fund; Head load workers welfare fund; and Agriculture workers welfare fund.

Further, Gujarat rural workers welfare board; Gujarat labour welfare fund, Tamil Ndau Construction workers welfare board, Tamil Nadu labour welfare fund, West Bengal labour welfare board; Utter Pradesh labour welfare scheme and Andhra Pradesh labour welfare fund are also catering the basic needs of unorganized sector population.

The welfare funds can be categorized into two : tax based and contributory. The funds executed and managed by Central government are tax—based where the those executed by the government of Kerala are mostly contributory. Further welfare funds of Central government have limited schemes such as health, housing and education. The welfare funds of Kerala government have many schemes. Including the said three schemes, old age pension, assistance for funeral expenses, interest—free loans for the marriages of daughters, educational assistance and medical facilities. In this way Kerala welfare fund schemes provide a much wider range of benefits, including many of the branches of social security that are included in the ILO convention concerning Minimum Standards of Social Security (Subrahmanya, 2000).

However, these welfare funds are suffering with financial crisis and the by limited their schemes. While discussing this Subrahmanya (2000) argued that the central and the Kerala models represent two extreme, one the minimalist approach, the other the maximalist approach. Neither can be consider ideal for the future development of welfare funds in India as far as benefits are concerned. He suggests preparation of standardized list of benefits which may be provided from the welfare funds and to priorities them, some what as follows: health care, invalidity, old age and survivor benefits, maternity and child care, educational assistance and housing.

BEEDI WORKERS WELFARE FUNDS—AN EXAMPLE

Existing Structure of the Board

Soon after the independence, along with so many other

industries, this particular industry also expanded and flourished in several parts of the country. Keeping the growing strength of the workers population in this industry, for the first time, as a constitutional obligation, a Welfare Fund was constituted under the Beedi Workers Welfare Fund Act, 1976 in order to facilitate the basic welfare measures for the beedi manufacturing workers and their family members. Broadly the welfare measures covered under this Act includes health, housing, education, recreation and family welfare.

To materialize the Beedi Workers Welfare Fund, cess was levied under the Beedi Workers Welfare Cess Act, 1976 and the cess won on the issue of tobacco obtained from Central Warehouse. Later on this system was modified by Beedi Workers Welfare Cess Amendment Act 1981 through which cess was levied on manufactured beedis at the rate of 10 to 50 paise per thousand beedis. Gradually the cess rate was altered several times (during 1987, 1995 & 1998) keeping the escalation of welfare and maintenances costs. At present it is Rs. 2 per 1000 beedis (wef. June 2000) and as per this rate of cess an expected annual income would be around Rs. 84 crores at the current level of production of beedis and the exemptions of Central Excise Duty and Cess (ref—Notification No. 33/82—GE, dated 28.2.1982 and amended by 78/86 and 35-87).

The collected cess amount deposited into the accounts of Consolidated Fund of India and based on the estimated requirements the amount will be sanctioned to the concerned Welfare Commissionrates. This estimation has to be subjected to the approval of Parliament and this fund is considered under non-plan expenditure.

In general, the organization and administration of this found is the primary responsibility of the Ministry of Labour. The Labour Welfare Organization of this ministry is shouldering the responsibility of administering this fund at all India level, majority in 14 States/Union Territories and for the administrative purposes the entire country was divided and grouped in to nine regions.

Each region is having a headquarters and the geographical distribution of these regions is as follows—

Headquarters	States/Union Territories comes under the region
Allahabad	Uttar Pradesh, Himachal Pradesh, Jammu & Kashmir, Punjab and N.C.T of Delhi
Bangalore	Karnataka, Kerala and Lakshadweep Islands
Bhilwara	Rajesthan, Gujarat and Haryana
Hyderabad	Andhra Pradesh, Tamil Nadu, Pondicherry and Andaman & Nicobar Islands
Bhubaneswar	Orissa
Jabalpur	Madhya Pradesh
Karma	Bihar
Nagpur	Maharashtra, Goa, Daman & Diu and Dadra & Nagar Haveli
Calcutta	Assam, Arunachal Pradesh, Meghalaya, Nagaland, Manipur, Tripura, Mizoram, West Bengal and Sikkim

To Director General is the head of the Labour welfare Organization and the Welfare Commissioner heads each one of the regions. The Central and State Advisory Committees, formed on tripartite basis are also functioning as coordinating bodies in administering the fund.

As per the labour statistics 2001 there are 44,11,275 beedi workers in India. Of them 36,89,116 were provided with identity cards through which they avail the welfare activities. Further out of the total beedi work force 85 per cent are women.

Welfare Activities

Following are the objectives of the existing welfare fund Act :

* Public health and sanitation, medical facilities and the prevention of diseases;
* Water supplies and facilities for washing;
* Educational facilities;
* Housing and recreation facilities including standards of living, nutrition and amelioration of social conditions;
* Family welfare, including family planning education and services;
* Such other welfare measures and facilities as may be prescribed;

To grant loan or subsidy to a State Government, a local authority or an employer, in aid of any scheme approved by the Central Government for the purpose connected with the welfare of workers engaged in beedi manufacturing;

* To pay annual grants in aid to the employer who provides to the satisfaction of the Central Government welfare measures and facilities of the prescribed standards for the benefit of workers engaged in beedi manufacturing; and
* Any other expenditure, which the central Government may direct to be defrayed from the Fund.

To justify the above objectives of the Act, various welfare schemes have been formulated and put into practice. Broadly they are as follows :

Health : Establishment of separate Hospitals and Dispensaries, including mobile units; Welfare Schemes for T.B. Patients including reservation of Beds in T.B. Hospitals and Domiciliary Treatment to T.B. Patients; Scheme for Cancer patients; Treatment of Workers suffering from Mental Diseases; Grant of Financial assistance to Beedi workers for purchases of spectacles; Leprosy Relief for Beedi Workers; Maternity benefit scheme for female Beedi workers; and Scheme for payment of extra monetary compensation for sterilization to Beedi workers.

Social Security : Group Insurance Scheme through cooperatives societies.

Housing : Building your own house scheme; Housing scheme for economically weaker sections; Scheme for grant of subsidy to cooperative societies of beedi workers for construction of work sheds or godowns or both.

Education : Award of scholarships to the children of beedi workers studying in class in V and above; Financial assistance for school uniform/text books and stationery to school going children studying up to class IV; Incentive scheme of passing final examination from high school onwards; Attendance incentive scheme to female students studying class V and above.

Recreation : Establishment of audio-visual sets/cinema vans/ exhibition of films; Organizing sports, games, social and cultural activities; Holiday scheme; Supply of T.V. Sets of beedi workers industries/cooperative societies; Establishment of community halls in beedi workers housing colony with colour T.V. Sets.

Under these major issues of welfare the following schemes are in operation —

Starting of static cum mobile static dispensaries; Scheme for reservation of beds in T.B. hospitals; Scheme for domiciliary treatment of T.B; Scheme for treatment of beedi workers suffering form cancer; Treatment of workers suffering from mental diseases; Scheme of leprosy relief for beedi workers; Grant of financial assistance for purchase of spectacles; Scheme for reimbursement of expenditure as a financial assistance to the workers suffering from heart diseases; Scheme for reimbursement of expenditure as financial assistance to beedi workers for kidney transplantation; Scheme for payment of monetary compensation for sterilization to the beedi workers; Maternity benefit scheme for female beedi workers; Group insurance scheme; Scheme for grant of subsidy and financial assistance to cooperative societies of beedi workers for construction of work sheds and godown; Grant of scholarship; Financial assistance to school going children of workers for supply of one set of dress and reading materials; Scheme to pay incentive to the children of beedi workers on passing final examination conducted by the board/ university from tenth class onwards; Scheme to provide incentive/ financial assistance on the basis of attendance in schools, colleges to the female students; Supply to T.V. Sets; Scheme for sanction of grant in aid for setting up of community centre in the residential colony of beedi workers; Scheme for excursion cum study tour of beedi workers to the holiday home; and Integrated housing scheme.

Financial Set Up—Income and Expenditure :

As mentioned earlier, the main source of finance is coming form the Beedi Workers Welfare Cess Act, 1976 which was amended couple of times by enhancing the cess amount according to the increasing survival and felt needs of the workers. At present the Rs. 2/- per 1000 beedis is the cess collected by the Central Excise Department (Wef— June 28, 2000). With this enhancement of cess, an additional amount of Rs. 42 crores is getting in to the Welfare

Fund by rising its total to Rs. 84 crores per year. Out of this total approximately 82 per cent of the amount has been sanctioned to the Labour Welfare Organization to cater the welfare needs of the workers and the remaining 18 per cent is being withheld by the Consolidate Fund of India.

The Labour Welfare Organization in turn, under priority basis disbursing this amount to the nine regional labour welfare commission-rates. Roughly the Labour Welfare Organization is spending 45-50 per cent on health sector, 25-35 per cent on education, 8-10 per cent on housing, 6-7 per cent on demonstration and 0.5-1 per cent on recreational activities.

With the above details it can be understood that the Labour Welfare Organization is giving much priority to health sector, which is off course the essential felt need of the workers. Next priority of the organization goes to education followed by housing and almost negligible amount is allotted for creating recreational facilities. A considerable amount (roughly 17 per cent) is also being spent on administration.

Administrative Set Up & Organizing The Fund :

Though the existing administrative set up is theoretically doing at its best, practically it has several operational and administrative problems. To be specific the existing system is highly bureaucratic and too centralized. It is not fully working under decentralized mechanism, for instance the entire Labour Welfare Organization is headed by the Director General who is having administrative powers but not financial powers. The financial powers are vested with the Labour Ministry. Either DG, or Welfare Commissioner, or Director as the administrators will have to depend on the Welfare Ministry for all financial matters and this is a time consuming process.

Coming to the organizing the fund, the total welfare programme for beedi workers are funded by the Central Excise Department is going into the Consolidated Fund of India and form there, after deducting certain percentage of amount (Approximately 15-20 per cent) towards its administrative and maintenance cost from the total collected cess, the remaining amount is made available to the Labour Organization for further disbursement between the nine regions.

In fact this fund comes under non-plan expenditure category and more importantly there is no economic contribution from government side. In general, non-plan expenditure may not essentially follow all normal government rules and regulations. Further, the estimated budget has to be examined by the committee and thereafter Parliament approval is needed. As a routing matter, all government rules are applicable to this fund even though government stake is not there and again, under hostility measures, government is imposing normal 10 per cent cut on beedi workers welfare fund. With such restriction coverage of number beneficiaries will automatically reduced. Further, Ministry of Labour has imposed ban on purchasing new vehicles and this reflected the health sector of the Labour Welfare Organization, especially the mobile medical units got affected. As such the available funds are not at all adequate to meet the welfare needs at substantial level. In this way several administrative and financial constraints exist in the administrating the beedi workers welfare fund.

The earlier part of this study critiqued the existing Beedi Welfare Fund model, suggested changes in terms of quality and attempted a first level income-expenditure budgetary analysis of the amount of financing required to adequately covering all beedi workers through the Beedi Workers Welfare Board.

The following section outlines a suggested approach based on some key principles, for proposed change in the functioning of welfare funds towards a more efficient and equitable system.

Proposed Model

Approach to Implementation

There are three key principles on which the implementation of the proposed decentralized model is based :

(1) Decision-making would move away from the Central Labour Ministry, down to the State level. The Beedi Workers Welfare Fund itself would need to be granted autonomous status, allowing, it to function as an autonomous body at both the Central and State level. For this, an amendment to the Beedi Welfare Fund Act would be required.

This autonomous body would not be a department of the Labour Ministry (as it currently is), but would instead be an independent, registered body with it's own identity and existence. However, officials from the Labour Ministry would certainly continue to be representatives on the Board of the new, independent entity.

(2) A high level of decentralization in the implementation of welfare schemes, with the maximum decision making and implementation responsibility resting with the workers. Implementation of schemes through the Beedi Workers Fund should be decentralized down from the Central level to State level (not regional level) boards. At the State level, implementation should be through a tripartite mechanism, involving the workers, employers and government, on an equal basis. (See next section on proposed management patterns).

For example, the beedi workers themselves could be trained to run their own creches (Children) and become trained "barefoot doctors" to increase outreach. This would serve two purposes; increase coverage while generating alternative employment opportunities for beedi workers, as well as enable services to be tailored exactly to meet workers's needs.

For this level of decentralization in implementation, those targeted by the welfare board, such as beedi workers, will need technical and managerial training and support. This can effectively be done through organizing the workers and supporting them to form their own groups, mandals, co-operatives or union.

Equally importantly, implementation of the Welfare Board's schemes should give due recognition to gender specific needs, especially in the case of informal sector trades dominated by women, such as beedi rollers. Workers' representation on the tripartite board should be in the same proportion as the number of women workers in the trade, e.g. 80% women in the case of beedi rollers.

(3) The State level board should have the maximum powers and flexibility. They should be empowered to identify

where clusters of beedi workers live an target these workers through appropriate, customized welfare measures. They should also support linking up these groups of workers with local, development organizations.

Management Mechanism

In order to adhere to the principle of decentralization, the welfare boards should be set up for maximum decision-making and implementation at the state level. There should continue to be a central advisory board (of the autonomous Beedi Welfare Fund), but this would only concern itself with broad managerial and financial policy matters. Financing may be multipartite, but the majority of administration, control and implementation should be at the state level, with further decentralization as follows :

A Welfare Fund Board at the state level with the following representatives in equal numbers :

* Workers Unions—representatives should not be chosen from central trade unions (as is the current practice), but should be representatives from local, state level unions of beedi workers themselves. One criterion for selection to the State Board should be that the representative is an actual beedi worker herself.
* Employers/employer's associations
* State—official from the Ministries of Labour, Health and Finance
* Central—Labour department

This state level board will be empowered to make all decisions relating to the provision of social security benefits to the target worker group, in the state. Ultimately, an umbrella legislation covering all informal trade groups, as in Kerala or Tamil Nadu could be introduced.

The Board will strictly monitor all services and activities. The Board itself will have committees at district level for decentralized implementation. These district level committees will also be tripartite in nature. Hence, the implementation structure will be as follows :

State Level Policy Board
Chair : State Labour Secretary
15 Members : 5 workers; 5 State & Central government representatives; 2 employers; 2 contractors

Each state board will develop norms for functioning and a manual, which will be discussed at Central level, before adoption.

The overall approach will be towards flexible management and programs, which are tailor, made for the workers. Each of the components of the services provided will be reviewed every month through a meeting of the State Advisory Board. Overall workers themselves should keep administration costs at a minimum, through decentralized implementation as far as possible. Speed and efficiency of the district level (and taluka level) implementation committees should be formally monitored, recognized and rewarded.

A major departure from the existing model in this proposed model is to decentralize the welfare boards down to the state level and train the workers themselves to implement and manage the majority of services on offer. For this, capacity building support in terms of organizing workers to form their own organizations, managerial support to run their own organizations and technical support to actually implement service delivery—for childcare, healthcare and housing, will be required.

Financing Mechanism

Financing the welfare board would be done through a multipartite financing mechanism, with equal contributions form the following :

* Cess on manufactured products sold;
* Employer's contribution (% on sales); and
* Worker's contribution (Rs. 100 per workers per year).

The state-wise cess contribution would be allocated, based upon the number of beedi workers actual steering committee, that meets regularly (at least once a month), to implement and monitor the welfare schemes. It will also monitor the collection of the funds and disbursement of the same down to the district and taluka levels, as well as monitoring the utilization of funds. The state board would have full flexibility in both the areas of fund raising and fund utilization, within the broad set of budget heads decided by the central advisory committee.

Currently, many Welfare Boards are administered at the central level, with the cess collected going into the Consolidated Fund of India. This makes it inefficient in three ways :

(a) Money is released as per the budget estimates submitted by the Welfare Board to the Ministry of Finance. Excess cess collections over the budgeted amount; remain in the Consolidated Fund, without payment of interest to the Welfare Boards. This results in substantial revenue loss of the Welfare Boards.

(b) As the money is collected and distributed centrally through the Consolidated Fund of India, it is subject to all the rules and regulations of the Ministry of Finance. For example, the recent austerity measures introduced by the Government, also apply to all expenditure by the Welfare Boards, although most of the financing is from sales, worker or employer's contributions, i.e. people's own money. This added bureaucracy and centrally imposed regulations on expenditure, leads to inefficiency in implementation.

(c) Currently, as the cess collected does not flow directly into an autonomous beedi workers' fund, but flows through the Consolidated Fund of India, the Finance Ministry retains a percentage (up to 8%) for their own "administrative expenditure." This amount rightly belongs in the workers's welfare fund and is unnecessarily being paid over to the Government.

The State will allocate funds to the districts, based upon district-wise numbers of beedi workers within the state.

Through a focus group discussion with 25 beedi rolling women, it clearly emerged that women were able and willing to contribute for a variety of services such as health, childcare and pension.

However, they wanted a good level of service in return and easy collection mechanisms. This is where the lessons learnt by micro finance institutions can be applied, as they have mastered the specially cash collection and delivery mechanisms required by the informal sector, e.g. doorstep collection, simplified procedures, involving people's participation, transparency, etc.

In fact, an additional source of capital funds for the Welfare Boards could be small savings generated from the workers themselves. Micro finance institutions such as SEWA Bank of BSIX, have found that the informal sector is a major market for small savings generating a total of 55% of total national saving os the Indian economy through very small individual balances. These savings could be mobilized from workers by forming self-help groups. If invested professionally, following the prudential investment norms of the RBI, this could be a substantial source of finance into the Welfare Boards, as well as mobilizing workers to form groups and make their own individual contributions into their workers' welfare fund. The workers interviewed stated that hey were willing to pay upto Re. 1 per day for services such as health, pension and childcare, each, i.e. a maximum of Rs. 30/- per month.

Finally, when it came to employer's contribution, past experience shows that this is difficult to collect, very erratic and involves high collection costs. Beedi workers's union organizers felt that it was difficult to collect employer contributions against the number of workers they employed, as they did not want to divulge this information (same experience with employer's contribution with PF). However, if they were charged a percentage of their total turnover, for contribution into a workers's welfare fund and had equal representation on the Welfare Board, then their contribution should be forthcoming.

In conclusion, it has been proposed a high level of decentralization down to the state level in the implementation of the welfare schemes, through an autonomous welfare board. In fact, the schemes could eventually be run by local organizations or trade unions while the state steering committee/board reimburses such organizations for scheme implementation and provides them with appropriate training as well as monitoring their performance (Vijaya Kumar and Smita Ghatate 2001).

Note : This version has been presented during the Workshop on GLOBALIZATION AND ITS IMPACT ON WOMEN WORKERS IN THE INFORMAL ECONOMY jointly organized by UNIFEM and SEWA Bharat held at UNDP. New Delhi (December 4-5, 2002).

Acknowledgment :

The author would like to thank Smt. Renana Jhabval, Shri R.K.A. Subrahmanya, Smt. Shalini Sinha and Dr. K.S. Bhat for their support during the preparation of this paper (This paper is a synthesized version of a study on Welfare Boards).

References :

Das, S.K. 2001, "A Better Deal, for Beedi Workers" report submitted to ILO, New Delhi.

ILO, 2000, "The Beedi Industry in India : An Overview" New Delhi : ILO.

Jhabvala Renana, 2001, "Towards a Concept of Basic Security" Ahmedabad : SEWA.

Jhaabvala Renana and Subrahmanya, RKA, 2000 "The Unorganized Sector : work security and social protection" New Delhi : SAGE.

Rodrick, D 1997 "Has Globalization Gone to Too Far?" California Management Review. No. 3.

Rugman, A 2001, "The End of Globalization". McGraw Hill

Sen, Amartya 2000 "Works and Rights", International Labour Review, Vol. 139, No. 2

Somavia 2002, "ILO Tackles Social Consequences of Globalization" speech delivered at World Commission on the Social Dimensions of Globalizations, Geneva : ILO.

Subendu Das 2001 "Globalization and Workers in Developing Countries : Can Social Partners become a model for industrial relations" Indian Journal of Labour Economics, Vol. 44 No. 3.

Venkataratnam 2001 "Globalization and Organized Labour" Editors Introduction, Indian Journal of Labour Economics. Vol. 44, No. 3.

Vijaya Kumar, S 2001 " Social Security in Indian Context" Discussion paper submitted to the study group of Second National Commission on Labour.

Vijaya Kumar, S and Smita Ghatate 2001 "Restructuring the Beedi Workers Welfare Fund : Conceptual Model" report submitted to the study groups of Second National Commission on Labour.

Vijaya Kumar, S and G. Subbayamma 2001, "Social Security for Unorganized Sector in India : A Need for Comprehensive Reforms", Indian Journal of Labour Economics, Vol. 44, No. 4.

8

Economic Security in Old Age for Vulnerable Populations : Retirement Systems and Life Course Perspectives

*Phoebe S. Liebig**

INTRODUCTION

Economic security in old age can be viewed from two broad perspectives. The first, more traditional approach focusses on the post-retirement phase. It emphasizes the current economic status of the aged: income levels, poverty and wealth, sources and shares of retirement income among different groups of elders (e.g., couples versus singles), and special treatment of income (e.g., concessions, tax "breaks"). The structure of retirement systems, their relationship with economic growth and development, and the extent to which reform is necessary to reflect societal changes (e.g., population aging, trends in family structure) are of particular importance.

Lifecourse Perspective. The second looks at economic security from the lifecourse perspective of aging as a social process over the

* *Associate Professor of Gerontology & Public Administration, University of Southern California, Los Angeles, USA.*

lifespan. The focus is on the *preretirement phase,* intragroup differences (e.g., gender, class) and the extent to which social structures and policies enhance economic security for some and not others. "Cumulative advantage or disadvantage" across the life course is a key issue (O'Rand, 1995), particularly for vulnerable populations, e.g., women, rural and urban poor, race, caste. Advantages that accrue to social location early in life, whether socioeconomic class or caste, allow individuals to gain further advantage; the gap between the privileged and the disadvantaged grows in old age (O'Rand, 1995)

Thus the lifecourse perspective examines measures that enable younger persons to escape poverty, e.g., income maintenance programs, Grameen Bank schemes, "sweatequity" housing. It emphasizes the effects of events (e.g., schooling, unemployment) experienced earlier in life on later behavior at older ages (e.g., income, health), with growing attention to transitions (e.g., widowhood, poorer health) that affect the oldest old (Myers, 1995). It also recognizes that economic security is threatened when the potential for work is disrupted by unemployment, short term injury, poor vocational skills, disability and skill obsolescence (Schulz, 1992, 75), as well as child rearing and eldercare provision. These contingencies have an impact on current livelihood and retirement income accumulation for all income groups, not just the poor.

This viewpoint also draws on the life cycle hypothesis (Ando and Modigliani, 1963) and its assumptions that consumption needs and income are unequal at different points over the lifespan. Simply stated, younger persons have consumption needs (e.g., education) higher than their incomes and thus borrow heavily. The middle-aged have rising earnings allowing for debt repayment and the acumulation of savings and assets, while for retirees, incomes decline and savings are consumed. Accumulation and expenditure of wealth (e.g., pensions, savings accounts, home equity) can be seen as stages in a lifelong developmental process, called the "wealth span" (Cutler, 2002), which has important implications for economic security in old age.

THE ISSUE OF ECONOMIC SECURITY IN OLD AGE

The issue of economic provision for people in their old age has confronted all societies throughout history (Schulz, 1992). In the past, this security depended almost exclusively on the family unit and to a lesser degree, on community/village resources. While the family is still a major support for elders worldwide—80 to 90 percent of elder care is provided by families—its nature has changed significantly. Decreasing family size, increased labor force participation by women outside the home, greater geographic mobility, marital instability, and the growing numbers and proportions of older people, especially of the very old who often require extensive social and health supports, have placed greater pressures on the family unit.

These pressures have, in turn, led to changing attitudes about family obligations, economic and other, even in nations where filial piety has been a time-honored tradition. There is a growing recognition that families are unable unassisted to deal with large-scale problems generated by economic development and global markets. Faced with these several challenges, families require support of nongovernmental organizations and government entities to help them sustain their obligations. While formal institutions have been given additional responsibility for helping families and in some instances, have taken over some traditional familial obligations, these efforts have been designed primarily to supplement and support families in their traditional roles, not to supplant them (Schulz, 1992, 78).

Today, economic security in old age centers on providing basic protections against losses of income in retirement due to partial or complete labor force withdrawal; assuring the financial stability of public and private retirement income systems, especially social insurance; and maintaining a fair and acceptable balance of costs and benefits across income classes, gender and age cohorts (Kingson and Williamson, 2001, 369). The major focus is on sources of retirement income, including welfare assistance, as the primary underpinnings of aged security, with attention paid to differing income levels and poverty (see, for example, Crown, 2001; Crystal, 1995; Vijaya Kumar, forthcoming; Schulz, 2000). However, other resources and concessions available to elders (e.g., access to medical care, family caregiving, travel discounts) have important impacts on economic well-being in old age (Crown, 2001; Vijaya Kumar, forthcoming). The special tax treatment of retirement income and assets of older households, as in the United States, can also play a major role in such wellbeing (Liebig, forthcoming).

POPULATION AGING

The task of providing adequate income protection for the aged is becoming increasingly difficult, in both industrialized and developing nations (Wheeler and Keamey, 1996; Schulz, 1992). Global population aging has been explosive, with 20 years added to the average lifespan over the last half of the 20th century, to its current level of 66 years. One of every ten persons is now aged 60 or above, the majority (55%) of whom are women. By 2050, one of every five will be in that age group and a century later, one of every three persons will be age 60+ (United Nations, 2000).

The older population itself is aging. The oldest old (age 80+) are the fastest growing segment of the elderly. Currently 11 percent of the older population, they will grow to 19 percent by 2050; 65 percent are female (United Nations, 2000). Longevity for women is greater than for men in both developed and developing nations. In the former, life expectancy at age 60 for females is 22 years, compared to 18 years for males; in the latter, it is 16 years for women, compared to 14 years for men (United Nations, 2000). In the early 1990s, life expectancy in southeast Asia was projected to increase to age 68 for men and age 70 for women in 2000 (Phillips, 1992). It is anticipated that this gender differential will persist, raising important issues about the economic security of women in old age but also at younger ages.

Due to declines in fertility and mortality, the velocity of population aging is even greater in newly developing countries in Asia and Africa than in developed nations of Western Europe and the New World, such as the United States, Canada, and Argentina (Brink, 1998). Thus, they will have less time than their industrialized counterparts to adapt to the consequences of population aging. In 1996, more than 43 percent of the world population aged 75+ lived in just four countries: China, India, Japan and the United States (U.S. Census Bureau, 1996). By the year 2025, Japan's proportion of persons 65+ will escalate to 23 percent (Hashimoto, 1992) and China and India alone will account for nearly 40 percent of all older persons in the world (Shuman, 1995). By 2050, 26.1 percent of China's population and 20.6 percent of India's will be age 60± (World Bank, 1997).

Despite gains in longevity, retirement patterns have not changed significantly. In many developing countries, agriculture is the dominant occupation; older people continue to work until no longer physically able. In rural India, for example, 65 percent of men and nearly 19 percent of women continue to work after age 60 (Rajan, Mishra and Sarma, 1999). In industrialized countries, retirement has become a socially accepted institution, largely due to the availability of retirement income. For the 65-69 age group, labor force participation rates for most developed countries are low, usually less than 10 percent for men and around 5 percent for women, with a few notable exceptions (Japan, 55 percent; Portugal, 29 percent) for males and (Japan 28 percent; Norway, 17 percent) for females (World Bank, 1997, 29). Some countries, e.g., China, India, have retained mandatory retirement at relatively early ages for non-agricultural workers.

In nations, such as the United States, where mandatory retirement has been abolished, retiring before age 65 persists, largely due to personal preferences, pension plan structure and access to employer-provided health benefits. Male and female labor force participation rates for ages 60-64 are 55 percent and 37 percent, respectively. These rates drop precipitately to 26 percent and 16 percent respectively at ages 65-69. One outcome of longer life expectancy and early retirement is that time for any wealth accumulation for retirement tends to be shorter, especially when extended periods of schooling are factored in, while the expenditure stage is longer (Cutler, 2002).

The immense task of providing income for ever escalating numbers of the aged, who are now living longer, has led to an array of approaches: welfare or social assistance; mutual benefit societies; employer liability programs; occupational and industrial pensions for public and private sector employees; voluntary and compulsory savings programs; social allowances or demogrants; and social insurance (Schulte, 1990; Schulz, 1992). Programs that support families, not just aged individuals, such as the recent U.S. National Caregiver Support Program and housing allowances for multigenerational families in several Asian nations (Liebig, 2001), have also emerged as ways to enhance old-age economic security.

RETIREMENT AND ECONOMIC DEVELOPMENT

All nations create retirement systems that are unique to their historical, political and economic development circumstances. Economic development is accompanied by new sources of economic insecurity that threaten individual social welfare. The long-term gains of markets often translate into short-term misery, especially in occupational shifts from farming and other self-employment to labor markets (Schulz, 1992). All economic systems relying on markets need ways to provide for those who cannot participate. While development of the global economy exacerbates these disruptions worldwide, effects can be localized. According to the World Bank, most of the emerging Third World economies are located in Asia and private investment capital is flooding the region (Stoesz, Guzzetta, and Lusk 1999), with varying, but often negative impacts on workers and retirees.

In many newly industrialized countries (NICs) and developing nations in Asia, such as Singapore, South Korea, China (including Hong Kong), India and Thailand, economic development has been the major thrust of social planning. Numerous Asian countries created a series of five-year plans to guide this process. The "four tigers" (Hong Kong, Singapore, Taiwan and South Korea) developed a style of authoritarian capitalism, through a combination of government-directed industrial policy, a disciplined workforce, and. strategically established tariffs (Stoesz et al., 1999, 13). This strategy resulted in annual growth rates ranging from 5.6 percent to 7.2 percent. Soon, Malaysia, Thailand and Indonesia followed suit, initiating heavy investments in education (especially in high-tech skills), rigorous encouragement of savings, an aggressive industrial policy favoring certain industries, and use of low-wage labor and Japanese capital and guidance (Stoesz et al., 1999, 14-15).

The two Asian nations with the greatest numbers of elders developed very different approaches. China moved from "market

Communism" to market socialism based on a high domestic savings rate, a strong central government able to determine and coordinate development policy, the engagement of a cohort of cooperative overseas Chinese managers adept at international capitalism, and a willingness to dismantle large state-run enterprises and rural communes to facilitate the emergence of a market economy. This strategy resulted in China's GDP growth of more than 10 percent per year over the past 15 years (World Bank, 1997). But it also has led to the need for interventions, too few in number, for millions of unemployed and displaced workers, e.g., Shanghai's Project 4050 that provides tax breaks and management guidance for unemployed state workers in their 40s and 50s who start their own businesses (Ni, 2002).

India took a different tack after independence, first inaugurating a strategy that favored nationalized industries and more skilled workers and keeping out cheaper imports from industrial nations. While this socialist development brought India heavy industry, it did little to improve the life of the typical Indian villager (Stoesz et al., 1999, 15). Due to disappointing economic performance in comparison with other Asian nations, in the late 1980s India undertook some reforms to diminish government influence in the economy, liberalize economic relations, and open trade to foreign countries. These steps generated increased economic growth, but still have had minimal benefits for the nation's poorest citizens (Stoesz et al., 1999, 15-16).

Until fairly recently, this economic development focus in Asian nations led to in attention to welfare delivery in general and services for specific groups, such as elders, in particular (Phillips, 1992). For the most part, the majority of NICs and developing nations fall into the residual category of welfare policy orientation, or the "social assistance welfare state" (Schulz, 1992). Basic means-tested benefits, combined with remedial services, have been targeted to needy groups and individuals such as the elderly, primarily those without families. Government expenditures primarily have been allocated to the long-term productive potential of the young.

Similarly, until the late 1970s and early 1980s, most developing nations were not very interested in aging issues. The position of the aged was seen as relatively strong due to family support, elders were a small proportion of the total population, and while older persons remained economically productive in agricultural economies, they were seen as resistant to change and therefore not appropriate for human capital investmeni in rapid industrialization (Schulz, 1992). Advocacy by the United Nations in the 1980s and the World Bank in the 1990s changed this scenario.

With an eye to the interactions of retirement income provision and economic development, the World Bank (1994) proposed a multipillar strategy to provide old age security. This consists of a publicly-managed, tax-funded mandatory plan to ensure a means-tested guaranteed pension; a mandatory, privately managed and funded savings plan, with government regulation; and a voluntary, unregulated savings system. Each pillar is designed to transfer purchasing power from the working phase to the retirement stage of the lifecycle. The resultant savings aggregations provide needed capital for economic development by the private sector or to government for providing collective goods and provide the economic underpinnings for pensions (Davis, 1995).

STRUCTURE OF RETIREMENT SYSTEMS

This article can only briefly summarize the structure of retirement systems, with the development of social insurance as the primary mechanism for ensuring economic security in old age in western nations. Occupational pensions and provident funds also have been important approaches, usually coupled with some kind of welfare assistance. For illustrative purposes, after a brief overview of Germany's prototypical system, the U.S. retirement system will be described and then the retirement systems in Asia, particularly China and India.

INDUSTRIALIZED NATIONS

In western European nations in the late 19th and early 20th centuries, industrialization and related social and economic changes created the need for public pensions and generated the economic surplus required to finance them (Williamson and Pampel, 1993). This led to the appearance of the social security welfare state, based on two key principles: universality and wage replacement to maintain continuity in pre- and post-retirement living standards for workers used to a high standard of living (Schulz, 1992, 87).

Germany. The structure of the German pension system became the template for most developed nations. In 1889, Germany was the first to enact a national compulsory old-age and invalidity pension system, building on an already existing welfare program and sickness and industrial accident insurance enacted in the early 1880s. Initially this old-age pension system had the following characteristics: earnings-linked, equal employer-employee contributions, minor redistributive aspects, low replacement rates with pension benefits below existing welfare benefits, relatively wide coverage (54 percent) of blue collar and some white-collar workers, and eligibility at age 70 (Williamson and Pampel, 1993). A separate pension system for white-collar salaried employees was added in 1911.

Subsequent reforms included replacement ratios designed to maintain a preretirement standard of living (1957); an early retirement option at age 63 with full benefits, coverage for the self-employed and housewives, and a redistributive "minimum wage" benefit (1972); and by the mid 1980s, coverage of virtually all private sector employees (Williamson and Pampel, 1993). Also the retirement age was lowered to age 65 and several provisions benefiting women added: in the event of divorce, pension credits earned by husband and wife are evenly split; retirement eligibility occurs at age 60; and one year of pension credit is given for each child. However, there is no special spouse or couples benefit. More recent changes include indexing benefits, the use of substitute periods (e.g., military service, unemployment, illness and pregnancy) and credits for care provision for children and elderly parents to calculate benefits. Separate programs cover miners, public officials and farmers, while some self-employed persons are covered by compulsory, privately financed pension programs administered by their professional associations (Williamson and Pampel, 1993).

United States. The U.S. retirement system shares many of the German system characteristics, via a tripartite approach — the "three-legged stool." A compulsory social insurance program is the foundation, augmented by corporate and individual tax incentives for voluntary occupational pensions and voluntary savings. Recent public policies (e.g., higher benefits for delayed retirement) have emphasized post-retirement earnings. A means-tested welfare assistance program operates as a "safety net" for those with inadequate income from other sources.

The Old Age, Survivors and Disability Insurance (OASDI) program, more popularly known as Social Security, was enacted in 1935. It is an earnings-linked, publicly administered system, funded on a pay-as-you go-basis by a compulsory payroll tax paid equally by employers and employees. The self-employed pay both shares, but get special income tax treatment. Like all social insurance programs, OASDI combines actuarial risk-spreading of private insurance with social adequacy; long-term security is guaranteed by broad-based government taxing power (Schulz, 1992). Initially, it was solely an old age program with limited coverage and minimal benefits; survivor benefits and disability insurance were added by 1950. An early retirement age of 62 was established first for women and then for men, with an actuarial reduction in benefits. A marriage must last 10 years for spouses to share retirement benefits. Coverage is now nearly universal, except for some agricultural workers and some state and local government employees. Unlike the German system, housewives are not covered in their own right and pension credits are not given for bearing children or providing family care. Separate retirement systems are available for elected officials, judges and special groups (e.g., civil service employees) who may also be eligible for OASDI.

Normal retirement is age 65, which will gradually increase to age 67 by 2027. Benefits are indexed by annual cost of living adjustments (COLAs) and are redistributive; low earners get a higher replacement rate than higher earners. Average monthly benefits vary: \$874 for a retired worker; \$1,454 for an aged couple; and \$841 for an aged widow(er). Since 1983, benefits for higher income recipients have been subject to income taxes. Some elders are totally dependent on Social Security for their income. It accounts for 42 percent of total income for all persons age 65+, mostly low- and middle-income households; 91 percent of all elders receive at least some Social Security income.

The development of the "second leg" of the retirement income stool, occupational pensions, actually preceded OASDI enactment. Municipal governments and then large firms started providing lump sum pensions in the late 19th century. State and federal employee pension systems were added in the early 20th century, when defined benefit plans guaranteeing specific benefit levels became dominant. Private sector employers, including the self-employed and very small firms, provide pensions voluntarily, but receive income tax incentives for doing so. Pensions allow employers to manage their labor force, as seen by the heavy use of early retirement incentive programs, designed to provide incentives to older—and usually more expensive—workers to retire.

The importance of occupational pensions as a retirement income source grew markedly in the 1960s and 1970s but even today, only 30 percent of persons age 65+ receive this type of income. Defined benefit plans tend to redistribute benefits from early leavers to late leavers and from those with broken work histories, e.g., women, racial minorities, part-time workers, persons with disability to white males. Less than one-fourth of all elderly households receive 70 percent of all pension income (Calasanti and Slevin, 2001). Only about half the U.S. work force is covered by such pensions which are rarely portable if a worker changes jobs. Regulation is fairly stringent to ensure that pension fund investments are reasonably safe; payments of vested (earned) benefits are made, even if a company goes bankrupt; disclosure to participants is adequate; and plans do not benefit only high-paid employees. Still loss of benefits occurs, especially in defined contribution plans where only contribution—not benefit—levels are guaranteed, and regulation is more relaxed.

Other characteristics of occupational pensions include: early retirement at ages 55 or 60 and restrictions on the hours retirees can work for their former employer before losing their pension benefits. Mode of payment and survivor benefits must be selected — they are not automatic as in OASDI — and provisions for splitting pension benefits upon divorce are resolved by the courts. At best, benefits are indexed on an ad hoc basis, although public employee pension plans are more likely to do so automatically. The voluntary nature of employer pensions results in modest rates of coverage and relatively small amounts of monthly income. Although a mandatory universal pension system (MUPS) was proposed in the early 1980s, it was never seriously considered by the U.S. Congress.

The "third leg" consists of individual savings and assets. Tax incentives, rather than compulsory savings as in many European systems, are provided to boost retirement savings and build up assets; however, they tend to benefit higher earners (Liebig, forthcoming). Since 1975, Individual Retirement Accounts (IRAs) have allowed individuals, even those with an occupational pension, to set aside $2000 annually on a tax-preferred basis and invest it without income tax penalties. Recent legislation has provided more tax incentives to make retirement savings more attractive, especially for workers in their SOs. Other proposals have included a mandatory Individual Account plan, administered by government and funded by additional contributions from workers, similar to provident funds in India.

The largest asset of all Americans, including the elderly, is their home. Tax policy is a major stimulant by allowing homeowners to deduct mortgage interest and local and state property taxes from their federal income taxes. This approach benefits the relatively affluent, largely because the value of the standard income tax deduction makes itemizing mortgage interest and property taxes a losing proposition for most low-income households (McCarthy, Van Zandt and Rohe, 2001).

About 80 percent of older Americans own their home, with a median value of $96,000 (U.S. Administration on Aging, 2001); homes consitute 42 percent of the net worth of those age 80+ (Radner, 1993). The home, however, is a relatively illiquid asset and elders are reluctant to take out loans against their home equity due to repayment problems. Since the 1980s, reverse annuity mortgages have been available from banks allowing elders who are property rich but cash poor to draw on that equity to provide a monthly stream of tax-free income and to remain in their homes until death or permanent relocation. However, lower-income elders typically own older homes of lesser value that require more maintenance, so the income group who could benefit most from this policy may get only very small amounts of income.

When the "three-legged stool" proves inadequate, social assistance is available. Welfare for U.S. elders was first provided by the states during the last part of the 19th century and late 1920s, similar to old-age pensions in India described below. These programs were incorporated into the social insurance law of 1935, that also included unemployment insurance and welfare for women and children. In 1974, the Supplemental Security Income (SSI) means-tested program was created for the aged, blind and disabled poor. It is a federal program that may be supplemented by the states. Even with state participation and benefit indexing, recipients—mostly women and minorities—are not raised to the official poverty level, even those who become poor for the first time in old age, i.e., widows. Like other means-tested programs, SSI carries a stigma, tends to be socially divisive and politically vulnerable, with high administrative costs, imprecise targeting and low participation rates among eligible persons (Schulz, 1992).

DEVELOPING/NEWLY INDUSTRIALIZED NATIONS (ASIA)

Few of the NICs and developing nations in Asia have developed universal social insurance programs. While this is gradually changing, these new ventures are not without difficulty, in part due to economic downturns. For the most part, pensions have covered specific employee groups, such as government and industrial workers, in keeping with economic development priorities in countries such as China, Singapore and India (Cheung and Vasoo, 1992; *Global Aging Report,* 1996; Subrahmanya, 1994). Singapore created a provident fund based on employer-employee contributions, with old age public assistance available for those who did not participate in pension plans. In the late 1990s, the fund experienced problems, necessitating relief for employers. Workers' wages were cut by 5 to 8 percent and employer contributions to the Central Provident Fund were reduced by half for workers age 55 and younger. However, workers in that age group were still required to pay 20 percent of their earnings, while those age 55 to 60 paid 12.5 percent and those age 60 to 65 paid 7.5 percent *(Global Aging Report,* 1999).

By contrast, Thailand was slow level to develop any kind of old age income support (Warnes, 1992). In December, 1998, the Thais inaugurated an Old Age Pension Fund requiring employees and employers to pay equal shares totalling 6 percent of employee salaries over 15 years to yield a pension representing 15 percent of the retiree's salary over the last 5 years. In March 1999, the fund was projected to collapse by 2029, due to the Asian economic crisis, and only 2 percent of employee salaries continued to be collected by the government (*Global Aging Report,* 1999).

China. In 1950, a formal pension system was established for enterprises with more than 100 workers via the State Council's Regulations on Labor Insurance. A contribution rate of 3 percent was funded by a small number of enterprises on a pay-as-you-go basis. These old-age pensions covered 50 to 70 percent of worker's wages and were managed by the All-China Federation of Trade Unions; 30 percent of the funds transferred to a national master fund seem to have provided some prefunding (World Bank, 1997). In 1955, a separate system was set up for employees of government units, nonprofits, and Communist party organizations, and in 1958, coverage was extended to enterprises with fewer than 100 workers.

This system was devastated by the Cultural Revolution of 1966.

Economic reforms began in 1978. New pension regulations were issued for state-owned enterprises, government workers, and nonprofits, with recommendations that large collectively owned enterprises follow the same rules. Several regulations were created to encourage early retirement and lead to a large influx of new urban workers: retirement ages of age 60 for men and age 55 for women were reaffirmed, minimum years of service were lowered to 10 from 20, and a job was guaranteed for one child after a worker retired. Higher benefits were related to longer length of service, a minimum monthly pension of 30 yuan was guaranteed and disability pensions were related to the final standard wage and extent of care needed. This led to a fivefold upswing in the number of retirees and a commensurate increase in pension costs.

Several pension reforms were issued in the 1980s, accompanied by employment reforms that established contract labor for new workers; current workers continued as permanent workers, with separate pension pools created for the two groups. Only contract workers were required to make individual contributions;

enterprises contributed to both pools. In many cities, workers in collectively-owned enterprises became members of pension pools; some provinces moved toward provincial-level pooling, generally only for state enterprise workers. In 1991, reforms called for individual contributions by all workers, experiments with individual accounts, an expansion of pooling, and the establishment of three tiers: a basic benefit, a supplementary benefit provided by financially sound enterprises, and individual savings (World Bank, 1997). In that same year a voluntary pension insurance system was introduced for farmers and workers in town and village enterprises *(Global Aging,* 1996). Accounts based on voluntary contributions are fully funded and turned over to counties to invest; at age 60, the money is turned into an annuity. About 50 million people participate, but contribute miniscule amounts which are unlikely to generate more than a 5 percent replacement of income after retirement (World Bank, 1997).

Further pension refinements in 1995 led to proposals for two models for the basic tier, with city and prefectures allowed (subject to provincial approval) to select a reform design. This has led to the creation of hundreds of schemes nationwide. A growing emphasis was placed on individual accounts, with a social pool responsible for those already retired and for current workers not fully covered by such accounts. These reforms were designed to provide urban retired workers with a minimum pension and pension pools at the municipal level *(Global Aging Report,* 1996).

China's pension system is largely urban-based, with extended families still the chief means of elder support, a situation similar to India's. Even in urban areas, coverage has largely focussed on the state sector; coverage of the non-state sector that accounts for more than 50 percent of employment, is very spotty. Contribution rates are high and very variable, with inadequate scope for pooling and portability. A high degree of pension system fragmentation is the result of wide dispersion of authority over pension policy and administration, reflecting the variety and complexity of the country's economy. Furthermore, system instability makes it difficult for workers and retirees to be certain about replacement rates and indexing of benefits (World Bank, 1997).

India. India's national retirement income system has been heavily shaped by its colonial experience and economic development goals after independence. It basically consists of provident funds and life insurance approaches, more recently augmented by a means-tested old-age pension. Social insurance approaches have largely been limited to worker's compensation and survivor benefits.

The British created a pension system for government employees in 1881 and a provident fund was created in 1925 to cover only civil servants and government railway workers. Workmen's compensation, India's first social insurance legislation, was established in 1923. A few employers introduced occupational pensions on a voluntary basis in the 1940s (Williamson and Pampel, 1993).

After independence and in keeping with economic development concerns, workers in the organized sector were provided pension coverage: first, civil service employees and then employees of major enterprises in key industries: factories, mines, oil fields, and employers with 10 or more employees. Many would have preferred a social insurance approach, but that was rejected due to the potentially heavy burden on the economy, employers and employees; instead the provident fund approach used by most former British colonies was adopted (Williamson and Tampel, 1993). The Coal Mines Provident Fund and the Employees State Insurance Act were passed in 1948.

The provident fund approach became dominant with the passage of the Employee Provident Fund in 1952, funded by minimum employee contributions of 10 percent of salary, matched by the employer; 12 percent annual interest is paid on deposits, with the fund administered by a board appointed by the national government. Employees can withdraw funds, on a non-refundable basis, to cover income needs during illness or disability and to meet various family obligations, including education and marriage. Maternity benefits, including a medical bonus, were enacted in 1961 for women working in factories, mines, plantations, and shops and other enterprises with 10 or more workers.

Several other programs were created in the 1970s for non-civil service workers in the organized sector. The Employees Family Pension Scheme was the first old-age social insurance law, in which the national government made contributions for payment of survivor pensions based on the income of the deceased worker. Participation is compulsory for members of the Employees' Provident Fund. The 1972 Gratuity Act took a previously voluntary benefit and made it part of the social security system, subject to collective bargaining (Williamson and Pampel, 1993). It covers most industrial workers, but not administrators, managers or civil employees of the national and state governments. The Employees Deposit-Linked Insurance also provides survivor benefits based on the balance in the worker's account at the time of death.

Both contributory and non-contributory approaches are used to provide civil service employees with economic security in old age. The former approach includes group insurance, established in 1982, and two provident funds to cover different categories of employees. Non-contributory mechanisms include a pension program for nonindustrial government employees, COLAs ("dearness relief"), disability retirement (invalidity), cashing out of unused leave, and service and death gratuities. These programs fall under the purview of the Central Civil Service Pension Rules of 1972.

India's provident fund approach has had a major impact on retirement income policy in other Asian nations, such as Malaysia, Singapore, Indonesia and Sri Lanka (Williamson and Pampel, 1993). This approach has proved popular with many developing nations, because these funds contribute to capital formation by investment in government securities to promote economic growth. They have the advantage of providing some economic security without draining scarce government resources or embarking upon a full-blown social insurance system that often gives rise to political pressures to pay pensions that are more generous than worker contributions can justify (Williamson and Pampel, 1993). The use of provident funds also probably found greater favor due to India's ethnic, religious and linguistic diversity; the shared risk and redistributive provisions of social insurance are more likely to gain popular support in more homogenous societies (Williamson and Pampel, 1993).

On the other hand, there are some downsides. Workers only have access to funds they have contributed; without shared risk, one receives only what one has put in. Thus provident funds do little to redistribute income from the more affluent to the poor, are less beneficial for very low wage earners and for those with irregular work histories (e.g., women, the uneducated, poorly skilled) and protections for dependents are usually inadequate. Lump sum payments are problematic; with longevity uncertain, funds can be depleted, leaving the retiree with little to live on.

But perhaps the most negative aspect of provident funds is their relatively low level of coverage. As of 1998, approximately 23 million persons were covered under organized sector pension plans (Vijaya Kumar, forthcoming). However, fully 90 percent of India's total workforce —the unorganized sector— are not covered by these pension schemes (Subrahmanya, 1994; Vijaya Kumar, forthcoming). Workers are primarily in the agricultural sector; wages are low, with little job security and the lack of year-round work (Vijaya Kumar, forthcoming). Retirement benefits are provided by five types of life insurance policies issued by the Life Insurance Corporation of India, primarily to provide family protection. Some combine savings for old age, both defined benefit and defined contribution plans, with family protection and premiums are deducted from the employees' monthly salaries. Some also involve employer contributions, but none are directly funded by the government. Most are not suitable for agricultural workers because the required contribution levels are too high.

In India, 80 percent of the aged live in rural areas; of those 40 percent live below the poverty level, with 33 percent just barely above (National Sample Survey Organisation [NSSO], 1998). To alleviate these problems, in 1957, the first state provided old-age pensions for destitutes; the last program of this kind was created in 1983. Initially, the payment ranged from 30 to 100 rupees; today, the range is from 60 to 300 rupees. Despite these efforts, only 16.5 percent of rural elders receive any kind of pension or retirement benefit, compared to 48.2 percent of urban elders (Rajan, Mishra and Sarma, 1996). In the 1980s, four states created old age pensions for landless agricultural workers; two states (Tamil Nadu and Kerala) developed special protections for deserted and widowed destitutes. They also provide semiannual clothing and weekly rice rations.

However, no nationwide program was in force until 1995, when the National Old Age Pension Scheme (NAOPS) was instituted. It was designed to smooth out geographic inequities by providing 75 rupees monthly to all destitutes age 65 and over, but with a national ceiling on numbers of recipients — at first, 5.4 million and now 6.9 million. While it was intended that NAOPS recipients would continue to be eligible for a state old-age pension, some states have diverted their funds elsewhere (Rajan, 2001). In addition, the national Annapuma scheme created in 1999 provides 10 kilos of rice or wheat for destitute elders via existing public distribution systems. Less than one percent of the national budget is spent on these two programs, compared to 6 percent expended on pensions (Rajan 2001). Both of them, like their state welfare assistance counterparts, have encountered cumbersome application procedures and problems with determining eligibility and irregular payments. The lack of administrative infrastructure to administer complex retirement income programs is an especially big problem in rural India (Williamson and Pampel, 1993).

In 2000, a voluntary system of funded personal pension accounts was proposed. Participants would make an annual, tax-free contribution of at least 500 rupees, to be invested in three types of investments offered by six fund managers. The payout would be a tax-free annuity at age 60, with early withdrawals permitted under some circumstances. Government contributions would be made if the individual participates for at least 10 years, with the final balance not falling below the total contributions (Pension Update, 2000). Again, it is not likely that many agricultural workers would avail themselves of this voluntary pension.

RETIREMENT SYSTEMS REFORMS AND THE LIFECOURSE PERSPECTIVE

All nations, especially developing countries like India, are faced with the daunting and risky task of trying to provide an adequate standard of living for their elders. As noted earlier, economic development and the global economy increase the need for social security programs, as well as the ability to fund them, but the pressures of population aging cause policymakers to tread lightly in this area. The World Bank proposal, "self-funded" social retirement systems, such as Chile's, and U.S. proposals for Social Security privatization, emphasize benefits more directly tied to contributions, with fewer intergenerational transfers from young taxpayers to older beneficiaries. These self-funded systems are essentially an intermediate form between social insurance and pension funds and provide vehicles for forced savings that are invested. They are defined contribution plans and expose workers to investment and inflation risk, without guaranteeing a minimum replacement ratio.

Thus, some kind of social security safety net - as proposed by the World Bank - is required (Davis, 1995), especially for the oldest old cohort who worked when wages were generally lower and who tend to "outlive" their incomes. One approach is means-tested welfare assistance which, as noted above, is subject to many negatives and often does not bring the impoverished up to an adequate standard of living. In some countries (e.g., the United Kingdom, Poland), publicly-funded age-based or care-based supplements have been introduced, so the very old do not fall behind (Williamson and Pampel, 1993).

But more importantly, self-funded systems continue the cumulative disadvantage experienced by low-wage in their younger years, into their retirement years. Because women constitute ever larger proportions of the aged, this issue is particularly relevant for females. Lifelong inequities for women become exacerbated in old age, leaving them with less financial security in retirement due to labor market discrimination or episodic employment patterns. The traditional domestic division of labor in most nations presents important barriers to employed women in terms of promotions, pay and pensions (Calasanti and Slevin 2001). In particular, adequate and subsidized child care and elder care, as well as pension credits for child rearing and family caregiving, enable women (and men who are engaged in the same roles) not to be penalized in their retirement years for undertaking these socially valued tasks during their working years. Self-funded pension systems will not work well for women, unless these and similar gender issues are addressed.

With few exceptions, women receive low wages over the life course, whether working continuously or intermittently. For example, U.S. women make 73 cents for every dollar paid to men (U.S. Census Bureau, 1999 as per Calasanti and Slevin, 2001). Occupational segregation also plays a role; women's jobs, primarily in the service sector, pay substantially less and offer less mobility and fewer benefits, such as occupational pensions. Furthermore, in many developing nations, the lack of educational opportunities for girls and women leads to poverty in early life and consequently in old age. Microcredit schemes, such as the Grameen Bank, and policy thrusts, such as India's Year of the Girlchild in the late 1990s, are of great importance in breaking this cycle.

Race/caste and ethnic relations lead to reduced educational opportunities, a lack of supportive neighborhoods, slums and crime. These lower class workers, recent immigrants and "guest workers" are often poorly skilled and paid subsistence wages. The latter, even if they pay into a social insurance system, are often precluded by their non-permanent status from collecting retirement income. In many developing countries, the prevalence of subsistence wages is exacerbated by multinational corporations going "offshore" in their quest for low-wage workers. The host countries may not have social insurance programs that sustain these workers in times of unemployment or disability due to sickness and accident. Furthermore, in nations where agriculture is still a major occupation and agricultural workers are not adequately covered by any kind of pension system (as in China and India), the biggest challenge is to create a retirement System that covers this particular group of low-income workers.

Given these issues, self-funded systems with mandatory savings are not a panacea and will not work unless wages are high enough to provide an adequate replacement ratio in retirement, and social insurance and employment-related programs are in place to cover those situations that disrupt labor force attachment (e.g., unemployment, disability, dependent caregiving) earlier in the lifecourse. Particular attention must be paid to the development of support programs and social insurance that recognizes the distinct employment-caregiving patterns of women. Without these, one possible scenario is greater numbers of the aged, especially those who received very low-wages, will be participants in means-tested pension programs, with even greater numbers of very poor, very old women worldwide in this 21st century and beyond.

In addition, for richer western nations, such as the United States, Italy, France and Germany, there are transition problems and attendant costs in moving from a pay-as-you-go system to a self-funded system. Perhaps one way to limit the growth of the former would be to add a second and third tier of self-funded plans on top of the social insurance system (Aaron and Reischauer, 1998). Politically and economically, this may be preferable to adding self-funded plans to a means-tested welfare program as has been proposed by the World Bank. Regardless, economic security in old age, especially for vulnerable populations, will continue to challenge the creativity, ingenuity and compassion of policy makers in all nations.

REFERENCES

Aaron, H.J. and Reischauer, R.D. 1998. *Countdown to reform: The great social security debate.* New York: Century Foundation Press.

Ando, A. and Modigliani, F. 1963. The life-cycle hypothesis of saving: Aggregate implications and tests. *American Economic Review 53* (March), 55-84.

Brink, S. 1998. Overview: The greying of our communities worldwide. In S. Brink (ed.), *Housing older people: An international perspective,* pp. 5-20. New Brunswick, NJ: Transaction Publishers.

Calasanti, T.M. and Slevin, K.F. 2001. *Gender, social inequalities, and aging.* Walnut Creek, CA: Altamira Press.

Cheung, P. and Vasoo, S. 1992. Ageing population in Singapore: A case study. In D.R. Phillips (ed.), *Ageing in east and south-east Asia,* pp. 77-104. London: Edward Arnold.

Crown, W. 2001. Economic status of the elderly. In R.H. Binstock and L.K. George (eds.), *Handbook of aging and the social sciences* (5th ed.), pp. 352-368. San Diego, CA: Academic Press.

Crystal, S. 1995. Economic status of the elderly. In R.H. Binstock and L.K. George (eds.), *Handbook of aging and the social sciences* (4th ed.), pp. 388-409. San Diego, CA: Academic Press.

Cutler, N.E. 2002. *Advising mature clients: The new science of wealth span planning.* New York: John Wiley & Sons.

Davis, E.P. 1995. *Pension funds: Retirement-income security, and capital markers, an international perspective.* Oxford: Clarendon Press.

Economic crises threaten retirement funds on three continents. *Global Aging 4* (4), 4-5. Hashimoto, A. 1992. Ageing in Japan. In D.R. Phillips (ed.),

Ageing in south and south-east Asia, pp. 36-44. London: Edward Arnold.

Kingson, E.R. and Wilhmson, J.B. 2001. Economic security policies. In R.H. Binstock and L.K. George (eds.), *Handbook of aging and the social sciences* (5th ed), pp. 369-387. San Diego, CA: Academic Press.

Liebig, P.S: 2001. International perspectives on housing frail elders. *Journal of Architecture and Planning Research 18* (3), 208-222.

Liebig, P.S. forthcoming. Tax expenditures: A different view of aging policy. *Southwest Journal of Aging*

McCarthy, G., Van Zandt, S., and Rohe, W. 2001. *The economic benefits and costs of homeownership: A critical assessment of the research.* (Working paper #01-02). Washington, DC: Research Institute for Housing America.

Myer, G.C. 1995. Aging and the social sciences: Research directions and unresolved issues. In R H. Binstock and L.K. George (eds.), *Handbook of aging and the social sciences* (4th ed), pp. 1-11. San Diego, CA: Academic Press.

Ni, C-C. 2002. Shanghai helping the hard-to-market help themselves. *Los Angeles Times,* June 8, A8-A9.

O'Rand, A.M. 1995. The cumulative stratification of the life course. In R.H. Binstock and L.K. George (eds.), *Handbook of aging and the social sciences* (4th ed.), pp. 188-207. San Diego, CA: Academic Press.

Overhauling pensions in China. 1996. *Global aging report, 1* (3), 6. Pension update. 2000. *Global aging report, 5* (3), 6.

Phillips, D.R. 1992. East and south-east Asia: Issues of ageing in the region. In D.R. Phillips (ed.), *Ageing in east and south-east Asia,* 1-21. London: Edward Arnold.

Radner, D. 1993. Economic well-being of the old old: Family unit income and household wealth. *Social Security Bulletin 56* (1), 3-19.

Rajan, S.I., Mishra, U.S., and Sarma, P.S. 1999. *India's elderly: Burden or challenge?* Delhi: Sage Publications.

Schulte, B. 1990. The role of social security in providing social protection to the very old: A comparative view. In *The social protection of the frail elderly,* pp. 45-76. Geneva: International Social Security Association (Studies and Research #28).

Schulz, J.H. 1992. Economic support in old age: The role of social insurance in developing countries. *International Social Security Review 45,* 75-101.

Schulz, J.H. 2000. *The economics of aging* (7th ed.). Dover, MA: Auburn House.

Shuman, T. 1995. Third world aging. In G. Maddox (ed.), *The encyclopedia of aging* (2nd ed) (pp. 934-937). New York: Springer.

Stoesz, D., Guzzetta, C. and Lusk, M. 1999. *International development.* Boston: Allyn and Bacon.

Subrahmanya, R.K.A. 1994. Income security for the elderly in India. *Bold* 4 (2), 28-29. United Nations. 2000 (May). The ageing of the world's population. www.un.org/ esa/ socdev / ageing / agewpopo.htm.

U.S. Administration on Aging. 2001. A profile of older Americans, 2001: Housing. www.aoa.gov/aoa/stats/profile/2001 /9.htm

U.S. Census. 1996. *Global aging into the 21st century.* Washington, D.C.: Author.

Vijaya Kumar, forthcoming. Economic security of the elderly in India: An overview. *Journal of Aging & Social Policy*

Warnes, A. 1992. Population ageing in Thailand: Personal and service implications. In DR. Phillips (ed.), *Ageing in East and Southeast Asia* (pp. 185-206). London: Edward Arnold.

Wheeler, P.M. and Kearney, JR. 1996. Income protection for the aged in the 21st century: A framework to help inform the debate. *Social Security Bulletin* 59 (2), 3-17.

Williamson, J.B. and Pampel, F.C. 1993. *Old-age security in comparative perspective.* New York: Oxford University Press.

World Bank. 1994. *Averting the old age crisis: Policies to protect the old and promote growth.* Oxford: Oxford University Press.

World Bank. 1997. *China* 2020; *old age security: Pension reform in China.* Washington, DC: Author.

9

Employees State Insurance Scheme : An Analysis of its Performance and Growing Resentment

*M. Mahadeva**

INTRODUCTION

Increasing dependence of human beings on institutional assistance for protection has been widely accepted. This was mainly to fulfil the basic needs of human beings, as they themselves are not in a position owing to backwardness. Over the years, the 'State', being overall representative of the society, also responded positively for such dependence of the disadvantaged groups. It has, besides extending the social as well economic protections, covered a large number of vulnerable groups under the various assistance schemes. Under the two important instruments of social security measures, i.e., social insurance and social assistance, the character of the State participation is both as a facilitator and a provider for the targeted groups. Being the principal guardian, the State has facilitated by institutionalising the social benefits through a number of legislations. Also, by building the institutional networking contributory social insurance is being provided with a number of contributors including the voluntary contribution of the beneficiaries. In such

* *Associate Professor, Institute for Social and Economic Change, Nagarabhavi, Bangalore 560 072.*

circumstances the contributors are the benefactors as well as beneficiaries. As provider, the state has extended the social assistance to the vulnerable group, as they are unable to obtain certain benefits on their own.

In India, social security is not a fundamental right but the same is intend to ensure under directive principles of State policy which aims at promoting the overall welfare of the people. Thus the social security packages are derived mainly from the legislations and collective agreements. The collective agreements have further created contracts between the State and individuals so as to exercise mutual obligations and benefits. However, a very distinct characteristic feature of the existing social security schemes is that each one follows a difficult set of definitions, packages, target groups, etc., and unfortunately the total coverage does not add up to a comprehensive whole (Johri 1982, Parthasarathi Shome, 1982). A major portion of India's population still remains uncovered although attempts are being made to extend certain benefits such as health and eduction for all. Yet other drawback in the existing social security is that only workers in the organised sector have been able to avail benefit, whereas the workers in the unorganised sectors that form the chunk of the population are yet to be covered under such benefits.

The Statutory provision of social security measures in India for the workers dates back to late nineteenth century with the passing of the Fatal Accidents Act of 1855. Under the Act the dependents of the workers who died in Industrial accidents could claim compensation if they could prove that the employer's personal negligence was the cause of accident. Thus the non-fatal injuries were not compensable. The first world war and its impact on industrialisation and the birth of the International Labour Organisation (ILO) have together by and large compelled the government to show its concern and create a conducive environment for workers. At about the same time, labour unionism becoming more strong, prominent, and in the wake of strong agitation for better working conditions, wages and protection, the Workmen's Compensation Act was enacted in the year 1923. It was intended to provide compensation for disablement of death arising out of an industrial accident or disease — as the Final Accidents Act was ineffective in terms of coverage or workers. This Act covered employees earning a monthly remuneration of up to Rs. 200, serving in railways, manufacturing industries, mines, shipping and building industry. The workers were entitled to a compensation in case of personal injury caused by accidents in the course of employment. However, no compensation was payable if the worker was injured (fatal or non-fatal) under the influence of alcohol or had willfully disobeyed or willfully removed safety appliances. The compensation was paid for temporary and permanent disbalement.[1] However, one of the greatest weaknesses of the Act was that employer was solely responsible for compensating the workers. This apart in the event of heavy liability, there was always a risk that the employer may not be able to discharge his liability.

Though these two Acts were major initiatives in the field of social security to industrial workers, they were not devoid of shortcomings. A major lacuna was that absence of serious commitment on the part of the employers. Especially under the Workmen's Compensation Act, lump sum compensation was provided to manual factory workers with no pledging from the employer's side. This has kept the workers away from being compensated for medical treatment. Maternity benefit was the second contingency of the social security although its genesis was only in one Presidency State. Unlike the previous Acts, cash benefit at a daily rate basis for seven to twelve weeks was given to the women workers in factories as part of maternity care. The benefit ranged from half a rupee per day to full daily wages. Although Bombay Presidency was the first to pass this Act in 1929, followed by Central Provinces, it took more than three decades to enact the Maternity Benefit Act to provide a uniform benefit all over the country. Even this Act was not free from deficiencies. There was no provision for medical aid before, during or after confinement. Also, since the employers were to provide the cash benefit under maternity care, married women were either refused to employ or were they discharged on pregnancy.

Further, although the need for health insurance for workers was felt during late 1920s in the wake of the high incidence of sickness and the monetary constraints of the workers, most provinces were

1. *The rate of compensation varied according to the monthly wages of the workers. While compensation for temporary disablement was paid at half monthly intervals, for permanent disablement like death, a lump sum amount was paid.*

not in favour of same. Nevertheless, on the suggestion of the Royal Commission on Labour (1929), government of India decided to introduce a tentative scheme on the basis of the single establishment in the places where medical facilities could be made available by the government provided the employers and workers were willing to contribute (Review Committee Report, 1966). In this regard, Bombay Presidency took initiative again and prepared a scheme of sickness insurance, which war contributory in nature. Accordingly, industrial workers were legally entitled to three weeks' sick leave with pay every year. However, due to short of health insurance measures the scheme did not provide any medical benefits. Subsequently during the next few years a tentative scheme of sickness insurance for factory workers was considered on experimental basis with limited scope. At the first instance, workers of the cotton, jute, textiles and heavy engineering industry were covered. On the basis of the experience, health insurance for industrial workers (Committee Report, 1944) was proposed. The scheme was compulsorily contributory to cover maternity and industrial injury benefits. These benefits were extended to the workers of all the perennial factories including the non-manual on the suggestion of ILO, with two-third of the costs of the medical benefits and cost of additional cash benefits should be Provincial/ State Governments.

EMERGENCE OF THE EMPLOYEE'S STATE INSURANCE

The Workmen's State Insurance Bill of 1946 took the shape of Employees' State Insurance Act, which was passed by the Domain Legislature in April 1948. Of the all social security measure in India, ESI is a prominent social insurance scheme, which is distinct in its character and comprehensive in coverage of labour class (ESI Guide, 1997). The scheme is predominantly self-financing by way of contributions of the employers and employees of the industrial, commercial and other establishments. Medical provision against sickness, temporary and permanent disablement benefits in the events of employment and industrial accidents and dependent's benefits to the insured as well as primary dependents are the packages of the scheme. Good networking institutions (hospitals, dispensaries for medical benefits and corporate body with local offices for administration and over sea purposes) have facilitated the insured and dependent persons to make use of the benefits. The scheme is prevailing upon the tenet of "pooling risks and resources". Workers of the factories/establishments contribute a certain percentage of their wages and derive benefits correpsonding to their needs. Thus made each contributor a benefactor and a beneficiary. The scheme is also unlike other similar insurance schemes. In the case of the other schemes, insured person contributes forwards a lumpsum pool on a clearly defined (monthly, quarterly, half-yearly and yearly) instalment basis and gets the benefits only after the payment of the last instalment. These schemes cover the risk for only the insured persons and in the event of the death of insured person/his/her nominee gets the lumpsum assured. Whereas in the case of the ESI, although every insured person contributes 1.5 per cent of the wages received, entitlement of the various benefits is being extended not only to the insured persons but also to their dependents (both direct and indirect).

The scheme is advantageous to both employers as well as employees. Employers under the purview of the ESI Act are exempted from all liability (of providing medicine facility to their employees of their dependents in kind or cash, reimbursement of actual expenses, lumpsum grants, provisions of maternity etc.). Besides, it is also argued that employers would have a well secured workforce which is an ingredient of higher productivity. But employers being the major contributors are only expected to deduct the employee's contribution and remit it to the ESI Corporation[1] along with their contribution of 4.75 per cent the total wages paid regularly without fail. Similarly the employees enjoy medical, sickness, maternity, employment injury and accident and dependent benefits. In addition to these, some of the subsidiary benefits are also being provided to the insured persons

1. *The ESIS has its own Corporate office in the national capital and its regional officers in most of the State headquarters. The Corporate office represents the overall interest of ESIS with the government and implement the policy decisions/changes from tinie to time. it is an apex body to administer the ESIS in the entire country. Similarly regional officers administer and supervise the schenie at the State level. ESIS is predominantly a self-financing scheme with the contribution both from employers and employees. Therefore, its relationship with the government (centre-States), although confined to policy matters, State Government shares a noniinal cost of niedical services and appointment of manpower in the* ES! *hospitals and dispensaries.*

to meet the social-economic contingencies. This category of benefits include funeral expenses, rehabilitation allowance, vocational rehabilitation and old age medicine. Further, one of the laudable features of the ESIS is a good network of institutions for administration of medical services to the insured and dependent persons. The scheme has its own hospitals with clinical facilities spread over to all the implemented area in the country besides annexes and beds reservation facility in the government and other hospitals. This apart, medical services and care are also provided through dispensaries and independent medical practitioners. Since a sizeable number of employees are exposed to the risk of employment injury and occupational diseases which are often hazardous and fatal, occupational diseases centres were also established in four major metropolis of the country.

The main focus of the scheme is to enable the labour class to lead quality life by extending social insurance and by increasing access to various means of basic needs. It is believed that such insurance and increasing accessibility have high social pay off to the designated target groups (Getubig and Sonke Schmidst, 1992). It is also an undeclared agenda of the scheme to arrest the existing disequilibrium in the availability to services (medical benefits) for contingencies like illness, disability, deaths etc., to the ESI covered workers. The Scheme covers in the first instance the workers in the non-seasonal factories using power in the manufacturing activities with 10 or more persons and non-power factories with 20 or more workers for wages. The Act empowered the State Governments to extend the provisions of the Act to other establishment also. At present the provisions of the Act have been extended by most of the State Governments to the establishment with 20 employees or more in cinemas and theatres, hotels and restaurants, transport agencies, newspaper establishments and shops, 10 or more number of employees in the beedi manufacturing establishments in the implemented areas and in slate pencil manufacturing units with one or more persons as worker/s. As far as the wage ceiling is concerned, the employees of the factories and establishment who are in receipt of wages not exceeding Rs. 6500 per month working in various factories and establishments are covered under the Act. Persons with daily wages upto Rs. 40 or Rs. 1200 per month working in various factories and establishment are exempted from contributing but are entitled to all the benefits with their employers' contribution.

ISSUES AND OBJECTIVES

Over a lapse of five decades of implementation of ESI scheme, there have been an overwhelming emphasis to a wide range of industries/establishments and employees on the one hand and development of the needed infrastructure provide medical services to the employees on the other hand. These strategies found to have yielded a perennial flow of revenue in the form of contribution, which in turn facilitated the authorities to develop medical infrastructure (hospitals, dispensaries and reservation of beds in other hospitals of ESI covered employees). However, at the same time there has been growing resentment on the part of the ESI employees. These resentment pertains mainly to the adequacy and quality of medical services in the ESI and in general hospitals. State Governments have taken the responsibility of providing adequate and qualitative medical services to the ESI employees, but have lagged behind their commitments. Poor supply of the scheduled medicines in the ESI hospitals has forced the hsopitalised employees to buy the prescribed medicines in the open market. To meet the requirement many have resorted to informal borrowing. It is also being argued that attention towards ESI employees in the hospitals is scanty and not in par with the contribution. Further, the same eagerness that has gone in for the development of medical infrastructure is missing in the case of medical services on the part of the ESI authorities. Concerns are growing over the excess bad capacity credit in the hospitals. Inadequate services have also party contributed for the dropping bed occupancy. Inability is being expressed for alternative medical services by the ESI authorities. Finally, employers, the principal financiers of ESI, are reluctantly shouldering the burden of contribution. Especially, employers of the small and medium scale industries/establishment are under financial strain. Higher ratio of employers' contribution has led to under-reporting of employees to escape the burden.

These issues can be classified as supply side as well as demand side. On the supply side no doubt the authorities have created the needed infrastructure but what is lacking is the medical attention and services towards the ESI employees while hospitalisation. Similarly on the demand side, the employees being the benefactors demand a qualitative and hassle free services, which have been hardly adhered to. These deficiencies are recurring for two reasons. First, the ESI authorities have no control over the medical services and the supply of curative medicines as the State Governments are responsible for the same. Second, lack of frequent and periodical supervision over the availability of services at the hospitals for the ESI employees. Although supervisions are conducted by the authorities to persuade the industries/establishments to come under the ESIS, but similar monitoring is missing on the hospitals and their services. The paper addresses these issues in greater detail. Specifically, the paper intends to assess (a) Industry-wise coverage of employers-employees, (b) Infrastructure developed vis-a-vis beneficiaries, and (c) Revenue-Expenditure pattern under ESIS. Besides, paper accounts the growing resentment on the part of the employees-employers. Selected for assessment as ESIS has an avowed objective of promoting welfare through security measures. Since the scheme intended to develop infrastructure as one of the pre-conditions for promoting welfare, the intention of the present exercise is to account as to how far the labour class respond to the same.

METHODOLOGY

The paper is based on the official data of ESI Corporation and primary informal discussions. The data pertaining to industry wise coverage of employers-employees, infrastructure development, beneficiaries, revenue-expenditure and other aspects have been collected from Statistical Abstracts and Annual Reports of ESI Corporation for the period between 1991-92 and 1997-98 separately for India and Karnataka. Since the study was conducted in Karnataka, the analysis also includes the experience of ESI in that Sate. Informal meetings and discussions have been held with trade union leaders, a limited number of employers and employees of different industries to elicit their response to the ESIS. A few ESI and other hospitals (with reserved beds of ESI labourers) have also been visited to account for the medical services. The data thus collected, discussions and personal visits, form the basis of anlaysis of this paper.

PERFORMANCE ASSESSMENT

At the outset, there are widespread differences in the coverage of employers and employees, under utilisation of infrastructure, general fall in the number of beneficiaries, etc. There has not been a commensurate growth in the total number of employees and employers covered under ESI between 1994 and 1999. The number of employers registered to have grown over 25 per cent which is four fold growth as compared to the employees, which has grown only at a little over 6 per cent during the period. The number of employers have increased from 1.75 lakhs in 1994 to 2.20 lakhs during 1999 and employees from 76.15 lakhs to 80.85 lakhs. In absolute terms there has been a net addition of 0.45 lakhs of employers and 4.7 lakhs of employees (Table 1) and the employers-employees ratio was 1:10.44 during the period under assessment. Similarly across industries under ESI coverage, by and large, there has been a moderate growth in the number of employers but a marginal fall in the number of employees excepting the units under paper and printing, commercial establishments, hotels and restaurants, cinemas and theatre. In the case of these units there was a proportionate increase both in the employers and employees and growth was phenomenal and far exceeding the average. Especially in the commercial establishments the growth was respectively more than three and fifteen times between the employers and employees. This is followed by paper and printing units (2.28 and 4.5 times) and hostel and restaurants (1.88 and 4 times). However, looking at the composition of industries in the ESI coverage, although textiles, engineering and miscellaneous units were predominant in terms of employers-employees coverage up to 1994, miscellaneous units have lost their position in favour of commercial establishments in addition to the other industrial giants. The coverage of employers establishment in addition to the other industrial giants. The coverage of employers-employees of textiles, engineering and miscellaneous was together anything around 46 and 50 per cent in the total upto 1994 and the same trend is being continued with 43 and 49 per cent with commercial establishments and new entrant by 1999. As a result of the emerged change, miscellaneous units which was the third highest sector of coverage of employers and employees under ESI has pushed down to fourth place with around 13 and 10 per cent in the total coverage. However, textiles and engineering units have continued to maintain their major share in the coverage, although the same was eroded in the recent years.

Table 1: Growth in the Industry-wise Coverege of Employees and Employers

Industry	As on 31.3.1994				As on 31.3.1999			
	Total No.of Employers	% to Total	No.of Employees (In lakh)	%	Total No.of Employers	% to Total	No. of Employees (In lakh)	%
Food Beverage in Tobacoo	11,305	6.4	5.87	7.7	13,698	6.23	5.56	6.88
Textiles	20,170	11.5	18.09	23.7	23,140	10.52	17.65	21.83
Leather and Rubber	7,220	4.2	3.00	3.9	10,389	4.73	3.10	3.83
Chemicals and Chemical Products	13,353	7.6	5.98	7.9	13,432	6.12	5.67	7.01
Non-Metallic Minerals	7,884	4.5	3.63	4.8	9,014	4.10	3.27	4.04
Metallic Minerals	16,116	9.2	6.47	8.5	19,775	9.00	6.28	7.77
Engineering	38,542	22.0	13.01	17.1	41,247	18.76	12.84	15.88
Transport	5,206	3.0	3,33	4.4	5,664	2.58	3.1 7	3.92
Paper and painting	8,240	4.7	3.01	3.9	12,941	5.89	3.83	4.74
Miscellaneous	21,703	12.4	6.78	8.9	28,420	12.93	7.66	9.47
Commercial Establishments	16,763	9.5	4.62	6.1	30,113	13.70	8.93	11.04
Hostels and Restaurants	6,973	4.0	2.01	2.6	10,247	4.66	2.49	3.08
Cinemas and Theatres	1,682	1.0	0.36	0.5	1,724	0.78	0.41	0.51
Total	**1,75,157**	**100.0**	**76.15**	**100.0**	**2,19,804**	**100.00**	**80.85**	**100.00**

Source : ESTC, Statistical Abstract, 1993-94 and 1998-99.

The erosion of employees in relative terms has resulted in decline in the average number of employees per employers. Although in absolute terms there has been a constant growth, employers-employees ratio has reduced. There has been a net addition of 0.72 and 23 lakhs of employers and employees but the ratio has reduced from 1:43 in 1991-92 to 1:39 in 1997-98, which was a net drop of four employees per employer (Table 2). Contrary to the above, the number of beneficiaries and average beneficiaries per employees have increased over the period. The total beneficiaries, as can be seen in table 2 increased from 237 lakhs in 1991-92 to 353 lakhs in 1997-98 a net addition of 116 lakhs or 49 per cent. Similarly, the average beneficiaries (insured persons and dependents) per employee has increased from 3.91 to 4.22. The situation as far as employer-employees ratio and average beneficiaries per employee is slightly different in Karnataka. The growth in the number of employers has constantly increased from 0.10 lakh in 1991-92 to 0.15 lakhs in 1997-98 and the employees from 4.31 to 6.47 lakhs during the period Similarly the beneficiaries growth was 46 per cent jacked up from 19.24 to 29.1 lakhs. The net addition was 0.05 and 2.18 lakhs. However the employer-employee ratio was constant at 43 but a marginal decline in employee-beneficiaries ratio from 1:4.47 to 1:4.33 during the period.

Creation of objective-oriented or service-based infrastructure for hospitalization and treatment of insured/dependent persons under ESI has been given overriding priority. There has been a constant addition to the existing infrastructure over the years. ESI hospitals and dispensaries have increased from 115 and 1,399 during 1991-92 to 179 and 1,450 in 1997-98, which was a net addition of 14 and 51 or 12.17 and 3.65 per cent. But by and large such attempts to increase the ESI annexes was lacking and their numbers have remained constant.Similarly 723 new beds have been added but while doing so, it is attempted to increase the bed strength in the ESI hospitals and annexes. In other words, reservation of beds in the other hospitals (one of the strategies to increase accessibility of medical service to ESI employees) has been discourage during the period of anlaysis. As a result, the bed strength in ESI hospitals and annexes has been increased from 80 per cent to 84 per cent and proportionately reserved beds in other hospitals have reduced. Contrary to the increasing

Table 2 : Growth in ESI Coverege and Infrastructure

(In Lakhs)

Year	Number of		No. of Employees per Employer	No. of Beneficiaries	Average No. of Beneficiaries per employee	ESI Hospitals	ESI Annexes	Number of Beds in				ESI Dispensaries
	Employers	Employers						ESI Hospitals	ESI Annexe	Reserved in Other Hospitals	Total	
					INDIA							
1991-92	1.41	60.58	43	237.03	3.91	115	42	17582	841	4546	22969	1399
1992-93	1.50	66.91	45	288.83	4.32	116	42	17988	841	4263	23092	1402
1993-94	1.62	66.59	41	286.93	4.31	118	42	18325	842	4181	23348	1427
1994-95	1.70	67.97	40	293.50	4.32	122	42	18429	842	4116	23387	1433
1995-96	1.91	67.97	36	203.35	3.00	124	42	18527	842	4101	23470	1440
1996-97	2.00	77.32	39	327.67	4.24	125	43	18695	867	3772	23334	1443
1997-98	2.13	83.62	39	352.90	4.22	129	43	18985	867	3840	23692	1450
					KARNATAKA							
1991-92	0.10	4.31	43	19.24	4.47	7	3	1100	84	551	1735	136
1992-93	0.10	4.31	43	19.25	4.47	7	3	1100	84	551	1735	136
1993-94	0.11	4.26	39	19.05	4.47	7	3	1100	84	551	1735	136
1994-95	0.12	4.99	42	22.32	4.47	7	3	1100	84	551	1735	136
1995-96	0.13	5.02	39	22.43	4.47	7	3	1100	84	551	1735	136
1996-97	0.14	6.76	48	28.50	4.03	7	3	1100	84	551	1735	136
1997-98	0.15	6.49	43	28.12	4.33	8	3	1150	84	551	1785	136

Source : Annual Reports of ESI corporation for various years and Statistical Abstracts of ESI.

capacity at the national level, efforts in increase the number of ESI hospitals, dispensaries, annexes and addition of new beds (excepting during 1997-98) are missing in Karnataka.

The disheartening feature of ESI infrastructure is the lack of corresponding increase in the occupancy rate vis-a-vis increase in the coverage as well as beneficiaries. In other words the infrastructure created, especially the beds was not fully utilised to their capacity (to their total bed days) as can be seen in the table 3. The number of beneficiaries per hospital and dispensary has increased 2.06 and 0.17 lakhs in 1991-92 to 2.73 and 0.24 lakhs in 1997-98. Similarly beneficiaries per bed have also been increased from 1.032 to 1,490. It need be specified again that owing to the regular increase in the number of beds, the number of bed days per year have increased from 84 lakhs to 86 lakhs. However the overall occupation rate was far below the expected level. It is less than half (i.e. 47 per cent) of the capacity created over the years. Both employers and authorities have contributed in their own ways for the below capacity occupation of beds in the hospitals. General reluctance for hospitalisation on the part of the employees and lack of need based capacity creation on the part of the employees and lack of need based capacity creation on the part of the authorities emerged as two major reasons. In addition to the inadequate service and attention, there has been a growing reluctance on the part of the employees to be the in-patients for curative treatment as hospitalisation would be burdensome to the families. It is argued that hospitalisation would mean unforeseen expenditure and loss of the work and income for the in-patient attendant. Besides, reluctance also for expecting the patient to be on the bed always or in the hospital premises during the period of hospitalisation. Therefore most employees (with whom discussion held) prefer to be out-patient for injuries and sickness as it facilitates them to attend to their domestic and personal works. Interestingly, it is not uncommon to avail sickness holidays and other related benefits on the part of a section of employees through false certification. There is also a fair degree of scope for arguments that bed capacity created in excess and unevenly by the authorities. Notwithstanding the fact of reluctance, bed capacity has been added continuously to the curative side of the medal services. In other words, intensive care wing (for treatment of life threatening diseases) of the medical services is relatively neglected in terms of bed capacity. But for the lack of information or data, bed capacity distribution between the curative and intensive care wings would have been very clear. However, it is improper to say that the present bed capacity is unnecessary as long as there is scope for introduction of services of special treatment in the .years to come. Additional capacity can also promote the coverage of employees who are at present not covered by ESIS. The situation in Karnataka is far better as far as the occupancy rate is concerned. This has been achieved by increasing the coverage of beneficiaries per hospital/ dispensary/bed without jacking up the capacity bed days, which was kept unchanged upto 1996-97. This strategy has helped in thinking the overall occupancy rate at 60 per cent, which is well above the national average. Despite of this, there has been marginal decline in the occupancy rate from 69.19 per cent in 1991-92 to 65.43 per cent in 1997-98.

Although the incidence of employees deemed exposed to various (sickness, temporary and permanent disablements, etc.) are very high as can be seen in table 4, their share has significantly reduced over the years. So also the cases of maternity and dependents benefits along with their claims. Persons exposed to sickness as well as disablements have reduced from 100 per cent to 87 per cent and from 94 to 93 per cent respectively. Maternity benefits claims per thousand insured women have also gone down from 27.5 to 21 per cent. By and large the same trend can be noticed in Karnataka also.

Unlike the other schemes, there has been a mismatch in the growth of revenue and expenditure under ESI, in which case the total revenue that comes as contribution far exceeds the total expenditure. Besides, percentage expenditure to the total receipts has drastically reduced during the period under review. The total revenue receipts as can be seen in table 5 have doubly increased from Rs. 692 in 1993-94 to Rs. 1510 crores during 1998-99. This was mainly due to increasing ceiling limit of coverage of workers from 1997 onwards. The contribution being the major source of revenue (80 per cent) has increased significantly from Rs. 496.38 to Rs. 1210.54 crores (144 per cent growth) during the period. Contrary to this, the totalexpenditure (medical as well as administrative) has not correspondingly increased. The overall expenditure growth is only 54 per cent (from Rs. 594 to Rs 916 cores) as against 118 per cent of revenue receipts. This has left a large chunk of revenue unspent.

Table 3: Infrastructure and Beneficiaries

(Figures in lakhs)

Year	Number of Beneficiaries Per Hospital	Per Dispensary	Per Bed	Total Number of Bed days Created	Occupied	%
			INDIA			
1991-92	2.06	0.17	1032	83.84	39.35	46.93
1992-93	2.49	0.21	1251	84.29	41.57	49.33
1993-94	2.43	0.20	1229	85.22	36.83	43.22
1994-95	2.41	0.20	1255	85.36	35.59	41.69
1995-96	1.64	0.14	866	85.67	39.17	45.72
1996-97	2.62	0.23	1404	85.17	39.30	46.14
1997-98	2.73	0.24	1490	86.48	45.44	52.54
			KARNATKA			
1991-92	2.75	0.14	1109	6.33	4.38	69.19
1992-93	2.75	0.14	1110	6.33	4.08	64.45
1993-94	2.72	0.14	1098	6.33	3.81	60.19
1994-95	3.19	0.16	1286	6.33	3.99	63.03
1995-96	3.20	0.16	1293	6.33	3.43	54.19
1996-97	4.07	0.21	1643	6.33	3.13	49.45
1997-98	4.02	0.21	1621	6.52	4.27	65.43

Source : Ibid.

Further, it can also be observed that the percentage expenditure to the total revenue has drastically reduced. The position in the case of Karnataka is by an large the same but the revenue expenditure; is narrowed down in the sense that about 92 per cent of the revenue has been spent on various activities upto 1993-94. But this trend did not continue during the subsequent years as the expenditure has reduced drastically to a little over half. This only means that a substantial amount of contribution is being collected from the employers-employees. This does not mean that the same is unspent. Rather a part of the surplus revenue is being used for upgradation of the services in the ESI hospitals and capacity creation for the super speciality treatment of the ESI workers. Secondly the remaining surplus revenue is being used as reserve fund to meet the expenditure of permanent disablement benefits, dependent benefits, medicare for age-old retired insured persons.

GROWING RESENTMENTS

At the outset, the ESI Scheme is being implemented jointly by the ESI Corporation and the State Government. Although ESI Corporation is fully responsible for the implementation of the scheme, the Act has provided a specific role to the State Government as the welfare of the employees comes under their purview. State Government appoint the manpower (Doctors, Nurses, Paramedical staff) and the supportive staff in the hospitals. Also, responsible for meeting a nominal cost (i.e., one-eight or 12.5 per cent) of medical services. This arrangement though divides the responsibility of implementation of ESI between the two agencies, but would pose a threat to the scheme if laxity on the part of one partner. ESIS is an example to have suffered laxity as it attracted only a casual concern of the State Governments. Laxity has led to erosion of faith of the employees over the scheme especially on the quality of medical services and the attitudes of the hospital manpower. Interestingly the authorities, union leaders and employees are the opinion that State Governments should give up their responsibility (sharing cost and management of power) to the ESI Corporation in order to improve the medical services. Alternatively it is argued that State Governments can continue to retain their position as overall authority by allocating annual budgetary resources (equivalent to 12.6 per cent of medical services) to ESI Corporation.

Despite increasing infrastructure under ESI, a good chunk of employees continued to be deprived of the benefits. There are two such categories of employees. First is the organised workers who are already under the purview of the definition but have not been brought under the ESI benefits. The other category of workers are those qualified (by the large) to be brought under ESI purview and benefits but working in the unorganised sector. Although in the absence of the data, it is difficult to quantify the exact number of workers in the unorganised sector, it can be broadly identified as construction workers, head loaders, stone cutters/crushers, quarry workers etc. These workers deserved to be brought under ESI coverage and benefits as their occupations are not seasonal and most of them work on daily wage basis. Above, all, these workers are also by and large exposed to various types of risks. Therefore to extend the coverage, the employers of these workers or the State Governments, could be persuaded to contribute for the same. As far as the uncovered organised sector employees are concerned, there are over 11 lakh employees working in 0.17 lakh non-seasonal factories/establishments and the same work out to around 13 per cent of the employees already under ESI benefits/ coverage.

Notwithstanding the well intended objectives of ESI there have been a number of misconceptions and apprehensions both on the part of the employers and employees. First of all, employers being the major contributor of the scheme felt that their share of the contribution is burdensome as they contribute 2.7 times higher than the employees contribution which is ranging from a minimum of Rs. 684 to a maximum of Rs. 3708 per employee per annum at the existing system of coverage. Owing to higher rate of employers contribution, a large number of factories/ establishment have reported stayed out of the purview of the scheme.

Especially, the employers of the medium and small scale industries/establishments wish to be out of the coverage as their capital investment is very small. In fact, over the years, higher rate of contribution of employers has given rise to increasing under reporting or not reporting cases of employees. Physical verification through personal visits on the part of the ESI authorities to impress the employees have gone without considerable successes. In most cases, the regular employees have been misreported as part-time casual labourers and their numbers have been under reported. Similarly, there has been a growing dissatisfaction among the employees of higher bracket income (say between Rs. 4000-Rs.6500 per month). It is being argued that high income employees was made to contribute to facilitate the low paid employees as well as to meet the administrative cost of the ESI establishments. Further it has also been argued that the contributions of employers and employees in the pretext of super speciality treatment (open heart surgery, kidney transplantation, cancer etc.) is said to be huge as compared to their incidence and expenditure. Other major apprehensions on the part of the employers are the labour absenteeism and legal implications. It is believed that a full-fledged implementation of ESI to their workers would promote labour absenteeism as they are entitled for a variety of benefits such as sickness or medical which in turn includes provision for leaves of absence with wage protection. Similarly non-complying with provisions and benefits may resort to legal course of action which would lead to a number of inconveniences including financial losses, which especially the employers of medium and small establishments may not withstand.

Also, there are a number of disincentives for employees to subscribe to ESI coverage with the existing arrangements of medical services. The services of the hospitals, dispensaries of ESI are no way different from that of any government medical centres. Under such circumstances, ESI workers felt to avail the medical services like any other citizens from the regular centres. Besides, lack of good reception for the ESI workers, good behaviour of the hospital staff, bureaucratic approach (in hospitalisation process, service administration etc.) on the part of the hospital authorities have been the added disincentives. In this regard, labour unions also share the similar feelings that inspite of being well paid (salary, non-practicing allowance) and more promotional avenues, the ESI doctors lack service mentality and commitment to the cause of the labour welfare. Above all, non-availability of prescribed medicines while on hospitalisation has caused a host of inconvenience to the ESI in patients. According to Pharmacopoeia, 750 medicines are scheduled to be made available to the ESI and other hospitals and dispensaries. But in reality, only 50-60 items of medicines are made available for the in-patient employees. Non-availability of scheduled medicines

Table 4: Incidence of Various Sickness, TDB and PDB and Claims

Year	% of the Employers deemed Exposed to Sickness	% of persons claimed benefit	Maternity benefit per 1000 insured women	% of employees exposed to TDB/TDB	% of TDB Beneficiaries claimed benefit at the end of the year	% of Dependent benefits claimed
			INDIA			
1991-92	100.00	19.63	27.52	94.32	1.41	0.70
1992-93	83.69	20.77	30.86	100.00	1.25	0.67
1993-94	94.82	23.48	28.29	100.00	1.37	0.71
1994-95	97.84	20.71	25.59	98.75	1.47	0.74
1995-96	99.21	18.97	21.95	98.63	1.41	0.78
1996-97	86.64	16.95	20.66	92.76	1.45	0.71
			KARNATKA			
1991-92	90.51	14.98	33.12	100.00	0.90	0.39
1992-93	93.50	16.74	36.58	100.00	0.87	0.45
1993-94	84.77	20.27	32.16	100.00	0.96	0.46
1994-95	85.97	15.76	32.10	92.59	0.89	0.41
1995-96	95.22	15.60	27.91	99.60	0.95	0.43
1996-97	74.70	11.69	31.65	83.33	0.75	0.33

Source : Statistical Abstract and Annual Reports far various years

Table 5: Growth in Revenue and Expenditure Under ESI

(Rs. in croresl

Particulars	All India 1993-94	All India 1988-99	Percentage Change	Karnataka 1993-94	Karnataka 1998-99	Percentage Change
A Receipts						
(a) Contribution	496.39	1210.54	144	30.58	95.28	212
(b) Interest on Contribuiton	00.54	1.87	246	0.05	0.53	960
(c) Miscellaneous	195.53	297.96	52	3.18	4.04	27
TOTAL	**692.46**	**1510.37**	**118**	**33.81**	**99.85**	**195**
B Expenditure						
(a) Sickness benefit	61.07	101.44	66	2.98	6.06	103
(b) Enhanced Sickness benetit	0.05	0.04	-20	-	0.01	100
(c) Extended Sickness benetit	4.49	6.12	36	0.10	0.31	2
(d) Maternity Sickness benefit	7.53	15.94	112	1 .03	2.52	145
(e) Disablement Sickness benefit	56.58	79.30	40	2.37	5.20	119
(f) Dependent Sickness benefit	18.71	38.73	107	0.76	1.38	82
(g) Funeral Expenses	1.07	1.68	57	0.05	0.11	120
(h) Medical benefit	337.44	443.96	32	19.23	29.72	55
(i) Other benefit	0.6	0.63	5	0.03	0.05	67
TOTAL	**487.54**	**687.84**	**41**	**26.55**	**45.36**	**71**
C. Establishment						
(a) Administrative	68.05	150.88	122	3.95	9.73	146
(b) Depreciation Repair Maintenance Hosptital Building	13.76	16.42	19	0.59	0.99	68
(c) Capital/construction Reserve Fund	24.85	60.62	144	–	–	–
TOTAL	**106.66**	**227.92**	**114**	**4.54**	**10.72**	**136**
Grand Total (B + C)	594.20	915.76	54	3.09	56.08	80
% of Expenditure To Receipts	85.81	60.63	–	91.96	56.16	–

has compelled the patient employees to purchase such medicines from outside the hospitals, which is an additional contingency expenditure. A group of low paid workers were even maintaining that they were forced to borrow from informal sources in meeting such contingency expenditure. Although such expenditure are reimbursable immediately, delay tactics have been reportedly employed in making such payments and workers may even forfeit the same for having not submitted such claims within a stipulated period.

POLICY OPTIONS

From the above discussion, a number of issues emerges for policy consideration. Although ESI is one of the noble schemes owing to its features, its full-fledged acceptatility by the employees and employers has been in doldrums. Especially, increasing discontentment among the employers of the small and medium term factories/ establishment and high bracketed income groups due to burdensome contributions has limited the coverage. Added to this, utilisation of the existing infrastructure below the capacity owing to a number of weaknesses as discussed elsewhere has detracted the scheme. But in order to achieve the above goals a few hard decisions are warranted in the years to come, which include structural changes and reforms within the scheme itself. It is all the more important to make the scheme attractive both by the employers as well as employees and self-sustaining. Facilitating environment is absolutely necessary to encourage the employers to voluntarily support for the social cause of security of the workers. There are two means of achieving the same. First by reducing the present level of contribution and refix the same at an accepted leveling consultation with the employers. Although matching contribution would be an ideal situation, over and above can also be thought of. But the employers contributions should be reduced from the present level of 2.71 times of the employees contribution. Fixing up of over and above the matching contribution is also justifiable in order to sustain the scheme as well as to build up the capacity in the medical infrastructure. Secondly, from the point of view of the employees, make the scheme and its packages 'optional' especially for the high income bracketed employees. This would facilitate them to avail the medical benefits from the non-designated ESI hospitals on cost-reimbursement basis.

Under such circumstances, the medical expenses could be restricted only to the extent of their employers' contributions. Besides if the high income bracketed employers opt for exclusion from the scheme, their entitlement should be restricted to only medical benefits. Yet another way of making the ESI scheme attractive is by including the employers of the small and medium scale establishment for the extension of medical benefits on contributory basis. This would serve as an impetus to these employers as benefactor as well as beneficiaries.

Optimum utilisation of existing infrastructure can also be ensured by various means. Chiefly by covering the left over employees and employers in the organised and by include the additional categories of employees in the unorganised sector, who are getting daily minimum wages and exposed to risk. Although there are hardly any evidences of covering the labourers of unorganised sector under similar schemes, still it makes sense to include them on humanitarian consideration. While extending the ESI benefits to the excluded unorganised labourers, State Government may be made as a principal contributor besides their employers as subsidiary contributors. Number of days of employment with risk and wage level should be the criteria for such cases. Ideally, workers in the unorganised sector of scheduled establishment employed for more than a week with minimum wages could be included. It is also necessary to constitute an "Enforcement Authority" at the State level to act as a watchdog and to pursuade/ follow up the inclusion of left over employees both in the organised and unroganised sector. Further, it is indeed necessary not to establish any more hospitals and create beds until the existing capacity is fully utlised. Similarly, cancellation of beds in the general hospitals would bring about effective utlisation of infrastructure in the existing ESI hospitals. In view of the fact of poor-service of manpower and inadequate supply of scheduled medicines in the ESI hospitals, alternatively ESI Corporation itself can take over all the hospitals, including the manpower and dispensaries in order to ensure better services to its employees. Capacity building in the ESI hospitals to undergo super speciality treatment is also a need of the hour. This would not only facilitate the close coordination between the ESI Corporation and hospitals but also minimises the workers dependence on other hospitals.

ACKNOWLEDGEMENT

This paper is based on the financial support of the Indo-Dutch programme on Alternatives in Development to the research project entitled "Social Policies and Legislation in India — From Independence to Structural Adjustments". The author is grateful to the seminar participants for their comments on this paper. The author also benefited from the discussions he had with Mr. Allampathi Venkataram, President, Bharatiya Mazdoor Sangh (Karnataka) and Representative of the Regional Board of Directors of ESI Corporation and Mr. Ravindranath, Deputy Director, ESIC. The research assistance of Ms. Leena is gratefully acknowledged. The author remains indebted to Professor B.S. Sreekantaradhya for his very useful comments on the earlier version of the paper.

REFERENCES

1. C.K. John (1982), Social Security in India — Issue and Prospects, *Labour and Society,* Vol. 7. No.2.
2. Parthasarathi Shome (1982), Social Security in India — The Economics of the. System, *Labour and Society,* Vol. 7. No. 2, pp. 105-135.
3. Employees' State Insurance Scheme, Review Committee Report, 1996.
4. B.P. Adarkar Committee Report on Employees' State Insurance Scheme, 1944.
5. Employees' State Insurance Guide Book for employers (1997), Director General, ESIC, New Delhi.
6. Getubig and Sonke Schmidst (1992), Rethinking Social Security Reaching out to the Poor, Asia and Pacific Development Centre, Malaysia.

10

Public Distribution System in India During the Last Five Decades

*M. Chakraborty**

INTRODUCTION

The Public Distribution System (PDS) can be visualised both as an anti-inflammatory as well as an anti-poverty measure. It is a system that strives to soften the hardships caused by inflation which leads to the erosion of purchasing power, particularly in the hands of the fixed income groups or those who are price takers. This system helps to maintain the real value of purchasing power in the hands of the poor, its impact can be effective as any conventional poverty alleviation measure.

Today, we lay stress on more production mainly in order that people gets the things they need at prices within their reach. It is not possible, always to provide all essential commodities required by common man.

In the welfare State, one of the primary duties of the State is to provide food security to its people. This becomes more prominent in

* *Faculty Member, National Informatics Centre Training Unit, Lal Bahadur Shastri National, Academy ofAdministration, Mussoorie. Dehradun, UP, INDIA, PIN 248 179.*

a country like India having high density population with cropping pattern mostly dependent on rains and no regular assured system of irrigation, due to which the availability of food stocks remains fluctuating over periods of time causing uncertainties. To overcome such eventualities and to provide assured supply of essential commodities, a system of Public Distribution has been devised and adopted in India since Pre-Independence days. PDS was introduced as an-operational mechanism for rationing in the wake of the Bengal famine of 1943. Now it has developed into a stable and a permanent feature of our strategy to control prices, reduce fluctuations and achieve an equitable distribution of essential consumer goods. Under the first plan the PDS confined itself to supplying the needs of urban areas and highly deficit rural areas, through a system of statutory rationing. In the forties and fifties the PDS was viewed initially as a rationing system to introduce scare commodities and later as a fair price system in competition with the private traders who were believed to be exploitative. The major foodgrain items covered under it continued to be wheat and rice.

THE EXISTING ORGANISATIONAL STRUCTURE

PDS is a mechanism whereby availability of essential commodities is assured within easy reach of the consumers in every nook and corner of the country. This is a retailing system where foodgrains, sugar, an other necessary items like kerosene oil and edible oil etc. are made available to the people of the State at affordable price to meet their minimum needs. Regular and timely availability of supplies is assured through close monitoring system so that PDS becomes an effective instrument of regulating and keeping under check various forces to play in the open market. Timely, assured supply on fixed and reasonable prices also help in controlling the fluctuating trends of market due to vagaries of weather and consequent changing prospects of the crops. Consequently, PDS serves as a constant and stable check on market forces and works as an effective price stabilising factor.

PDS also serves as an effective instrument of social welfare and indirectly contributes to development of' rural population at large and the poorest of the poor in particular who cannot afford to buy necessary and essential items from open market. PDS thus contributes in its own way in ensuring minimum standards of health, especially for the less privileged. By assuring availability of foodstuffs and their necessities of life within easy access of the rural poor, matching with their buying capacity. PDS also serves as an instrument of Rural Development especially in far-flung and inaccessible areas. The PDS thus operates in conjunction with the Agricultural Price Policy.

OBJECTIVES OF THE PUBLIC DISTRIBUTION SYSTEM

The role of PDS has become more important because of its involvement in production, procurement and logistics to ultimate distribution through retail outlets.

The PDS acts as the main agency for the handling of food grains on behalf of Central Government to procure a sizeable portion of the marketed surplus from farmers on behalf of Central and State Government.

It is also minimises inter-seasonal, inter regional price variations, and builds up buffer stocks of food grains means of internal procurement and imports.

To give an outline of objectives a diagram is given below:

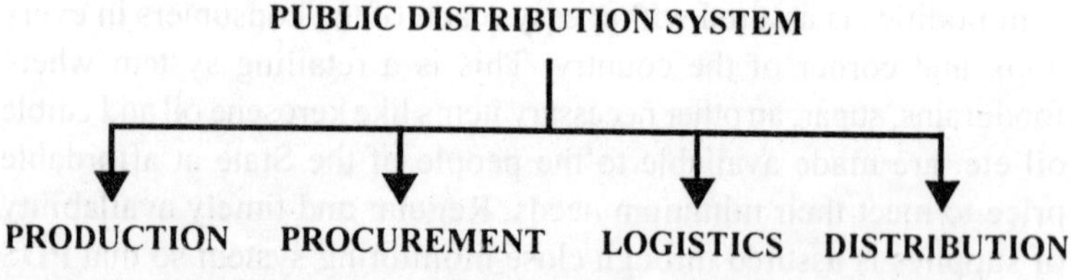

THE PROCUREMENT OF PDS

The PDS comes under the "Food and Supply Department" of the State Government. The chief executive at the State level is the Director of District Distribution Procurement and Supply. The District Controller of Food and Supply and the Sub-Divisional Controller, Food and Supply are responsible for effective monitoring of the system at the District and Subdivision levels respectively. The Inspectors, Sub-Inspectors of Food Supply who hold their office at Block level, sub-divisional level and District level assist them. Under the present system of procurement of PDS stock from Food Corporation of India (FCI) depot and subsequent distribution to different Fair Price Shop (FPSs) in the State. The State allocation of foodgrains and levy sugar received from the Central Government and allotted to different Districts on the basis of feeding strength of each District. On an average about 15-16 million tonnes of foodgrains are issued by Food Corporation of India (FCI) to the states at a uniform Central Issue Price (CIP) which is much less than the economic cost incurred by the Central Government by way of procurement, storage, transport and distribution. The difference between the economic and the Central Issue Price (CIP), called the consumer subsidy is borne by the Central Government. Allotment and Off-take of Rice (TPDS) and Wheat (TPDS) from Central Pool from April 2000 to June 2000 is given in the Table - 1 and Table - 2. Also Allotment and Off-take of Rice and Wheat from 1995-96 to 1999-2000 (Financial Year wise) given in Table - 3. .Month-wise allotment of Sugar from 1994-95 onwards is given in Table - 4. Allocation of Sugar (State-wise) during 2000 (PDS only) is given in Table - 5.

Main source of obtaining foodgrains for meeting the requirement of PDS is Food Corporation of India (FCI). In some States, levy sugar is also supplied by Food Corporation of India (FCI), while in other States, sugar is directly obtained from sugar mills. Monthly allocation of foodgrains and levy sugar for each State is made by the Ministry of Food and Civil Supply, Government of India and thereafter, the supply is lifted after making prepayment to Food Corporation of India (FCI). In some states, such supplies are lifted by the Department of Food and Supplies directly from Food Corporation of India (FCI) from their District depots. In such cases the corporations make available further supplies to the department or its outlets/private (Fair Price Shop (FPSs) on requisition being preferred by the concerned authorities of Food and Supplies Department. Allocation and off-take of foodgrains under Public Distribution system/TPDS in earlier years is listed in Table - 6.

The aim of the Food Management Policy of the Government of India has been monopoly imports procurement from domestic producers, trade regulations price control etc. FCI carries out its functions through its own network. The purpose of food policy is equitable distribution of supplies at reasonable prices.

Procurement of food grains is one of the food management policies. It is one of the essential aspects of the food security policy.

It serves the objective of price security to the farmers, which include them to sustain production level. Procurement operations are carried out by the Food Corporation of India (FCI) and the State agencies in consultation with the State Governments. Procurement prices are based on support prices announced by the Department of Agriculture and Co-operation. Table - 7 gives the procurement data of rice and wheat during the last seven years. Since 1965 the Food Corporation of India (FCI) has managed procurement. In some states procurement of foodgrains is directly being done through various agencies/ cooperative organisations The State Governments are under no bonds in determining the methods of procurement. Stocks thus procured are contributed to the stock pool of Food and Supplies Department for distribution through PDS. This practice is usually resorted to various States to provide support price to the agricultural class and to prevent chances of distressed sale, which may prove as a disadvantage to the agriculturists. The Government of India adopts a combination or any one of the procurement methods:

- Upon market purchase
- Pre-emption Purchase
- Monopoly procurement
- Levy system

Co-operatives function through these agencies for the further procurement of food grains. The prices are fixed by the Government on the recommendation of Commission for Agricultural Costs and Prices (CACP) for FCI, which has several regional offices for administration.

OPERATIONAL SYSTEM

Besides maintaining few main nodal stores at State level, a fairly large network of stores and sub-stores exists at District, Tehsil and Block levels and even below block level in sensitive and remote areas. Supplies, after being received from Food Corporation of India (FCI), are channelled to these stores and sub-stores according to their monthly quota/requirement. From these stores the supplies are dispatched to the Fair Price Shop (FPS) according to their allocated quota, under close supervision and monitoring of the supervisory staff.

Table 1 :

(Rice - 2000-2001)

Statement Indicating Allocation And Offtake of Rice (TPDS) From Central Pool from April, 2000 To June, 2000

(In '000 Tonnes)

Sl. No	States/Uts	Grand Total Erpm April, 2000 To June 2000 (P) Allotment				Offtake			
		Bpl	Apl	Addl	Total	Bpl	Apl	Addl	Total
1	ANDHRA PRADESH	226.680	461.760	399.600	1088.040	219.499	218.557	0.000	438.056
2	ARUNACHAL PRADESH	4.200	17.580	0.000	21.780	3.270	8.826	0.000	12.096
3	ASSAM	114.360	77.820	20.000	212.180	92.195	4.487	0.000	96.682
4	BIHAR	206.160	23.760	0.000	229.920	48.244	0.299	0.000	48.543
5	DELHI	0.000	40.830	0.000	40.830	0.000	0.926	0.000	0.926
6	GOA	1.560	10.710	0.000	12.270	0.312	7.069	0.000	7.381
7	GUJARAT	48.000	54.000	127.682	229.682	30.965	0.926	0.000	31.891
8	HARYANA	0.000	0.000	0.000	0.000	0.000	0.000	0.000	0.000
9	HIMACHAL PRADESH	0.000	15.690	0.000	15.690	0.000	0.238	0.000	0.238
10	JAMMU & KASHMIR	28.200	37.530	0.000	65.730	9.683	2.912	0.000	12.595
11	KARNATAKA	138.000	111.000	86.000	335.000	136.190	95.331	0.000	231.521
12	KERALA	92.100	343.860	0.000	435.960	113.950	23.790	0.000	137.740
13	MADHYA PRADESH	144.000	31.050	- 0.000	175.050	108.859	0.668	0.000	109.527
14	MAHARASHTRA	126.960	67.140	0.000	194.100	78.052	6.914	0.000	84.966
15	MANIPUR	7.800	8.580	0.000	16.380	4.168	2.543	0.000	6.711
16	MEGHALAYA	8.580	28.590	19.014	56.184	8.242	0.773	0.000	9.015
17	MIZORAM	3.180	20.430	0.000	23.610	3.180	20.064	0.000	23.244
18	Nagaland	4.620	25.890	0.000	30.510	4.094	0.237	0.000	4.331
19	Orissa	190.920	11.160	128.982	331.062	180.601	0.322	0.000	180.923

Table (Contd.)

20	PUNJAB	4.080	0.840	0.000	4.920	0.028	0.000	0.000	0.028
21	RAJASTHAN	1.500	2.340	17.573	21.413	0.231	0.010	0.000	0.241
22	SIKKIM	2.040	8.910	12.000	22.950	0.000	2.559	0.000	2.559
23	TAMILNADU	274.740	115.320	0.000	390.060	284.213	35.786	0.000	319.999
24	TRIPURA	13.860	27.360	0.000	41.220	14.407	3.740	0.000	18.147
25	UTTAR PRADESH	189.000	33.600	0.000	222.600	0.000	0.000	0.000	0.000
26	WEST BENGAL	132.420	32.190	0.000	164.610	9.012	9.098	0.000	18.110
27	A & N ISLANDS (@)	0.900	7.050	0.000	7.950	0.000	0.693	0.000	0.693
28	CHANDIGARH	0.120	0.510	0.000	0.630	0.000	0.000	0.000	0.000
29	D & N HAVELI	0.720	0.540	0.000	1.260	0.239	0.480	0.000	0.719
30	DAMAN & DIU	0.120	0.330	0.000	0.450	0.040	0.050	0.000	0.090
31	LAKSHADWEEP (@)	0.000	1.635	0.000	1.635	0.000	0.000	0.000	0.000
32	PONDICHERRY	3.900	0.870	3.000	7.770	2.105	0.000	0.000	2.105
	TOTAL	1968.720	1618.875	813.851	4401.446	1351.779	447.298	0.000	1799.077
	CRP/BSF	0.000	5.072	0.000	5.072	0.000	1.891	0.000	1.891
	DEFENCE	0.000	31.236	0.000	31.236	0.000	20.311	0.000	20.311
	BHUTAN	0.000	5.550	0.000	5.550	0.000	0.000	0.000	0.000
	GRAND TOTAL (ALL-INDIA)	1968.720	1660.733	813.851	4443.304	1351.779	469.500	0.000	1821.279

(P) = PROVISIONAL

(@) = Allocation for these two States are made annually

NOTE : Additonal Allocation is being made at Economic cost. Additional Allocation to Andhra Pradesh, Gujarat and Rajasthan is made at BPL rates.

(SOURCE: *FCI)*

Table 2 :

(Wheat - 2000-2001)

Statement Indicating Allocation and Offtake of Wheat (TPDS) from Central Pool from April, 2000 To June, 2000

(In '000 Tonnes)

SI. No	States/Uts	Grand Total Erpm April, 2000 To June 2000 (P) Allotment				Otttake			
		Bpl	Apl	Addl	Total	Bpl	Apl	Addl	Total
1	ANDHRA PRADESH	0.000	24.000	0.000	24.000	0.000	2.809	0.000	2.809
2	ARUNACHAL PRADESH	0.420	1.590	0.000	2.010	0.000	0.259	0.000	0.259
3	ASSAM	0.000	30.900	0.000	30.900	0.000	0.390	0.000	0.390
4	BIHAR	309.240	35.640	0.000	344.880	107.583	0.468	0.000	108.051
5	DELHI	0.000	127.920	0.000	127.920	0.000	0.083	0.000	0.083
6	GOA	0.720	5.070	0.000	5.790	0.000	1.272	0.000	1.272
7	GUJARAT	72.000	88.500	191.523	352.023	85.182	2.074	0.000	87.256
8	HARYANA	43.980	2.160	0.000	46.140	11.767	0.000	0.000	11.767
9	HIMACHAL PRADESH	25.560	9.600	0.000	35.160	4.058	0.115	0.000	4.173
10	JAMMU & KASHMIR	8.880	22.080	0.000	30.960	4.237	5.810	0.000	10.047
11	KARNATAKA	34.500	27.750	20.000	82.250	34.267	24.589	0.000	58.856
12	KERALA	0.000	113.160	0.000	113.160	0.000	12.546	0.000	12.546
13	MADHYA PRADESH	176.040	37.950	0.000	213.990	27.784	0.110	0.000	27.894
14	MAHARASHTRA	235.800	124.140	0.000	359.940	124.708	8.032	0.000	132.740
15	MANIPUR	0.000	5.130	0.000	5.130	0.000	0.000	0.000	0.000
16	MEGHALAYA	0.000	3.000	0.000	3.000	0.000	0.094	0.000	0.094
17	MIZORAM	0.000	3.030	0.000	3.030	0.000	0.896	0.000	0.896

Table 2 (Contd.)

18	NAGALAND	1.140	4.620	0.000	5.760	0.771	0.350	0.000	1.121
19	ORISSA	0.000	0.000	90.000	90.000	22.681	0.000	0.000	22.681
20	PUNJAB	21.720	4.530	0.000	26.250	0.655	0.000	0.000	0.655
21	RAJASTHAN	128.700	98.040	333.889	560.629	77.652	0.285	0.000	77.937
22	SIKKIM	0.000	0.300	0.000	0.300	0.000	0.350	0.000	0.350
23	TAMIL NADU	0.000	0.000	0.000	0.000	0.000	0.759	0.000	0.759
24	TRIPURA	0.000	3.840	0.000	3.840	0.000	0.000	0.000	0.000
25	UTTAR PRADESH	384.000	66.510	0.000	450.510	0.000	0.050	0.000	0.050
26	WEST BENGAL	141.900	194.100	0.000	336.000	100.194	9.134	0.000	109.328
27	A & NISLANDS(@)	0.420	2.040	0.000	2.460	0.000	1.147	0.000	1.147
28	CHANDIGARH	0.960	2.910	0.000	3.870	0.000	0.000	0.000	0.000
29	D & N HAVELI	0.180	0.150	0.000	0.330	0.060	0.060	0.000	0.120
30	DAMAN & DIU	0.060	0.120	0.000	0.180	0.006	0.000	0.000	0.006
31	LAKSHADWEEP (@)	0.000	0.126	0.000	0.126	0.000	0.006	0.000	0.006
32	PONDICHERRY	0.000	0.060	1.500	1.560	0.000	0.717	0.000	0.717
	TOTAL	1586.220	1038.966	636.912	262.098	601.605	72.405	0.000	674.010
	CRP/BSF	0.000	8.538	0.000	8.538	0.000	2.225	0.000	2.225
	DEFENCE	0.000	36.261	0.000	36.261	0.000	22.468	0.000	22.468
	BHUTAN	0.000	5.100	0.000	5.100	0.000	0.000	0.000	0.000
	GRAND TOTAL (ALL-INDIA)	1586.220	1088.865	636.912	3311.997	601.605	97.098	0.000	698.703

(P) = PROVISIONAL
(@) = Allocation for these two States are madeannually
NOTE : Additonal Allocation is being made at Economic cost. Additional Allocation to Andhra Pradesh, Gujarat and Rajasthan is made at BPL rates
(*SOURCE:* FCI)

Table 3 : Statements Indicating allotment and Offtake For Rice and Wheat from the central Pool (Financial Year-wise)

SI. No	States/Uts	Financial Year (April, 1995 to March, 1996)				Financial Year (April, 1998 to March, 1997)			
		Rice		Wheat		Rice		Wheat	
		Allotmen	Offtake	Allotmen	Offtake	Allotment	Offtake	Allotment	Offtake
1	ANDHRAPRADESH	2620.00	2159.10	192.00	102.70	2540.00	1946.80	180.00	127.30
2	ARUNACHAL PRADESH	102.70	90.60	7.20	5.40	109.20	100.70	7.20	5.50
3	ASSAM	568.00	434.50	360.00	351.70	648.70	520.90	355.50	301.90
4	BIHAR	381.60	23.50	705.60	227.30	389.60	37.50	713.06	438.70
5	DELHI	240.00	26.50	840.00	153.20	240.00	113.60	700.00	574.70
6	GOA	78.00	44.80	42.40	23.40	90.00	59.50	37.20	32.60
7	GUJARAT	409.00	208.60	835.50	425.00	376.00	276.40	690.90	624.20
8	HARYANA	53.56	6.40	209.48	62.40	52.00	21.80	208.16	131.30
9	HIMACHALPRADESH	131.00	45.20	144.00	98.20	122.80	86.50	140.00	119.30
10	JAMMU & KASHMIR	528.00	271.70	360.00	115.90	528.00	353.70	360.00	149.00
11	KARNATAKA	1443.12	942.90	360.00	219.50	1453.12	1110.00	356.00	286.70
12	KERALA	1800.00	1170.60	585.00	557.40	1847.00	1530.00	572.50	544.10
13	MADHYAPRADESH	580.16	204.60	583.92	136.60	613.68	302.90	605.624	31.1046
14	MAHARASHTRA	858.00	359.70	1100.00	610.50	858.00	553.60	1010.00	850.10
15	MANIPUR	120.00	32.90	32.40	28.20	120,00	58.90	32.40	31.30
16	MEGHALAYA	172.00	164.40	28.00	27.70	190.00	181.90	29.50	26.50
17	MIZORAM	94.00	93.70	24.00	23.30	92.05	88.60	23.50	20.90

Table 3 Contd.

18	NAGALAND	72.5O	71.00	18.20	21.60	81.20	89.40	8.60	8.30
19	ORISSA	790.00	365.70	420.00	238.50	1012.00	592.90	451.00	419.60
20	PUNJAB	16.65	2.00	155.00	8.00	18.00	1.60	121.00	54.00
21	RAJASTHAN	52.00	8.70	1453.92	459.30	59.00	16.70	1358.37	1141.30
22	SIKKIM	57.60	43.10	12.30	9.90	60.10	60.90	10.70	11.30
23	TAM1LNADU	1590.00	1745.10	310.00	174.20	1903.50	7866.50	287.20	217.20
24	TRIPURA	194.40	148.70	21.60	9.60	194.40	150.10	21.60	14.80
25	UTTARPRADESH	549.60	209.50	1185.60	225.70	532.20	359.30	1140.40	894.90
26	WESTBENGAL	856.00	447.10	1098.60	842.30	800.00	517.10	1071.00	904.50
27	A & N ISLANDS	30.00	0.00	9.00	0.00	30.00	0.00	9.00	0.00
28	CHANDIGARH	3.60	1.10	21.60	1.00	3.60	2.10	21.60	7.90
29	D & N HAVELI	6.00	1.60	2.75	0.70	6.00	1.50	3.00	0.60
30	DAMAN & DIU	6.70	0.90	2.15	0.20	7.20	1.40	2.40	0.20
31	LAKSHADWEEP	6.30	4.70	0.50	Neg	6.30	6.60	0.50	0.30
32	PONDICHERRY	24.00	2.00	9.00	Neg	25.00	4.10	9.00	0.00
	TOTAL	14434.49	9332.90	11129.72	5159.40	15008.65	11013.50	10536.97	8370.10
	CRPBSF	18.00	17.10	30.00	25.00	18.001	8.80	30.00	31.70
	DEFENCE	143.78	102.20	134.03	105.90	112.50	100.90	135.00	112.40
	BHUTAN	22.20	8.70	20.40	2.30	22.20	9.70	20.40	6.20
	GRANDTOIAL (ALL-INDIA)	14618.47	9460.90	11314.15	5292.60	15161.35	11142.90	10722.31	8520.40

Table 3 : Statements Indicating allotment and Offtake For Rice and Wheat from the central Pool (Financial Year-wise)

Financial Year (April, 1997 to March, 1998)				Financial Year (AprIl, 1998 to March, 1999)				Financial Year (April, 1999 to March, 2000)			
Rice Allotmen	Offtake	Wheat Allotmen	Offtak	Rice Allotment	Offtake	Wheat Allotmen	Offtake	Rice Allotmen	Offtake	Wheat Allotment	Offtake
2309.00	2000.07	183.00	125.29	2350.400	2116.278	137.000	123.832	2300.400	2282.454	741.000	99.208
107.86	89.31	7.11	5.76	109.200	94.193	7.200	5.750	109.200	101.442	7.800	5.331
590.85	438.31	323.08	793.94	620.000	555.050	363.600	311.867	670.000	529.183	213.900	219.155
489.80	156.31	788.40	513.74	507.360	235.778	831.040	714.313	507.360	236.540	861.040	679.827
174.30	100.34	661.47	532.02	164.680	112.680	694.800	560.151	154.680	75.462	724.800	3.849
76.80	51.95	32.30	27.10	75.960	59.967	33.720	31.136	75.960	45.308	33.720	11.775
308.00	178.75	741.65	519.31	356.000	251.362	494.000	403.543	292.500	165.578	739.500	292.506
5.00	4.10	178.55	98.44	0.000	0.000	156.600	75.367	0.000	0.000	156.600	53.298
134.99	90.07	131.02	115.66	144.867	93.980	139.695	126.551	146.760	64.694	142.440	54.949
430.76	296.56	290.59	167.74	386.532	318.270	364.548	138.204	433.266	332.380	364.548	45.166
1024.52	833.94	260.00	248.84	940.000	888.058	300.000	279.758	900.000	793.896	420.000	229.929
1827.36	1607.38	389.04	370.93	1789.840	1625.876	452.640	433.026	1743.840	1265.904	452.640	235.909
3.50	297.27	584.90	308.91	417.200	305.994	503.880	319.815	412.200	315.728	503.880	70.678
678.40	562.37	1251.80	987.43	722.480	666.083	1178.160	093.646	762.480	675.568	1208.160	1074.253
101.40	45.19	25.66	27.61	122.520	42.955	32.600	30.982	125.000	46.226	23.220	1.414
199.28	152.89	26.54	28.70	209.576	182.364	29.520	29.578	207.576	192.096	14.460	15.124
106.21	95.05	16.94	17.70	125.076	123.149	24.060	23.733	125.076	88.511	14.080	14.797

Table 3 : Contd.

108.97	92.22	28.73	29.24	125.800	114.790	38.060	37.646	125.100	113.559	23.490	19.457
715.405	50.84	299.00	207.19	656.980	575.793	-435.000	401.863	1169.855	856.8244	20.000	168.180
12.60	1.82	91.30	14.18	11.520	0.780	61.560	8.336	11.520	1.981	61.560	5.644
56.86	4.17	901.30	451.44	47.470	5.431	839.560	449.092	15.860	2.704	633.220	241.010
77.38	52.05	5.68	5.32	87.720	63.015	10.680	8.485	87.720	70.013	2.090	1.398
1359.71	1261.92	244.60	124.48	1310.760	1282.723	360.000	228.849	1814.760	804.269	360.000	164.387
167.33	153.49	17.90	14.49	200.000	182.902	21.600	17.582	197.500	150.484	17.160	7.421
521.59	320.98	1214.82	867.206	32.400	462.496	1319.040	1002.941	739.700	363.715	1529.440	336.453
536.90	315.98	1193.20	927.66	567.250	249.710	1047.350	959.636	518.600	199.501	1061.100	744.277
30.00	0.20	9.00	0.10	30.000	0.000	7.500	0.023	30.000	25.95	79.00	07.485
2.94	2.08	17.58	5.27	3.600	1.726	21.600	4.637	3.600	0.026	21.600	0.000
4.95	2.78	1.98	1.32	6.600	3.758	3.000	2.010	6.600	1.376	3.000	0.357
4.38	3.34	1.50	0.69	7.200	1.453	2.400	0.743	7.200	0.790	2.400	0.029
8.70	3.11	0.50	0.89	3.150	2.620	0.252	0.271	6.300	7.298	0.504	0.202
20.14	0.00	4.82	0.00	26.000	1.647	9.000	0.146	24.000	10.043	9.000	1.750
1265588	976484	992402	693859	12758141	10620881	9919665	7823512	13724613	10819510	10175352	4855218
18.00	12.89	30.00	20.89	18.000	10.475	30.000	11.985	20.290	11.290	34.152	14.293
135.80	116.12	140.00	98.041	36.596	106.436	144.996	106.770	125.000	109.521	140.004	110.760
22.20	7.17	20.40	22.84	22.200	5.415	20.400	6.791	22.200	10.645	20.400	15.258
12831.88	9901.02	10114.42	7080.36	12934.937	10743.207	10115.061	7949.058	13892.103	10950.966	10369.906	4995.529

Table - 4 : Monthly Allotment of Levy Sugar

(In Lakh Tonnes)

YEAR	OCT	NOV	DEC	JAN	FEB	MAR	APR	MAY	JUN	JUL	AUG	SEP	TOTAL
1994-95	3.80	3.49	3.37	3.77	3.88	3.65	3.37	3.36	3.27	3.41	3.51	3.72	42.60
1995-96	4.03	3.60	3.49	3.69	3.70	3.72	3.70	3.71	3.73	3.73	3.75	4.31	45.16
1996-97	4.25	4.06	4.13	4. 11	3.77	3.70	3.70	3.68	3.68	3.74	3.75	4.02	46.59
1997-98	4. 16	3.71	3.70	3.73	3.72	3.70	3.71	3.71	3.71	3.71	3.70	3.93	45.19
1998-99	4.08	3.73	3.80	3.72	3.74	3.70	3.71	3.71	3.71	3.72	3.74	3.94	45.30
1999-2K	4.12	3.80	3.71	3.79	3.74	3.82	3.82	4.46	4.46	4.17	4.18	—	44.07

(*SOURCE: SUGAR RELEASE* SECTION)

Table 5 : Monthly Allocation of Levy Sugar During 2000 (P)

SL No.	STATES/Uts	MAR., 2000	APR., 2000	MAY, 2000	JUNE, 2000	JULY, 2000	AUGUST, 2000
1	ANDHRA PRADESH	28.30	28.19	31.74	31.74	30.46	30.46
2	ARUNACHAL PRADESH	0.61	0.61	0.82	0.82	0.82	0.82
3	ASSAM	15.75	16.48	18.20	18.19	17.21	17.21
4	BIHAR	36.75	36.75	42.74	42.75	40.59	40.59
5	DELHI	12.08	12.08	17.16	17.17	13.01	13.01
6	GOA	0.51	0.51	0.67	0.67	0.54	0.54
7	GUJARAT	17.58	17.58	20.24	20.24	18.01	20.50
8	HARYANA	7.00	7.00	8.31	8.35	7.54	7.54
9	HIMACHAL PRADESH	3.32	3.32	4.58	4.65	4.33	4.33
10	JAMMU & KASHMIR	5.57	5.53	6.91	7.01	6.92	6.92
11	KARNATAKA	19.14	19.14	21.88	21.88	20.50	20.50
12	KERALA	12.37	12.37	13.60	13.60	12.86	12.86
13	MADHYA PRADESH	28.19	28.19	33.35	33.37	32.08	32.08
14	MAHARASHTkA	33.57	33.57	38.32	38.32	33.76	38.27
15	MANIPUR	1.34	1.33	1.75	1.76	1.76	1.76
16	MEGHALAYA	1.26	1.26	1.67	1.68	1.68	1.68
17	MIZORAM	0.51	0.51	0.67	0.68	0.67	0.67

18	NAGALAND	0.86	0.86	1.16	1.16	1.16	1.16
19	ORISSA	13.47	13.48	15.12	15.12	15.63	14.76
20	PUNJAB	8.85	8.66	9.93	9.94	8.66	8.66
21	RAJASTHAN	18.81	18.81	22.48	22.48	21.14	21.14
22	SIKKIM	0.29	0.29	0.38	0.38	0.38	0.38
23	TAMIL NADU	23.75	23.75	26.04	26.04	23.83	23.83
24	TRIPURA	1.98	1.98	2.61	2.61	2.61	2.61
25	UTTAR PRADESH	59.24	59.14	70.85	70.85	69.04	69.04
26	WEST BENGAL	29.10	29.05	33.26	33.26	30.45	30.45
27	A & N ISLANDS	0.28	0.28	0.38	0.38	0.38	0.38
28	CHANDIGARH	0.39	0.39	0.53	0.53	0.16	0.16
29	D & N HAVELI	0.06	0.06	0.08	0.08	0.08	0.08
30	DAMAN & DIU	0.04	0.04	0.06	0.06	0.06	0.06
31	LAKSHADWEEP	0.08	0.08	0.11	0.11	0.11	0.13
32	PONDICHERRY	0.47	0.46	0.63	0.63	0.63	0.66
	BHUTAN	0.31	0.31	0.31	0.31	0.31	0.31
	ADJLTSTMENT+FCI	—	—	(–) 0.36	(-) 0.36	—	(-) 6.00
	GRAND TOTAL (ALL-INDIA)	381.83	382.06	446.44	446.46	417.37	417.55

(P) = PROVISIONAL

SOURCE : DIRECTORATE OF SUGAR

Table 6 : Foodgrains Allocation and Offtake Under the Public Distribution System/TPDS

(Million Tonnes)

Year	Wheat		Rice	
	Allocation	Offtake	Allocation	Offtake
1991-92	10.36	8.83	11.36	10.17
1992-93	9.25	7.85	11.48	9.69
1993-94	9.56	6.09	12.41	9.10
1994-95	10.91	5.11	13.32	8.01
1995-96	11.32	5.81	14.61	9.75
1996-97	10.71	9.35	15.10	12.04
1997-98 (P) (April - Feb	10.11	6.35	12.83	9.04

(P)- Provisional

Socurce : Economic Survey 1997-98

Table 7 : Procurement of Wheat and Rice (Central Pool)

(Million Tonnes)

Marketing	Wheat (April - March)		Rice (April - March)	
Year	Qty,	% Change	Qty.	% Change
1991-92	7.75	–29.9	9.24	–21.3
1992-93	6.38	–17.7	11.79	26.6
1993-94	12.83	101.1	13.65	15.7
1994-95	11.87	–7.5	13.40	–1 .8
1995-96	12.33	3.9	9.95	–25.7
1996-97	g.14	–33.6	12.22	22.8
1997-98 (April - Feb.)	9.30	14.2	12.51*	

*as on April 17, 1998

Source : - Economic Survey 1997-98

POPULATION COVERAGE

At present there is universal coverage under PDS according to 1991 Census except in case of "Identified Areas" covered under Revamped Public Distribution System (RPDS), where the foodgrains are being provided to the entire rural population according to 1991 Census. Revamped Public Distribution system (RPDS) was launched in January 1992 to strengthen the existing PDS in far flung, difficult and other identified backward areas. Initially the scheme was launched in 1752 blocks, which has been extended now to 2446 blocks. Upto November 1995,15238 additional ration shops were opened and 64 lakh new ration cards were issued to the people in Revamped Public Distribution system (RPDS) areas. Achievements in both the schemes are more than 100 per cent. 54,491 shops in the backward areas provided facilities of doorstep delivery of foodgrains to ensure timely availability. Additional storage capacity of 5,31,766 MT has been created in difficult and backward areas to ensure adequate supply of foodgrains throughout the year. Allocation of foodgrains for Revamped Public Distribution system (RPDS) areas was increased by 40 per cent and Central Issue Price (CIP) was further reduced by Rs. 50 per quintal. It has made PDS more meaningful for the people who have low purchasing capacity. The PDS is implemented in the country with the understanding that the supply of grain would be done by the Centre while the distribution would be done by State Government to cover the entitled population. It is also observed that the State always received lesser supply of food than the demand. If the scheme for food at half rate to the people falling in the below poverty line (BPL) was to implement, the dual card system had to be undertaken to avoid its misuse. Starting in early 1950's with the sole purpose of providing succour to the needy people, the PDS has hardly achieved the goal.

SCALE

Scale of foodgrains and sugar to be provided under PDS to an individual per month is fixed by the prescribed authority which is Government of India or in some States, the State Government itself. In some other States, this authority has been delegated to the District Food Controllers, which itself provides a good leverage to the local authorities to mould the system to meet the local requirements and to make it adjust to the changing needs according to the demand, availability and market forces.

Each household covered under PDS is provided a ration card that indicates the name of the head of the family, details of other family members and related particulars. Each adult is termed as a "Unit" in this card and the minor below the age of 3 years, is termed as a "Half Unit". Total number of Units, for which a particular ration-card is issued in urban or rural areas, is written on this card itself. By producing this card, people can draw their quota of ration from the Fair Price Shop (FPS) against cash payment.

PRICE AND SUBSIDY

The end retail sale price of foodgrains and sugar is fixed by the State Government from time to time after taking into account the price at which Food Corporation of India (FCI) makes the commodities available. Every effort is made to keep the end retail prices under PDS uniform throughout the State irrespective of the location of the Fair Price Shop (FPSs), and the transportation, by whatever mode.

No direct subsidy is being made available under PDS at present but a lot of indirect subsidy is involved at various stages to maintain and sustain the PDS. In the first instance the process of procurement and availability of foodgrains etc. at District Headquarters by Food Corporation of India (FCI) involves a good deal of subsidy. Secondly, the cost incurred in sending the supplies from District Headquarters to the stores/sub-stores and Fair Price Shop (FPS) is borne by the State Government, Lastly, for maintaining uniform and reduced end retail prices of foodgrains under PDS, a lot of subsidy is being provided by Government of India and the same is being supplemented by the respective State Government. F.P.S. level prices of foodgrains in various states are given in Table-8.

CENTRAL ISSUE PRICE

The Central Issue Prices (CIP) for the PDS have not been revised since 1st February 1994. Central Issue Price (CIP) for PDS for wheat was Rs. 402 per quintal (Rs. 352 per quintal for Revamped Public Distribution System (RPDS) and for rice Rs. 537 per quintal for common variety, Rs. 617 per quintal for fine and Rs. 648 per quintal for supper fine quality respectively. The detailed data is shown in the Table - 9. Some of the states have fixed the prices for PDS and Revamped Public Distribution System (RPDS) even lower than the Central Issue Prices (CIP).

Table 8 : ISSTJE Prices at Fair Price Shops in State/Uts

(Rs. per Kg.)

SR. No.	STATES/UT	BPL Wheat	BPL Rice	APL Wheat	APL Common $	APL Rice Gr. A	As on
1	ANDHRA PRADESH *	–	5.25	9.00	–	12.00	26.7.2000
2	ARUNACHAL PRADESH	3.00	4.00	5.00	NA	–	–
3	ASSAM®	–	6.53-6.59	8.74-9.29	–	13-13.26	12.1.2000
4	BIHAR	5.10	6.48	9.84	–	2.89	1.4.2000
5	DELHI	–	-	9.50	–	12.30	1.4.2000
6	GOA	–	6.30	9.50	–	12.40	1.4.2000
7	GUJARAT *	2.00	3.00	8.00	–	10.00	5.2.2000
8	HARYANA	5.00	-	9.50	–	–	1.4.2000
9	HIMACHAL PRADESH	5.00	7.20	9.80	–	13-13.50	1.4.2000
10	JAMMU&KASHMIR®	5.10	6.50	9.50	12.00	12.50	1.4.2000
11	KARNATAKA *	5.00	6.40	9.80	–	12.75	1.4.2000
12	KERALA	–	6.40	9.50	–	10.40	1.4.2000
13	MADHYA PRADESH ®	5.00	6.40	9.75	–	12.75	1.4.2000
14	MAHARASHTRA ®	4.00	5.40	9.80	–	13.50	1.8.2000
15	MANIPUR	–	4.00	7.60	7.64	9.77	Feb 1999
16	MEGHALAYA	–	6.40	9.60-10.00	11.85-12.15	12.30-13.60	1.4.2000

Table 8 : Contd.

17	MIZORAM	–	4.00	7.90	7.50	9.55	31.3.2000
18	NAGALAND	3.00	4.00	5.10	6.10	7.60	1.12.98
19	ORISSA	–	6.50-5.00	-	–	12.90	1.4.2000
20	PUNJAB	4.58	5.96	9.06	–	11.86	1.4.2000
21	RAJASTHAN	3.00	4.00	7.00	–	9.70	5.3.1999
22	SIKKIM	–	6.40	9.50	–	12.50	1.4.2000
23	TAMIL NADU	2.00	3.50	9.75	–	NA	1.4.2000
24	TRIPURA	–	6.40	0.75	12.05	12.75	1.4.2000
25	UTTAR PRADESH	3.00	4.00	7.00	7.50	9.55	8.3.1999
26	WEST BENGAL	5.00	6.40	9.70	–	12.60	1.4.2000
27	A&N ISLANDS	5.00	6.40	10.15	–	12.90	Mar2000
28	CHANDIGARH	4.87	6.28	10.12	–	12.44	1.4.2000
29	D & N HAVELI	5.00	6.40	9.70	–	12.40	30.4.2000
30	DAMAN & DIU	5.00	6.40	9.90	–	12.80	1.4.2000
31	LAKSHADWEEP	3.00	4.00	7.35	–	9.55	Jul 99
32	PONDICHERY	–	4.00	9.50	–	12.30	1.4.2000

TPDS not launched in Delhi and Lakshdweep.

NA. - Not available (to be intimated by the State Government.

$ - Applicable only to J&K, Himachal Pradash and hilly areas at North Eastern States including Sikkim and. Uttar Pradesh.

* - Additional subsidy Borne by State Government.

- Differs from area to area.

(SOURCE : PD II Section)

TRANSPORTATION AND STORAGE

Transportation and storage from the procurement centres to the regional depots is the responsibility of the Food Corporation of India (FCI). Transportation is generally arranged through private contractors. Lifting of grains from the regional depots to the issue centres is mainly the responsibility of the Civil Supplies Corporations of the State Governments. From the issue centres to the Fair Price Shop (FPSs) it is the responsibility of Fair Price Shop (FPSs), except in some states like Andhra Pradesh where the State Government up to the Fair Price Shop (FPSs) provides transportation. Proper storage of such large stocks is an important aspect of PDS. The main aim is to keep costs down and to prevent deterioration in stocks. The various agencies involved and facilities utilised are : Food Corporation of India (FCI) regional depots, Central Warehousing Corporation, State Warehousing Corporation, Godowns of Civil Supplies Corporations, Cooperative Societies and private godowns.

DISTRIBUTION SYSTEM

In most of the sates, there is a vast, well-knit system of retail outlets covering every remote corner of the State. Besides Government run Fair Price Shop (FPSs), there are retail outlets run by Co-operative Sector as well as by Private Sector on commission basis. The amount of commission payable to the Cooperative/Private Sector and other terms & conditions varies from State to State according to the local requirements. The fixation of the total quota to be supplied to each state is determined by the Central Government. The issue price charged at retail level is fixed by the Central Government. This makes uniformity throughout the country. The distribution at the retail level is done through the Fair Price Shop (FPSs), which works under a license from Civil Supplies Department of the State Government. District level officials take decision about the location of the Fair Price Shop (FPSs). Local political pressures also play an important role in this decision. Commodities to be covered are generally fixed by the State Government, but the Central Government has listed wheat, rice, sugar, kerosene oil etc. as essential items, while State Government can add other commodities depending upon the local situation. At the national level, an Advisory Council on PDS has been set up to monitor the working of the PDS. At the District and

Block levels a consumer advisory committee has been set up to look into the problems of consumers. In some states mobile Fair Price Shop (FPSs) for interior remote areas have been arranged. In Andhra Pradesh as on 1-9-1997, there were 39,715 Fair Price Shop (FPSs), ont of which 6,974 were in urban areas and 32,741 in rural areas.

Table 9 : Central Issue Price of Foodgrains

(Rupees Per Quintal)

Effective From		Common	Fine	Superfine	
Rice	01.02.1994	537	617	648	FOR P D S
* *	01.06.1997	–	650	750	FOR APL FAMILIES
		350	350 .	–	FOR BPL FAMILIES
			GRADE "A" (##)		
**	01.12.1997	550$	700		FOR APL FAMILIES
		350	350		FOR BPL FAMILIES
	01.04.2000	590	590		FOR BPL FAMILIES
	29.01.1999	700,$	905		FOR APL FAMILIES
	01.04.2000	1135$	1180		FOR APL FAMILIES
WHEAT	28.12.1991	280			FOR PD S
	11.01.1993	330			FOR PD S
	01.02.1994	402			FOR PD S
**	01.06.1997	450/250			FOR APL/BPL FAMILIES
	29.01.1999	650			FOR APL FAMILIES
	01.04.1999	682			FOR APL FAMILIES
	01.04.2000	900/450			FOR APL/BPL FAMILIES
C. GRAINS	01.10.1990	199			FOR P. D. S

(**) = If Any State/Ut is Not Ready to Implement the TPDS even by 31 .5.1997 The Cip of Wheat & Rice Issued to that State/Ut from 1.6.1997 will be only at the Rate Applicable to APL Families

(APL/BPL) = For Families Above/Below Poverty Line

($) = Applicable Only To J&K, H.p., N E States, Sikkim And Hilly Areas of Uttar Pradesh

(##) = With Effect From 1.12.1997, Rice Has Been Categorised Into Common & Grade "A" Only.

(Source : Policy-i Section)

There is a reservation of 15% for scheduled castes, 6% for scheduled tribes, 25% for backward classes and 3% for physically handicapped in the allotment of Fair Price Shop (FPSs) in Andhra Pradesh. Similarly, in Rajasthan, as on December 1997, total 18,488, Fair Price Shops (FPSs) were functioning in the State, out of these 13994 shops were functioning in the rural areas and remaining 4494 in urban areas. A number of shops are further allotted to be functioned in Co-operative as well as in Private Sector.

Ration cards are issued in favour of every household after due enquiry about their place of residence, number of units in the family, range of annual income etc. The Inspectors and Sub-Inspectors usually conduct such enquiry at the village level and certificates of verification of the particulars are also obtained from the elected representatives of the people.

Millions of people were covered by Fair Price shops (see Table -10). About 2000 cards are allotted to one ration dealer for locality which may, however, vary depending on the proximity of localities from the ration shop. The dealers are appointed by the sub-divisional officers undergoing due process as laid down under the rules framed by the State Government from time to time.

Food grains and other commodities are allotted to the ration dealers by the Sub-Divisional Controller of Food and Supply on the basis of the number of ration cards tagged to the dealer. The ration dealers in their respective areas issue cereals to the ration cardholders. The Inspectors and Sub-Inspectors are responsible for ensuring maintenance of proper accounts by the ration dealers in respect of transactions of all the items. All particulars relating to withdrawal of ration commodities and stock held by the dealers are sent to the Sub-Divisional Controller in a prescribed Performa, who sends these records to the District Controller of Food and Supply for onward transmission to the Directorate of Food and Supply for compilation and record. The particulars and figures regarding total number of ration cards, withdrawal of the commodities by the card holders and the stock held by the dealers have to be maintained meticulously since the total requirement for a District will have to be assessed on the basis of these particulars.

ADMINISTRATIVE SET-UP & SUPERVISORY MECHANISM

Effective supervisory mechanism has been devised for all levels which ensures that the stocks are transported and maintained in the stores/ sub-stores as well as Fair Price Shop (FPSs) according to the requirements worked out on the basis of strength and scale of ration sanctioned by the prescribed authority. It also ensures through periodical inspection that the ration of good quality is made available to the people in time, regularly, according to the needs of the people and also on the prices fixed by the Government.

Table 10 : Statement Indicating Statewise No. of Households BPL Households. Fair Price Shops and Ration Cards

	Population % (1999) (In lakh)	BPL as per expert group	No. of Households (1999) (In lakh)	No of BPL House-Holds (1999) (in lakh)	Fair Price Shop			Ration Cards (in lakh)			No. of cards per FPS	Reported as on
					Rural	Urban	Total	BPL	APL	Total		
ANDHRA PRADESH	746.17	25.68	156.43	37.78	32860	7578	40438	113.25	51.53	164.78	413	Apr 2000
ARUNACHAL PRADESH	11.55	40,86	2.34	0.77	842	103	945	0.82	2.6	3.42	366	Mar 2000
ASSAM	258.78	40.86	44.39	19.06	28687	3660	32347	18.82	23.7	42.52	131	Apr 2000
BIHAR	981.22	54.96	159.29	85.90	47293	10242	57535	84.26	88.74	173	301	Nov 97
GOA	15.47	14.92	3.1	0.38	429	161	590	0.07	3.02	3.09	522	June 2ooo
GUJARAT	475.51	24.21	86.30	19.95	10518	3750	14268	33.9	71.96	105.86	741	June 2000
HARYANA	195.46	25.05	31.03	7.33	5182	2521	7703	5.68	37.74	43.42	545	June 2000
HIMACHAL PRADESH	65.45	40.86	12.26	4.26	3616	279	3895	2.77	9.27	12.04	309	Apr 2000
JAMMU & KASHMIR	97.09	40.86	18.42	6.17	2237	689	2926	3.36	10.12	13.48	461	Sep 97
KARNATAKA	514.36	33.16	93.18	28.75	14912	5400	20312	64.60	47.18	111.79	550	May 2000
KERALA	319.82	25.43	60.57	15.35	12279	1982	14261	20.58	41.62	62.2	434	June 2000
MADHYA PRADESH	783.46	42.52	138.67	53.34	20489	3652	24141	43.65	134.18	177.83	737	Mar 2000
MAHARASHTRA	901.22	36.86	175.33	60.45	35005	10802	45807	58.13	135.96	194.09	424	June 2000
MANIPUR	24.41	40.86	4.70	1.30	1753	175	1928	0.67	1.13	1.8	93	June 97
MEGHALAYA	23.59	40.86	4.35	1.44	3257	572	3829	0.97	0.98	1.95	51	Mar 97
MIZORAM	9.22	40.86	1.62	0.53	771	232	1003	NA	1.66	1.66	154	Apr 2000
NAGALAND	16.29	40.86	2.92	0.95	138	213	351	0.96	1.05	2.01	573	Mar 99

TABLE - 10: (Contd.)

ORISSA	355.35	48.56	67.30	31.82	20824	3841	24665	41.23	39.85	81.08	329	Dec99
PUNJAB	232.76	11.77	39.32	4.30	9514	4401	13915	4.91	49.12	54.03	388	May2000
RAJASTHAN	526.39	27.41	87.15	21.66	14386	4557	18943	22.87	80.93	103.8	541	Feb2000
SIKKIM	5.41	41.43	1.02	0.34	519	359	878	NA	NA	0.66	75	Oct 97
TAMILNADU	612.55	35.03	137.65	45.79	20625	5889	26514	64.88	91.59	156.47	588	June2000
TRIPURA	36.65	40.86	6.99	2.31	1185	174	1359	2.31	4.55	6.86	505	May2000
UTTAR PRADESH	1663.64	40.85	267.47	95.48	64393	12326	76719	95.48	159.96	255.44	333	Jul98
WEST BENGAL	779.72	35.66	143.33	46.59	15673	4842	20515	46.11	109.13	155.24	757	Oct 98
A & N ISLANDS	3.74	34.47	0.79	0.22	286	118	404	0.12	0.74	0.86	213	May 2000
CHANDIGARH	8.60	11.35	1.96	0.18	47	183	230	0	2.12	2.12	922	Apr2000
D & N HAVELI	1.84	50.84	0.35	0.14	78	N.A.	78	0.16	0.16	0.32	410	Jun 2000
DAMAN & DIU	1.35	15.8	0.25	0.03	7	6	13	0.02	0.27	0.3	2231	May 2000
DELHI	134.18	14.69	26.73	2.96	428	2739	3167	NA.	36	36	1128	Mar2000
LAKSHADWEEP	0.69	25.04	0.11	0.02	21	14	35	N.A.	0.13	0.13	343	May 2000
PONDICHERY	10.76	37.4	2.16	0.65	163	233	396	0.90	1.64	2,53	641	June 2000
Total	9812.7		177.48	596.2	368417	91693	460110	731.43	1238.63	1970.8	428	

The supervisory staff also ensures that the salesman maintains proper record of the sale and the sale proceeds are regularly remitted in Government.

MONITORING SYSTEM

A close monitoring system is essential to ensure that good quality ration/essential commodities reach the people in time. To ensure this, a set of Performa's has been devised to collect information regarding "INPUTS" as well as "OUT-PUTS" regularly on monthly basis. Each Fair Price Shop (FPS) & the Sub-store provide this OUTPUT information in first week of each month to the next higher authority. After consolidating it for all such centres operating under his control he sends the same in consolidation, from the entire area under his control to his controlling officer. This process is repeated at every level and reaches the Head of the Dept. by end of third week of each month. The operations of the Fair Price Shop (FPSs) are supervised and monitored by food inspectors.

TARGETTED PUBLIC DISTRIBUTION SYSTEM (TPDS) FOR THE POOR

Targetted Public Distribution System (TPDS) has been launched from 1st June 1997. About 32 crore people who are below the poverty line will get rice and wheat at subsidised price.

BENEFICIARIES OF TARGETTED PUBLIC DISTRIBUTION SYSTEM (TPDS)

The poor and vulnerable sections of the society identified as living below the poverty line who will normally include: landless agricultural labourers, marginal farmers, rural artisans/craftsman like potters, tapers, weavers, blacksmiths, carpenters, etc. in rural areas and persons earning their livelihood on a daily basis like porters, rickshaw pullers and hand cart pullers.

SALIENT FEATURES OF TARGETTED PUBLIC DISTRIBUTION SYSTEM (TPDS)

- About 32 crore people Below the Poverty Line (BPL) to get Rice and Wheat at about half the Central Issue Price.
- 10 Kilogram of foodgrains per family per month will be issued to all Below the Poverty Line families (BPL) at highly subsidised rate.

- Outgo of foodgrains under Targetted Public Distribution System (TPDS) is likely to be 184 lakh metric tonnes (LMT) in a year against 153 lakh metric tonnes (LMT) a year. The additional quantum will go to states where poverty is acute.
- The prices at which the foodgrains are to be issued to states will be Rs. 3.50 per Kilogram for rice and Rs. 2.50 per Kilograms for wheat.
- The subsidy involved under the restructured Public Distribution System is about Rs. 9000 crore for the Central Government.

On May 1997, Prime Minister of India announced that the PDS is an integral part of efforts towards poverty alleviation. The Government has now significantly modified this system to meet the special needs of the states with the highest concentration of the poor. The system will cover a population of 32 crores living below the poverty line. This system can succeed only if all the agencies involved work with commitment. The State Government, in particular has a very important role to play in implementing the system.

Minister of Food and Civil Supplies, Agriculture, Consumer affairs and Public Distribution Government of India, announced that the poorest section of the society are the ones who are very badly hit by such rise in prices of foodgrains. According to the estimate of Planning Commission, the number of such persons below poverty line is about 32 crores. Since in this section of the society, which is acutely affected by the change in the economy, Government is keen to protect them from the vagaries of the market to the extent possible. With this view, Government has decided to streamline the PDS with its focus on the poor. Thus under this Targetted Public Distribution System (TPDS) 10 Kg. of rice or wheat per month per family will be given to all families below the poverty line at about half the central issue prices. This new system can succeed only if the people and all political parties cooperate. Otherwise the scheme, because of its inherent pitfalls, will lead to heavy drainage of Government funds by diversion of the foodgrains meant for the poor to open market. The huge number of excess ration cards and number of families not utilising their entitlement of foodgrains, all lead to this diversion. If there is no proper check and vigilance in the issue of cards for the poor. There may be more bogus cards. PDS is maintained under the dual responsibility of Centre and State Government. The State Government has responsibility to see that the foodgrains issued by the Centre Government is made accessible to the people. The success of the system depends upon the interest and involvement of the State Government.

On 30th September, the Prime Minister of India announced in the Chief Minister's meeting that there should be a collective approach towards strengthening of the Targetted Public Distribution System (TPDS) which was a new experiment to make a dent in the poverty.

A review of Targetted Public Distribution System (TPDS) is necessary in order to make it acceptable in different states. The system, which is accepted by a State, should also be sustainable over a period of time. Sustainability is a function of coverage, scale of allocations, unit economic cost of foodgrains and unit subsidy which together determine the amount of subsidy that the exchequer is required to bear. The main complaint about Targetted Public Distribution System (TPDS) is the very low allocation of foodgrains i.e. 10 kgs per BPL family per month. The scale needs to be raised to 20 kgs. This system has adversely affected the tribals of Madhya Pradesh.

The Central Government supplied wheat and rice to the states at the following Central Issue Prices (CIP) for below poverty line (BPL) and above poverty line.

(APL) families during 1997-98.

Central Issue Prices (CIP): Rs. I Kg.

	Wheat		**Rice**	
		Supper Fine	**Fine**	**Common**
BPL	2.50	–	3.50	3.50
APL	4.50	7.50	6.50	

The dimension of the Targetted Public Distribution System (TDPS) being implemented since 1st June, 1997 is detailed below in tabular form:

Targetted Public Distribution System 1997-98

			BPL	APL	TOTAL
1.	No. of families in lakh		586.64	Not Fixed	1 645.76
2.	Allocation of Foodgrains (LMT)				
	Total		70	104	174
		Rice	37	62	99
		Wheat	33	42	75
3.	CIP (Rs./Kg)				
	Rice	Common	3.50	.	
		Fine	3.50	6.50	7.15
		Supper Fine	-	7.50	Weighed
	Wheat		2.50	4.50	Average
4.	Eco. Cost (Rs. 1Kg.)				
	Rice	Common	8.45	8.45	9.00
		Fine	8.88	8.88	Weighed
		Supper Fine	9.27	9.27	Average
	Wheat		7.61	7.61	
5.	Unit Subsidy (Rs. 1Kg.)				
		Rice	5.50	1 .85	
	Wheat		5.10	3.10	
6.	Total Subsidy (Rs/Crore)				
		Rice	2035	1147	31-82
		Wheat	1683	1302	2985
	Grand Total		3718	2449	6167

REVIEW OF THE PDS

The Performance of the PDS has not been uniform in the country. In some states the administration is weak, corrupt to the public needs. In these states deficiencies noted include huge shortage of stocks, fake supply entries in ration cards, diversion of commodities for sale to open market and bogus ration cards.

The PDS suffers from irregular and poor quality of foodgrains made available through Fair Price Shop (FPSs). The position in rural areas in these aspects is much worse than urban areas. Official statistics on the trend in rural urban distribution are not available. Major proportion of foodgrains is distributed in urban areas as compared to rural areas.

Most of the Fair Price Shops (FPSs) are economically not viable. The main reasons for this are low rate of commission, high cost of overheads, under weighing at the warehouse supply points and poor quality of supply stocks leading to unsold stocks.

The distribution of essential commodities through the PDS is so meagre that it can hardly suffice the need of a family. And even for this the consumers have to make repeated visits to the ration shops in their respective areas. Most of the time they come back empty handed with assurance that ration would be made available to them sometime next week. The modus operandi of the fair price dealers is to refuse ration to the card holders on one pretext or the other as many times as you can. This will make the consumers tired and harassed who would automatically stop coming to the ration shops and go to the open market.

The PDS in rural areas has not been given much attention. It was only in the sixth plan that explicit attention was given to rural areas.

CONCLUSION

In a welfare State the economists, planners and public have always hailed the PDS in general. PDS as it works at present seems to be coming up against its inner contradictions. It is given the task of keeping down prices to the consumer and also ensures payment of remunerative prices to the producer. The system has grown out of a particular historical situation which no more obtains in the country. Unfortunately, the system also did not receive adequate attention of the mass media for its modernisation. There has been criticism occasionally about the qualitative and quantitative aspects of the ration commodities but no suggestions about the improvement of modernisation of the system as a whole emerged so far. It is time now that the planners should pay attention for revamping of the PDS, which helps sustenance of millions of people in our country. This will require modernisation of the system by way of computerisation and effective monitoring at all levels for eliminating the drawbacks, which are inherent in the system. India requires eradication of poverty and raising almost half population of poverty above poverty line and also to innovate agricultural methods to meet the increased demands of growing population.

REFERENCES

Acharya K.C.S., 1983 Food Security System in India, New Delhi: Concept Publishing Company.

Bhatia B. M., 1983 A study in India's Food Policy, Malaysia : Asian and Pacific Development Centre.

Birla Institute of Scientific Research Economic Research Division, New Delhi, State in Foodgrain Trade in India, Vision Books.

Bora P. M., 1982 Food Administration in India, A Study of Indian State, Delhi: Ajanta Publications.

Chary A. Krishnama and Renuka C., 1991 Managerial problems facing fair price shops, Kurukshetra, December.

Chopra R. N., 1981 Evolution of Food Policy in India, New Delhi: Macmillan India Limited.

Economic Survey 1996-97.

Economic Survey 1997-98.

Guromoorthy T.R. 1992 Public Distribution System - a boon for rural people, Kurukshetra, May.

Kabra Kamal Narayan and Ittyerah Anil Chandy, 1992 The Public Distribution System in India, New Delhi: Eastern Books.

Koshy Abraham, 1991 Malfunctioning of the Public Distribution System: An Empirical Analysis, Vikalpa the Journal for Decision Makers, Vol. 16, No. 1, January-March.

Madi KR. 1991 Public Distribution System in India, Southern Economic, July 1.

Mishra Bhagabat, 1985 Economic of Public Distribution System in Food-grains, New Delhi: Ashish Publishing House.

Ninth Five Year Plan (1997. 2002), Vol. II.

Rao A. Muralidhar, 1991 How does PDS work in rural areas, Kurukshetra, December.

Singh U.K., 1991 Public Distribution System, New Delhi : Mittal Publications.

Sud Surinder, 1992 Making Public Distribution System More Effective, Yojna, April 15.

Tyagi Ramesh G., 1997 Management of Interlinkages: The Public Distribution System in India, Public Enterprise, Vol. 6, No. 3.

Union Budget 1997.

11

Canadian Perspective on Housing Development: Lessons for the Indian Context

*M. Mahadeva**

INTRODUCTION

Under the changing economic circumstance, market facilitation for the production of various social and economic goods and services has gained momentum. Besides in the most advanced and industrialised countries, market has increased its involvement (with investment) in economic sphere slowly in developing countries also. Mismatch between the public financial services and increasing demand for goods and services by a variety of consumers together with shrinking role of the governments have increased pace of market facilitation in these countries. Housing being both a social or merit and economic good, its production is largely dominated by private sector both in the developed as well as in the developing regions. Governments due to resource shortage and due to huge requirement of investment to meet the total housing needs have increasingly facilitating various players (production agents) in the

* *Associate Professor, Institute for Social and Economic Change, Nagarabhavi P.O., Bangalore-5600 72, India. Email: mahadeva@isec.ac.in.*

housing market with conducive environment. This conducive environment has enhanced opportunities both for production and consumption of housing benefits by different income consumers. On uninterrupted basis, finance which is one of the principal housing inputs is being supplied to consumers on affordable price by different financial institutions. Similarly a large number of private developers have been encouraged to take up land development as well as house construction activity. These positive measures have resulted in alleviating housing deprivation and in some cases brought about housing surplus. Governments on the other hand have redefined their commitment to only the persons of dire need. Housing subsidies and other incentives as the instruments of government intervention have continue to be the housing hopes of the most vulnerable groups notwithstanding their inadequacy and untimely. Interestingly governments in developing countries also gradually embracing the market facilitation for production of housing for various consumers. But unfortunately governments have given sufficient indications to reduce their role in housing largely without creating a facilitating environment for different players in the market. For example, a full-fledged and broad-based housing finance system is yet to be developed for increasing accessibility. Household savings are yet to become a principal source for housing investment. Housing financial institutions are in various stages of consolidating their role in the market. Above all, structural inadequacies like dichotomy and disparities in the application of resources are flourishing. Similarly with regard to residential lands, the public designated institutions have failed to live up to their own expectations. Legal hurdles are continuing to be the obstacles for large scale development activities of private actions. Thus as a result, considerable number of households especially of most deserving and vulnerable persons have been left in lurch without a hope of fulfilling their housing dreams.

The above account is a typical examples of a well developed as well as a mediocre market mechanisms in housing development respectively in a developed and in a developing countries. Canada is one such country to have embraced the market for the production of housing benefits at a large scale for the Canadians. Market support strategies were employed (Carter 1997, Prince 1995), over four decades to minimize the housing deprivations. In addition to the market facilitation, government has also shouldered the responsibility of meeting the housing needs of vulnerable groups. On the one hand market has been facilitated to produce adequate number of housing units to a large majority of Canadians and Government (mostly the federal) at the same time assumed the role of a provider to the people whose housing needs had not been met by the normal housing market. As part of the facilitation to the private sector measures were initiated to involve the major financial giants to supply the mortgage finances to the homebuilders (individuals, institutions etc) on continual basis. Mortgage insurance facility to the housing loans has been introduced ever since considering housing as a merit good as part of the securitisation of assets. Besides to promote housing activities and demand, ownership and rental sectors have been supported with financial assistance, subsidies and fiscal incentives. Creation of the Canada Mortgage and Housing Corporation (CMIHC) as an apex body to administer public funds has further facilitated the housing market. Although by and large the private sector is continued to play a bigger role in the housing market, decreasing role of the government over the years (especially from late 80s) has focussed the public action more towards meeting the housing of dire needy. Gradual reduction in the public investment and housing subsidies, withdrawal of fiscal incentives introduced during early 70s, have augmented the uncertainties. Increasing participation of governments at various levels (provincial and local municipalities) in the production of housing benefits to the most desired person has prompted the Federal Government to act as a lender of the last resort. As against this, Indian context is a classic example of market approach without a conducive environment for housing production. It is evident from the recently approved sectoral policy document. The National Housing and Habitat Policy (1998) has indicated to eliminate houselessness and bring about housing surplus, but largely without proposing any structural changes.

With this backdrop, the overall purpose of the paper is to draw lessons of the housing development strategies of Canada for the Indian context. Especially the paper addresses the issue as to how a facilitating environment could be created to maximize the housing production in India. Since financial mechanisms including the fiscal incentives have influenced the household decisions in Canada, their detailed examination would be an immense use for the Indian context. In the light of the positive outcomes in the housing production, the analysis make the case for the support of the market to create surplus in housing in view of the fact that the government alone is not able to meet the total need, more so in India. The paper is divided into four parts. Second section provides a Canadian perspective of housing development emphasizing the various financial mechanisms. The third section reviews the various outcomes of housing market with regard to housing surplus. The final section endeavour to present a number of lessons for India mainly with regard to changes needed in the financial sphere to fulfill the housing dream of the needy.

PART II

Housing through Market Facilitation

Canada is of course a democratic country, which has strongly adopted mixed economy approach in the production of social welfare. This has been ensured with a greater participation of market in the production and distribution of social and private good such as housing. The ideology has been neither total privatization nor wholesale participation of the government in the production and distribution of the housing benefits to various income groups. As Ramesh Mishra (1990) points out the objective of mixed economy approach "is to contain and reduce the role of the government in social welfare and to encourage non-governmental organizations and agencies.... Which in turn reduces the pressure on government financing, less bureaucracy, more decentralization, more community involvement and greater participation." Correspondingly, the production of housing units privately by the individuals as well as by the institutional builders has been very well supported financially and encouraged fiscally over a last few decades. In fact the long-term objective of the Canadian housing philosophy has been to ensure dwelling of a decent standard to all Canadian at prices they can afford that has been sought to achieve through grants and loans to developers and consumers. Again the overall purpose of such continuous support of the government to the private housing production industry and market is only to ensure healthy flow of funds for residential buildings and production of adequate number of homes.

The attempt to reduce the financial burden on the part of the government and greater participation of the Non-government agencies in terms of investments have been by and large achieved during 80s and 90s. This period was marked with reduction in residential public expenditure (relative terms) (Hulchanski 1990). If the erosion of residential expenditure during 80s and 90s is analysed first, it gives an indication of eroded importance of housing sector in the investment priorities of the country. The residential expenditure as percentage of the gross domestic expenditure has fallen from 5.97 percent in 1981 to 5.18 percent in 1999, although the fall was severe during 1995-96. Precisely, the residential expenditure (RE) has not increased corresponding to the increase in the Gross Domestic Expenditure (GDE) over the years. Notwithstanding 163 percentage growth in the GDE between 1981 and 1999, the RE registered to have grown only at 2.29 times as against an impressive growth of 2.63 times of GDE in the economy. Second, but further disappointing factor is the erosion of the role of the public sector and a drastic cut in the housing expenditure in the overall residential expenditure. Over two decades the share of the public sector investment has reduced from $ 436 million in 1981 to a mere $ 134 million in 1999. In percentage term, the same has fallen from 2.03 to less than half a percent or 0.27. The public expenditure cut in the housing sector has been more severe during late 90s in which the share was reduced to only half a percent and a gradual reduction even in that as can be noticed in table 1. As has been explained elsewhere the overall focus of the housing development strategy is to augment the role of the private sector and reduction of public expenditure in housing. Inferentially, there has been a phenomenal increase in the share of the private sector. It can even be said that the entire housing production is in the hands of private sector. The contribution of the private sector in the total residential expenditure has been doubled from $ 21077 million in 1981 to $49064 million in 1999 and in relative terms also the same has increased from 97.97 percent to 99.73 percent during the period.

Table 1 : Gross Domestic and Residential Expenditure (Public-Private) 1981 -1999 (Millions of Dollars)

Year	Gross Domestic Expenditure	Residential Expenditure Total	Public	Private	Col 3 as% Col 2	Col 4 as% Col 3	Col 5 as% Col 3
1	2	3	4	5	6	7	8
1981	360494	21513	436	21077	5.97	2.03	97.97
1985	485139	25696	285	25411	5.30	1.11	98.89
1990	678135	42247	471	41776	6.23	1.11	98.89
1995	807088	36312	176	36136	4.50	0.48	99.52
1996	833921	39717	133	39584	4.76	0.33	99.67
1997	873947	45193	125	45068	5.17	0.28	99.72
1998	895704	45030	125	44905	5.03	0.28	99.72
1999	949400	49198	134	49064	5.18	1.27	99.73

Source: CMHC 1999 Canadian Housing Statistics

The second tenet of housing development strategy is the creation of the facilitating environment for various players in the market. The chief purpose was to increase the housing production in the ownership as well as in the rental sectors in response to the growing demand from various segments. In fact one of the outcomes of the housing strategies implemented over five decades is the significant part of the rental housing stock in the pro-profit private sector. Most importantly, a vast majority of private rental units were not only subsidized but were given ownership status to their occupants as they were registered as condominiums during their construction period (Miron 1995, Hulchanski 1990). However notwithstanding the diminishing share of the rental units in the total stock, about three households in every ten lived in rented accommodation according to 1996 census. The dominance of the owner housing in the total stock has been achieved successfully by evolving a very strong housing finance system with four different pillars, (a) Private financial institutions (b) Mortgage loan insurance (c) Subsidies and (d) Lower interest rate and down-payment.

Private Financial Institutions (PFIs)

Private financial institutions consist of a host of corporate bodies which encompass the Chartered Banks (CBs), Life Insurance

Companies (LICs), Trust Companies (TCs) and Mortgage Loan Companies (MLCs). MLCs were initially started as subsidiaries of charted banks as the former were not allowed to make conventional mortgages until 1954 (Lawrence, 1974). These institutions are closely regulated by the federal and provincial authorities and assigned to each of them a specific resource constituency. CBs raises short-term deposits, LICs sells insurance bonds concerning to life, property and casualties and TCs manages trust and pension funds besides raising resources through term deposits (Fallis, 1990). Although each of these institutions has their own specific investment avenues, lending housing mortgage loans has been made a mandatory as back as 1950s and early 1960s. At the same time these institutions have also given freedom to determine the volume of funds to be made available for mortgage lending. There are a number of other institutions mostly consists of individuals, non-institutional bodies whose business is primarily a residual in nature, response to market influences and for their own personal considerations. Straight forwardly, it can be said that the mortgage lending for residential activities come from the private financial Institutions that constitute a significant portion in the total, which will be discussed in the latter stage.

Mortgage Loan Insurance (MLI)

The development success in the housing production is largely attributed to the insurance coverage of residential mortgage loans. The Canadian Housing Legislation 1954 insured all the mortgage loans made by private investors against borrowers' default. Mortgage insurance is one of the major steps towards securitizing the assets! investment. In fact mortgage insurance has infused a greater confidence among the private investors to participate in a very significant scale in the mortgage lending activities over the years. Even though the public mortgage insurance scheme (1954) was covering only the loans of new constructions, over the years the loans for the acquisition of an apartment and purchase of existing building have also been incorporated. Similarly, level payment mortgage and conventional mortgage methods were introduced during the immediate years of the scheme with a major difference in the loan-value ratio (90-95 percent in the case of the latter and 60 percent in the case of former respectively). However from mid 1960s they have been made identical (Fallis 1990, Ibid). Accordingly, the amortization period ranges between 25 and 30 years with 90-95 percent loan-value ratio and more importantly on identical interest rates and terms. Mortgage loan insurance is made available to all homebuyer through the CMHC approved financial institutions on the payment of the fees towards application and a premium. The insurance premium is between 0.5 percent and 3.75 percent of the loan amount, which depends on the size of the down payment. Further the premium can be paid as a lump sum or added to the mortgage loan (CMHC 1998). Flexibility to reduce the mortgage cost is an added advantage to the homebuyers. Payment of mortgage weekly or biweekly ensures the homeowners not only the reduction in principal but also saves interest. Yet other way of adequate financing of housing is through Mortgage Backed Securities (MBS). The National Housing Act (NHA) ensured a risk free investment, for residential mortgages, which are insured by CMHC. These securities have made available a pool of funds to benefit homebuyers at competitive rate of interest. These securities also offers higher rate of interest and security as an incentive to the investors.

Rental and ownership subsidies have also influenced the production of housing units up till 1980s, although a major part of them were reduced during 90s. As George Fallis (1990) illustrates, there were three types of housing subsidies. Under the first, households or families were allowed to dwell in the government owned buildings on payment of rent, which used to be 25-30 percent of total family income. However rents, thus collected were not in accordance with mortgage payment as well as operating cost of the buildings and hence federal and provincial governments have together shared the burden. In addition to this, tenants were also allowed to rent the units in the privately owned or buildings of non-profit organizations. Under such circumstances, tenants were charged only a rent geared to income, obviously which was below the market rent. Secondly, supply of rental units through non-profit organizations (cooperatives, municipal housing corporations, religious and other ethnic associations) was another form of secured dwelling to the tenants, which were constructed on subsidized loan and interest basis. Of late these organizations are supported with insurable loans with the assistance of CMHC to reduce the mortgage interest to 2 percent. Finally, rehabilitation subsidies were provided to the building owners, which needed a major repair. The purpose was to enhance the health of the buildings to ensure safety dwelling for additional 15 years. Below market rate loan up to CN $ 12,000 per unit werre supplied on a rental agreement with government. Full forgiveness of the loan was also allowed if the post rehabilitation rents were 50 percent or more below the average market rents. Similarly to that of rental subsidies, ownership subsidies were also provided although they were not substantial enough. Grants for first time owners and renovation assistance to meet the major repairs to improve the building's life up to 15 years were made available. Mortgage insured loans up to CN $ 10000 in urban areas and CN $25000 in rural areas with forgiveness are also being provided if owners continue to stay for 5 years after renovation. Second incentive was income tax exemption of saving for down payment up to a maximum of CN$1,000 per year and a lifetime total of $10,000. Although over the years these exemptions were withdrawn, the capital gains on the sale of an owner-occupied house are also exempted (Hulchanski, 1990).

Interest Rate and Down Payment

Other non-structural factors that influence the behaviour of housing consumers are the interest rate on mortgage loans and down payment. The general tendency is higher the interest on mortgage loan and the down payment lower the propensity to invest or postponement of owing a house and vice-versa. It is important to note that latter is the case of Canada in the sense that mortgage loans have been made available at fairly cheaper rate although they were at the higher side in the 80s. As can be seen in the table 2, there has been a phenomenal drop in the rate of interest on mortgage loans over a period of twenty years. Especially the decadal fall was more during 90s for all the three-term periods. The interest rates have been slashed down by 2.15 times from the average 14.39 percent for the period 1980-84 to 6.69 percent during 1995-1999 for one-year term. Similarly by 2.07 times from 15.24 average percent to 7.36 percent for three years term and by 2.02 times for 15.55 average percent to 7.71 percent for five years terms during the same period. Further the decadal fall registered at 1.59 fold, 1.53 fold and 1.50 fold for one, three and five years respectively. Furthermore, fall in the interest rate has turned out to be a boom for housing owners during 2000. The eleven months average interest of mortgage loan was considered to be the cheapest in the last 21 years as the same was 6.87, 7.49 and 7.80 percent for one, three and five years mortgage loans respectively. Yet other advantage within the interest rate is term period. The logical argument is that more the term period lesser the interest payment and vice-versa, as the difference in the interest rate further gets reduced if the mortgage term is for longer period. Not withstanding the direct relationship between the difference by period and interest rate, the table further depicts that 3 to 5 years terms of mortgage is found to be cheaper than 1 to 3 years. Longer the mortgage period further reduces the installment payments and ensures tension free income adjustments in the families.

Table 2 : Rate of Interest on Mortgage Housing Loans By Term Period 1980-2000 (In Percent)

Period	One Year	Three Years	Five Years	Difference Between		
				1-3yrs	3-5yrs	1-5yrs
1980-1984	14.39	15.24	15.55	0.85	0.31	1.16
1985-1989	10.98	11.35	11.64	0.37	0.29	0.66
Decadal Average	12.68	13.29	13.59	0.61	0.03	0.91
1990-1994	9.22	9.97	10.45	0.75	0.48	1.23
1995-1999	6.69	7.36	7.71	0.67	0.35	1.02
Decadal Average	7.95	8.66	9.09	0.71	0.43	1.14
2000*	6.87	7.49	7.80	0.62	0.31	0.93

* Figures are for 11 Months from January to November

Source : CMHC

Down Payment is an important component of the total housing cost, which is the difference between the housing cost and the loan amount. In other words, down payments are the consumer's contribution of the housing cost. Although down payment component is an accumulated savings of the low and moderate income families to realize the dream of owning a house, high income families pays the same without a specific saving mechanism. Many times even the high-income families also obtain housing linked savings as an instrument of Income Tax exemption if the same is induced by the state. Down payment besides serving as seed money of the housing project can also influence the housing related decisions of the families, in the sense that larger the down payment requirement lower is the housing demand (Lawrence, 1974, p36 Chap 3) and vice-versa. Similarly, it need not be said that down payment also varies the loan component and lower repayment and vice-versa) Not withstanding the fact of higher amount of mortgage loan repayment, Canada has successfully reduced the size of the down payment over the years in order to check the postponement of home purchase by the average families. Down payment requirement of single and semi-detached new homes has been reduced from 39 percent in the early 1960 to 25 percent in the late 60s (Carter 1997, p606) and further from 10 percent in 1991 to only 5 percent at present on CMIHC-insured mortgages of the purchase price of the unit (CMHC 1998, p3).

Besides facilitating the various players of the private sector through a number of financial mechanisms to ensure continuous flow of funds for housing activities by the federal government, similar attempts can also be seen at the provincial as well as at municipality levels. A number of institutions and community-based organizations have been nurtured at the local and provincial levels to produce housing benefits both for owner occupation and for rental purposes. Similarly, various developmental mechanisms have given greater role to the private initiatives. Financial assistance, subsidies, grants and supply of serviced lands are the tools employed to involve private and community organizations to produce, manage and improve the housing at these levels. As Carter (pp6l7 — 624) describes there have been community based housing schemes meant to provide non-profit rental and cooperative units for first time buyers. Private sponsors are required to earmark 60 percent of their units to the households of the core needs. Remaining units have to be rented to low-income families on 30 percent rent of their income and for moderate-income families on near to local market rates. Partnership groups were also encouraged with 100 percent capital financing to provide affordable self-contained housing to homeless individuals (youth, single mothers etc) to live independently. Further individual homeowners and private builders have also been provided with grants to take up renovation of the badly deteriorated dwellings, reconstruction, conversion of non-residential buildings into housing units, construction of additional new dwellings etc. Furthermore a number of municipalities have facilitated housing activities at their level mainly through self-financing which also includes subsidies, fiscal exemptions and by donating the serviced land on lease basis at below market price to the individuals as well as non-profits and community organizations. These agencies are encouraged to take up new construction and improvement of the existing dwelling units. Yet a number of municipalities have even changed regulations, administrative approval procedures to facilitate the housing activities on private initiative basis.

PART III

Impact of Market Facilitation

At the outset, the outcomes of the mortgage led financing system in the housing sector are the result of the continuous emphasis of the policy initiatives for over four decades. Housing development strategies commencing from mid 1950s characterizes the multifold increase in the investment under the protected environment as well as the housing stock in the ownership and the rental sectors. It can be said that major part of the investment has come from the leading financial giants which is long-term in nature with low capital risk. This section of the paper emphasizes housing production by the market in relation to the total investment. First important outcome of the market-supported strategies was the volume of investment. Housing sector has seen a total investment of over 5000 billion dollars between the period 1974 and 1999 on an average of 192 billion dollars per year. Over 93 percent of the total investment has come from the private sector (71.58 percent of institutional and 22 percent of non-institutional) and the rest from the government agencies. This itself shows the relative position of the private sector in the housing market. Although the share of the government source in the total investment is by and large constant at 6 percent during the period, institutional source has further strengthened its dominance by increasing its share from 63 percent in 1974 to 72 percent in 1999. However the non-institutional share including individuals has weakened its position from 32 percent to 21 percent (see table 3). With in the institutional source, the chartered banks have emerged as the dominant force in

Table 3: Growth and Source of Residential Mortgage Credit By Lending Institutions-1974-1999 (Millions of Dollars)

	Private Financial Institutions				Others	Government Agencies & Corporations			
Period	Charted Banks	Life Insurance Companies	Mortgage Loan companies & Trusts	Total (2+3+4)	Individuals, Non-Institutional Corporate & Other Companies	CMHC	Pension Fund	Total	Total (5+6+9)
1	2	3	4	5	6	7	8	9	10
1974	7387	4698	11138	23223	11823	-	1905	1905	36951
1980	104446	43657	121024	269127	122635	-	25300	25300	417062
1990	542010	120944	439924	1102878	335747	9664	68945	78609	1517234
1999	1638810	180984	377719	2197513	634702	144105	71343	215448	3047663
Total	2292653	350283	949805	3592741	1104907	153769	167493	321262	5018910
percentage	(63.81)	(9.75)	(26.44)	(71.58)	(22.01)	(47.86)	(52.14)	(6.40)	

Source:CMHC (1999) Canadian Housing Statistics

the mortgage investment owing to their wealthy resource base and institutional networking. With an exception in the early 1970s due to prohibition on mortgage investment, the chartered banks have established their position by supplying over 38 percent of the total institutional investment by 1980. Between 1980 and 1990 the banks virtually established their dominance and by the end of 1999 the total supply was around three-fourth of the total mortgage loans. On the other hand the mortgage loan companies being the subsidiaries and traditional financial intermediaries for mortgage investment, their relative position has eroded due to the full-fledged entry of chartered banks. Mortgage loan companies have held only 17 percent of the mortgage investment by 1999. Similarly Life Insurance Companies, although over the years the investment has increased in absolute terms, the relative position has significantly eroded as they supplied only less than 10 percent of the investment.

The second outcome of the market support strategy is the owner occupied and detached single housing stock (see table 4). From 1971 to 1999 the total housing stock has increased by 1.83 fold or 83 percent. The increase in the housing stock was substantial between the period 1971 and 1981 as compared to the rest of the reference period. The increase was 38 percent during 1971-81 but in the subsequent period the same was dropped to only 14 percent. Similarly the growth was further dropped to only single digit i.e., to 8 percent and 7 percent during 1991-96 and 1996-99 respectively. This overall increase in the housing stock has also brought about a phenomenal increase in the owner occupied stock as well as detached single units over the years. Owner stock and single detached units have increased their share in absolute terms although the relative growth is moderate in the total stock. The owner occupied stock has increased over two fold from 3630 thousands to 7359 thousands and in percentage term it has increased from 57.39 and 63.70. The period between 1971-81 was considered as boom for *ownership* housing as much of the success is achieved only during this period. In fact the growth in the ownership housing stock was much higher (at 41 percent) than the total housing stock increase for the period. For rest of the period the growth has fell from 23 percent between 1981 and 1991 to just 6 percent between 1996 and 1999. There has also been more or less two fold increase in the detached single units. These units have increased by 97 percent between 1971 and 1999. Akin to that of owner occupied stock, the substantial increase in the construction of single detached units has registered during 1971 to 1981. Although the growth rate was by and large the same to that of owner stock for rest of the period but between 1996 and 1999 the same has grown at 8 percent, which is slightly higher than the owner stock for the period. It is also clear from the table that attached double units have also increased their share in the total housing stock during the period of analysis. Notwithstanding the similar growth pattern of attached dwelling stock vis-a-vis detached and even owner occupied, the increase in the case of attached stock is over three fold. Attached stock has increased from 5.90 percent in 1971 to 10.50 percent during 1999.

Table 4 : Housing Stock by Tenure and Type, Canada 1971-1999 (Figures in thousands)

	1971	1981	1991	1996	1999
Total Housing Stock	6325	8757	10018	10820	11553
Owner Occupied Stock	3630	5123	6304	6948	7359
	(57.39)	(58.50)	(62.93)	(64.21)	(63.70
Rental Housing Units	2695	3634	3714	3872	4194
	(42.61)	(41.50)	(37.07)	(35.79)	(36.30)
Type of Dwellings					
Detached Single	3276	4615	5432	5949	6458
	(51.80)	(52.70)	(54.21)	(54.98)	(55.90)
Attached Double	373	613.	791	987	1213
	(5.90)	(7.00)	(7.90)	(9.12)	(10.50)
Row Units	168	226	229	236	231
	(2.65)	(2.58)	(2.29)	(2.18)	(2.00)
Apartment Units	2508	3303	3566	3648	3651
	(39.65)	(37.73)	(35.60)	(33.72)	(31.60)
Percentage of Mortgage of the Owner Stock	51.20	52.17	53.03	54.70	52.59

Source : Computed from various published census reports of Canada since 1971 and Canadian Housing Statistics 1999 (CMHC)

It goes without say that the substantial increase in the owner occupied, single detached and attached units has come at the cost of rental, apartment and even row units stock. Precisely, the relative share of the rental apartment and row units in the total housing stock has constantly decreased due to increasing construction of ownership as well as single units in about three decades. The expansion of housing units in these three segments (absolute terms) has failed to retain the supremacy that was established until 1971. Because the relative importance of the rental units has dropped continuously from 42.61 percent in 1971 to 36.30 percent in 1999. Similarly the apartment units from 39.65 percent to 31.60 percent during the period. Importantly a substantial drop was registered during 1981 to 1991 in the case of rental sector and was during 1996 to 1999 in addition to 1981 to 1991 in the case of apartment units. The drop was -4.43, —2.23 and —2.12 percent respectively of the rental and apartment units. Row units have also last their share marginally from 2.65 percent in 1971 to 2 percent in 1999.

The factors that have contributed to increase in the home ownership (and also detached single dwelling units) over the years are a question of significant importance. Independent family formation being the major determinant, the censuses for the different periods has accounted a continuous addition (see table 5). Especially family households have increased by 2.75 million in absolute figures or a little over 58 percent between 1971 and 1996. Of the three different constituents of independent family households, the growth is eye catching among the husband and wife families in the sense that this category account to a majority (1.82 million) in the total net increase or over 66 percent. Similarly, the other segments of family households although share the success equally (more or less) spouse with single child and parent or two children or two parents families have added 0.74 million followed by 0.73 million of the families of spouse with children. However the significance of the other constituents in the independent family household is being eroded over the years from 23.35 percent in 1971 to 9.24 percent in 1996. As John Miron (1995, p. 583) argues husband-wife couple and an other person aged 20 or older are the potential households to occupy a separate dwelling. It is further argued that there exists a positive relationship between the increase in family income and housing consumption.

Correspondingly, census 1996 clearly indicates the increase in annual income of not only economic families with two or more persons but also among the married couples, two parent families with children and married couple with other relative's families. Especially the average income after tax has increased between 1991 and 1998 by 6.49 percent in the case of economic families. Significantly, the average income of the married couple families exceedingly increased by 8.85 percent than that of economic families followed by 7.72 percent (two parents families with children) and 7.10 percent (married couples with other relatives), during the above period.

Table 5: Growth of the Independent Families (In Million)

		1971	1981	1991	1996
1	Population	21.57	24.34	27.30	28.85
2	Households	6.04	8.28	10.02	10.82
(A)	Family Households	4.93	6.23	7.23	7.68
(a)	Husband-wife families	1.58	2.40	3.13	3.40
(b)	Spouse-children families	1.04	1.40	1.67	1.77
(c)	Spouse-single child & parent or two children or parents	1.06	1.53	1.73	1.80
(d)	Other families	1.25	0.90	0.70	0.71
(B)	Non-family Households	1.11	2.05	2.79	3.14

Source: Censuses 1971, 1981, 1991 and 1996 CMHC — Canadian Housing Statistics

Thus, with increasing income among the most potential households, higher loan-value ratio, lower rate of mortgage loans and lower level of down payment have also enhanced the housing opportunities especially from early 80s. In addition, fiscal incentives mainly in the form of tax exemptions under Registered Home Ownership Programme (RI-lOP) and withdrawals from the Registered Retirement Savings Plan (RRSP) for down payment of housing cost and others have strengthened the hands of homebuyers (Nick Van Dyk, 1995). Yet, Direct Subsidy programmes such as the Assisted Home Ownership Programme (AHOP) have also increased the opportunities by accumulating the capital required for down payment of a house for the young people.

Last but the most important oulcome of the market supported strategies is the housing units production vis-a-vis the total households. In about three decades, the continued supports have posted surplus in the housing production (see table 6), in the sense that housing units exceeded the number of households (of both family and non-family). During the period under review, there has been a total completion of 5.57 million housing units as against a total of 5 million households which leaves a surplus of 0.57 million units. A substantial part of the surplus in housing production has been witnessed during nineties and seventies. The total production was in the order of 1.31 and 2.47 million households as against 1.03 and 2.24 million households and thus lives a surplus of 0.28 and 0.23 million units. Also the market had produced the surplus during eighties, the same was far less as compared to seventies and nineties. Further, even if it is presumed hypothetically that all family household occupy the most preferred single detached, double attached and row units because of their relative advantages, there exists still a surplus of 0.43 million units as the production of the units far exceeds (1.02 million) against a total family households of 0.59 million during nineties. By and large, the same arguments holds good for eighties also, although the surplus is almost half of the nineties.

PART IV

Lessons for the Indian Context

What are the lessons that could be drawn from the Canadian experience of market facilitation in housing development? Housing is a 'collective good' than a 'social good' in Canada, produced largely by the market with a strong support of the public action for the benefit of the consumers. Government has become a true facilitator of the market and the last resort than a direct provider excepting for the targeted lowincome households and in meeting the needs of the special segment of population. One of the pre-conditions of the housing success is the continuous and adequate flow of funds for housing activities, which the Canadian public action has successfully achieved it without developing a specialized housing finance system. Asset securitisation measures (mortgage investment insurance) have boosted the private financial institutions to expand their investment avenues. Financial incentives (lower rate of interest, less down payment and higher loan-cost ratio) have contributed in their own ways in meeting the housing needs over the years. India is one of the developing nations, which came out with a public action on housing (GOI 1998) recently which is intend to bring about a surplus in the housing production and to create a conducive environment to facilitate the various players in the housing market especially the private sector. Besides the policy also intended to expand the mortgage market, as part of the overall financial market to meet the financial needs of the sector. Towards achieving these objectives, Canadian experience of housing development with market support could be a direction to the Indian context. Before the discussion on the specific lessons to be drawn to the Indian context, it is important to address as to why India needs these lessons? This question can be answered with the following three reasons.

Table 6 : Housing Completions and Household Growth 1971-1999 (Figures in lakhs)

	1971-1981	1981-1991	1991-1999
1. Net Increase in Households	22.40	17.37	10.26
Average household increase	2.24	1.74	1.14
2. Net Family Households	12.98	10.03	5.90
Average family Households	1.29	1.00	0.66
3. Net Non-family Households	9.42	7.34	4.36
Average Non-family Households	0.94	0.73	0.48
4. Net Dwellings Completion	24.66	17.92	13.12
Average Dwelling Completion	2.46	1.79	1.46
5. Net Dwellings Surplus (7-4)	2.26	0.55	2.86
Average Surplus	0.22	0.05	0.32
6. Net Single Detached Completion	-	10.47	7.76
Average Single Units Completion	-	1.05	0.86
7. Net Double Attached Completion	-	0.73	0.94
Average Double Units Completion	-	0.07	0.10
8. Net Row Units Completion		1.23	1.49
Average Row Units Completion	-	0.12	0.16
9. Net Apartment Units Completion	-	5.49	2.93
Average Apartment Completion	-	0.55	0.32

Source : Census Reports for 1971, 1981, 1991 and 1996; and CMHC (1999), Canadian Housing Statistics.

Note : '-' indicates not available

Limited Public Action : The Constitution of India, as in the case of Canada, has vested with the 'State Government' a middle level tier a major responsibility of meeting the housing needs of the people. Union Government at the same time is expected to take lead in designing the housing development strategies from time to time reflecting the different needs of the people and to evolve the housing finance mechanisms. However in practice the housing strategies employed over four decades immediately after independence were not only ad hoc but also failed to reflect the overall needs of the sector as well as the people. Housing production and supply mechanisms have been by and large uncorroborated with family formation and subsectoral needs. This has led to a huge gap between the construction and growing needs. Similarly the State Governments have continued to share only a limited part of their resources while implementing centrally sponsored target oriented housing schemes. They have failed in evolving their own strategies to meet the total housing needs of the people. Further although self-housing practice could be a potential method, creation of a conducive environment to facilitate different players in the housing market is yet a dream. In other words, although private sector shares a major component in the total investment in the housing sector it has been left to itself. Land being one of the principal inputs of. housing, paucity of funds have left a large chunk of the same unserviced in urban areas (World Bank, 1985). Similarly in rural areas residential site owners (largely distributed under site cum construction assistance scheme) have been left in lurch owing to financial difficulties.

Weak Financing Systems : One of the State sponsored dichotomy is the development of the specialised housing finance institutions along with the commercial banks to finance the housing activities. Although simultaneous existence of housing financial institutions and commercial banks has brought in a greater degree of competition, but have failed to reach a wide range of builders especially the common man in rural areas. Each of them are competing for resource mobilisation and refinancing with separate lending procedures, interest rates, amortization period, etc. Commercial banks with huge branch network have established predominance in household's savings mobilisation and cater to the housing needs of the people largely in urban areas. Whereas, HFIs mobilise resources from the capital market and refinances the same at slightly higher rate of interest. The amortization period is generally varies between 15 and 20 years in the case of HFIs besides less down payment in highly deserving cases. Commercial banks on the other hand lends generally up to 15 years and 75 percent of the construction cost of the houses. Thus the prospective house builders are caught between the two different housing finance systems in urban areas for relative advantages (or disadvantages). While at the same time, both the systems have failed to broad base their activities and to minimize the informal financing practices (let alone replace it) especially by the low and nearer middle income families. It is important to note that both the systems are catering only the income class families that too in urban areas and as a result the financial needs of the non-income people have either neglected or unserved. It is because of these structural weakness and practical difficulties in the housing finance systems, the informal financing of housing is perpetuating at higher scale especially in rural areas.

Eroded Confidence and Lack of Security for Investment : The second State sponsored 'directed investment" under anti-poverty programmes over four decades has generated aversion including eroded confidence on the part of the poorer sections owing to growing incidence of non-repayment of loans. This has also resulted in its own way on housing finance in rural areas. There has been an enhanced apprehension on the part of the financial institutions in meeting the housing financial needs of the poorer sections because of its long-term nature, non-repayment incidence. Together with the eroded confidence, lack of protective measures to securitize the institutional investment for housing especially the doubtful loans in the events of borrowers default have further impeded the situation and strengthened the withdrawing process. At this juncture, government as an overall representative and provider for these sections, should device a range of alternative measures. One such alternative is the mortgage insurance, which was altogether missing in the Indian context. In this regard, notwithstanding the intention of the NHHP to bring about measures to protect the institutional investment for housing, the inordinate delay would further deprive the housing benefits to the low and middle income in general and poorer sections in particular.

The Canadian experience of housing development with deep market support need not be a lesson in toto for the Indian context as there is wide range of differences between these two countries, especially in regard to the importance attached to housing development and housing consumers are concerned. Clearly there are affordable and unaffordable housing consumers in India whose needs can be met by the market and the government respectively. In terms of the size of these consumers, although the unaffordable poor constitute to a little over 40 percent of the total population (World Bank, 1999) the market needs to be facilitated in order to meet the housing needs of the other consumers. In that direction, the Canadian experience as described below could be a direction for the Indian context as they are the potential instruments of increasing the housing stock (including among the low income and poorer sections) and thereby minimize the housing deprivation.

1. Considering the size of the each type of the consumers (Income class and non-Income class) of housing, it is immensely necessary to consider housing a collective as well as social good rather than only a collective good as in the case of Canada. Market could be a chief agent of production of the collective good for the consumption of income class; of course the players needs to be supported with as discussed in the coming paragraphs. The market needs to be given an impression that it enjoys the support of the public action and the same would be protected at times of crises or need. Further government being the chief provider of the social good for the consumption of the non-income class can also produce the same with the help of the private action as in the case of Canada. In which case a large number of non-profit organizations are being supported to implement the social housing programmes for the exclusive consumption of low-income groups of those of the excluded persons of the market. In India, the already existing non-profit organizations like housing cooperatives could be a better alternative to implement the social housing programmes. At present the fullest potentials of the housing cooperative societies, whose numbers are more than 80,000 (NABARD 1996) have been untapped as they were left to

themselves hitherto. These societies being the people's organization can better reflect the needs of the low-income groups.

2. Development of a strong mortgage system to finance the housing activities in the ownership as well as rental sectors is a necessary pre-condition. Mortgage finance could be a part of the overall financial market as can be seen in Canada instead of developing a separate housing financial system (as is in India over last two decades with limited success). Commercial banks as the chief household saving agent could be a suppliers of mortgage loans for housing as they have a strong resource base. Such a proposition would minimize the ambiguities in the different interest structures as followed by HFIs and commercial banks at present. This would also strengthen the Central Bank to evolve a uni-interest structure under one umbrella for mortgage loans and others. The new mortgage financial arrangements would eventually call for a merger of the existing Housing Financial Institutions (HFIs) with the National Housing Bank (NHB) as an apex body and further with the general financial system. It is necessary to mention at this juncture that a significant part of the success especially the mortgage loans have come from the private financial institutions in Canada without evolving a separate financial system. The Housing and urban Development Corporation of India (HUDCO) a principal designated agency for housing could be reorganized as a mortgage developer, a guarantor and an implementing authority of social housing programmes of the government, on the lines of the Canada Mortgage and Housing Corporation (CMHC). Make available the mortgage loans at lower rate of interest with the lowest down payment would be an impetus for the expansion of ownership housing. This would also promote rental sector, which is an important segment of the housing market.

3. Investment protection against the risks would bring about more mortgage loans to the different housing consumers. The same can be ensured with the development of the

mortgage insurance scheme to provide security to the mortgage financial institutions in the event of the borrowers default. The modus operand of the scheme could be that every mortgage loaner should pay the insurance premium of a certain percentage of the loan amount to be paid either as lump sum or could be added to the mortgage loan repayment schedule. In India, as mentioned elsewhere not only the need for the reorganization of HUDCO to oversee the mortgage operations including the securitization of financial assets is warranted but also the development of the alternative strategies to ensure a decent housing to the citizens.

4. Besides the supply side, the demand side should also be strengthened to motivate the people to meet their housing needs. This can be done through a number of fiscal incentives. Mainly the tax exemptions would go a long way for the homeowners. It would be an additional strength to the first time homeowners, if they were provided income tax exemption for a major part of the payment of the principal as well as interest on mortgage loans. It would be a further boost if they enjoy the benefit of concessions in the stamp and registration fees. Capital gains exemption for the proceeds of the sale of ownership units could be encouraged up to a desirable extent although the same promotes a certain degree of speculation. Housing linked savings needs to be promoted at large scale with similar fiscal incentives. This would not only promote the thrift but could even a down payment of the mortgage loan, as has been operated in Canada. Although in India, some of these exemptions are already extended to the home owners from the beginning of 80s a lot more needs to be done in the years to come especially in promoting the household savings for housing and stamp and registration besides continuing the on-going exemptions. Because foregoing a part of the revenue income to fulfill a social cause of housing would be a better strategy than discouraging fresh investment, which has an administrative expenditure.

REFERENCES

1. Tom Carter (1997), Current Practices for Procuring Affordable Housing: The Canadian Context, *Housing Policy Debate* Vol 8. issue 3, pp 593-631.
2. Michael J Prince (1995), The Canadian Housing Policy Context, *Housing Policy Debate,* Vol 6, issue 3, pp 721-758.
3. Ramesh Mishra (1990), The Collapse of the Welfare Consensus—The welfare state in the 1980s. *Housing the Homeless and poor, New Partnership among the Private, Public and Third sector (Ed)* George Fallis and Alex Murray, University of Toronto Press, Canada), pp 82-114.
4. David J Hulchanski (1990), Canadian Government Housing Expenditures: A Ten Years Review, *Canadian Housing,* Vol 7, No 1, pp 19-22.
5. John Miron (1995), Private Rental Housing: The Canadian Experience, *Urban Studies,* Vol 32, No 3, pp 579-604.
6. Lawrence B Smith (1974), *The Postwar Canadian Housing and Residential Mortgage Markets and the Role of the Government,* University of Toronto Press.
7. George Fallis (1990), Housing Finance and Housing Subsidies in Canada, *Housing Studies,* Vol 27, No 6, pp 877-903.
8. Canada Mortgage and Housing Corporation (CMHC) (1998), *Your Housing Experts,* pp 2-4.
9. Nick Van Dyk (1995), Financing Social Housing in Canada, *Housing Policy Debate,* Vol 6, issue 4, pp 815-848.
10. Government of India (1998) *The National Housing and Habitat Policy,* Ministry of Urban Development Housing.
11. World Bank (1985), *Urban Housing in India,* Staff Working Paper, Number 730.
12. World Bank (1999), *World Development Report,* Oxford University Press, P.
13. National Bank for Agriculture and Rural Development (1996), *Statistical Statements Relating to Cooperative Movement in India,* Part II: Non-Credit Societies, Mumbai.

ACKNOWLEDGEMENTS

The research on which this paper is based was funded by the Canadian International Development Agency (CIDA) through the Development Studies Programme of the Shastri Indo-Canadian

Institute (SICI). Neither CIDA nor SICI endorses the view expressed herein. The author is grateful to CIDA and SICI for the financial support and the University of Toronto, especially CUCS for academic affiliation. This work would not have been possible without the support of Prof David J Hulchanski, Director CUCS, who was my academic contact person and benefited by the academic discussions and comments on the paper, for which the author is indebted. Similarly the help and support of MS Swarnalatha Vemuri, a social worker, Dr Lori Muddrick Donnon (SICI), Mr Robert Genier (CMHC), Ms Grace Ramirez (CUCS) and Supriya Shekar, Jayashekar Mambally during my stay in Toronto are gratefully acknowledged. However, the author alone is responsible for any mistakes.

12

Gender Justice: A Study of Policy Approaches

B. Meena Rao and*
*S. Uma Devi**

An individual with indisputable rights of liberty and freedom is the fundamental dream behind universal equality. Given that every human being is equal to the other, it implies that a man and woman are taken as inherently equal. But the whole world knows this is not how it is. Throughout the world women have usually fewer rights and a lower social status than men. The traditional role of a wife and mother dominates and most woman's lives center around their households. Hence, women the world over, are still demanding for equality and justice because of the widespread discrimination they face in all walks of life. Accordingly, many policies and programmes are being drafted with some awareness of their marginalized position. Today, gender analysts are paying special attention to the wide-ranging frameworks regarding the perspective, approach and strategies advocated at different forums for understanding and combating women's unfavourable placement in the society. (Dagar

* *Associate Professor, Dept. of Politics and Public Administration,*
* *Associate Professor, Centre for Criminal Justice, Andhra University, Visakhapatnam, A.P. India.*

Rainuka, 1998). This paper attempts to throw some light on the development of different conventions, declarations, laws, rules and regulations for the global to the national and to the state level which have been introduced specifically to meet the needs which the women were hitherto denied.

The agenda of all global deliberations has been engendered. Now the focus is on equal participation of men and women in all walks in life. It has been globally accepted that a social transformation is necessary to establish gender justice. Nonetheless, the United Nations Report (1997) on the status of women worldwide states that, "the reality of women's lives throughout the planet indicate that gender equality in all its manifestations remains a long way off. Women are still the group of people who undertake the bulk of the unpaid work which is done in the society, live in greatest poverty, control the fewest resources, and (most of whom) are hardly educated even to the primary school level" (Dagar Rainuka 1998). This adverse placement of women in the society is the result of rigid behaviour and suppressive customs against the female sex. To cite a few examples:

- Roman Catholic press and bishops in several countries like Africa, Ireland, Italy, the United States, the Philippines and Brazil have been exploiting their religious authority to obtain sexual favours from nuns, in some cases to rape and subsequently obliging the victims to seek an abortion. (William Phillip, 2001).
- Women in Kuwait still do not have the right to vote, though they have been campaigning for it for thirty years. In 1999, the Amir decreed that women should have full equal rights but the parliament rejected it.
- Widows in Africa are considered bad omens, excluded from auspicious events and made to undergo tortuous rituals. They have no right to inheritance or custody of children, but can be 'inherited' by other men in the family and are sexually abused.
- South Korea suffers a balance of trade deficit of more than two billion dollars. In order to compensate for this the

government forces young women to sell their bodies in order to directly earn foreign exchange.

- Saudi Arabian Constitution prohibits women to drive automobiles believing it to be a source of undeniable vices.
- A British woman police sergeant has claimed that it is common practice for male colleagues to rubber stamp new female arrivals at a station on thier breasts and buttocks with the official station stamp.
- According to an I.L.O. study, women receive only one-tenth of the world's income and less than one hundredth of the world's property and perform nearly 2/3 of its work hour.
- "Market driven growth policies" are undermining women's right. In many of the countries, it is women who are losing jobs in the face of growing unemployment. They are being denied equal opportunities and access to health services with cut backs in social sector spending.
- Among industrialized countries the Japanese and Canadian women top the list of those in low paid jobs.
- In the Ukraine, formerly a part of the Soviet Union, 80 per cent of those currently unemployed are women. And in countries such as Zimbabwe, macroeconomic restructuring has led to the growth of the informal sector which employs mainly women and young girls. "Women," according to the report of the Women's Environment and Development Organisation, "are the shock absorbers for structural changes."
- In Pakistan the testimony of two women is equal to that of one man as evidence and to prove rape, at least four adult Muslim males have to be eyewitnesses. As that situation is near impossible, rape in Pakistan is rarely proved and rapists roam free. (Rashtra Mahila, 2000).

Against this background, it is only predictable that, from different quarters of the world gender analysts have focused attention for providing access to facilities and means and eliminating discrimination and violence on the basis of sex, which is a global phenomena and concern (Dagar Rainuka, 1998). Right from the late 1700s and early 1800s many thinkers have stressed on the importance of liberty, equality and reason of every individual. On the eve of the French Revolution (1789-1799) the Marquis de Condorcet, a French philosopher spoke in favour of women's right to vote. The British author Mary Wollstonecraft argued for women's rationality and equality with men in her book, 'A Vindication of the Rights of Women (1775-1783). Mill (1869), challenged the hierarchy of monarchy, the order of the church and natural fortitude and replaced it by the "conception of individuals as free and equal beings emancipated from the ascribed, hierarchical bonds of tradition" (Mill 1975). This new intellectual atmosphere helped justify women's rights to full citizenship.

The first-wave of feminism questioned women's exclusion from citizenship rights, education and employment, and not only gained women some legal, political and economic rights, but importantly, brought into focus women's impoverished status and the need to improve it. The challenge was taken up by the second feminism wave which campaigned for the legislation of equal rights and focused attention on women's discrimination in employment and politics on grounds of sex. During the last five decades efforts towards gender equality have succeeded in making at least visible this unfavourable status of women as a result of which women movements have become a truly global phenomenon.

The concern to eliminate all obstacles that stand in the way of enjoyment by women of equal status with men is reflected in the strategies of international agencies such as the United Nations. The Commission on the Status of Women (CSW) was established as a functional commission of the Economic and Social Council on June 21, 1946 to prepare recommendations to the Council on promoting women's rights in political, economic, civil, social and educational fields. The Commission began with 15 members, and now consists of 45 members elected by the Economic and Social Council. It makes recommendations to the Council on urgent problems requiring immediate attention in the field of women's right and the object is to promote the principle that, men and women shall have equal rights. The Commission's mandate was expanded in 1987 by the Council in its resolution 1987/22. Following the 1995, Fourth World Conference on Women, the General Assembly mandated the Commission to integrate into its work programme, a follow-up process to the conference in which the Commission should play a catalytic role, regularly reviewing the critical areas of the Platform of Action (UN Website on Women watch).

The declaration of the International Women's Year by the United Nations General Assembly in 1975 could be considered as the turning point. Since then, a mobilisation process began, which resulted in the adoption on international covenants and instruments, national policies and plans, and grass root activism for achieving gender equity (UN, 1998) and generated many debates on the status of women. The year marked a call of action to ensure the full integration of women in the total (economic, social and cultural) developmental efforts (Mustafa & Singh, 1998).

The International Women's Decade (1975-85) was marked in the history as a period of intense data gathering activities on women's economic role and participation pattern in family and society. (Lalita, 1996). While the International Women's Day is the story of ordinary women as makers of history, it is rooted in the centuries-old struggle of women to participate in society and social change on an equal footing with men. The idea of an International Women's Day first arose at the turn of the century, which in the industrialised world was a period of expansion and turbulence, booming population growth and radical ideologies. Since those early years, March 8th, the International Women's Day has assumed a new global dimension for women in developed and developing countries alike. Recently in 1999, in its effort to make International Women's Day a "day to remember" UNESCO had appealed to the media worldwide to give editorial charge of news on this day to women. In a special appeal, UNESCO Director-General Koichiro Matsuura has said," If journalists, the media and the organizations that represent them come together to make this initiative a success, then for the first time in history, a day's news output in both print and broadcasting, throughout the world will fall under the editorial responsibility of women" (Rashtra Mahila, 2000).

The growing international women's movement has been strengthened by four global United Nations' Women's Conferences. The first world conference on women was conducted in 1975 in Mexico (i.e. Plan of Action). The theme of the conference was threefold: equality, development and peace. (Dhawan, 1995). It was emphasized at this conference that discrimination against women violates (a) the principle of equality of rights and respect for human dignity, (b) is an obstacle to the participation of women on equal terms with men, in the political, social, economic and cultural life of their countries, (c) hampers the growth of the prosperity of society and the family and makes more difficult the full development potentialities of women in the service of their countries and of humanity, and that "... the full and complete development of a country, the welfare of the world and the cause of peace require the maximum participation of women on equal terms with men in all fields." (Shah, 1995) The conference forwarded various suggestions for the recruitment, nomination and promotion of women in various branches of government, public bodies, trade unions and pressure groups. In 1980, a mid-decade conference was held in Copenhagen, Denmark (i.e. the Programme of Action). In this conference, discussion revolved round three more factors namely, education, employment and health (Khan 1998).

From July 15th to 26th 1985, a world conference to review and appraise the achievements of the UN Decade for Women was held in Nairobi (Kenya). The Nairobi Conference (Forward Looking Strategies) was built on the earlier world conference on women, also on the work of the UN Commission on the status of women and on the activities and ideas of the worldwide women's movements. These strategies were designed to serve as guidelines for the creation of a new world order based on equality, development and peace. Some of the measures were intended to affect women directly. It was stressed at the conference that, 'women by virtue of their gender, experience discrimination in terms of denial of equal access to the power structure that controls the society and determines development issues and peace initiatives,' and noted: 'for equality to become a reality for women, the sharing of power on equal terms with men must be a major strategy.' It also emphasized that success in this area would depend "upon whether or not women can unite to help each other (Chowdhury, 1994).

The Fourth World Conference on Women in Beijing in September 1995, (i.e. Platform for Action) was the largest conference ever held by the United Nations with some 17000 participants representing 189 States and more than 2,500 non-governmental organizations. Besides the already identified areas of women's neglect, the Beijing conference identified some more critical areas of concern for today's women. These are, poverty, violence, armed and other conflicts, human rights, mass media, environment and development. The commitments made by different representatives in Beijing reflect the understanding that women's equality must be a central component of any attempt to solve the world's social, economic and political problems (Rashtra Mahila, 2000). The conference emphasized the importance of governmental and non-governmental organizations in educating women to exercise their civil, political and social rights. It was also pointed out that in this process of consciousness raising, efforts would have to be made to fix definite time-bound targets and even resort to a quota system. In spite of all this, women everywhere continued to be marginally represented in decision-making processes which have a direct impact on them.

The world community has also identified violence against women in its various forms as a clear violation of women's rights. And in accordance with this in many countries, provisions guaranteeing enjoyment of human rights without discrimination on the basis of sex have been included in their constitutions or integrated into the legislative reforms. Discriminatory legal provisions have been repealed and legal literacy and other measures are introduced to alert women of their rights and ensure their access to those rights.

The Convention on the Elimination of all Forms of Discrimination Against Women (CEDAW) was adopted in 1979 by the UN General Assembly. This is directed towards national legislation to ban discirimination against women in all spheres — political, economic, social, cultural and civic. This is often described as an international bill of rights for women. Consisting of a preamble and 30 articles, it defines what constitutes discrimination against women and sets up an agenda for national action to end such discrimination. The Convention is the only human rights treaty which affirms the reproductive rights of women and targets culture and tradition as influential forces shaping gender roles and family relations. Countries that have ratified or acceded to the Convention are legally bound to put its provisions into practice. The Convention which entered into force on September 3, 1998, has as of October 2000, 166 state parties. Keeping in step with the Convention twenty three nations observed the Human Rights Day on 10th December 1999, by signing a legal protocol that would enable women for the first time to submit sexual discrimination complaints directly to the UN as well as protest against other violations covered in the Convention. This landmark protocol would allow women to bypass the national governments and have the UN Commission on the status of women investigate their grievance. The Commission would then attempt to persuade the respective governments to rectify the abuses. (Rashtra Mahila, 2000).

It was universally agreed that female sexual exploitation was interrelated to factors such as poverty and the cultural devaluation of women. Any steps to combat trafficking it was felt must assess and understand the background of poverty, and the lure of money that leads women and children to prostitution. These factors are being recognized and attempts have been made to form networks around these issues at the latest World Congress on Commercial Sexual Exploitation of Children (Stockholm, 31 August, 1996).

In November 2000 for the first time the Security Council tailored a resolution on the impact of war on women and girls. Then open Council session, initiated by Namibia followed a closed-door meeting where members listened to women from Somalia, Sierra Leone and other war zones call for protection against rape and sexual abuse, punishment for the perpetrators and equality with men in peace efforts. The Security Council has adopted unanimously its first resolution, recommending women in war zones to get special treatment as victims of conflicts and be partners at the negotiation table. The resolution urges Secretary-General to use women as chief envoys to pursue peace talks or head peacekeeping missions. Mr. Kofi Annan has been asked to carry out a study on the impact of war on women and girls and the role of women in "peace-building and the gender dimensions for peace processes and conflict resolution." (Times of India, 2000). From the Commission of Status on Women —1946, declaration of International Women's Decade — 1975-85, the Plan of Action, the Programme of Action, Forward Looking Strategies, and the Platform of Action, CEDAW and now women to be a part of peace talks are a few attempts made by the UN to improve the status of women throughout the world. All such conferences under the aegis of the United Nations has helped make a rallying point for coordinating efforts to demand women's rights and participation in the political and economic process. Thus, where once women fought to put gender equality on the international agenda, gender equality is now one of the primary factors shaping that agenda.

NATIONAL POLICIES

A significant result of international initiatives and UN meetings on women, in so far as Indian women are concerned, is a visible shift from viewing women as targets of welfare policies to their emergence as a critical factor of development. The scattered or piece-meal approach to the advancement of women, unrelated to policies and strategies for economic development is now replaced by an integrated participatory approach. A new holistic approach emphasizing on the needs, aspirations and choices, of the women was adopted for bringing them into the mainstream of national development programmes.

Resistance to women's oppression in India neither began nor ended with British colonial rule but had its roots in the Indian social structure and cultural heritage. The Prevention of Sati Act was enacted in 1829 which out-lawed widow burning. Widow remarriage was legalized in 1856 through the efforts of social reformers such as Raja Ram Mohan Roy and Dayanand Saraswati. By the beginning of the 1900s women's movement became more aligned with the nationalist political campaigning in India's freedom struggle. The leaders of the freedom movement viewed the emancipation of women as a part of the greater movement for social and political liberation. An Indian Women's Conference organized in 1904 took an active part in the boycott of foreign goods in 1905. In the twenties and early thirties the All-India Congress Committee constituted study groups on women's issues.

By 1927, three major nationwide organisations, the Women's India Conference (1917), National Council of Women (1925) and the All-India Women's Conference (1927) were all discussing major women's issues and social problems concerning them.

In 1929, Indian women earned rights to property and inheritance equal to men's rights. In the Karachi session of the Indian National Congress in 1931 a resolution was adopted on fundamental rights which incorporated the concept of equality of sexes. The National Planning Committee constituted by Subash Chandra Bose under the chairmanship of Jawaharlal Nehru prepared a report highlighting many of the modern-day concepts of equality of sexes and gender justice. With this historical background our founding fathers did a brilliant job in ensuring justice in the Constitution.

The preamble to the Constitution, interalia, assures justice — social, economic and political, equality of status and opportunity and dignity of the individual. The fundamental rights guarantee women's equality under law (Bandyopadhyay, 2000). The Constitution of India guarantees equality of sexes and in fact grants special favours to women. These can be found in three articles of the Constitution. Article 14 says that the government shall not deny to any person equality before law or the equal protection of the laws. It further empowers the state to adopt measures of positive discrimination in favour of women to assist them to overcome the cumulative socio-economic, educational and political oppression faced by them for centuries. Article 15 (1) declares that government shall not discriminate against any citizen on the ground of sex only. No citizen shall be barred from roads, shops, hotels or public places on the grounds of sex only. Moreover, Article 15 (1) directs the state to make any special provision in favour of women and children. Article 16 guarantees that no citizen shall be discriminated against in matters of public employment on the grounds of sex only (Anthony, 1989).

The Directive Principles of State Policy provide for affirmative action for securing adequate means of livelihood for men and women, equal pay for equal work, protection of health and strength of workers — men, women and children — from abuse, just and humane conditions of work, raising the level of nutrition, maternity relief and conditions of work, ensuring decent standards of life and full enjoyment of leisure. The Directive Principles affecting women are laid down in article 39. It says, "The state shall, in particular, direct its policy towards securing:

(a) That the citizens, men and women equally have the right to an adequate means of livelihood - Article 39 (a)

(b) That there is equal pay for equal work for both men and women - Article 39 (d)

(c) That the health and strength of workers, men and women, and the tender age of children are not abused and to make provision for securing just and humane conditions of work and for maternity relief - Artilce 42.

Though the principle of 'equal pay for equal work' is not expressly declared by our Constitution to be a fundamental right, but it is certainly a constitutional goal. Directive Principles, as has been pointed out in some of the judgements of the Supreme Court, have to be read into the fundamental rights as a matter of interpretation. Taking collectively these provisions spell out the basic right to equality of women in India as individuals (Anthony, 1989). The Constitution of India also makes provision for the reservation of women at the local government level. It states:

(a) Not less than one-third (including the number of seats reserved for women belonging to the Scheduled Castes and Scheduled Tribes) of the total number of seats to be filled by direct election in every panchayat to be reserved for women and such seats to be allotted by rotation to different constituencies in a panchayat - Article 243 D (3)

(b) Not less than one-third of the total number of offices of chairpersons in the panchayats at each level to be reserved for women - Article 243 D (4)

(c) Not less than one-third (including the number of seats reserved for women belonging to the Scheduled Castes and Scheduled Tribes) of the total number of seats to be filled by direct election in every municipality to be reserved for women and such seats to be allotted by rotation to different constituencies in a municipality - Article 243 T (3)

(d) Reservation of offices of chairpersons in municipalities for the Scheduled Castes, the Scheduled Tribes and women in such manner as the legislature of a State may by law provide - Article 243 T (4)

However, the Indian state's policy approach towards women has not been wholly guided by these constitutional rights and directives. If it had it would have shown in the First Five Year Plan itself. In the early stages of our plan era, women as a target group did not receive any convincing treatment.

The First Five Year Plan (1951-56) focused on the need to provide adequate services for women's welfare. It planned for development of maternal and child health and family planning services. In 1953 the Central Social Welfare Board (CSWB) was established which symbolised the welfare approach to women's problems, and subsequent establishment of state Social Welfare Advisory Boards to promote and assist voluntary organisations in the field of welfare of women, children and the handicapped. In 1956 the CSWB started a Scheme of Condensed Courses of Education for Adult Women and a Scheme for Socio-Economic Programmes for Women.

The Second Five Year Plan (1956-60) emphasised the need for special attention to problems of women workers. Recognizing that they were less organised these women were organised into Mahila Mandals, to act as focal points at the grass-root level for the development of women. The Plan stated that women should be protected against injurious work and it also suggested speedy implementation of the principle of equal pay for equal work, provision of facilities for training to enable women to complete for higher jobs and expansion of opportunities for part-time employment and to provide the facilities of creches. The Maternity Benefits Act, 1961, was enacted at the end of this Plan.

The main thrust of the **Third Five Year Plan** (1960-66) was on the expansion of girl's education, which continued in the **Fourth Plan** (1969-74). Measures to improve maternal and child health services, supplementary feeding for children and nursing and expectant mothers were also introduced. It was in the early 1970s that Crash Schemes for Rural Employment, Food for Work Programme, Drought Prone Areas Programme, and Desert Development Programme were initiated, aiming at strengthening the rural base of the economy. Though these schemes seemed to be gender-neutral, they were male-biased. They were targeted at men as the heads/earners of the families, with the assumption that benefits to men will trickle down to the rest of the family members. The Committee on the Status of Women in India (CSWI) was appointed by the Government of India in 1971 having a three-fold objective: (a) to evaluate the changes that had taken place in the status of women as the result of the constitutional, legal and administrative measures adopted since independence, (b) to examine the impact of the complex processes of social change on the various sections of Indian women and (c) to suggest measures which would enable women to play their full and proper role in building up the nation (Ministry of Education and Social Welfare, 1974). In 1972, a Central Scheme of Assistance for Construction of Hostel Buildings for Working Women was initiated. The scope of the Scheme was widened in 1980, by including a provision for day care centers for children.

The **Fifth Five Year Plan** (1974-79) showed a shift from welfare to development. This was largely because of the influence of the International Women's Year (1975) and International Women's Decade (1975-85). The new approach aimed at an integration of welfare with developmental services. A Report of the Committee on Status of Women in India (CSWI) called 'Towards Equality' was published by the Department of Social Welfare in 1974. In order to operationalise the recommendations of this report, a Blueprint of Action Points and National Plan of Action for Women were formulated in 1976. The Plan emphasised the need to train women in need of income and protection. In 1975 the CSWB started a Scheme of Assistance to Voluntary Organisation for Creches for Working and Ailing Women's Children and a Scheme for Vocational Training of Adult Women. The Ministry of Social Welfare started a scheme for setting up Women's Training Centres or Institutes for Rehabilitation of Women in Distress in 1977-78. In 1976, a Women's Welfare and Development Bureau was set up in the Ministry of Social Welfare. In the same year, the Equal Remuneration Act was enacted. The development schemes that were being launched parallel to the welfare schemes for women were again gender-neutral. A direct attack on poverty was launched by initiating the Integrated Rural Development Programme (IRDP) in 1978-79. Credit from banking institutions and subsidy from the government were given to rural families below the poverty line, for self-employment and income generation. Under the IRDP, a special place was accorded for Training Rural Unemployed Youth for Self Employment (TRYSEM). The National Rural Employment Programme (NREP) was introduced in 1980 and the Rural Landless Employment Guarantee Programme (RLEGP) in 1983. Unfortunately, rural women were only marginally visible in these programmes that targeted them.

In spite of the Directive Principles of State Policy up to the Fifth Plan there was no effort to see women as human or productive entities. "The statistical 'purdha' concealed the full extent of their participation in these sectors and their contribution to the national domestic product, and this made them invisible persons to the policy planners." (Bandyopadhyay, 2000).

For the first time the **Sixth Five Year Plan** (1980-85) introduced a separate chapter on women. This plan adopted a multi-disciplinary approach with a three pronged thrust on health, education and employment. It stressed on economic independence, giving of joint titles to husband and wife in all asset transfers, including of land, house sites and other economic units, a public policy package that included ownership rights and enforcement of wage laws. During the tenure of Rajiv Gandhi as the Prime Minister, the government took a positive stance towards women, may be because of the massive mandate he received from them in the 1985 election. The Department of Rural Development announced a 30% quota for women in all anti-poverty programmes for the rural areas and a special programme called 'Development of Women and Children in Rural Areas' was introduced providing for collective action by rural women. The department also sensitised public servants on gender issues which received support from other related departments. The effort of a sympathetic Prime Minister heading the government, to introduce a 'special component' approach for women was turned down by the cabint.

The **Seventh Five Year Plan** (1986-90) continued on the lines of the previous plan while reference was made regarding the rights and privileges of women. The main thrust of the Plan was in making women realise their role in the process of development. The developmental programmes for women continued with the major objectives of raising economic and social status and to bring them into the mainstream of national development. A significant step in this direction was the identification and promotion of beneficiary oriented programmes for women. The Seventh Plan also had a separate chapter on women this time titled 'Socio-Economic Programme for Women'. It focused on the concepts of equality and empowerment of women which was expressed by the International Decade for Women.

During this period a number of policies and programmes focused on mainstreaming women's issues. The National Policy on Education which was released in 1986, had a chapter on 'Education for Women's Equality', which in fact began the women's empowerment phase in India. The Twenty-Point Programme against poverty, adopted in 1986 also included a point on equality for women. The National Perspective Plan for Women 1988-2000 was published by a Core Group set up by the Department of Women and Child Development under the Chairperson, Mrs. Margaret Alva, providing government leadership. In the same year, the National Commission on Self-Employed women published 'Shramshakti' which is a comprehensive study of the working and living conditions of poor women, in rural and urban areas, under the Chairperson, Mrs. Bhatt, providing a non-government leadership.

These efforts influenced the **Eighth Plan** (1992-97) which shifted the focus from development to empowerment. In 1990 the National Commission for Women Act was enacted and two years later the National Commission for Women was set up as a national apex statutory level body to review the Constitutional and legal safeguards for women which recommends remedial legislative measures, facilitates redressal of grievances and advises the government on all policy matters affecting women. In 1991 a National Plan of Action for the SAARC Decade of the Girl Child (1991-2000) was formulated by the Department of Women and Child

Development. In 1996 the Draft of the National Policy for the Empowerment of Women was finalised.

As a follow-up of the Fourth World Conference at Beijing, "Growth with Equity" has been adopted as the theme of the **Ninth Plan** (1997-2002) and the following are the main objectives : (a) Generation of adequate productive employment and eradication of poverty. (b) Provision for basic minimum services of safe drinking water, primary health care facilities, universal primary education, shelter and connectivity to all villages in a time-bound manner. (c) Promoting and developing people's participation through Panchayati Raj Institutions, Cooperative and Self-Help Groups and (d) Empowerment of women.

A dispassionate analysis of all the five year plan efforts for development of the women and reducing their drudgery would reveal that in many aspects, the urgency was not fully appreciated and that the schemes were implemented in an extremely routine manner.

Acknowledging the limitations in using law as an instrument of social change, policy makers have been compelled to adopt discrimination in favour of women. As mentioned earlier, the 73rd and the 74th amendments reserving 33 per cent seats for women at the panchayat level, among other provisions, was a historical step in this direction. A case involving adultery illustrates the point that laws favouring women will be valid, though it may be discriminatory against men. Abdul Aziz was charged with adultery under the IPC. According to this law, a man who has sexual intercourse with a woman without her husband's consent is committing adultery and is punishable for a term of five years in jail. But the woman shall not be punishable, even as an 'abettor' or one who helps commit the crime. Abdul Aziz argued that this was discrimination on the ground only of sex and thus violated the Constitution. The Supreme Court rejected the argument, pointing out that under Article 15, the government could make special provisions for women in their favour. It also stated that the discrimination in favour of women was deliberate, in view of the social position of women in this country.

The case shows that special provisions of law favouring women can be passed by the government. Thus reservation of seats for women in an election to a municipality was upheld by the courts. A rule enabling women to be released from jail on bail, but not men in the same circumstances, was also held valid. Punishment for outraging the modesty of a woman was held valid though there is no such law for men. Where admission to a mixed college was restricted not merely on the ground of sex but also to develop a women's college in that town, the restriction was held valid. The rule that service of court summons can be only on an adult male member of the family was also held valid as it favoured women. Therefore, the government can discriminate in favour of women but it cannot discriminate against women (Anthony, 1989).

The "intrusion upon the privacy of a woman", according to section 509 of the Constitution, is punishable. But there are very few instances in which a woman has complained or the police have punished a person for such intrusion. If a man enters a woman's house or room, and threatens, insults or annoys her, he can be charged with criminal trespass (Sections 441 and 442).

The Indecent Representation of Women (Prohibition) Act, 1986 bans titillation picture on hoardings, packages, books, slides and films. Indecent representation is defined as the "depiction in any manner of the figure of a woman, her form or body, or any part thereof, in such a way as to have the effect of being indecent, derogatory or denigration or is likely to deprave, corrupt or injure public morality".

The commission of Sati (Prevention) Act, 1987 makes glorification of sati a serious offence. This act was passed to quell protests against the burning of Roop Kanwar on the funeral pyre of her husband in Deorala, Rajasthan. Even before this Act, the glorification of sati has been held to be abetment of suicide and thus a crime under the penal code. There has been consistent defiance of the law by a section of the people, and the government has not shown the will to enforce the law.

The Government amended the law on rape and introduced the Criminal Law (Amendment) Bill in 1980, which was ultimately passed as an Act in 1983. For the first time the Criminal Law (Second Amendment) Act, 1983 gave legal recognition to domestic violence by making cruelty inflicted by the husband or his relatives an offence.

Section 498A says, "Whoever being the husband or the relatives of the husband of a woman, subjects such women to cruelty shall be punished with imprisonment for a term which may extend to three years and shall also be liable to fine". Another important enactment is Section 304B. It has been inserted in the IPC by the Criminal Law Amendment Act passed in 1986. It created a new offence of dowry death. The offence under this section is punishable with a minimum of seven years and a maximum of life imprisonment. The accused booked under the section will have to prove their innocence. Section 174 was also amended to provide that in case a woman dies or commits suicide within seven years of marriage, it is mandatory for the police to order a post-mortem and other investigations. Further, the Law of Evidence was amended to provide that if a married woman commits suicide within seven years of her marriage, the presumption in law will be that the husband or his relatives abetted the crime - Section 306 (Gandhi Anjali, 1997).

Section 160 protects women from unnecessary harassment at the hands of policemen who make enquiries in criminal cases. While the police can call for the attendance of male witnesses at the police station, "no male person under the age of 15 years or woman shall be required to attend at any place other than in which such male person or woman resides". That means a woman need not go to the police station to give evidence but the concerned policemen must meet her at her house. Unfortunately, ignorance of this rule has resulted in several tragedies involving poor and illiterate women.

When a woman involved in crime has to be examined by a doctor for evidence, only a lady doctor or someone under her supervision can do so (Section 53). If a criminal hides in the house of a woman, who according to custom does not appear in public, the police cannot enter the house or break it open unless they tell her that she is at liberty to withdraw and afford her every reasonable facility to withdraw (Section 47). When summons cannot be served on a person, it can be served only on an adult male member of the family and not a woman (Section 64). If a woman sentenced to death is found to be pregnant the High Court shall order the execution to be postponed, and may, if it thinks fit, commute the sentence to imprisonment for life (Section 416). Although all laws are not gender specific, the major provisions of many laws affect women in quiet significant ways. These include: the Special Marriage Act, 1954; the Family Court Act, 1984; the Dowry Prohibition Act, 1961 (amended in 1984 and 1986); the Child Marriage Restraint (amended) Act, 1976; the Equal Remuneration Act, 1976; and the Medical Termination of Pregnancy Act, 1971.

In a patriarchal society, where gender equality still remains a distant dream, the recent judgement of the Supreme Court upholding the rights of widows to parental property is most welcome. The Apex Court has ruled that a "destitute" widow daughter without any income of her own or no estate of her husband to fall back upon can claim maintenance from her father or mother. So long social tradition had legitimised inheritance of paternal property by the sons only and the hapless destitute widows had to depend for their subsistence on the men in the family —be it the father, the husband or the son. Now by reinterpreting Section 19 of the Hindu Adoption and Maintenance Act, the Supreme Court has given financial independence to women. The judgement of the court confers an independent and personal right against the father during his lifetime or against the mother if the daughter is unable to maintain herself out of her earnings or other properties (Rashtra Mahila, 2000).

Along with this, the recent recommendation of the Law Commission to the Government to amend the Hindu Succession Act 1956, to allow women to get an equal share in the ancestral property will go a long way in giving women opportunity and freedom to be masters of their own destination outside male supervision and control. The amended act would make daughters co-parceners like sons so that they would be entitled to get their share of the ancestral property as a matter of birthright (Ibid.). Taking suo moto notice of certain provisions regarding the property rights of Hindu women under the Act in relation to laws governing the inheritance or succession of property amongst the members of a joint Hindu family, the Commission has said, "social justice demands that a woman should be treated equally both in the economic and social sphere. The exclusion of daughters from participating in co-parcenary property ownership merely by reason of their sex is injust."

The Law Commission has also suggested elimination of discrimination against women in laws pertaining to inheritance and succession of ancestral property under the Mitakshra system of joint Hindu family that permits only males to be the members of the co-parcenary and the devolution takes place by survivorship rather than succession. The Commission has further suggested deletion of Section 23 of the Act which places restrictions on the daughter to claim partition of the dwelling house. The Commission hopes that once the daughter is entitled to her property rights the dowry system would end and the condition of women would improve. The proposed changes if implemented will have far-reaching social and legal implications. With an equal share in their ancestral movable and immovable property, including the family business, it would result in women's economic empowerment and enhancement of their stature in the society. Indeed the Supreme Court's judgement and the recommendations of the Law Commission will trigger off changes, that in the long run will create tangible space for women to stand on their own feet (Ibid.)

As we can see meticulous care was taken by planners and policy makers, in bringing women into the mainstream of development. But it must be borne in mind that this process is painfully slow due to the inherent traditional biases. The writing on the wall is for everyone to see — mere legal sanctions are just not enough. Awareness and knowledge of women's rights to equality has to be created not only among women but in the society as well. According to the Encyclopedia of Women's Development, legal aid programmes for women, have to be developed which are not litigation oriented. These must consist of (a) creating legal awareness amongst the people and especially women, by making them aware of the rights/duties conferred upon them by various legal aids programmes, (b) holding Legal Aid Camp where lawyers go to different centers and give them free advice, (c) conducting para-legal training programmes for social workers and voluntary agencies and mobilising them for supportive action, and (d) supporting public interest litigation, by which social workers can participate and carry forward the legal aid programmes for women. The constitutional vision of gender justice can be realised only by a set of multiple strategies in which the states are also involved. Thus, for the improvement of the status of women, strong intervention from the state is essential (Institute for Environmental Development). India, being a democracy and with decentralisation of powers, it becomes necessary for the state also to take up policies and programmes for the development of women. Several states have formulated their own policies for the advancement of women.

ANDHRA PRADESH STATE POLICIES

To bring about all-round development of women the Andhra Pradesh state government is making efforts in this direction. Such intervention has been in various ways for the protection of women's rights by passing suitable Acts or making appropriate rules, along the national lines. But till the 1980s the state as independent unit has not done much on its own. Broadly four major streams have dominated the developmental strategies of Andhra Pradesh since its formation in 1956.

The early fifties focused on community development schemes organised mostly by promoting the co-operative sector but unfortunately women had no role of benefit. The late fifties witnessed land reforms and redistribution as a strategy. Certain parts, especially Telangana, saw massive peasant uprising and women played a major role in the reprisal. But in the Tenancy Act wherein cultivators of the lands were given ownership women were not considered. Even in the Acharya Vinobabhave's 'Bhoodanam Movement' women had no share. While land reforms have not been able to bring all excess ceiling surplus lands, even in the lands distributed there is no separate record of women beneficiaries. It is only now that the A.P. State Government has made an effort to give pattas in the name of women. It may be noted here that Andhra Pradesh was formed in 1956 and by that time First and Second Five Year Plans were already formulated at the national level. As Andhra Pradesh was just then formed and in the initial stages, it simply followed suit.

The sixties showed the advent of Green Revolution Technology. The post-harvest processing usually performed by casual women wage workers was displaced by the mechanisation process. In the seventies, keeping in line with the Centre's policy DRDA and IRDP have been implemented by the state for those below poverty line.

As we have seen in the early plans, i.e. till sixties priority was given on the whole to rural reconstruction, but no single programme worked successfully because of overenthusiasm to cover many developmental programmes under one umbrella. They were neither successful in social development nor in agricultural developmental through Green Revolution. In all these Plans emphasis was on acceleration of economic growth as a strategy for improving living standards of the people. Hence, from late seventies planners realised that poverty is the root-cause of failure of all developmental programmes. Many studies emphasised on the fact that poverty continued to rule at very high levels — as high as over 50 per cent of the nation's population.

Realising the importance of the mechanism of percolation a Women's Cooperative Finance Corporation was set-up in 1975 for providing the needy women skill training and extending loan facilities for augmenting their earnings and thereby to improve their economic status. It may also be mentioned here that in the year 1987-88 a separate commissionerate in the Secretariat was created for advancement and empowerment of women — monitoring, reviewing and evaluating various programmes intended for development of women. Besides women's development it looks after the child welfare and nutrition, welfare of the physically and mentally handicapped, and aged and disabled. The imposition of the State ban on sale of arrack on October 2, 1993 was a landmark decision in furthering the process from development to empowerment and this in turn inspired the state government to formulate an Action Plan for women 1994-2000. It can be said that now there was a shift from 'Women's Development' to 'Women's Participation' in articulating her demands.

The main objective of the A.P. State Action Plan for Women 1994-2000 is to integrate women at all levels in the mainstream of development and economic activity. It is a commitment of the State Government focusing primarily on 22 sectors amongst which women development and child welfare is included. The Action Plan accepts SHE has the right to survive, has the right to be free from poverty and exploitation, has the right to equality, dignity, freedom, opportunity, care, protection and development so that SHE, "shall not only endure but triumph". The state government had declared the year 1997 as the year of "Gender Equality with Social Justice". Further, realising that the women's question has to be resolved on all fronts and has to be a prime player in the centre stage of development, the State Government had taken a historic decision to prepare and implement a women's Sub-Plan 1997-98. The objective of the Sub-Plan is to allocate minimum 1/3 of the total budget outlay of each department for programmes and projects for women.

In addition to the safeguard guaranteed by the Centre, the state has formulated a few more policies for safeguarding the interests of women. A brief review of some of the Acts and programmes are enumerated below to give an idea of the range of legal protection available to women in Andhra Pradesh and it can be said with pride that these are first of their kind in the entire country.

1. Equal property right for daughter and son under the Hindu Succession Act since May 1986, to uphold the fundamental right of equality before law and to put an end to social inequality of women.
2. A.P. Devadasis Act 1988, bans the practice of dedication of women as Devadasis, Jogins, Basavins, etc.
3. The A.P. Factories Rules, 1950 provides under Section 73-76, for creches where more than 30 women employees are working (Section 48).

The various state programmes and policy initiatives in Andhra Pradesh state are as follows:

1. 33% reservation of seats in Panchayati Raj Institutions.
2. 30% reservation in government and other public sector jobs.
3. Free education up to graduate level.
4. Entrustment of fair price shops.
5. Grant of individual or joint land and house site pattas.
6. Purchase of agricultural land in the name of Scheduled Caste and Tribal women.
7. Minimum 30% coverage under loaning by Financing Corporation, viz., the S.C., B.C., S.T., P.H.C., Minorities Corporation and the State Finance Corportation.

8. Implementing Girl Child Protection Scheme with an annual outlay of Rs. 25 crores.
9. Reserved 33 per cent or 1/3 of the jobs in the non-traditional category of conductors and drivers in A.P.S.R.T.C.
10. Establishment of Mahila Courts (at Hyderabad, Vijayawada, Vishakhapatnam) (G.O. Ms. No. 9, dt. 12-3-1996) to deal with offences against women.
11. Establishment of family courts in several districts (Hyderabad, Vishakhapatnam, Tirupati, Kurnool, Secunderabad, Vijayawada, Warangal).
12. On the lines of National Commission for Women Act 32 of September, 1996, the State Government constituted a State Commission for Women in May, 1999.
13. To improve the condition of women and to make them the architects of their own future, the State Government organised Mahila Janma Bhoomi for the first time in Andhra Pradesh on May 1st, 1999.
14. In July 1999, another innovative scheme entitled 'Deepam' was proposed by the State Government to liberate the women from the daily ordeals of collecting fire-wood and to relieve them from the travails in the smoke filled kitchens. Under this scheme 10 lakh gas connections were to be issued to rural women. The State Government has decided to deposit Rs. 1,000/- per connection (100 crores for 10 lakh connections) as refundable deposit to the oil companies (The Hindu, 1999).

There are also schemes for training for employment like STEP (Support to Training and Employment Projects) which seeks to empower groups of poor women in traditional sectors. Another programme IGA (Income Generation Activities) has been taken up in phases. The latest addition is the launching of 'Janani', a welfare scheme aimed at helping pregnant women in the State. The scheme envisages financial assistance and medical treatment to pregnant women and other benefits accruing to them. The scheme provides a monetary benefit of Rs. 500/- if the women undergo sterilization and extension of the girl child benefit scheme to the child in the family (The Hindu, 2001). Endless efforts are being made to amend the Constitution and to provide legal guarantees to safeguard women and their interests. The recent amendments to sections 125 and 127 (1) of the Criminal Procedure Code to enhance the divorce maintenance from Rs 500/- to Rs. 1,500/-is a case in point.

However, there are limits to the extent to which changes can be effected by law. Attempts at bringing about changes in the status of women through either legislation or judicial activism can achieve little success without an accompanying change in the social and economic structures and the culture of the society.

Though the legal position of Indian women is better than in most countries of the world, they face inequalities in various forms and are denied equal opportunities for personal growth and social development. They are burdened with discrimination which in turn perpetuates their low status. Millions of our women are ignorant or just unable to enjoy the many rights and privileges that have been conferred on them. The need of the hour is awareness amongst the women and change in the perceptions of the law enforcement agencies, without which even the most progressive of legislation will be reduced to a dead letter.

REFERENCES

Anthony, M.J., 1989. Women's Rights, p. 10. Hind Pocket Books, New Delhi.

Bandhyopadhyay, D. 2000. "Gender and Governance in India", *Economic and Political Weekly,* Vol. XXXV, No. 31, July 29-August 4.

Chowdhury, Nazma, 1994. "Women in Politics in Empowerment", *A Journal of Women for Women,* Vol. 1, Dhaka.

Dagar Rainuka, 1998. "Intervening for Gender Justice", *The Indian Journal of Social Work,* Vol. 59, No. 4.

Dhawan, S.R., 1995. "Fourth World Conference on Women, Beijing, 1995: A Conference to set Women's Agenda to Next Century", *Kurukshetra,* Vol. XLIII, No. 11, August.

Gandhi Anjali, 1997. "Violence Against Women with Reference to 498A and 304B, Indian Penal Code", *The Indian Journal of Social Work,* Vol. 58, No. 4, October.

Institute for Environmental Development Studies, *International Encyclopedia of Women's Development,* Vol.4, Lucknow, p. 24.

Lalita, N., 1996. "Women's Empowerment through Cooperatives", *Social Welfare,* Vol. 43, No. 6, September.

Ministry of Education and Social Welfare, 1974. "A Report of Department of Social Welfare", *Government of India,* New Delhi, December.

Mill, J.S., 1975. "The Subjugation of Women", Universal Press, London.

Mustafa K. Mujeri & Lisa Singh, 1998. "Impact of Increase in Income on Gender Relations within the Household: A Cross-Country Analysis", *Towards Gender Equality: CIRDAP,* Dhaka.

Rashtra Mahila, 2000. *"News from Abroad",* Vol. 3, No. 2, July.

Rashtra Mahila, 2000. *"Women to Make News on March 8th",* Vol. 3, No. 15, March.

Rashtra Mahila, 2000, Vol. 3, No. 16, March.

Rashtra Mahila, 2000. "U.N. Protocol on Women's Rights Signed", Vol. 3, No. 14, July.

Rashtra Mahila, 2000. Vol. 3, No. 19, June.

The Hindu, 1999. "A Glow in the Lives of Rural Women", July 8.

The Hindu, 2001. *"Janani Scheme for Women",* June 2.

The Times of India, "Women in Battle Zones to be Part of Peace Talks: U.N.", 2000, September 22.

U.N. U.N. Website on Women Watch.

U.N., 1998. "Towards Gender Equality, Poverty. Rights and Participation", *Report of the Regional Workshop.*

Vidyaben Shah, 1995. "Towards Equitable Society", *Social Welfare,* May.

William Phillip, 2001. "Prices Force Nuns in having Sex", *Guardian Weekly,* March 29- April 4,S.S.

Zarina Rahman Khan, 1998. "Political Participation of Women: The Problematic", *CIRDAP,* Dhaka.

13

Human Communities and Cultural Tradi tions : An Integrated Pattern in Development Strategies

*R.M. Sarkar**

I

Man as a social animal is specifically characterised by his cultural heritage. This heritage is the outcome of long term interactional activities in the perspective a his variegated hazards and anxities which came into force in the path of his struggle for existence througl time and space. It was through a continuous combat with the unfavourable surroundings — both biological and cultural — man could win over the success in putting down the unwanted and unfavourable factors that raised their heads obstructing his smooth progress. In course of that combative attitudes and functional processes man could have been able to find out conspicuous ways and means to adjust himself with the earthly happenings and thus his life was processed and became perfectly efficacious through the emergence of a new and novel thinking and working pattern known by the term culture. Thus, culture is regarded as the human form adaptation. It is to be noted

* *Editor, Man in India, Mayurakshi, Baghajatin Park, Kolkata - 700094, India.*

that adaptation is the key concept in the living world. In plant kingdom it is obviously present and it functions through the structural modifications enabling the plant to survive in the specific condition of the habitat. Among the animals it appears through the two dimensional ways — structural modifications as well as development of inherited patterns of behaviour. But in case of man it is seen that the neurological structures are highly characterised by complications. These are less stereotyped and thus these unitedly are capable of the development of variegated reaction patterns. Moreover, man is endowed with intellectual activities, he is provided with the unique powers for associating memory reflections facilitating to modify his behaviour in the arena of experience. Because of man's gregarious mode of behaviour together with his ability to speak fluently and thus helping broad-based communication, as well as his specific tendency to pass on the cumulative effects of his efforts and experience to the next generation, so human patterns of living thus became conspicuously different from those of other animals. As no animal other than man has got the ability to transmit the benefits of acquired knowledge and earned experience to the succeeding generations, so culture is regarded as the unique phenomenon pulsated in the life and activities of man.

The culture is uniquely human — and human beings have become the unique animal by the possession of this specific phenomenon. In human, culture interacts with biology giving rise to an integrated picture of biocultural setting of human life and work. The process of hominisation is an excessively long-term and highly complicated happening that is engaged in transforming animal into human species. Thus, it is the result of synthesis between biological and cultural evolution patterns. Mention may be made that whereas biological evolution is universal to all the species of the living world, biocultural evolution is effective only in the case of man. Thus, culture is not only unique to man but it is an inevitable trait for this existence constituting a categorical difference from other animals.

Culture is present at all levels of human existence but it is seen to be patterned according to the thoughts and ideas of the human communities concerned. It is called by the term 'patterned ideas' which became embodied in the group tradition and objectified in language, tools and institutions. These patterned ideas are seen to dominate the behaviours of the members of a particular culture group. In the analysis of any social system and the psycho-philosophical patterns of the group within a cultural setting, it is inevitable to study the traditional features that have been influencing the social sentiments through time. The literal meaning of tradition is transmission through generations. Thus, the inherited customs, beliefs and thoughts, institutions, dress, ornaments, laws, songs and tales are traditions. The knowledge, beliefs, values, standards, folkways and mores as a whole which are found useful to the human group are ultimately embodied in the group tradition. This group tradition is such an essential factor in the social system and the cultural perspective that the society concerned out and out declines to sacrifice those traditional values during any sort of directed change meant for overall development of the society. Man is specifically regarded as tool making animal and at the same time he is value making machine — one is related to material culture and the other is to spiritual culture. This spiritual culture greatly shapes and work behind the formation of traditional behaviour-patterns.

The cultural traditions of different human groups have characteristics of their own which have been modelled according to the belief-patterns and thought-patterns of the groups concerned. Thus, the cultural traditions of the people in a particular group have given rise to a specific value-attitude system which is needed to be honoured properly at the time of implementing any welfare measure for their all-purpose development. The upliftment programme must not neglect the traditional values and attitude of the people for whom these are meant. Otherwise, the whole attempt may cut a sorry figure. In every society we find that all the members prize and desire certain things and work together in order to get these. It is the duty of the planners to know the factors that are universally desired or valued in a particular society. It may be pointed out that a large number of schemes regarding the welfare of the people have failed to bear fruits due to the lack of previous enquiry regarding the traditional values and attitudes of the communities concerned. Human communities, it is to be noted that, are developed in a common territory and rared up in a spirit of shared way of life. As a permanent local aggregation of people, the community is characterized by having diversified, as well as having common interests. Human community represents a sentiment— there is always a well-feeling here. This living together attitude gives the members of the community common thinking patterns and value-attitude systems which are ultimately integrated into the inner recess of live of the people. Each and every community has got is own thoughts, beliefs, ideas, customs, superstitions, folkways and myths. All these features are in an intermingling situation and thus these give rise to the integrated traits that are subject to transmission through generations. Tradition is culture-specific and it is moulded and patterned according to the life-philosophy of the people. The tradition which is processed through cultural patterns and perspectives forms cultural traditions — the governing forces in a particular community. The workers employed in the welfare activities in relation to a particular human community must take special interest in understanding the various facets of the cultural traditions of the people concerned. It is always desirable that the personnel attached with developmental activities must pay proper respect to the beliefs and thoughts of the people. Otherwise, the people concerned will not be understandable to the personnel employed in development activities. In any sort of development programme the personnel attached to it and the people to be developed must be mutually compatible — they must understand each other so that there may be the regular occasion for amicable relation processed with reciprocal perceptibility.

Life is everywhere need-oriented. There are some essential and inevitable needs required for survival of life on earth. In the very first instance we find a lot of common needs shared by both men and animals. Thus, there are needs for food getting, shelter arrangement, protection from attack of others, sex gratification, reproduction, health, in addition to needs for breathing, excretion and other physiological processes. Like other animals man satisfies these primary needs in the day to day life. But whereas among other animals the satisfaction of primary needs are done through instinct and biological capabilities, in man this situation is conducted through the imposition of culture — a unique trait developed in man in course of his line of advancement from non-human ancestry. Human efforts for food getting are characterised by the inventions and discoveries of a lot of circumstances which helped them to devise their material belongings that have been adjusted with the surroundings in a highly effective fashion to make the process less difficult. Through the efficient endeavour for adjusting with harsh climatic conditions men could become the inhabitant at almost all sorts of environmental situations of the world. In these cases, imposition of cultural activities became the most essential issue for bringing the various adverse conditions to his favour. In course of time these activities had developed the technological devices which collectively constituted the fruitful arena of human survival. According to Malinowsky, human society and culture are best understood as an assemblage of contrivances for the purpose of fulfilment of their sociological and psychological needs. It is seen that organic needs of human beings are commonly processed with other non-biological needs known as derived and integrative needs. Unlike other animals the basic needs are categorically satisfied through the devising of multifarious ways and means. The most important characteristic features in this regard are that the human beings have regularised their day to day activities through the formation of biological as well as social groups. Their life became group-oriented and that group was fashioned through various norms and regulations that had been formulated in the light of their day to day observations and practical perceptions. In these perspective of his adjustment with the surroundings man differs strikingly from other animals because of the fact that these are regulated by cultural features. These needs are seen to have derived from the conditions of human collective patterns of living. Thus, these are derived needs — the reflections of human collective enterprise. As because the collective mode of life and activities required organisational patterns, so there has automatically developed tradition-oriented cooperating modes of behaviour and different machineries of social control. Then there are occasions when needs are in demand for the expression of collective sentiments. It has been seen in the workings of the human social system that there exists some form of interrelated needs producing cultural responses for satisfying the requirements for recreation and for aesthetic expression. This situation indicates that there are certain needs which are in integrated relation with certain types of cultural responses. Therefore, these needs have been termed as integrative needs focusing the social values, norms, religion, mythology, ritualistic performances, language patterns together with different forms of symbolism. The variegated phenomena — biological and social —that have been processed into the desire for satisfaction of the diversified human needs together form the rule of conduct which are honoured most by the society and the people concerned. These ultimately take the form of cultural traditions which run down through generations and the people attached to these are pledged normally and sentimentally to preserve these without any sort of distortion.

In each and every society the relation between human needs and cultural responses is characterised by a specific patterns which differs from one society to another. The network that constitutes in the perspective of the relationship between needs and cultural responses is specifically influenced by value-orientation and psychocultural trends. A particular society is under obligation to follow these socio-cultural patterns and in no circumstances these are to be dishonoured. Anthropologists distinguish two universal features of human social behaviour on which all the cultural responses connected with different needs are based. One of these is recognised as the collective endeavour which is characterised by group formation having traditionally transmitted norms; and the other is related to the devising of various institutions. The collective endeavours belonging to the first factor function in a regularised fashion, these do not work in an anomalous condition; rather the total phenomenon is governed by well-knit cultural traditions giving rise to these institutions. These institutions are obliged to obey a body of rules and regulations. People form such institutions in their direct response to the surroundings for sake of their trouble-free existence despite various adversities.

In the sphere of social science, development is a significant word. It does not restrict itself only to the growth and progress from the existing status but many things more. In the attempt for development of any community or human group for raising its manner of living and thereby helping it to resist various odds and anxieties there must be some sorts of well-defined strategies. These strategies, it is to be noted, should be chalked up in the background of the total way of life of the population group concerned. The life pattern and the development activities in relation to a human group are based on multidimensional factors and the principal elements working within these are identified as population perspective, organisational patterns, environmental influences and technologies devices. In order to have the integrated aspect of these factors in the formation and working of a human social system there must be an all-rounded attempt to study the biocultural as well as socio-cultural background in which the society concerned as a whole gets its identity in the broader social system. The development strategies must always be characterised by the need-based philosophic principles, as we have seen that, the human needs are the direct outcome of long-term interactions with the material as well as spiritual world. Until and unless these two specific dimensions are analysed and carefully looked into no practical success can be achieved through the efforts made in respect of development of the human elements and social settings which come into the picture. Development strategies must be directly based on the specific interpretation of the needs of the society and in the anthropological domain these needs are known as felt needs. Felt needs are the reflections of peoples' mind which are constituted through the long-term and complicated process of interactions with the physical and socio-cultural surroundings in which the people concerned live and work for existence. Special emphasis should be given on the point that these needs of the people are intimately attached with the mental pattern and categorically processed by sentimental consequences. Thus in developing the strategies for development care should be taken to see that these are being formulated keeping the total perspective of the concerned society clear in the context of the peoples' indigenous life-ways and thought-ways. At the very outset, the goal for a particular development planning should be well-defined and which must be understood properly by the personnel designing the framework for development. It is required that the people to be developed should be studied implicitly from close quarters in an unbiased way and with the categorical analysis of the information thus collected the needs of the people concerned can be identified. The study of such kind must be conducted within the institutional framework of the community/society in question.

It has been proved true that economic development and technological change are impeded by cultural traditions brought forth in the background of various institutional factors. It is due to this any item in the programme of development must not go against the cultural traditions of the peoples concerned. Otherwise, the very attempt for bringing any developmental change would be out and out rejected by the people. Scientific procedures for development speak in favour of peoples' participation into the programme through the acceptance of the mode of approach. Peoples' participation is possible and practicable only when the facets of the developmental progamme are supported by the people for whom these are meant. To get whole-hearted acceptance of the people to be developed there is an essential requirement to understand the felt needs of them in the background of the social system. Thus a deep-based study on the behaviour-patterns of the people becomes the essential issue.

Development differs exclusively from what is known as instant relief. There is also a great difference between development work and welfare activities. There is no doubt about the fact that all these efforts are aimed at beneficence to human beings but whereas these are for short-term benefit of the people principally through monetary assistance thereby creating some improvement of not only the economic but side by side with this there is always an earnest appeal to make amelioration of the socio-cultural perspectives and thinking patterns. The developmental workers, in the strict sense of the term, believe in the all-round improvement of the human element as the balanced changing situations of all the spheres of life which is the only key to success for human development activities. This is the whole truth and until and unless it is properly understood in the actual context it would be next to impossible to bring any real improvement in the line for which we have been fighting through time and space. Full exposure to human life is effected when it is focused through the light of the integrated actions between ecology and environment. These two factors are always seem to be in the effectual process of influencing the different facets of socio-economic life; moreover, these penetrate into the psycho-philosophical setting of the community as a whole giving rise to an explicitly integrated cultural patterns. The culture of any community must be assessed in the background of the ecosystem in which the community concerned has been flourished and engaged itself to eke out its existence. The natural resources on which the community depends are to be explored and the relationship between man and nature should be studied so that their importance in the developmental activities is not neglected. In the development strategies the concept of eco-cultural process must be given due priority for a good result. From our past experience it has been seen that such a step has never been taken for keeping close linkage between human element and the total eco-system, rather in the name of development the basic ecosystem concept has been out and out neglected. At the time of making any improvement in the basic pattern of life of any rural/tribal community it must be the duty of the development personnel to evaluate the pattern of adjustments of the people with the total ecosystem. A holistic study and integrated analysis of the rural/tribal ecosystem are highly effectual in understanding actual pattern of exploitation of the natural environment by the people to maintain their livelihood. All these communities, rural and tribal, have got their traditional method of harnessing natural resources through the application of indigenous knowledge. Mention should be made that this indigenous knowledge is forwarded to many other spheres like informal education, treatment of diseases, maintenance of safety and protection in adverse situations in life, controlling the irregularities of natural forces, conservation of forest and the like. Care should be taken to see that in the name of improvement and betterment this indigenous knowledge system may not be disregarded and thereby exclusively thrown down. Most of the time the imposition of allien thoughts on the indigenous communities creates the problems in the attempt for development. The total disregard of the traditional culture by the development strategies formulated in the urban dominated perspectives is the root cause of failure of so many development programmes. These specific strategies categorically fail to detect the felt needs of the people to be developed and thus very naturally needs of the outsiders get eminent position here which the people under the development programme cannot appreciate. This lack of appreciation does a great deal in extinguishing the spirit of the people under such programme and thus the development endeavour becomes ultimately delinked from the people for whose benefit it has been framed. Sometimes it is seen that various governmental organisations as well as non-governmental organisations working separately on the different developmental issues in a particular community are not processed through coordination which causes puzzling conditions for the illiterate simple rural/tribal communities. All these situations very naturally hurt the sentiment of the indigenous people who, as a matter of course, try to get rid of those 'developments'.

II

In most of the development policies in India related to the tribal as well as rural communities it is seen that the basic issues connected with the felt needs are not properly and effectually taken into consideration. Various development strategies for the down-trodden communities have been sincerely made since the independence of India and in spite of their specific implications these have failed to bear the requisite fruits. Lots of money were spent, there were various formalities for the implementations of the work plans, though there was sufficient seriousness from the part of the governmental administration but the proper goal could not be reached. From the close study into the problematic issues and through the analysis of the different phenomena it is revealed that in these cases the developmental plans have failed to appreciate the felt needs of the people concerned. A conspicuous gap has always prevailed between the people and the development workers, and due to the lack of any linkage between these two groups of people there has resulted this unfortunate situation. The people brought under the developmental programme could not accept the various facets of the changing situations and naturally they were deviated from the main line of the activities concerned. As a natural consequence the implementation of the said programme became a routine work. However, the development strategies must honour the needs of the people. If it is not done, the whole attempt in spite of due sincerity and seriousness would cut a sorry figure. When it is seen that the working patterns related to the effective attempts for development of the suffering humanity are going against the cultural traditions of the people, it is definite that total effort would be futile. This specific observation can be proved through the study and analysis of the way of life of the Birhors and the very attempt for their development. The Birhors - a nomadic hunting-gathering tribe exemplify a tradition-oriented tribe in Jharkhand, having forest-based life and activities. Forest ecology has shaped their life-philosophy in such a way that a detachment even for a moment makes them embarrassed.

Their totalistic life is governed exclusively by the forest-centred environment, forest becomes the part and parcel of their way of living. It is for this reason their identity has been intermingled with the forest — they are known as Birhors or the men of the forest *(Bir* mean forest and *hor* stands for man).

Birhor life and thinking patterns can best be understood in terms of their ecological settings which govern their economic and socio-religious domain. As a key factor in the shaping of the cultural patterns in any human society ecology is characterized by multifarious action-oriented facets which are seen to be interlinked with the different thought ways and life-ways of the people. Owing to continuous interactions with the natural surrounding man could develop specific value patterns which are found to prevail a close-set integration with the philosophy of life. This particular philosophical orientation is the architect of human distinctive culture-specific pattern known by the term cultural ecology. Ecology and humanity are two interrelated and interdependent facts of existence. This situation dates back to the prehistoric times. The prehistoric men had to find out various ways and means to adjust themselves with the surroundings. They had to make close observations on the natural happenings to see the behaviour patterns of different animals, to understand the nature and extent of variegated vegatations for the sake of their existence. Thus proper understanding of any human community needs the evaluation of its interactional patterns with the environment both biotic and physical — through time and space. The process of human existential activities is highly characterized by the modes of adjustment and the ecological surroundings. The cultural-ecological method of studying people especially those who are directly dependent on natural circumstances is ineviatable in proper evaluation of the culture traits that have been developed centering round the totalistic life-situation. Until and unless this situational context is properly understood the full needs of the people concerned can never be brought into light. This inability to highlight the specific requirements of the people to be developed causes to grow a negative approach towards the programme for development. The programme for work thus very naturally becomes a routine activity and a considerable gap is created between the people brought under the development programme and the personnel working towards development. The strategies for development must not allow to grow such an embarrassing state of affair, otherwise it wold cause to create conspicuous pitfalls in the path of work.

Birhor culture is the result of multidimensional interactions between man and nature. Forest ecology is so much forceful in Birhor life that forest and Birhor have become synonymous. It is for this reason the Birhors identify themselves as the men of the forest. Economically the Birhors are known as the hunter gatherer tribe subsisting solely on forest products. The traditional economy, therefore, is needed to be studied through the adoption of ecological models. The Birhors are characteristically a nomadic community, their way of life is highly influenced by wandering philosophy. This specific philosophical orientation is the outcome of their continuous interactions with the multiplex forested ecology. The Birhors are always on the move and this moving character indicates the unique pattern of their cultural adjustment. The ecosystem of the Birhors embraces the diversified biological components constituting biological communities with their abiotic environment. Within this ecosystem the nomadic Birhors could have been able to satisfy the basic needs of their life — their economic life has not only processed through the direct impact of the eco-system centering round the forest of Chotanagpur plateau but also their social and spiritual life has been pulsated with dynamic potentialities.

In the background of this eco-cultural setting the life and activities of the Birhors have flourished in small tradition bound villages — the tandas — in the midst of hills and dales of Chotanagpur. The *tandas* are specifically characterized by the possession of conical leaf huts known as *kumbas.* In each tanda there are 10 to 15 kumbas. The constructionof the kumbas is not difficult for them. The raw materials like twigs, leaves and creepers are collected from the forests. These are cut down from the forests indiscriminately. Kumba making has got a specific technology which is learnt by the Birhors through traditional knowledge and understandings that run down through generations. The kumba is the manifestation of indigenous scientific perception. The conical structure is thatched with leaves of trees and these are tied up by creepers in such a way that a single drop of rain water does not percolate through the thatched roofs and walls of the kumbas. There is always a strict vigilance in searching out any misfortune of such kind i.e.percolation of rain water not for protecting the inhabitants of the huts and the materials within from wetting but for maintaining the very purity of the leaf huts. Percolation of rainwater through the roof and walls of these huts is regarded as the pollution of the total habitational unit. The kumba is not only regarded as the place of living for the family members but also it is said to act as the resource centre for spiritual influence which is thought to be essential in keeping the inmates of the hut free from all sorts of evil activities of the malevolent impersonal powers. In the floor space of each kumba a small stone slab representing the clan god — Bonga Ora is implanted. It is firmly believed by the Birhors that the Bonga Ora protects the inmates of the huts concerned from all sorts of hazards and anxieties. During the dead hours of night when a number of malevolent spirits hover through the region, they are obstructed by the bonga ora residing in the kumba to enter there and therefore, these injurious spirits can not do any harm to the sleeping persons within the kumba. Thus bonga ora creates an inevitable part in the total existence of the Birhors. Moreover, he guides the Birhors in finding out a prospective area for hunting and gathering during the movement of the band. The band, constituted by 10 to 15 uniclan nuclear families, is guided by the *Naya* — the Birhor priest— who is believed to be spiritually animated by the *Bonga Ora.* At the time of disease and especially during the time of epidemics substantial help from the *Bonga Ora* is sought to resist the calamity. When scarcity of food becomes conspicuous the *Bonga Ora* is approached through the supernatural way by the priest on behalf of the people to bring an end to that trouble due to which the very existence is at a stake. Thus the household units of the Birhors, the centres for performing the basic activities for proper living, must be provided with the sacred seat of *Bonga Ora.* This specific mentality has become the essence of Birhor life-philosophy it has penetrated into the traditional patterns forming the specific cultural traditions.

The Birhor tanda in spite of its temporary existence is not an unsystematic assemblage of the family based huts — the *kumba.* The tanda is always uniclan in nature. This tanda is under the administrative domain of traditional headman or the *Naya.* He has got the double-headed authority — the headman and the priest. He is assisted by the *Kotwar* and who is responsible for organising hunting expeditions which are done on band level. There is another important personality —the *Mati.* He is the traditional medicine man and thus incharge of the whole supernatural affairs. He is to detect the causes of disease through occult practices and thereby to suggest the measures for curing these which is also done through supernatural way. These officials of the tanda are directly linked up with the principal economic pursuits i.e. hunting of forest animals and gathering of forest vegetative resources. There is a firm belief in the Birhor life-ways that the success in hunting is directly dependent on the grace of supernatural deities. Thus there is always an urgent necessity to keep proper connection with these supernatural powers. It is the duty of the *Mati* to maintain the close linkage between the Birhors and the supernatural world.

The ecology of the region together with the economic pursuits of these people jointly have given rise to a specific situation of uncertainties which are confronted with by the Birhors through the adoption of supernatural means. Food quest amongst the Birhors has been designed in such a way that they very commonly regard forest as their store house and thus food materials can easily be collected from these as and when required. They are to move about for that collection strategy which has resulted in their mind a kind of nomadism. From the earliest time Chotanagpur ecology has been providing the Birhors the rich food zone but their hunting-gathering philosophy has made them nomadic because nomadism has something to do with the hunting-gathering economic pursuits. In spite of rich food zone collection it may become uncertain sometime as there is no guarantee in achieving success in all sorts of hunting efforts. Under these specific circumstances the Birhors' way of life has become characteristically oriented with supernaturalism.

In addition to the collection of food materials directly from the forest the Birhors have got a traditional handicraft related to a particular creeper very frequently available in Chotanagpur ecological zone. The creeper, popularly known as *chop (Bauhinalia scandens),* is collected by them and from the fibres of which they prepare a type of strong rope. It has a great demand in the local market. With this specific handicraft, conditioned by indigenous methodological principles, the Birhors have been keeping regular connection with the agricultural communities of the region amongst whom such rope has got a great demand. Chotanagpur ecological region has stimulated inquisitiveness in the minds of the Birhors to harness its diversified and rich vegetative qualities of the herbs that grow so wildly and vigorously in the forested areas of Chotanagpur. Through a continuous course of trial and error these particular people could develop the knowledge of herbal medicines which they have processed through indigeneous way. Their innate capacity to identify various vegatative species and the indigenous skill to apply these according to the nature and condition of disease have attracted many advanced agricultural communities of Chotanagpur ecological setting for keeping contact with the Birhors. This particular situation has given the Birhors an opportunity to come in close contact with the people of other communities having different socio-economic life.

Birhor village organisation is specifically conditioned by the nomadic philosophy of the community together with the close set impact of supernaturalism. Village life is interconnected with forest setting. The physical as well as psychic linkage with the forest ecology forms the substratum of Birhor life-philosophy. Due to uniclan nature of the traditional Birhor village all the inhabitants find themselves within a consanguineous bondage where everybody link himself in a secured position because of mutual understanding and deep-rooted relationship patterns. In the nomadic and uncertain life these people need kin-oriented groundings so that during the time of calamity especially in the food quest an unfortunate family may get economic support from the other families. As members of the same clan there always prevail a brotherly feeling which helps each and every Birhor to fight with the unfavourable circumstances. It is for this reason the Birhors feel pleasure in living in uniclan village. The tanda or thetraditional Birhor village has been keeping constant and integrated linkage with the forest ecological setting from time immemorial and due to which the total social atmosphere of the inhabitants of Birhor tanda is seen to be perfectly oriented in the line of ecocultural adjustment. Various traits of culture have been intermingled with ecological characteristics. They can not think a slight severance even for a moment with the forest atmosphere. Thus the village of the Birhors has been continuous with the forest. The village is systematically administered by the clan god and here again comes the advantage of the uniclan tanda. When only one clan lives in a village setting there will be a common clan god. This situation in the ritualistic domain binds the families together. In addition to the *kumbas* created for living and working, within there are special kumbas in the tanda which are dedicated to the clan gods and other spirits. All sorts of ritualistic activities, conducted during the different times of the year, are held within these special kumbas.

The *kumbas* become inevitable to the Birhors because of the fact that these are comfortable for living during all the seasons. There are the results of successful adaptive endeavours for coping with the different circumstances. The thick layers of leaves knitted in a skilful way and covering the wall and roofs of the *kumbas* help the inhabitants to avoid the tremendous heat of summar months in Chotanagpur Plateau. During hot days the interior of the *kumba* remains cool because of construction technology conducted in the indigenous way, while at the time of tremendous cold outside in winter the inside of the *kumba* is felt warmer due to the thick cover of leaves laid over the conical huts. The Birhors have very limited clothings and thus without this sort of natural warmth created within the *kumba,* the Birhors will fail to thrive. This is the specific feature of their cultural adaptation to the environment, and this sort of innate propensity has penetrated into their value-attitude system forming a distinct cultural tradition.

As because all their requirements in mental and psychical domains are satisfied by the forest, so forest has become their inevitable unit of existence. All the facets of life of the Birhors are directly influenced and fashioned by forest environment. In the major phases of life like social, economic and religious, they can not go beyond the forest. The vastness of forest, its calm and pleasant atmosphere as well as the greeny and lustrous environs have jointly design their nature loving mentality. This state of affair instigate them to think themselves as the men of the forests in the strict sense of the term. They like to identify themselves as part and parcel of their immediate nature — the green and endless forests. The boundless forested region with green canopy inhabited by diversified species of animal in Chotanagpur of the past period worked as the dominating factor in shaping a specific tribal personality and universal group character which ultimately developed in them a specific philosophy as well as a psycho-cultural understanding enabling them to think themselves as kings of the forest. This "Kings of the forest" trait has taken a significant position in the cultural tradition of the Birhor and this phenomenon is so widespread and so integrated in their totalistic pattern of life that all sorts of development programme which have been implemented with a view to help the tribe overcome their present day ill-fated situation cut a sorry figure. The people for whose benefit these programmes are meant have failed to pay and respect or attach any seriousness to the endeavour as the different facets of the programme go against their cultural traditions. This leads to futility of the whole effort for development. An analysis of the total situational context would reveal that owing to non-acceptability of the various traits of the development programme by the tribal people concerned the total endeavour taken up by the governmental organisation with due seriousness has failed to achieve the positive result.

III

Chotanagpur forests like many other forested regions in India became the victim of a most unfortunate natural destruction like deforestation. The forested region of Chotanagpur fell under the evil activities like indiscriminate cuffing of trees on the one hand and total negligence in the maintenance of essential requirements for the existence and growth of forests since long time past on the other. These factors jointly caused a great deal in thinning the forests first and finally complete disappearance in many cases. Owing to the thinning of the forests the forest-living animals, the principal food items of the Birhors, faced calamities in their very survival and ultimately they had to take departure from this world. The total situation very naturally created an unbearable condition in the life and activities of the Birhors. On the particular ill-fated condition of their severance from the age-old integrated pattern of close-set relationship with the forests the Birhors became bewildered. Being perplexed in consequence of the demolition of the tradition bound economic pursuits as well as the destruction of their peaceable habitat framed up with the blessings of benevolent deities the Birhors had to give up all their hopes and aspirations in life and ultimately they became a destitute.

The thinning of the luxuriant forested regions of Chotanagpur, actually speaking, rapidly enhanced due to the impact of coal and other allied industrial units. Richness of mineral in the whole of Chotanagpur belt attracted the attention of various industrial organisations towards this landmass and which started lifting of mineral wealth from the deeper layers of the earth. As a necessary consequence the extensive forest cover of the region became the first victim and then as a chain reaction it affected the forest-living animal as well as the tribal people especially the hunters-gatherers. The processis is still continuing. The disappearance or excessive thinning of the forests has resulted an abrupt change in the forest ecology. In courseof time forest ecosystem has been totally disbalanced and as per the law of nature the situation has severed the reciprocal patterns of linkage amongst living-nonliving, living-living and nonliving-nonliving elements.

In this untoward state of affair the principal hunting-gathering tribe like the Birhors had been thrown into a very unfortunate circumstances and finding no other alternative to procure food by simple collection from the natural resources they had to starve. Hunger became their all-time companion and as a very simpleminded, nature-loving and destiny-oriented human community the Birhors lost all the aims and ambitions in their life. The indiscriminate utilisation of the forests and even hunting of the forest-living animal and collection of roots, fruits and tubers from the forests became prohibited, of course with conspicuous tribal concessions, by the imposition of the National Forest Policy in 1952. Owing to the enunciation of the Forest Act by the Govt. of India the Birhors have been completely debarred from cutting the trees for the construction of their traditional huts-the *kumbas*. This restriction has very naturally affected their social organisation centred round the *tanda*-based community life where *kumbas* form the essential units. Want of animal in the so-called forests has thrown them in great disaster and the administrative ban arising out of the Forest Act has added salt to the existing injury. In this anomalous situation they have failed to understand what is to be done. They have got no knowledge of any other occupation save and except hunting and gathering so that in times of emergency they would switch over to that.

After the promulgation of the National Forest Policy when the Birhors became the victims of the policy of severance of man-forest interrelationship, the administration of the country came to their help. On seeing the wretched condition of the Birhors the then Govt. of Bihar came forward to shoulder the responsibility of providing the ill-fated Birhors alternative ways and means for their survival. It was in 1956, when the Govt.of Bihar with the direct sponsorship from the Govt. of India started the effort for changing the life of those affected humanity. It was decided that a broad-based rehabilitation work should be conducted through which the basic and traditional pattern of life of the Birhors would be changed. In order to serve the purpose Birhor Rehabilitation Programme was framed up in 1956 under the auspices of the Govt.of Bihar. The principal efforts were centralised on the following points:

1. The Birhors were to be resettled. It was thought that if their wandering habit could be checked up and specific steps could be taken up to sedentarize them in resettlement camps specially designed for the purpose, these people would be able to engage themselves in the practice of food production. In this way their long-term dependence on forest for food through hunting and gathering would necessarily be stopped.
2. In the resettlement camps the Birhors were to live within the brick-built houses allotted for each family. The roofs of those houses were to be covered by baked tiles locally known as *khapra.* It was thought that if the Birhors get full-fledged permanent houses, having two rooms and a verandah, they could not take the pain of cutting trees from the forest to build leaf houses, and thus there would be no propensity amongst them to move about leaving frequently the temporary huts. Sentimental connection with the permanent houses would very naturally develop amongst them than the trend of sedentism.
3. For the purpose of making them perfectly sedentarized community the programme was made more integrated by providing each Birhor family, within the resettlement camps, lands for cultivation together with bullock and allied

agricultural implements. Moreover arrangements for kitchen gardens were made by the side of each settlement provided for the Birhor families so that they would be encouraged to grow crops off an on as per their requirements. It would gradually bring an end to their practice of collection of roots and tubers from the forest.

4. The traditional Birhor *tandas* with leaf-made *kumbas* were replaced by the newly constructed resettlement colonies having brick-built modern houses.

   Those government sponsored colonies were populated by bringing various Birhor families from their different temporary settlements the *tandas*. In these newly constructed colonies there were provisions for community houses, dancing platforms, public well and tubewells, training centres for learning agricultural activities so that the ill-fated tribal community would be attracted towards these colonies which automatically would minimise their connection with the forest for subsistence.

Through the Chotanagpur region and specially in the Birhor concentrated areas such types of resettlement colonies started growing up through the direct initiative of the Govt. of Bihar and those were time to time supervised by the administrative official under the said government. The main intention of those camps was to dissociate the Birhors from the forest and to help them develop a self-sufficient village life in the same ecological zone without destroying the elements of ecology. The ecology-economy relationship patterns in the traditional way of life was discouraged in that newly introduced method of subsistence and there was an effectual attempt to make them understand the proper utilisation of ecology for economic benefit through food production.

But the Birhors have not shown any positive sign to support the efforts that have been made since long time past. Practically speaking, life in the resettled colonies has become monotonous and it has failed to give any inspiration to the Birhors. The Birhors have failed to adjust with the new surroundings so carefully and seriously designed and processed for them by the organisors and in no time it has been observed that being unable to fit themselves with the changed situation many families have fled away during the stillness of night. It has become impossible for them to accept the changed situation within the resettled colonies as these very often neglect the traditional norms. The programmes for rehabilitation have been whole-heartedly focused to improve the economic condition of the tribe without giving any respect to their indigenous beliefs and practices. The organisors of the development programmes are always in the line of making some concrete attempts to change the uncertain life of the tribe based on hunting and gathering, and thereby to help them getting rid of extreme poverty that they have been facing since long time past.

Hunting-gathering tribes have got a specific pattern of their on. Obviously, there are many uncertainties in the mode of life but these people are not afraid of it. The uncertainty is their basic understanding of life and every step of which has been beautifully adjusted with that specific trait of food quest. Some conspicuous types of resistance, both physical and cultural, are set against this phenomenon so that they need not bother for uncertainty. Poverty is the daily companion of these people and, mention may be made, that poverty can never overpower them. Amongst the Birhors poverty is a self-imposed phenomenon thus it is not regarded as a hurdle for their life but a mode of existence. It is for this reason they attach less importance to it; what is more important is the problem of living. They are in favour of utilising the nature as per their will and convenience. It is objectionable, according to them, to put any restriction in the free utilisation of natural properties. They are against surrendering their freedom by mere allurement of getting so-called comfort in living. The programme of resettlement, it has been seen, has challenged that freedom. The resettlement colonies are patterned with routined activities to give special stress on the food growing activities as well as to stop the wandering habit of these nomadic group of humanity. These situations have exerted a tremendous blow to their understandings. Nomadism is such a mode of behaviour in which the life is conditioned by certain traits that are ultimately developed into wandering philosophy. The nomadic communities, it is to be observed, that are not haphazard and unsystematic in their movement, rather these follow a regular and planned line of wandering through the region in which the people belonging to the nomadic communities live and work. Nomadic hunters-gatherers are commonly organised into small bands that are linked up with the patterns of interactions based on mutual understanding. Each of the bands signifies itself as the categorical economic unit and thus the total economic organisation of the band-based community is centred round intra and inter-band cooperation conditioned by group activities. Among the Birhors each band is uniclan — members of a particular clan are united in a band which is not only an economic unit but also a socio-religious group having a particular clan god. The clan god or *Bonga Ora* is the guardian deity of the band and during the movement through the different places the *Bonga Ora* is carried by the band leader on his head. It is believed that *Bonga Ora* directs them supernaturally in selecting the hunting camp site. When the temporary *tanda* is to be established he actively assists them in searching out the prospective hunting and gathering zone. The *Bonga Ora* protects them from all sorts of hazards and anxieties both in natural as well as supernatural spheres. Thus their close spiritual association with the *Bonga Ora* inside and outside the living units is an inevitable factor in the maintenance of the day to day life and activities.

Considering the total situational context of the traditional nomadism-oriented hunting-gathering way of life in the indigenously fashioned tanda organisation on the one hand, and the modern sedentism — influenced food producing activity–dominated life on the other, it is seen that there has developed a conspicuous clash of values between the tradition-based indigenous and the modernised and imposed life-ways and thought-ways. The brick-built houses are no doubt based on modern technology and these are well constructed and safe but to the Birhors these are not safe because of the absense of *Bonga Ora* in these. They think these houses are not fit to live in during the night as the different malevolent spirits hovering around would get easy and instant entry in these houses due to the absence of *Bonga Ora* and thereby would put the Birhors in acute distress. Therefore, in many of the resettled colonies it has become the common practice to raise kumbas by the side of the brick-built houses. On enquiry, it is known that the day time can be spent in the brick-built houses but during the night it is essential to take shelter inside the kumbas for keeping themselves away from the evil influence of injurious deities. It is to be noted here that the Birhors have failed to accept the newly introduced house because of their nontraditional framework — these are culturally alien to them and so the tradition-bound *Bonga Ora* can not be established inside these houses. Thus these houses have failed to make any sentimental connection with these people for whose benefit these are meant.

The imposition of the factors for sedentism to make an end of the age-old traditional nomadism amongst the Birhors has put a deep mark in their life-philosophy. It is a fact that resettlement is not a solution to nomadism. It is to be mentioned that these people are always on the move not because of the fact that they cannot provide permanent shelters for themselves but because it is their life-style which has been designed according to their mode of food quest and pattern of exploitation of the nature. Traditionally, they are to cover a larger food zone extending over a vast region and hence it instigates nomadism. Nomadism amongst the Birhors is the essence of life-it has been penetrated into the value-patterns of the people as because total life-activities rotate round this phenomenon. Nomadism constitutes an inevitable factor in the culture traditions of the Birhors. This situation of life has performed closest integration with the surrounding ecology. Thus the three factors like man, ecology and nomadism are interlinked as well as interdependent in such an integrated pattern that one is unseparable from the other. If any of these factors is delinked from the integrated whole there will be an event of disequilibrium in the cultural settings of the people. Moreover, the resettled colonies have been designed in such a process where there is clear-cut sedentary life and the newly set colonies are seen to be inhabited by the families which are brought from different traditional *tandas* without maintaining any sociocultural norms which govern the nature of population in the *tandas*. The temporary *tandas* with their nomadic features have abruptly been transformed into the resettled colonies with amalgamated population belonging to different clans. This situation has led to some sort of anomaly in the social organisation of the Birhor resettlement colonies. The complete dissociation between the Birhors and the forest ecology has become a specific concern in the Birhor Rehabilitation Programme. A group of people having traditional multifaceted interdependence with the forest-based ecology can never be developed without allowing them to think for a moment about the forest. In reality, it has been done so and as a necessary consequence of which the Birhors in the resettled colonies find themselves in a stuffy atmosphere which is detrimental to the development programme as a whole. It is time for evaluating the whole situation directly related to the failures in the efforts for changing the life-situation of the Birhors and thereby to help them resist the unfavourable circumstances as faced by them. It must be noted that while framing up the programme for development through rehabilitation of any human community special provisions should be made to pay respect to the indigenous philosophic principles directly connected with the cultural traditions of the people concerned. The Birhor Rehabilitation Programme implemented throughout the Chotanagpur region pinpoints a very miserable state of affair. The very response of the Birhors towards the resettlement colonies raised after conspicuous troubles has become disheartening. The changed ecological and social setting that are newly developed for remoulding the life and activities of the Birhors have been proved out and out non-adaptive to these people as they do not find any emotional linkage with the newly introduced settlement pattern. Allotment of agricultural lands has become futile to them as they still follow the different world views regarding food quest. It is beyond their conception that a small plot of land can be utilised for getting food. They are still happy to think themselves as the "Kings of the forests." It has become a common scene today that in spite of living in the resettled colonies the Birhors in groups are going out for hunting and gathering. Therefore, it can be said with certainty that any sort of imposition of changing situation neglecting integrated cultural traditions of the people concerned is proved to be a meaningless attempt and hence it should be given up at the very outset.

REFERENCES

Andrewarta, H.G. & J.S. Bruner (Eds.) 1984: *The Ecological Web.* Chicago, Chicago University Press.

Bhowmick, P.K. 1990: *Applied-Action-Development Anthropology.* Calcutta, Institute of Social Research.

Bicchieri, MG. (Ed.) 1992: *Hunters and Gatherers Today.* New York, Holt, Rinehart and Winston.

Bornstein, M.H. & J.S. Bruner (Eds.). 1989: *Interaction in Human Development.* Hillsdale, N.J. Lawrence Eribaum.

Bose, N.K. 1972: "The Birhors", In *Some Indian Tribes.* New Delhi, National Book Trust.

Fagan, B.M. 1985: *People of the Earth,* Toronto, Little, Brown and Company.

Fox. Richard, C. 1969: Professional primitives: hunters and gatherers in Neuclear South Asia, *Man in India,* 49(3), Ranchi.

Kumar, H.D. 1995: *General Ecology.* New Delhi, Vikas Publishing House.

Leacodk, E & Richad Lee (Eds.) 1982: *Politics and History in Band Societies.* Cambridge, Cambridge University Press.

Lee, Richard, B. & Irven Devore 1968: *Man the Hunter.* Chicago, Aaldine.

Malinowski, B. 1944: *A Scientific Theory of Culture,* Chapel Hill, University of North Carolina Press.

Moran, E.F. 1982: *Human Adaptability-An Introduction to Ecological Anthropology.* Colorado, West View Press.

Moran, E.F. (Ed.) 1984: *The Ecosystem concept in anthropology.* A.A.A Selected Symposium, Washington D.C.

Piddington, R. 1952: *An Introduction to Social Anthropology.* London, Oliver and Boyd.

Rasmussen, K. 1947: The Seal Eskimos: Simplicity through poverty. In *A Reader in General Anthropology.* Ed. by C.S. Coon, New York, Henry Holt and Company.

Roy, S.C. 1976: *The Birhors - a little known jungle tribe of Chotanagpur.* Reprint edition, Ranchi, Catholic Press.

Saraswathi, T.S. (Ed.) - 1999: *Culture, Socialization and Human Development: Theory. Research and Application In India,* New Delhi, Sage Publications.

Sarkar, R.M. 1986 : Sedentarization of the Nomadic Birhors. *Van yajati,* 34(1), New Delhi.

Sarkar, R.M. 1990: From Nomadism to sedentism - adaptation and response as exemplified by the Birhors of Chotanagpur. *Man In India,* 72(3), Ranchi.

Sarkar, R.M.1993: Ecology, Culture and Social Disorganisation - The Birhors of Chotanagpur, in *Peoplc of India,* Ed. by S.B. Roy and Asok K. Ghose, New Delhi, Inter-India Publications.

Sarkar, R.M. - 1997: Forest Ecology and Cultural Development-Reflections from the life of the Birhors of Chotanagpur. In *Contemporary Society - Tribal Studies,* Ed. by G. Pfeffer, and D.K. Behera, New Delhi, Concept Publishing House.

Sinha, D.P. 1958: Cultural Ecology of the Birhors. *Journal of Social Research,* 1(1), Ranchi.

Vidyarthi L.P. - 1981: *Tribal Development and Administration.* New Delhi, National Publishers.

14

Sustainable Social Development : Myth or Pragmatic Reality*

G.C. Pande[1], *D.C. Pandey*[2]

1.1 SUSTAINABLE DEVELOPMENT: THE CONNOTATION

The World Commission on Environment and Development (1983) appointed Mrs. Gro Harlem Brundtland, the Prime Minister of Norway, to go into the problem of global crisis and survival potentialities of mankind in context of challenges of development strategies. The concept of sustainable development emerged from the Brundtland report (1987) entitled, "Our Common Future" submitted to U.N. General Assembly. It defines the concept as development which meets the needs of the present without compromising the ability of future generations to meet their own needs. Here the discussion centres round the needs of the mankind in specific sense of essential needs of the world poor, and the environmental demands. The progressive transformation of economy and society is termed as development. The growth potential is exploited for meeting the needs but the needs of all are not cared about because of the nature of social, economic and political organizations.

---

1. Professor Enieritus, Dept. of Economics,

2. Reader, Dept. of Geography, Kumaun University, Nainital, Uttaranchal State. India.

The tribals and scheduled castes in India share less of the prosperity due to institutional barriers and cultural reasons. These disparities and inter-group econo-social differentials wear an environment not conducive to growth. Absence of the basic capability building inputs, like education, health, nutrition, access to productive resources like land, and institutional supports create the environment unfavourable to conducive growth and sustainable development. The physical environment can attain sustainability by use of hydel, wind, solar, photovoltaic and nuclear energies, and the switch over from carbon intensive fuels is in favour of sustainability.

The social justice and minimum needs strategies of development are sustainable. Afforestation strategies in very large scale are sustainability supporting strategies which negate the impact of ecological degradation. The impact of new technologies like information technology and bio-technology are likely to spoil the economic ecology causing enormous fall in incomes of developing countries and positive gains to the owners of these technologies in the West. The genes and the germ plasms taken nearly free from developing countries for bio-technology research shall be resold to them at enormous costs, leading to augmented disparities.

This pattern of exploitation tallies with the exports of fossil fuels from the developing countries in the past century which promoted the disparities relegating the developing world to third grade colony of 'sub-human's. Dualistic character of world economy is a non-sustainable model.

Applying this line of argument to the dualistic character of development within Indian society we can trace the seeds of unsustainable disparities. The economy and society has dualistic pattern varying from most advanced export-enclave pattern to the crude tribal pattern and each has its independent enclave intensifying prosperity and acute poverty respectively due to technology differentials. The former has the pattern of western consumerism based culture while the later has to toddle round the crude traditional ways of living and deprived of the very essentials of cultured life. This status of differentials is a non-sustainable model for consistent growth of Indian society as well as the economy. Unless the wastages and vulgarities of consumerism are controlled, there is little hope for a sustainable development of human civilization.

Sustainable culture, sustainable economy, sustainable society, and sustainable development have something in-common. These work for democratic, egalitarian, non discriminatory, morality of proved values, and non declining utility, non declining resource stock and non-growing pollution levels. Sustainable development is an art of eating the cake and having it too. The development can be sustainable for its two values; intrageneration and intergeneration equity. We have to raise present output as well as leave stock of resources for posterity. We must keep the productive resources equally effective and in same quantum as we inherited. The tenets of sustainable strategy may include, among other things, the following:

(i) Preventing pollution (ii) Checking deforestation (iii) Afforestation in large scale (iv) Substitute wood and timber by metals (v) Recycle water (vi) Recycle paper (vii) Treat plastics (viii) Use fewer vehicles (ix) Come to simplicity of fewer needs (x) Work for atmospheric cleaning (xi) Avoid drug abuse, terrorism, and violence (xii) Protect biodiversity (xiii) Protect land and water (xiv) Restore degraded land (xv) Enrich ground water (xvi) Introduce efficient water management (xvii) Raise living standards of poor (xviii) Raise nutrition levels of poor (xviv) Control draughts by reserves and rain harvesting (xx) Encourage poly culture and substitute monoculture (xxi) Replenish loss to soil by raising new crop and preserve genetic diversity.

World Development Report (1992) noted that without adequate environmental protection development will be undermind and without development environmental protection shall fail. Alleviating poverty is a moral imperative and prerequisite for environmental sustainability.

The major question posed by sustainable development controversy is whether the present mode of development is sustainable over the long run or it is doomed to complete disaster due to the rapid pace at which this mode is rendering the basic resources unusable? If it is true, which dimensions and notions regarding development need to be reformulated or relegated all together? The second issue is regarding the development of the sustainability quality of earth by overcoming the limitations imposed by present state of technology or working resource use patterns, and social structure which imposes limitations on the ideal use of resources, and fails to enable nature to sustain present human civilisation any more. The sustainability is approached from three different angles; (a) economic or individual (b) environmental, the surroundings which make human survival possible and, (c) social: which means the organization and pattern of living wherein the nature distributes its fruits to the biotic-a biotic world. The economic approach to sustainability means eating the cake stomuch full as well as having the cake for future consumption. It maintains the stock of capital to see that future supplies are well ensured before consuming a part for the moment. Social sustainability maximises the optimum social justice and egalitarianism so as to benefit all in semi-equal manner so that society grows and prospers without endangering the source of supplies from nature.

Environmental sustainability emphasizes (Childial S. and Shekhar Pandey, 1999) stability for the biological and physical systems. Socio-environmental linkage gives rise to issues of intergeneration equity and common interest of mankind to save nature. The econo-environmental interface raises the issues of valuation and internalisation of environmental costs. The socio-economic interface deals with the vital matters relating to targeted relief to the deprived against the loss incurred to him by environmental damage. The geographers have been reaching a form of development which helps nature to help man and other creatures, as parts of ecology. Such model avoids a development which is militating and conflicting with upkeep of natural regeneration capacity. The main aim of development is to enable nature to protect the human civilisation as well as the framework of nature as a whole. Childial and Pandey (1999) stressed on four catagories of the social propensities, (a) Prospensity of society to proceed with development irrespective of its impact on environment; (b) Propensity to withhold development to protect environment; (c) Propensity to support both and co-ordinate at the conflicting points by relative greater advantage to sustainability; (d) Propensity to damage both the environment as well as the development by abuse of procreative faculties and population expansion.

1.2 SUSTAINABLE TECHNOLOGY FOR FUTURE GROWTH

The sustainable development model is interrelated with a sustainable technology which means that uses a non-exhaustible source of energy and which does in no way impair the environment by its products, by-products, effluents, or emission of smoke and gases. In modern sense, there can't be a model of technology which does not hit the environment. The primitive tribal technologies seem to be closer to the sustainable model of technology and that too can operate with hardly a millionth part of global population today in fully grown forest cover everywhere. Modern civilisation with so grown international trade, can't, all of a sudden, be reverted to tribal model of being in tune with nature. Modern living has the global dependence with regard to raw materials as well as the finished products. How this can be put to reverse gear to adapt purely to local supplies and limited modes of consumption? Bio-energy may have some answer to domestic energy needs. This, obviously, brings us to the conclusion that "mass-scale production:, which is a must in capitalistic system of today, is the root of our ills.

This mode can't do without endangering the sustainability. It needs so much of energy that the petty sources can't supply. The conventional techniques of production are not efficient enough to feed the united world of today. This means, that the current technologies are not sustainable because these are bound to hit environment by all the kinds of pollutions. The faster these grow, the earlier will be the end of our civilisation. The experts feel that revitalisation of conventional labour intensive technologies is possible by modifications in environment friendly direction. In that case the consumption levels, trade, and related activities shall have to be dropped enormously for which political concensus shall be essential. Even if developed, the solar, wind, bio-geo-thermal, energies will not be able to meet the requirements of modern world. The hydro-electric power assures little hope and this needs to be remodelled for the future needs.

The model of end-use devices determines the actual consumption of energy and proper attention here can economise the resources to a big extent. Small firewood can cook more food than greater wood in an inefficient cooking and heat-use device. The same is true for big industrial spheres where the end use devices are poor as in India because these were imported when the power was much cheaper. Technological growth needs tuning with needs of sustainability.

1.3 INTERGENERATION EQUITY IN OPPORTUNITIES

Sustainable development means a development which can be well afforded over a very long perspective without endangering either the resource-base on which the development stands or the human survival. It is termed 'sustainable' because nothing is going to obstruct its sustence in a long perspective. It is possible, if the style, mode, content, and impact of activities, leading to such development or the operation of such development, does nothing to impair the resources that lead to its survival. There maybe a type of development which is affordable over a foreseable future due to emerging competitive needs and exhaustible non-renewable nature of its imputs or self-negating impact of development itself. A development must afford to its innumerable future generations at least the same capacity and capability to prosper, maintain the level of consumption, retain the vigour and vitality of life with ever increasing choice-horizon, and maintain the variety and diversity of environment, as it promises to the present generation. The development opportunities and potentialities have their basic foundation on the pace of resource-consumption. If the resource-base is unending for billions of years, like sun-shine, it is unlikely to exhaust and cause problem in sustaining the development. Hydroelectric generation on rapid flows or solar energy in tropical areas do not seem to hit the sustainability. But the clearance of vast forest covered areas in the sloppy mountain tracts for making water reservoirs in unstable rocky geological formations is not free from the risks of large-scale land slides and great devastations by floods.

Development, progress, and economic growth today may reclaim extended tracts, utilize water flows for crops, irrigation, hydel generation, tourism, and huge structures of dams and reservoirs, etc. leading to augmentation of income and high average consumption. But do these ensure the same or higher in come for future without inviting catastrophe by disturbed ecological order? What mechanism has been evolved to rectify the disturbances created by these projects in naturally grown forests, to rehabilitate the soil, stabilize the rocks, and regulate the flow of water in the fast flowing streams which are likely to enundate the reservoirs in very short time ahead. Once the enundation by debris, soil, sand, gravel and rock-pieces starts, the reservoir shall fail to accommodate the water which may push the entire structure to give way. The gushing water stock to low lands may also wash away the human habitations, and result in floods of still greater devastating force. The sustainable development in this sense ensures that the activities enhancing income and comforts of mankind today should not be giving birth to dangers of spoiling the resource potential for future generations. The land fertility, environment, splendour, underground water level, green canopy, biotic life-forms, the oxygen content of air, air moisture, etc. must be protected by activities under the, present development.

The over exploitation of soil, removal of soil cover, deforestation, uprooting of soil bindings grasses, anihilation of thorny bushes of dry areas, and excess pressure on water resources, excess-dressing of soil by dangerous herbicides, insecticides, and fertilizers of any kind, etc. is likely to turn the lands into unrectible deserts of future. Therefore, the present development enthusiasts must take adequate care to see that in a hurry to make fast gains, the quality of land should not be allowed to deteriorate whether by erosion or desertification. The water is the source of life on earth but this resource is getting the rarest of all attention in spite of the fact that 4/5th part of the globe is water. The shortage of potable safe drinking water is a major problem. Water has to be kept free from all types of pollution so that life on the earth could sustain. The life forms in marine wealth is also likely to eliminate, if the quality of water is polluted for raising current consumption and living comforts of humanity today. The dimension of macro-level consciousness for protection of life resources in order to accord sustainability to current human civilisation has been raised in serious voice only recently, though even 5000 years before Chirst, the call for such alertness had been raised in Veda and later epics. What is special in this approach relates to acceptance of the exhaustable nature of non-renewable resources of earth.

It has been well identified today that the development pattern, development method, and development direction adopted by mankind everywhere, whether the highly progressive societies or the lagging humanity on road to modern growth, has been a sort of decoity, plunder, loot on the non-renewable resources of earth which shows that the future generations of mankind and other life, is likely to be deprived of their right to live. Because without air the life can't sustain itself and the pace at which we are polluting air on earth, is so fast that shortly the life on earth shall have to die of suffocation and for dearth of inhalable oxygen. Environmental degradation and depletion of rare resources of non-renewable nature, has endangered the survival over a long range. If the existing technology and pattern of development continues at present pace involving enormous burden on non-renewable resources, the future generations are like to suffer an unmendable loss of their, right to survive. The pace of depletion of natural rare resources is alarmingly high today and is likely to reach phenomenally high levels when the developing countries, so seriously trying to follow the advanced economies, attain their goals. This shall be at the cost of the rare resources like water, soil, lush green forest, inhaleable clean air and the ecology of survival.

1.4 SUSTAINABILITY OF LIVING SPACE

'Shrinking of ozone layer' is the illustration which adequately demonstrates how the humanity in near future shall have to bear the consequences of the bad deeds of their ancestors undertaken on the excuse of development. Present development is 'over spending' of non-renewable resources so as to leave nothing for the future except the lifeless extended deserts without water, greenary, splendour, or any sign of natural life forms. The danger has been revealed in the form of various abnormalities in the natural phenomena over the past several years. The symtoms of destruction, disturbed ecology, polluted environment, exhaustion of the regenerative capacity of nature, and irreparable loss to life systems by the deeds of development enthusiasts round the globe, are getting more evident. Neither the use of hydroflurocarbons shall eliminate from present set of technologies nor the shrinking of 'ozone layer' shall be controlled. This obviously, suggests that the direct radiation of ultra violet rays shall destroy all life on earth in near future. The 'sustainability' of development in the wake of such dangers is seriously impaired. Humanity shall not be able to maintain its affluence at existing levels over future. More dangerous than this is that the existing pace and form of development is likely to endanger the survival of any form of life.

The emission of industrial wastes, garbage, atomic fossils, radio-active remnants, effluents from chemical industries, tanneries, and so on, has hazardous impact on soil, water, air, and the other resources. The development strategies everywhere today have to go for these to compete well with the developed world. The pollution already accomplished by developed nations is enough to force the future mankind to live a miserable life of uncared creatures in highly unfavourable conditions. The smoke pollution and gas pollution emitted by the existing industrial installations in west and the developing countries alike, is likely to make the air so polluted that human beings, as other creatures, shall find no pure oxygen in all the times to come. The rivers are polluted by effluents, the seas and oceans by the vast waste materials of current civilisation, the greenaries all around are eliminating due to deforestation and desertification, and the snows on the lofty mountain ranges, the north and south poles, and the glacial regions are melting away by global warming. The experiments towards war-technologies, the making of bombs and other destructive materials, known as development today, are likely to reduce the beautiful earth planet to the heap of ashes. The danger is well identified and recognised by all, still, the so called development for destruction continues.

Sriniwas Gowda (1992) very rightly observed, "Environmental degradation-ranging from soil erosion, desertification, air pollution, to shrinking of ozone layer, pollution of the world's rivers and oceans, global warming and deforestation is drawing phenomenal attention of the academicians and policy-makers". The discussions have long been triggered and some policy level conclusions have been arrived. The policy making circles round the globe have been appealed for incorporating "Environmental Protection" as major objective and in no circumstances infringement of environment protecting regulations be allowed in any development activity whether production, consumption, exchange, trade or manufacturing. These considerations may be adopted as intrinsic parts in every policy. The environmental safeguard are not enough, rather environmental reform should be taken up as a merit in each policy because the future of the earth and its life resources depends on how much of reform is actually implemented to rectify the committed wrongs. The loss, caused to environment in any form by any development activity or non-developmental acts of humanity for various reasons, has to be met by the reformist action.

There should be a built in mechanism in the development projects to offset the environmental costs of humanity in the supply of a service or commodity. The other major policy dimension to environmental safety relates to the efforts laid down for the control in the human fertility. We are aware of the consequences of the population growth on the economic lot of the human beings as well as on the resources in short supply. The over breeding is related to the fate of the womenfolk, care of the girl child, education of the girls, job-alternatives available to girls, participation of women in the actual policy-making, and the technologies within an easy access of mothers to restrict fertility. The reproductive behaviour is actually determined by the status of women, significance attached to her various roles in society, an the safety and longevity assured to women regarding survival of their children. The women liberation drive in the present day life of women in the west suggests that women, by nature, do not choose to bear children as a matter of their own choice and sweet will. By and large the women want to free themselves of this burden and share with the males in shaping the society to still higher levels of welfare for all the life-forms. Women are the best guardians of nature and human culture together, therefore, their active participation is like to assure the humanity a brighter future than that of their male counterparts. Women, in some tribal societies, exercise the roles of decision-making to greater extent than in most developed democracies of the non-tribal populations. Steps to improve the status of the life resources are to be taken by state initiatives and private efforts by collaborating organisations.

The lavish use of water in modern living specially in urban culture is bound to end up the underground water and pollute all the flowing streams to the extent that human life shall be endangered by water born diseases and for shortage of potable water everywhere. The fumes of coal burning, smoke of firewood burning, dust storms, lead laden gas in the air, vehicular smoke, etc has already rendered the human breathing difficult. It has in fact led to diseases of all kinds, respiratory diseases, eye-burning, skin problems, etc. The soils, impoverished by erosion, or polluted with dangerous chemicals and excessive exploitation have gradually lost fertility and are likely to fail in feeding the ever increasing human numbers. Here is the role of policy-making with environmental considerations.

The tribal communities in absence of education, the dearth of knowledge and macro-approach, have everywhere been resorting to shifting agriculture and destruction of forests by fellings and fires. It is a practice which could help a handfull wild-life addicts and isolated primitive people in the past. In the new set of things the tribals have multiplied, forests have come under the state control deforestation is proved derogatory to the up keep of environment. Therefore, the liberties of shifting cultivation can not be permitted. But the tribals have their needs and a given culture within which they operate. the obvious environmental needs demand regulation of tribal liberties by settling them for stable agriculture. The tribal terraces in many cases tend to cling to the steep heights with decent of 50 to 60 degrees. Such terracing encourages the land slides and rapid erosion of soils. Obviously, to save the soil and mountains sides, an environment protection policy shall impose restrictions on terracing above 40 degrees slope in hills. The tribal agriculture, mostly dry farming, has some special advantages for the protection of the bio-herbal diversity and retaining the indigenous seeds of crops which do not use any sort of chemical fertilizers or insecticides or pesticides. Such crops are naturally less dangerous for human consumption than crops using intensive doses of insecticides.

Palni, Maikhuri and Rao (1997) rightly observed, "The significance of agrobiodiversity as a key component in maintaining the life and culture of the local people has been well recognised the worldwide. Bio-diversity is the source of risilience and regeneration and is necessary for the sustainability of agro-ecosystems."

1.5 ENVIRONMENTAL CARE FOR SUSTAINABILITY

Economists commonly agree that building the pollution prevention in to new investments would any way be cheaper than adding them later. New technology has to be less polluting than the old one. Any new pattern of life adopted has to be less impairing and far less injurious to environment. The civic and tribal settlements equally have to grow and develop in tune with the needs of environmental care. The cost of clean technologies have to be borne to avoid catastrophe for all. The linkage between safe environmental growth and economic growth over a long run is well recognised and to this extent, humanity can afford slowing down of immediate pace of growth than endangering the future for good. How far the economic growth shall have to suffer by picking up environmental safeguards as costs and how far the safer environment is likely to add to human welfare in the long range has yet to be ascertained at macro-level. Who should bear the cost of rectification of already spoilt environment and to what extent the regeneration system of nature would be enough to mend it, are the debatable questions while the agreement seems to emerge in policy based alignments of development and environmental care. Those who have higher incomes and consumption levels today are technically eating at the roots of environment which reduces the capacity of nature to maintain this civilisation in future. In this sense the income augmentation by greater output means encashing the future incomes in advance with huge discounts at the cost of those unborn generations whose case, there is no body to represent today. The lavish living today is like lavish spending by living on loan from future generations.

Any macro-economic accounting is bound to change if we deduct the costs of environmental damage in total incomes. To this extent, national income or global income reported today stands rectification and revision. Income generated by large scale deforestations and polluting water, air, soil, natural landscape by transport and tourism, and polluting underground water by pumping poisonous insecticides into soil, etc. are all illusory and misconceptions. The thermal power projects producing so much of power are actually converting the coal based energy into electric based energy because coal deposits are dwindling day by day. The petroleum is nearly exhausting and all the important minerals and deposits of nature are eliminating as the material wealth of the world is increasing. Once the metals are completely exhausted and minerals ended up, petroleum consumed, the future generations will not be able to prolong existing style of living and consumption. It adequately proves that the overall present and future resource balance sheet should be prepared and a strategy of sustainable development is adopted by mankind globally.

Human civilization can't sustain without the life supporting mechanism around the living organism. The supporting mechanism spread around the life forms is termed as environment. Life feeds itself, thrives and grows on the support of this mechanism. The quality of life is decided by the quality of the supportive resources. Soil, water, energy, air, and the peace besides the beauty of nature are important factors. The erosion, pollution, cantamination, exhaustion, rarity, degradation of these resources make the environmental deterioration. The qualitative deterioration of environment is the beginning of human misery, discomfort, disfiguring, lacking efficiency, stunted physical growth, and social life full of conflicts and disturbed peace emerging from tensions and pressures. A line of action towards development which causes the environmental deterioration, therefore, leads us to disaster. this does not ensure sustainability of civilisation over the long run.

The wider experience of mankind after 19th century illustrates the unsustainabler models of economic growth in so far as the developments have caused pollution, degradation of resources, wastages of irreparable nature, elemination of nonrenewable resources, and a general mismanagement of resources leading to human misery (Pandey, 1999). Sustainable development strategy is likely to revise such a model of development which disturbs the ecological balance of nature. The new strategy has to take a holistic view of development and drop the sectoral piece meal approach of development. The strategy affords adequate care for regeneration of oxygen by the special emphasis on green cover. It puts up efforts for keeping the water unpolluted and conserve water resources in such a way that the need of biotic and aboitic world is met in greater measure. Watershed management approach, for instance, is a part of such sustainable development strategy which protects the drift of soil to ocean and works for up keep of soil fertility. Without moisture the plants can't grow and thrive while without plants human being can't survive. The sanitary and hygeinic arrangements, which keep the water of rivers, lakes, ponds, ravines, underground water table and the water springs, neat and potable, are also a part of sustainable development. Steps to generate social and economic harmony and building of egalitarianism by opening opportunities of contended life for all wings of society also enter the theme of sustainable development. Such a society can survive long without international contradictions.

1.6 CONSERVATION OF RESOURCES FOR SUSTAINED GROWTH

The presumption of endless resource endowment by nature has to be forgotten and the prevalent practice of treating the environment as exogenous factor in growth has to be relegated to dust bin. It is well established that economists have to treat environment as an endogenous factor which is affected by human deals and their form, volume and character. The ecology is the supreme of the all arrangements of nature which makes a dent on the social and economic life as well as on the physical composition. If the pace of consumption of natural resources continues unresticted and unregulated on the excuses of economic growth and even increasing output, then the future shall be doomed to misery, stagnation and also utter disaster. Meadow's analysis in 'Limits to Growth' has explicitly placed the limitations in forefronts and expressed a humble warning against the current wastes and huge garbage of fossiled products. A true sustainable development strategy, thus, emphasizes on economising, recycling and regulated planned use of the rare resources of nature. This has actually led to recycling of water, minerals, metals, fuels, etc. the technologies are being searched to attain these goals at low costs. The promotion of the pace of the regenerative capacity of nature is very uneasy task as there can't emerge a method of quickening process of formation of petroleum, carbons, etc. in the stock of nature.

Conservation and upkeep is one of the known methods of prolonging the life of endangered resources. The restoration of ecological balance is said to be an important way. The experts believe that man and nature have to exist together and supplement each others survival. Man and his welfare is looked after by the nature. But the human attitude to the nature is of a crazy child. The degradation of environment is the outcome of man's crazy behaviour. Sustainability argument suggests that a harmonious relationship between nature and man has to be evolved for human good. Environment friendly technologies can make this relationship more cordial and mutually supporting. The status to the renewable resources is no way encouraging either. The resources which can be multiplied, planned and regenerated as per need are also in debilitated status. The deserts have emerged due to human excesses with the nature. In fact more and more areas which were greenaries once, are being desertified by the deforestations on a large scale and the dearth of water harvesting and water storage have led to desertification. In Gujarat and Rajasthan as also in some parts of Maharashtra in India, the draught conditions are far more frequent now. The victims of these draughts have to leave home with bag and baggage and herds for searching water every summer. These dimensions come-up as the issues for the future growth.

The tribal communities in the past truly followed the model of sustainable development. They used the products but protected the forests and used water while protected the streams. The intervention policy of the British rule took forests under the Government control and resorted to very large scale felling of trees to fill the treasures of the colonial regime. It was no more an individual use of forest for household needs. It was commercial use of the timber without replacing the stock. The same policy was followed by the following regimes except a change in regard to intention of replenishing these by new plantations. It was done nominally and the forest cover declined sharply over the first three decades after Independence. Between 1981-91, 42000 hectares of closed forests were cleared for logging. The other forests, deforested during this decade were in 37000 hectares in various states. Illicit fellings also continued. The actual forest cover discovered by Remote Sensing Satellite has been found in only 12 percent while the requirement prescribed by National Forest Policy (1952) and National Commission on Agriculture (1976) was stipulated as 33 percent. The tribal population's rights of Forest use were minimised. The tribes saw all this helplessly, closer access of forest officials led to exploitation of tribals. Tata Energy Research Institute (1997) reported that there was a net decline in availability of fresh water by two thirds and net degraded land area rose by almost

80 million hectares between 1947 to 1997. The varieties and diversity of forest wealth gave way to mono-culture of select species.

It is indeed difficult to reconcile the three different interests regarding future of forests; (i) the livelihood interests of the tribal communities (ii) commercial interests of government and contractors (iii) environmental protectionists. Similarly, in the exploitation of marine resources, the petty fishermen used seas as livelihood earning source who have been side tracked by mechanised trawlers of commercial class. The commercial use has less egalitarian impact and greater concentration impact while commercial scale operation makes huge profits leaving nothing for the future. They do nothing to regenerate the resource. Sustainability is possible either by reverting back to reduced consumption or by searching out alternatives of consumption. The natural resource exploitation rate has been several times faster than the pace of regeneration which has led us to this stage. The planners and the so called welfare governments could never foresee this disequilibrium. The present generation has been over eating on the share of coming generation. Barbier (1987). Lele (1991), Nadkarni (1996), Hinterberger (1997) and Solow (1993) raised the controversy of intergeneration equity.

1.7 CULTURAL ADJUSTMENTS FOR SUSTAINABLE DEVELOPMENT

Sustainbilay is a cultural problem of adjustment of habits of living, consumption, and pace of exploiting resources not exceeding the pace of regeneration. Where the two ends of withdrawal and refilling are coordinated and bear knife-edge equilibrium relationship, the sustainability criterion is met. In the context of western economies the sustainability is disturbed by the technology and industrial growth and in less developed areas of Latin America, Africa and Asia sustainability is seriously threatened by ever growing population which keeps on increasing pressure on the non-renewable as well as renewable resources irrespective of the regenerative capacity of nature. The deliberate changes, leading to pro environment changes in policy and programmes of development can, of course, help in protecting and optimising the regeneration and can save the environment as well as the renewables as resources. But economy and conservation together with recycling technologies can only be the sort of help in protecting the non-renewables. Unfortunately the developing economies are not as much users of non-renewables as they are exporters. All useful rare minerals are exploited for exports so that these economies meet their foreign exchange needs as well as needs of growing population. These economies have yet to grip over the technology to produce enough food for their growing population. What would be their future when nonrenewable resources are exhausted and the population multiplied several times? Similar is the case of the tribes where the consumption is growing and dependence on their rare resources is not tending to diminish where as the official dependence on their resources has also overgrown. With elimination of forests, and the water streams drying up in the mountains areas, the tribes will find no sustenance particularly when their population will have multiplied several times specially in the wake of the new medical facilities and sanitary arrangements coupled with increasing hygienic awareness. The onslaught on the natural environment does not seem approaching an end. A vast part of humanity is yet to gain by use of the fossil fuel energy like petroleum and other mineral wealth of nature. Gradually the economic development is bound to bring them in the fold, which shall further accentuate the pace of their depletion. Advanced economies also do not seem to be in a mood to impose any self control on such consumption. In some countries there are small efforts to develop some non-exhaustible and renewable sources of energy like solar, tidal, geo-physical, wind etc. The firewood and forest development would be a sizeable source for domestic needs at least in the rural peripheries but the forests are in great danger of being eliminated due to demand pressure of wood, forest products etc. and the for greater pressure for land under forests for industrial, housing, and agricultural purposes. This model is surely non-sustainable for long future.

Economic growth is essential for affording the surplus that should be invested towards mending the past mistakes regarding environmental damage. Economic development can't be discarded as a damaging phenomena. This together with a sound environmental management can be complementary to each other. World Development Report (1992) rightly noted that "Without adequate environmental protection, development will be undermined: without development environmental protection will fail"... It has been widely witnessed that the benefits of rising incomes are offset by the costs imposed on health and quality of life by the increasing pollution. The future productivity can be jeopardised if rising incomes today result in the soil degradation, depleted aquifer and destroyed eco-systems. The World Development Report found that alleviating poverty is a moral imperative and a pre-requisite for environmental sustainability. The poor are both the main victims and agents of environmental degredation.

Environmental damage shall be saved by stricter population control and upward revision of the living standards of the poor classes. This is more true for the scheduled tribes and scheduled castes in India. Much of the future of sustainable development depends on the pace at which their living conditions are improved, status elevated, their unemployment is solved and the population is kept within manageable limits. The World Bank report also notes with care that, "The evidence indicates that the gains from protecting the environment are often high and that the costs in foregone income (for choosing simplicity model) are modest if appropriate policies are adopted." Policies for efficient growth can complement those for environment protection. For instance, improving education for girls may be the most important long term environmental policy in the developing world, since educated women have smaller families and are able to make better use of natural resources.

How far this is followed by the policy making circles in India in specific reference of scheduled tribes and the scheduled castes shall be examined in the main body of this book. Strong public institutions are also essential for ensuring better results. There may be certain situations when a choice shall have to be exercised to opt either income growth or the environmental protection. Only a careful assessment of benefits and costs of alternate policies can make a right choice. The pollution affects the vulnerable classes several times more than the richer counterparts. Therefore, a check of pollution of water, air, soil, atmosphere, etc. shall bountifully benefit the poor in the safeguard of health, nutrition and housing. The scheduled caste population and the tribals shall be highly benefitted by official help towards their fertility control and rising levels of consumption.

The tribal communities and the scheduled castses have gained by expansion in irrigation facilities in the last five decades. They have shared the gains in terms of increased output and diversified output besides the rise in cropping intensity in their small holdings and they are, by and large, working as agricultural labourers or share croppers. Any way, irrigation permits the growing of three to four crops a year on the same land, therefore, creates productive employment for men, women and children of these vulnerable sections of society.

The irrigation projects are also facing increasing challenges from the farming groups in some areas of India, China, Thailand and United States. The dams and large irrigation systems are causing water logging, salinity, disruption of water table, damage to fisheries, and displacement of people inhabiting the areas submerged by new reservoirs and irrigation schemes. In the later seventies the trade off between relieving today's poverty and hunger through massive manipulation of water cycle and its natural systems and the attendant environmental and ecological costs of such development, came under scrutiny. The social disorientation caused by resettlement of affected population and damage to natural environment were the major complaints raised against the major irrigation projects.

The excess of water irrigation than required for each crop led to deterioration in the quality of land. It is indeed difficult to quantify all the social, environmental, and ecological costs related to human interventions in fresh water systems. It is certainly a fact that imprudent use, poorly developed irrigation arrangements, badly designed irrigation plans, etc. had some adverse effects on environment of these areas. The soil moisture rose to high levels and alteration in quality of underground water was reported in some cases. China, Egypt, India, Mexico, Pakistan, former USSR and Western United States have reported decline in productivity of soils in the excess irrigation areas. Water logging is reported from various parts resulting in salinity. This is due to the lack of proper drainage and water management. World Bank studies in these areas found that water logging and salinity reduced productivity by 30 percent. Sustainability needs saving of land against water logging.

Malaria and Bilharzia have affected the irrigated areas due to stagnant waterpools. Jaundice and other diseases rise-up in water logged areas as in Khatima, SitarGanj, Gadarpur. Nanakmatta areas of UP Terai where the tribal populations (around 72 thousand people) and scheduled castes (around 1,14,000 people) are affected by these ailments off and on. Bilharzia (Schistosomiasis) is caused by carrier vector from an aquatic snail which penetrates human skin. It causes a lot of human misery by damage to liver, bladder, lungs, nervous system and overall endurance. This problem has grown faster after the irrigational installations. China, Egypt. Sudan and Tanzania have reported considerable fall in labour productivity by this disease. Leaving the adverse effects of irrigation apart, the tribals and depressed wings of society are reported benefitting enormously by irrigation. In Thailand, the benefits of irrigation to the environment were substantial because it attracted large segments of population conventionally away from the general population, those generally devoted to "slash and burn" form of shifting cultivation, for organised stable agriculture. It was specially so regarding the tribes in the hilly tracts. In India as well, nearly 1,87,000 population of scheduled castes and 1,72,000 tribes have been settled in the irrigation project areas who have stepped on higher living standards in recent years. The reallocation of water to the dry land areas of Rajasthan, Gujarat etc. can bring a revolution in the life of the tribes and ignored parts of humanity in India.

Sustainable development strategy has to be biased in favour of social equity and coordination in welfare promoting measures so that the social environment and economic environment attains at least some degree of egalitarianism. The gains have to be percolated to the tribal communities and the scheduled caste populations in very large scale. Environmental care is based on the care of the last column of society who live with soil and the forests and who can provide safety to the diversity and variety to the wild life.

1.8 REMODELLING FOR SOCIAL EQUITY & SUSTAINABLE GROWTH

Sustainable development demands a future oriented remodelling of policies, programmes and society. We are aware that very vast tracts of arable fertile land in India have been diverted to the development of residential colonies, industrial complexes and playing grounds while every body is aware of the felt shortage of arable agricultural land in the country specially in the wake of the ever growing human numbers. It has been almost forgotten that these growing numbers shall require livelihood mostly in agriculture and food and raw materials shall be needed in increasing quantity in future. The Land Acquisition Act needs a revision in the light of this dangerous tendency. Expropriation of good, level, fertile, lands for non agricultural uses like public schools, universities, industries, parks and cremation grounds are almost a non-sense in Indian reference. This, obviously, reduced the bread creating capacity over future. Comprehensive food security system has been evolved in India, which is a plus point. The optimisation of yields from soil has to be a significant part of our policy. It is known that major parts of the country are under dry land farming and there is no hope of extending irrigation to all parts in near future.

Thus, the emphasis must focus round the development of appropriate technology for dry land farming which ensures multiple cropping and retain the crop diversity as well as nutrition supply even in odd conditions of draught. The richer and developed parts of humanity in India has the irrigation facility on its soils. The poorest of the poor, tribals, scheduled castes, backward communities and far flung sections manage with the dry land farming. 73 percent of cultivated area is believed to be under dry farming in India which contributes around 42 percent of food. If appropriate techniques are devised to promote forests around, to increase moisture holding and retaining properties of soil, and managing water storage from the scanty rainfall, the life of the tribals, scheduled castes and other lagging sections of Indian society can be considerably improved. The sustainable development includes the augmentation of crop yields in dry lands which not only ensures food augmentation but also ensures the crop-diversity and diseases-resistent crops. The prime need of the country is to promote oil seed production, pulses production, ground nut production, and production of coarse gains. Infact, tribal areas and lagging areas have specialisation in raising these even in very odd conditions of low rainfall. The investments in research towards dry land farming techniques shall directly help the country, and more to the tribals and scheduled caste populations.

Some alertness is emerging in this regard in recent years. Use of seed cum fertilizer drills, improved seeds of coarse crops, plant protection measures have helped the crop yields in some areas. Fertilizer use has also emerged in some areas of relatively greater soil moisture. India has 13 percent of world's semi arid tropics which require dry land farming research. Development of semi-irrigated areas and crop-life saving by emergent water-deposits should also be managed. Sorghum, pearl millet, pegeonpeas, chicken pea, ground nut, oil seeds, pulses, need special research for dry land areas which can significantly change the fate of tribal communities, scheduled castes and other backward communities. It is marked that 1/3rd of the dry lands in India are very degraded soils which attract less than 500 mm rains. The other 1/3rd part receives rainfall exceeding 1500 mm and these have serious water management problems. These include the black soils of cotton-cropping also. Nearly 40 percent of dry lands (around 100 million hectare area) have only shallow depth and these have faced soil erosion also. The dry land farming has rainfed crops which need timely tillage, planting, optimum plant population to save soil moisture, effective weed control, and efficient fertilizer use. In dry land, these need greater judgement and correct application. Techniques need to be developed for preserving soil moisture against evaporation. The tribes and scheduled castes population need intensive extension services for education on dry land farming.

Sustainable development of human society demands the reaching of the amenities to each wing of the society. The amenities not only relate to the modern living and comforts of life which promote the enthusiasm, efficiency, and capabilities of mankind to handle their day to day problems effectively like nutrition, food, medical, potable water, electricity, etc. but also covers the amenities of human resource development. The tribal and scheduled castes population in India is least dressed with these amenities so far. There have been some efforts in the past five decades for improvement in their living conditions, occupational persuits, resource development and in their overall participation in national main stream of ecosocio-cultural and political life. Much of the success in attaining a sustainable model of social development depends on modernisation and cultural change among the tribal populations and the lagging classes.

1.9 RESOURCE USE AND SUSTAINABLE DEVELOPMENT

Development in its true connotation is the process of getting to maturity, growth, refinement, gathering strength for making strides in upliftment and promotion of human welfare. When it is used in context of sustainable growth it means the furtherance, betterment, elaboration, enlargement and improvement in human welfare status which can be a continuous process without being obstructed by fluctuation or a droppage for dearth of affordability on the part of resources or capabilities of human beings. The concept is interreleated with optional utilization of avenues, potentialities and resources. A sustained growth is a continuous march of mankind to superior state of refinement and affluence. But sustainable development is the process of refinement that can be possible over the prolonged future in unrestricted and unobstructed flow over time. What causes this is not the smooth supply of resources on which the unrestricted human efforts shall continue operating. It is something more. A cultural refinement of human resource, better institutional arrangement, and higher ideals of mankind which guide the course of action, are a part of this process. It might require a different mind setting and frame of attitudes which leads to sustainable culture. Herman Kahn (1980) feels that the end of authoritarian, charismatic sacredism, and end of irrationality saves the path of development. How to make this process sustainable, needs the deeper analysis of factors related to unhampered growth. Injustice, suppression, subjugation, oppression, exploitation, discrimination etc. cause the aggravation of constraints and tensions. For sustainability therefore, more egalitarianism is warranted. Greater sharing in gains of human effort shall help the sustainability. More coordinated social, political and cultural adjustments are essential to ensure sustainability as claimed by Brundt Commission (1987).

Development is closely related to sharpening of productive capacity of resources. These may be land, soil, water, air, environment, the constituents which make the creation including the biotic and herbal life, the beauty resources, their inter-resource reactions, and in totality, the environment. How one form of life feeds the other form is the exchange mechanism that sustains the life in the world. Human being can make the growth and civilisational development sustainable by conserving, sharpening, developing and promoting resource utilisation with superb institutional growth to ensure equity, intra-generational and inter-generational. The resources are the gifts of nature and these have a limited carrying capacity. Sustainability may be seen in the light of the demand human society poses before the nature and whether such demand is very much within the carrying capacity. If the demand and use of resources is faster than the regenerative capacity of nature, the resources exhaust at faster pace. This makes the limiting factor in sustained growth. The non-renewable resources get extinct and the growth based on these have to eliminate by this ultimate limitation. The dynamism of human race shall be tested by how fast it is able to change its resource-base if metals exhaust, coal exhausts, petroleum exhausts and so on.

There shall not be any possibility of changing the life resources like water, air, soil, atmosphere, etc. These shall ultimately stop growth process of human civilisation. The sustainable development, thus, means the pattern which can continue in future unobstructed by pollution of earth, depleted productivity of soil, atmosphere etc. These shall ultimately stop growth process of human civilisation. The sustainable development, thus, means the pattern which can continue in future unobstructed by pollution of earth, depleted productivity of soil, contamination of potable water, poisoning of all products of soil (herbs, cereals, vegetables) by insecticides and pesticides, endangered survival on habitat by radioactivity caused by atomic and nuclear-explosions. How are we going to ensure that these barriers will not emerge for future generations? The fundamental question of sustainability emerges here. Our lavish and wasteful approach to resource utilisation today expedites the process of exhaustion of non-renewables or their pollution to the irreparable state. This means we are leaving a world for our future generations which shall not have pure air. Smoke, dust and acid laden gases will suffocate the future generation. The earth shall get unproductive and sterile. There shall not be any potable water left to quench their thirst. If our present technologies continue, the marine life, birds and even insects shall not be able to sustain on earth. Sustainable development, therefore, searches for a sustainable technology, sustainable culture, sustainable consumption level and the sustainable institutional order of society.

The optimal use of soil, land, water, air, forests, rocks, minerals biotic and abiotic life, etc. can be done by optimal development of human resource who will manage the earth. The economizing of rare resources, substitution, avoidance of all wastes, and expediting the regenerative capacity of nature for recouping the loss of renewable resources shall be essential. Sustainable technology shall make way for sustainable development.

An effort on the lines of regeneration can be seen in the afforestation programmes of India. The area under forests is being again planted with trees as may be noted from the table below.

Forest Afforestatlon In India

(Lakh hectares)

Five year plan	Afforested area	Comulative afforested area
First Five Year Plan (1951-56)	00.52	00.52
Second Five Year Plan (1956-61)	03.11	03.63
Third Five Year Plan (1961-66)	05.83	09.46
Annual Plans (1966-69)	04.53	13.99
Fourth Five Year Plan (1969-74)	07.14	21 .13
Fifth Five Year Plan 1974-78)	12.21	33.34
Gap year Plan (1979-80)	02.22	35.56
Sixth Five Year Plan (1980-85)	46.50	82.06
Seventh Five Year Plan (1985-90)	88.70	170.76
Gap Year Plan (1990-91)	07.01	177.77
1992-97	86.13	263.90

The rehabilitation of forests and soil resources, and water management conservation and rain harvesting including the storage and diversion of rives to dry land deserts by canals can ensure a great good to the future generations. The degraded land and degraded forests need treatment by scientific methods. Nearly 1215.8 lakh hectare land in India awaits treatment and utilisation. The sustainable development needs the treatment of degraded resources. Madhya Pradesh, Maharashtra, Rajasthan, Gujarat, Karnataka and Andhra have the major part of our degraded areas. 73 percent of crop-land is farming and devising proper technology for upgrading productivity in dry lands shall be a leap forward for sustainable development.

1.10 CONCLUSION

'Social sustainability' is a relatively new concept, it connotes weaving of those environs, conditions, and compatibilities which constitute the preconditions for building a tension-free, growth oriented and integrated society. A socially sustainable society is the only kind that can sustain itself over a long cherished span without internal conflicts, cohesive forces, oppression,resentment and disorder. Sustainability demands equity, democratic structure, interestrata coordination, mutual respect, intergroup amicable relations besides a free access to cling to the citadels of power, prestige and leadership. Experience has revealed that no society can sustain itself with continual oppression, autocratic whims of constituent wings, suppression of free will, and denial of opportunities to the hardworking creative components of society for indefinite period. In order to ensure social sustainability all Governments have a claim to be ideal welfare states, striving for the objective of ensuring a decent and progressively enlightened life of all human beings. Welfare states are inclined to protect such natural environs and conditions wherein all wings and sub-wings of the society materialise their dreams of progress within the framework of the broader convas of national main stream of cultural, political and sociallife. Welfare states act towards arresting the socio-economic and technological lag of the weaker components. This is how the stagnation and degradation of society is checked. Unification, integration, egalitarian character, democratic structure, and promotion of collaborative efforts for quicker growth are ensured by deliberate policies and programmes. Collaboration, coordination, mutual support, and strengthening of unifying forces are the instruments for promoting integration. In order to make the society a single united consistent whole, the constituent wings have to shun the destructive mutual rivalries, inter-wing antagonism and conflicts. The welfare state as a spokesman of entire society has to stand a guard for protection of the weaker wings and the slow and the lagging social components. All wings must grow and prosper at par and dedicate themselves to the common committed objectives.

Indian society holds the pride of bearing unity in great diversities of cultural ethos and the united common concern of all varying cultural wings for the committed support to the national ethos of mutual appreciation, mutual trust, mutual support, tolerance and common goal of building a vibrant and progressive society. Indian national culture is represented by the supreme value systems and life styles finding expression in diversified forms. Liberty and freedom of choice is the central theme in Indian culture. In most of the countries of the world, the aggressive intolerant dominant cultural streams ruled strictly to annihilate the divergent wings so that they have a single uniform pattern of cultural life. From its very inception, Indian culture preserved the values of tolerance, mutual appreciation, accommodation for divergence within the frame of national culture. This has led to the enviable enrichment of the main stream of cultural life. Indians have drawn a very large variety of tenets from cultural systems of the world and interwined them to make a strange admixture of varieties of cultures. The highly appreciable aspect of the 'Unity in Diversity' is that the varying ethnic constituents of Indian society have their distinguished identity which is well cared for and preserved with recognition.

Social sustainability ensures growth opportunities to all its components in an egalitarian pattern. National development policy and the programmes devise ways of equitable distribution of avenues of growth, it introduces the appropriate doses of growth incentives, offers the net work of infrastructure where the varying cultures find an easy expression, encourages collaboration and cooperation among the constituent cultural wings. Social reforms, educational push-up, access to science and technology strengthen the forces of modernisation and appropriate rationalisation. Social integration and sustainability is tending to grow much faster after Independence. The development programmes and welfare schemes have brought the divergent wings under a common fold of growth orientation.

There are several hurdles on way to high levels of social sustainability and closer integration. Inter-wing socio-economic differentials and disparities are by far more glaring today. Technological growth has, infact, widened the disparities in the inter-wing pace of growth. Even within the wings, intra-wing disparities are fast growing. Technology has helped the more alert and development conscious resourceful groups in their bid for growth while the other groups which have no access to these avenues for want of resource development, education, technology, infrastructure, and absence of initiative, dash, and enthusiasm, are left deprived of opportunities for growth. this state is not congenial to social sustainability. There are some institutional bottlenecks, structural barriers, inherent disadvantages, and disabilities which seem to hinder the equitable growth of all cultural wings of Indian society. There are several location specific, community specific, cultural situation specific, and habitat specific challenges which seem to obstruct the growth of some identified isolated ethnic entities. The inter-social strata and economic strata relations have often been roots of much hated oppression. The status of the scheduled castes, scheduled tribes, backward classes, etc. has indeed undergone a significant change over the past, yet some of their sub-wings still deserve attention of the welfare state for special treatment.

The hurdles on way of social sustainability which are location or habitat specific, have to be tackled by vigorous developmental action. Development of physical resources and man-power resources in these locations by affording appropriate infrastructure is likely to ensure rapid growth, the structural and institutional barriers may demand appropriate Parliamentary enactments, executive enforcements and gathering of mass support in favour of rationalised behaviour and modernisation. Empowerment of the relatively disadvantaged social wings and promotion of their alertness for change for progress would be necessary. Infact empowerment has two distinct dimensions; (a) Raising of the ambition line so that the weaker wings are not satisfied with only mediocre achievements, and (b) Capacity building for better performance and protecting their interests against the social miscreants. The welfare state has a role of guardian of the weaker wings at this stage,to ensure free and fair participation of the weaker in the main stream of national life. The experience along the development of scheduled castes and the backward classes has adequately proved the efficacy of policy measures in ensuring social justice for social sustainability. In some instances, the habitat of the isolated tribal entities has been destablised and ecologically so degraded that even the best efforts fail to yield adequate nutrition, this requires vigorous action to improve the environs, ecology, and quality of resources. Reaching of greater technology input in such areas would be advisable.

The main crux of the problem lies in development of human resources and their capability building without which their entitlements in the exchange based competitive economy can not possibly grow. The success of technological overhauling depends a long way on human resource quality. Nomadism needs a high degree of social treatment, schooling of children, orientation for settled agriculture, animal husbandry and crafts. The wider experience of development enthusiasts regarding Gujjars, Bawarias, and Muguthangies has suggested that stability promotes capital formation and economic growth. Human resource development has a prime role. Thus, social sustainability has much a closer link with the pace of human resource development.

Interstrata oppression and exploitation can be wisely handled by legislative action and strict enforcements for immediate control. Inheritable bonds of life long slavery of guileless poor tribal wings, bonded labour of weaker sections, heavily indebted enslaved labour, mortgaged human beings including women and girls, and trading on the innocent child labour by the merciless landed class and money lenders is prevalent as a rampant practice in Indian society in spite of a legal ban on slavery. This needs to be curbed with strong hand. Administrative laxity and judicial dilatory methods have to be handled more sternly in the interest of ensuring social sustainability.

The poorest of the poor in Indian society are often victims of misfortune, calamities, an mishaps and they have no social security against such risks and neither they have any savings to fall back upon. Floods, hail storms, droughts, crop diseases, keep on reducing these sections to penury and starvation which is the root cause of their heavy debts. The state of unemployment pushes them in the cruel hands of the exploiters. This needs attention of the welfare state. Schemes like RLEGP, NREP, Employment Guarantees, etc. have been of immense help in some areas. Adequate social insurance against such odds may be devised and afforded to these groups at very low costs. The unfortunate wings are often constrained to religious conversions for their helplessness. This can be better handled by socioeconomic protection of the poor by social security.

A suitable coordination model has to be found out to accommodate the tradition and value oriented life styles with modern materialistic and technology oriented system. Greater winning of confidence and activated supports with intensive educational spread can help removing the skeptic attitudes, helplessness, defeatism, and the debilitated ambition of isolated wings of Indian society. Indepth understanding of these cultures and value systems can help in devising an appropriate model of support net-work befitting the felt needs traditions and values of the farflung ethnic isolated entities in India.

ACKNOWLEDGEMENT

Author is highly grateful to the UGC for sponsoring major research project on occupational shift, and changing status of employment, income and investment levels among the socially lagging wings of society in Uttaranchal.

REFERENCES

Brundtland Harlen Gro, 1987. Our Common Future, U.N. Assembly Proceedings: Sustainable Development, 1987.

Ghildial & S.C. Pandey, **1999.** Theme of Sustainable Development: Towards Conceptual Clarity; Ed., G.C. Pande and D.C. Pandey, *Environmental Management & Development;* Anmol Publications, New Delhi (pp. 409-415).

Gowda, Srinivas, M.V., 1992. Technologies for Sustainable Development, *Southern Economist,* Vol. 31, No. 3, 1992 (pp. 21-24)

Palni, L.M.S., R.K. Maikhuri & K.S. Rao, 1997. Conservation of Himalayan Agro-Eco Systems, *Issues & Priorities,* Technical Paper - V, GBPIHED, Kosi-Katarmal, Almora.

Pande G.C. & D.C. Pandey, 1999. Environmental Management and Development, *Op. c:t;* (pp. 43-62).

Barbier, E.B., 1987. Concept of Sustainable Economic Development, *Environmental Conservation,* Vol. 14, No. 2, 1987.

Lele Sarach Chandran, 1997. Sustainable Development, A Critical Review, *World Development,* Vol. XVIX, No. 6, 1997.

Nadkami, M.V., 1996. Political Economy of Sustainable Development, Review of Development & Change, Vol. 1, No. 01, Jan-June, 1996.

Hinterberger, F., Lucks, and B.F. Schnidt, 1997. Material Flows Versus Natural Capital, What Makes an Economy Sustainable? *Ecological Economics,* Vol. 23, No. 1, October 1997.

Solow, R., 1993, Sustainability: An Economist's Perspective, Ed., Robert Dorgman & N.S. Dorfman, *Economics of the Environment: Selected Readings,* Third Ed., New York, 1993.

Govt. of India, 1992. *The Eighth Five Year Plan,* 1992-97, Planning Commission, New Delhi, Vol.1, (p. 7).

Tejwani, K.G., 1989. A Perspective on Soil and Water Conservation Research in India, Ed., Tejveer Singh & J. Kaur, *Studies in Himalayan Ecology,* Himalayan Books, 1989, (pp. 190-91).

Negi, S.S., 1983. Need for Conservation Based Rural Development Strategy in Himalayas, *Journal of Rural Development,* Vol. 2, No. 1, 1983, (pp. 138-143).

Agrawal, A., R. Chopra et.al., 1982. *The State of India's Environment: A Citizen's Report,* Centre for Science and Environment, New Delhi, 1982, (pp. 27-35).

Ackerman, W.C., 1967. *Ecology: The Sobering Science,* Trans, Geographical Union, Vol. 48,1967 (pp. 809-10).

Berreman, G.D., 1977. Ecology, Demography and Social Strategies in Eastern Himalayas, Case

Study, Ed. in Himalaya, Ecologic Ethnologic, Vol. I, Centre National De la Recherche Scientifique, Paris, 1977, (pp. 453-480).

Commoner, B., 1970, Ecological Facts of Life, Ed; in H.D. Johnson, No. Deposit, No Return, Man & His Environment, Addison Wesley, Rading, Mass., 1970 (pp. 8-35).

Boremann, F.H. & G.E. Likens, 1969. The Watershed Eco-Systern Concept & Studies on Nutrient Cycles, Ed. in G.M. Van Dyne, The Eco-system Concept in Natural Resource Management, Academy Press, New York, London, 1969, (pp. 76).

Singh, J.S., & OP. Chaturvedi, 1981. Ecology, Environment & Development, Ed. J.S. Singh, S.P. Singh & C. Sastri, Science & Rural Development in Mountains, Gyanodaya Prakashan, Nainital, 1981, (pp. 47-73).

Hogger, R., 1977. Cultural Systems & Ecological Crisis in Nepal, Ed. in Himalaya: Ecological Ethnologie, Vol. I, Centre De la Recherche Scientifique, Paris, Op. cit.

Watt, K.E.F., 1968, Ecology and Resource Management, A Qualitative Approach, McGraw Hill, New York, 1968, (p. 420).

15

Agricultural Development in India and its Impact on Poverty Reduction

*K. N. Selvaraj**

I. INTRODUCTION

India being primarily an agricultural economy, desired emphasis has been given to his sector over a period of time, which resulted in sustainable growth in agriculture. Though policy packages employed in agriculture to increase food grains production food surpluses reported from time to time may not always mean food reaching the vulnerable sections of the population[1] due to poor economic status. Insecurity in food is bound to assume growing importance for several reasons particularly in the context of change in structural reform polices (Ahluwalia, 1978; Gaiha, 985; Roy, 1997; Ravallion, 1998). Since agricultural sector continues to be a tradable sector, any likely changes in exports and imports, investment in new technology and rural infrastructure, income and employment in agriculture,

* *Department of Agricultural Economics, Centre for Agricultural and Rural Development Studies, Tamil Nadu Agricultural University, Coimbatore 3.*

1. *India has the dubious distinction of being the fastest growing country with an annual growth rate of 2.2 per cent and a projected population of 1.26 billions by 2016AD.* (Venkataraman. 1998).

agricultrual prices and food grain production have far reaching effects on food security. Nevertheless, the focus today is to assure basic food security to the people, improve the abysmally low nutritional standards and create surplus for poverty alleviation and creation of jobs[1] to improve the economic status of lower strata of population for better to food through making changes in policy frame work. The paper is organized into eight sections viz., food demand and supply, trends in rural poverty incidence of rural poverty and agricultrual growth, agricultural investment and performance employment elasticity of agriculture and implications.

Table 1: Producton of Food grains in India

Year	Rice	Wheat	Coarse cereals	Total cereals	Total pulses	Total Food grains
1990-91	74.29	55.15	32.70	162.13	14.26	176.39
1991-92	74.68	55.69	25.99	156.36	12.02	168.38
1992-93	72.86	57.21	36.59	116.66	12.82	179.48
1993-94	80.30	59.84	30.82	170.96	13.30	184.26
1994-95	81.81	65.77	29.88	177.46	14.04	191.50
1995-96	79.98	62.10	29.03	171.86	12.31	180.42
1996-97	81.74	69.35	34.10	168.11	14.2	199.44
1997-98	82.53	66.35	30.40	179.28	12.98	192.26
1998-99	85.99	70.78	31.46	188.23	14.81	203.04
1999-00*	88.55	70.10	29.36	188.01	13.55	201.56
CGR**	1.97	3.05	-0.17	1.78	0.69	1.85

*- As on 27.3.2000

* * - Estimated compound growth rate (per cent)

Source : Agricultural Statistics at a Glance, 2000

II. FOOD DEMAND AND SUPPLY

There was impressive growth in production of agricultural commodities due to resilience of agricultural technology, which

2. Of the projected population of 1.26 billions, 380 millions are unemployed. It was estimated that by the turn of the century hundred million jobs will have to be created with an annual growth of four per cent in contrast to two per cent at present. Evidences show that of the four per growth in employment, three per cent may have to come from agriculture and allied activities.

brought out substantial increase in productivity of crops. The compound growth rates (Table 1) indicated that both production and productivity of almost all the crops exhibited significant growth over the years. The growth is mainly due to planned investment made in agriculture through expansion of irrigation facilities and spread of fertilizers and credit outlets coupled with favourable/remunerative product prices.[1]

The demand for food articles depends on growth of population, income per-capita, distribution of income, elasticity of demand for food (price and income) and other requirements. Through it is argued that among the twin forces, that determine the rate of growth of demand for food, an increase in the growth rate of population leads to a direct increase in the growth rate of total demand for food and growth in per capita income increase rate of growth of demand for food grains albeit at a lower rate.[2] In the process of development (Srinivasan, 1987), it is increasing per capita income that is the dynamic factor underlying the growth in food demand (Mellor, 1983)[3]

3. According to World Development Report (1990), India can reduce poverty to 25.4 per cent by 2000 AD. The Human Development Index or Human Poverty index development by United Nations, which takes into account vulnerability to death at early age, prevalence of illiteracy, access health systems, availability of safe drinking water and adequate food, indicates that India had a low rank of 123 out of 160 countries in 1990 and the position further fallen to 138 among 175 countries in 1997.
4. Because of the elasticity of per capita demand for food being less than unity.
5. There are distinct phases in the development process that have a bearing on food demand. In the early stage of economic growth, people are poor and mortality rates are high, leading to moderate growth in population and slow growth in per capita income. As per capita income grows, population growth also goes up. Rising income combined with increasing population lead to much higher demand for foodgrains, particularly derived demand for cereals due to high income elasticity of demand for livestock products. In this phase,food supply has to take a qualitative jump. In addition to increasing domestic food supply through extensive application of new technology, in this phase, more reliance on food imports is necessary. Finaly, it is only at a later stage of development when population growth rates decline sharply and growth in income beings to have little effect on demand forfood, in which meeting food demand becomes manageable and even surpluses can emerge.

The rapid growth in population in the country results in a rapid growth in demand for food grains. It is observed from the demand estimates that the country to be self sufficient in food grains production, the growth rate of domestic output should henceforth accelerate to 3.5 to 4 per cent per annum from the level of 2.7 per cent per annum achieved during the last forty years period, 1949-50 to 1989-90 (Bhalla, 1995). Given the situation India has to produce a minimum of 230 to 240 million tonnes by 2001. The annual growth in food grains production was 2.67 per cent (1967-68 to 1995-96), 2.86 per cent (1980-81 to 1995-96) and 1.70 per cent (1990-91 to 1996-97) (Economic Survey, 196-97). These figures reveal that the incremental output per year must be more than what the country realised today (Table 2). Our analysis using the demand estimates of Radhakrishna and Ravi (1990) indicates that there would be deficit in food supply, which was 47.17 million tonnes 2010 (Table 3).

Table 2: Indian Foodgrain requirements (million tonnes)

Commodities	2010
Rice	107.29
Wheat	79.57
Other cereals	34.89
Total cereals	221.75
Pulses	28.46
Total food grains	250.21
Milak equivalent.	107.21

Source : Radhakrishna and Ravi (1990)

This indicates that the rate of growth in domestic output should be increased to 2.1 per cent during 2010[1] respectively from the present level of 1.85 per cent achieved during 1990s (Table 4). The country has to produce an additional output of 4.72 million tonnes of food

6. In order to be self sufficient in food grains production, the growth rate of domestic output should increase to 3.5 to 4 per cent per annum from the level of 2.7 per cent per annum achieved during the forty-year period. 949-50 to 1989-90. Hence, India must produce a minimum of 230 to 240 million tonnes by 2001 compared with the peak production of 176 million tonnes recorded in 1991 (Bhalla, 1995).

grains per year to meet the growing demand in 2010 from the present level of production of 203.04 million tonnes, which was the highest output recorded during 1998-99. Among the food grains, the availability of pulses increase only at the rate of 0.69 per cent per annum, whereas the required rate of growth was found very high with 6.75 per cent in 2010. The country has to produce an incremental output of pulses at the quantum of 1.37 million tonnes per year to meet the demand in 2010.

Table 3 : Demand-supply Gap of Foodgrains - India (million tonnes)

Commodity	Supply*	Gap — 2010
Rice	88.55	-18.74
Wheat	70.78	-8.79
Coarse cereals	36.59	1.70
Total cereals	188.23	-33.52
Total pulses	14.81	-13.65
Total food grains	203.04	-47.17

* Maximum output realised during 1990s was assumed as supply.

Table 4 : Required Rate of Growth to Meet the Demand — India

Commodities	2010 - per cent
Rice	1 .94
Wheat	1.18
Coarse cereals	—
Total cereals	1.65
Total pulses	6.75
Total foodgrains	2.11

The required rate of growth in output was computed based on highest output as base[7].

7. *The formula for future projections using compound growth rate is given by $F_p = \beta_V (1 + r/1\,00)^n$, where, F_p is future estimate, β_v refers to base year value, r denotes compound growth rate in per cent and n is the number of years to be projected. The required rate of growth was estimated using the above formula, which is given as*

$$r = \left(\frac{F_p}{\beta_v}\right)^{1/n} - 1 \times 100$$

III. TRENDS IN RURAL POVERTY

There are extensive and disquieting literatures (Desai, 1986 Ahluwalia, 1978, 1986; Rath, 1996) on quantifying the poverty line and absolute poverty in terms of the absolute number or the proportion of population below poverty line. A recurring theme in much of literature (Ahluwalia, 1978, 1986; Lal, 1976; Bardhan, 1986; Ravallion and Datt, 1996; Gaiha, 1985) is to find the relationship between trends in rural poverty and agricultural growth. There is a debate on the methods of measurement of poverty and its dimensions during the last three decades[1]. The interest of this paper, however, centres around the trickle down effect of agriculture growth in minimising the incidence of poverty without resorting much to the methods of estimation of poverty line and absolute poverty. The principle sources of data for this investigation are the 50th round consumption surveys conducted by NSS, secondary data collected from various statistical issues of India and studies of rural poverty.

8. Indian planning commission recommended in July 1962 that the national minimum per-capita consumer expenditure in India should be Rs. 20 (at 1960-61 prices). Bardhan (1970) stipulated Rs. 15 per capita per month for rural and for urban Rs.25 per capita per month. Minhas (1970) used similar approach in estimating the rural poverty. Dandekar and Rath (1971) fixed minimum income level, which may be called poverty line, on basis of some objective criterion such as adequate food. They used the norm of 2250 k.cal per day as suggested by Sukhatme (1965) and Nutrition Advisory Committee (1978). Bardhan (1974) and Rudra (1974) used balanced diet approach and Rao (1977) suggested balanced diet approach preferable to calorie intake approach. Planning Commission (1979) indicated that 2250 k.cal norm does not take into account age sex and occupation. As a result this is likely to vary sizably between rural and urban and it suggested 2435 k.cal for rural Indian and 2095 k.cal for urban based on age, sex and occupational features. Minhas (1993) applied behaviouristic approach to the estimating of calorie level for calculation of rural and urban poverty. It is also argues that a minimum level of per-capita income (or expenditure) to demarcate the poor from the rest cannot be an immutable one, but will depend upon the level of economic development of the society as well as its climatic environment and social values (Dandekar and Rath, 1971).

Primarily to conform to past trend without attempting to justify the measurement of poverty, the poverty line was computed based on minimum consumer expenditure level and consumption expenditure level guaranteeing minimal nutritional standards (Table 5). Accordingly, the poverty line based on consumer expenditure level of Rs. 15 per person for 30 days at 1960-61 rural prices (Ahluwalia, 1978) and expenditure level providing the norms of 2250 K.calories per day (Rath, 1996) was used. Planning Commission estimates were used for regression analysis. Applying consumer Price Index (CPIAL)[9] for Agricultural Labourers to the base year, estimates of poverty lines for each of the year were also computed.

Table 5: Per capita requirement of food articles*

Food article	Requirement per capita per day (kg)	Requirement per capita per year (kg)
Cereals	0.403	147.00
Pulses	0.082	30.00
Total foodgrains	0.485	177.00
Greenleaf vegetable	0.114	–
Root vegetables	0.085	–
Other vegetables	0.085	–
Total vegetable	0.284	103.66
Fruits	0.09	32.85
Sugar	0.07	25.55
Oil	0.04	14.31
Milk	0.28	102.20
Fish and meat	0.04	14.31
Eggs	8.41gm	3.07 (75 nos)

* Expected to provide 2500 calories - ICMR recommendaton

9. These estimates are obviously subjected to all the limitations arising from the use of the Consumer Price index for Agricultural Labourers as the price index. This separate Consumer Price indices were used for India and Tamil Nadu.

Table 6-8 present alternative estimates of the percentage of the rural population below the chosen poverty line. The years of rapid growth in the Indian economy coincided with reduction in poverty. As average annual increases of 3.4 per cent in GDP in the first half of the 1970s accelerated to rates of 5.9 per cent in the last of the 1980s (World Bank, 1989) and 7.10 per cent in the early 1990s (Economic Survey, 1996-97), the incidence of poverty recorded notable decline and there is considerable potential for towards reducing poverty in India to 25.4 per cent by 2000 AD (Venkataranam, 1998). According to Planning Commission (1998),[1] the annual average rate of decline of the poverty ratio in India during the period 1973-74 has been 2.05 per cent in rural areas and on the basis of the growtih rate experience between 1993-94 and 1996-97, the incidence of poverty has been worked out to 30.55 per cent in 1996-97 and 18.61 per cent in 2001-02 (Table 9).

Table 6 : Rural poverty line and percentage of rural population below poverty line based on calorie norm (2250 calories)

Year	Rural poverty line at current prices (Rs.)	Percentage of rural population below poverty line
1961-62	170	30.9
1971-72	398	–
1977-78	648	47.7
1983	1267	57.6
1987-88	1973	67.0
1993-94	2248	69.73
1996-97	2300	70.20
2001-2002	2318	70.36

Source: Complied from Rath (1996)
The estimates between 1993-94 and 2001-02 were computed based on past trend.

10. Planning Commission adopted a comprehensive method, that is the Squared Poverty Gap (SGP), to measure the intensity of poverty during the 20 years period (1973-74 to 1993-94). The SGP is composed of not only the poverty ratio and the poverty gap ratio, but it also captures the consumption distribution of the poor as measured by the coefficient of variation.

Table 7 : Rural poverty line and percentage of rural population below poverty line based on consumption expenditure level

Year	Percentage of population below poverty line	No. of persons in lakhs
1973-74	56.4	2613
1977-78	53.1	2642
1983-84	45.7	2520
1987-88	39.1	2319
1993-94	37.3	2440
1996-97	30.55	–
2001-02	18.61	–
2006-07	9.64	–
2011-12	4.31	–

Source : Planning Commission estimates compiled from Dutt and Sundaram (1998). Figures from 1996-97 to 2011-12 are projectionsof Planning Commission.

To provide an evidence for asserting a trend in increase or decrease in rural poverty over the period,[1] all the three estimates (calorie norm, consumer expenditure level estimates of Ahluwalia, 1978, and Planning Commission, 1998) were used and the results are reported in Table 10. These results indicate an evidence of presence of discernible trend in the incidence of rural poverty in India. The earlier studies reported a mixed picture in incidence of rural poverty in India. The trend analyses of Ahluwalia (1998) provided no evidence for asserting a trend increase or decrease in rural poverty in India over the period as a whole (1957-58 to 1973-74). However,

11. The time pattern of the incidence of poverty: Three alternative estimates were used to find out discernible trend in the percentage of the rural population below the poverty line. A linear time trend is fitted. *E-I or F-II or E-III* $= \beta_0 + \beta_1$ *TIME* $+ U_t$ *where, E-I - percentage of rural population below poverty line based on calorie norm (Rath, 1996), E-II - percentage of rural population below poverty line based on consumer expenditure level (Ahluwalia, 1978) and E-III - percentage of rural population below poverty line based on consumer expenditure level (Planning Commission, 1998). Time refers to time variable,* β_0 *and* β_1 *are the respective constant and slope coefficients and* U_t *is the stochastic disturbance term with classical normal assumptions,* $U_t (0, \sigma^2)$.

Bardhan (1971) reported an increase in the incidence of poverty over the sixties, which appears as an upswing in a pattern of cyclical variation. On the other hand, Minhas (1990) reported a decline in the percentage of rural population in poverty over the period 1956-57 to 967-68. These differences are due to identifiable differences on. some key issues in estimating rural poverty. Piecewise regression analysis or application of Chow test (Gujarati 1995) is the better analytical method to identify the differences in the incidence of rural poverty in the sub-periods. Our analysis shows that the presence of any discernible trends in the incidence of poverty obviously implies an increase in the absolute numbers of people in poverty because of the

Table 8 : Rural poverty line and percentage of rural population based on Ahluwalia (1978) estimates

Year	Poverty line (Rs.)	Percentage of rural population in poverty
1956-57	14.6	54.1
1957-58	15.1	50.2
1958-59	–	46.5
1959-60	15.3	44.4
1960-61	15.0	38.9
1961-62	15.5	39.4
1963-64	17.7	44.5
1964-65	21.3	46.8
1965-66	23.3	53.9
1966-67	28.5	56.6
1967-68	30.9	56.5
1968-69	27.8	51.0
1970-71	28.8	47.5
1973-74	42.9	46.1
1977-78	49.90	47.2
1983	61.35	48.61
1987-88	83.25	50.06
1993-94	124.50	51.86
1996-97	192.45	52.78
2001-02	218.71	54.35

Source : Compiled from Ahluwalia (1978)
Estimates between 1977-78 and 1996-97 were computed using the respective Consumer Price Inde for Agricultural Labourers (CPIAL) for India.

growth in rural population over the period. The results of trend equation fitted to planning commission estimates show a trend decrease in the incidence of rural poverty in India. The Gird Ratio[1] of food articles (-0.246) estimated using the 50th round data of NSS show that the difference in amount expended on food articles lessened due to distribution of per capita income (Table 11). The Gini ratio worked out to 0.469 for non-food items.

Table 9 : Comparison of estimates of poverty — India (percentage of populaton below poverty line)

Year	Rath (1996)	Ahluwalia (1978)	Planning Commission
1977-78	47.7	47.20	53.1
1983	57.6	48.61	45.7
1987-88	67.0	50.06	39.1
1993-94	69.73	51.86	37.3
1996-97	70.20	52.78	30.55
2001-02	70.36	54.35	18.61

Table 10 : Trends in Rual poverty — Estimates of linear regression

Particulars	β	SE ($A\beta_1$)	t ratio	Probability Commission
E-I ($R^2 = 0.92$)				
Constant	48.984	1 .089	44.980	0.0000
TIME	1.2671	0.0909	13.938	0.0000
E-II ($R^2 = 0.62$)				
Constant	46.225	0.5323	86.842	0.0000
TIME	0.2158	0.0345	6.262	0.0000
E-III ($R^2 = 0.98$)				
Constant	57.781	0.4644	124.416	0.0000
TIME	-1 .0874	0.0325	-33.457	0.0000

E-I - Calorie norm of 2250 calories (Rath, 1996)

E-II - Consumer expenditure level (Ahluwalia, 1978)

E-III - Consumer expenditure level (Planning Commission, 1998)

12. The mathematical form of Gini Index is given as

$$\frac{\Delta}{2u} = 1/n(n-1)\sum_{i=1}^{n}\sum_{j=1}^{n} / X_{ik} - X_{jk} / \text{ or}$$

$$G = 1 + 1/n - \frac{2}{n^2 - Z}\sum_{i=1}^{n}(n+1-i)Y$$

IV. INCIDENCE OF RURAL POVERTY AND AGRICULTURAL GROWTH

The explicit model of the determinants of rural poverty should explain the observed changes in rural poverty over the period. In this context, it is obviously relevant to consider the rate of agricultrual growth as an important factor influencing the incidence of rural poverty. By postulating that an important determinant of the extent of rural poverty is the growth in agricultrual sector, a cause and effect relationship was established between incidence of rural poverty and agricultural growth. Agriculture is not only the dominant source of income in rural areas, and besides, the scale of non-agricultural income generating activity in rural areas almost certainly depends upon the level of agricultural production. Hence, do we expect a trickle down effect in the rural economy? Thereby increases in agricultrual production per head reduce the incidence of rural poverty. To understand this experience in India, whether the growth of agricultural output has only just kept pace with the growth of rural population, the log trend equations[1] were fitted to per head production of foodgrains, agricultural production and net domestic product / gross domestic product. The results are reported in Table 12. The results is almost stagnation in output per head, in India, which can be seen from the table reporting time trends fitted to different indices of output per head of the rural population. The coefficient of time variable of per capita net availability of foodgrains is -7.9650 with probability level of 0.0958. But, the coefficients of trends variable of gross domestic product per capita show an upward trend in gross domestic product per capita. The exponential growth rate was 3.59 per cent for India and Ahluwalia (1978) reported a stagnation in output per head particularly in the case of national net domestic product per capita and he argued that this stagnation parallels the observed lack of any trend improvement in the incidence of rural poverty over the period and was one of its principal causes.

13. $log\ (FPIP) = \beta_0 + \beta_1\ TIME + u_t$
$log\ (APIP) = \beta_0 + \beta_1\ TIME + u_t$
$log\ (GDPAP) = \beta_0 + \beta_1\ TIME + u_t$
Where, log (GDPAP orFPIP)-food grains production index per capita, APIP - agricultural production index per capita and GDPAP - gross domestic product in agriculture percapita, measured in constant prices.

Table 11: Food and non-food expenditure per person for a period of 30 days

Fractile group	India — rural		
	Food	Non-food	Total
0-5	73.88 (72.93)	27.42 (27.07)	101.30 (100.0)
5-10	96.11 (73.27)	35.07 (26.73)	131.18 (100.00)
10-20	112.53 (73.06)	41.49 (26.94)	154.02 (100.00)
20-30	128.78 (72.28)	49.39 (27.72)	178.17 (100.00)
30-40	143.82 (71.64)	56.93 (28.36)	200.75 (100.00)
40-50	157.64 (70.29)	66.63 (29.71)	224.27 (100.00)
50-60	173.87 (69.32)	76.97 (30.68)	250.84 (100.00)
60-70	190.44 (67.44)	91.94 (32.56)	282.38 (100.00)
70-80	212.77 (65.55)	111.80 (34.45)	324.57 (100.00)
80-90	245.00 (61.94)	150.56 (38.06)	395.56 (100.00)
90-95	284.53 (57.02)	214.50 (42.98)	499.03 (100.00)
95-100	371.07 (42.39)	504.27 (57.61)	875.34 (100.00)
All	177.77 (63.17)	103.64 (36.83)	281.41 (100.00)

(Figures in parentheses are percentages)

Source Servekshana,Oct-Dec, 1996)

Gini Ratio

Food - 0.246

Non-Food - 0.469

Total - 0.335

Table 12: Exponential time trends in output per capita

Particulars	β_1	SE (β_1)	t ratio	Probability level
(i) Log (FPIP)				
Constant	-1 .6959	0.0242	-69.998	0.0000
TIME =	0.0091	0.0015	6.006	0.0000
$R^2 = 0.59$				
(ii) Log (APIP)				
Constant	-1 .7244	0.0223	-77.416	0.0000
TIME $R^2 = 0.76$	0.0123	0.0014	8.824	
0.0001				
(iii) Log (GDPAP)				
Constant	1.6581	0.0983	16.863	0.0000
TIME $R^2 = 0.57$	0.0353	0.0016	5.748	0.0000

The relationship between the incidence of poverty and agricultural growth over the period was examined through regression analysis. We used planning commission estimates of incidence of rural poverty (percentage of population below poverty line) for regression analysis and the results are compared with earlier studies. It is hypothesized that the incidence of rural poverty depends upon the level of net domestic product per capita.[1] Further, an alternative hypothesis that the incidence of rural poverty depends not only on the current year's level of net domestic per capita but also on the level in the previous year, is also tested[2]. There are other factors operating in the rural economy, which influence the incidence of rural poverty. This hypothesis was tested including time as an additional variable)[3]

14. *Improved agricultural performance, measured as an increase in the gross domestic product in agriculture per head of rural population at constant prices (GDPAP), is definitely associated with reduction in the incidence of poverty. The trend equation is given by*
$PPBL_t = \beta_0 - \beta_1 GDPAP_t + u_t$
Where, PPBL percentage of population below poverty line and GDPAP — gross domestic product per capita.
15. $PPBL_t = \beta_0 + \beta_1 GDPAP_t + \beta_2 GDPAP_{t-1} - + u_t$
Where, $GDPAP_{t-1}$ is the lagged (one year) gross domestic product per capita. Ahluwalia (1978) used average value of the current and previous year rather than introducing both as independent variables.
16. $PPBL_t = \beta_0 - \beta_1 GDPAP_t - \beta_2 GDPAP_{t-1} - \beta_2 Time + u_t$
To find out the underlying time trend in the incidence of rural poverty after allowing for changes in poverty incidence associated with changed GDPAP, the above equation was estimated.

There are relations between changes in nominal prices of some commodities consumed by the poor and their real incomes. The changes in the nominal price of the consumption basket of the poor had a far greater and more immediate impact on their ability to cross the poverty line than on their incomes, whether they are producers of these commodities or farm labourers. This is due to the rural poor's small share in the marketed agricultrual surplus; rigidities in rural wages, which increasingly monetised; and the wide spread dependence of the poor on market purchases for consumption needs (Narain, 1961). Therefore, in our analysis two more equations[1] were estimated by adding price as an explanatory variable to GDPAP and TIME. For, price, the Consumer Price Index for Agricultural Laboruers (CPIAL) was included as explanatory variable and another equation was estimated using index number of wholesale price of food articles (WPIF).

As shown in Tables 13, the coefficient of the variable GDPAP is negative and highly significant. Introduction of lagged GDPAP improved the explanatory power of the equation substantially ($R^2 = 0.45$ increased to 0.55) and then regression coefficient are again negative and the coefficient of lagged variable of GDPAP was significant (Probability level = 0.392) indicating that the incidence of poverty depends also on the level of GDPAP in the previous year. The results further suggest that there is an underlying time trend in the incidence of poverty after allowing for changes in poverty incidence associated with changes in GDPAP. There is a clear evidence of an inverse relationship between rural poverty and agricultural performance.

---

17. *The equations were estimated after logarithmic transformation.*

$$LPPBLt = \beta_0 - \beta_1 LGDPAP + \beta_2 LCPIALt - \beta_3 LTIME + u_t$$

$$LPPBLt = \beta_0 - \beta_1 LGDPAP + \beta_2 LWPIF - \beta_3 LTIME + u_t$$

The temporal variation in the incidence of rural poverty was assessed after making allowances for the changes in the incidence of poverty associated with agricultural performance and the normal price of the rural poor's consumption basket. TIME as an explanatory variable was included to identity the influence of host of factors like employment generation due to investment on socioeconomic overheads in rural areas, development of cottage and village industries, growth of the territory sector in rural areas resulting from agricultural development, land reforms, development of cooperative institutions and growth in health education and other services.

Table 13: Incidence of rural poverty and Agricultural Growth in India - OLS Estimates

Particulars	β_1	SE (β_1)	t ratio	Probability level
Constant	60.454	4.000	15.114	0.0000
$GDPAP_t$	-1.7029	0.3995	-4.263	0.0000
$R^2 = 0.45$				
Constant	62.213	3.777	16.473	0.0000
$GDPAP_t$	-0.7086	0.5834	-1.215	0.2380
$GDPAP_{t-1}$	-1.2120	0.5511	-2.199	0.0392
$R^2 = 0.55$				
Constant	59.923	0.5477	109.409	0.0000
$GDPAP_t$	-0.2025	0:0854	-2.372	0.0279
$GDPAP_{t-1}$	-0.1585	0.0860	-1.844	0.0801
TIME	-0.9863	0.0313	-31.565	0.0000
$R^2 = 0.99$				
Constant	5.9760	0.2447	24.417	0.0000
LGDPAP	-0.1051	0.0432	-2.435	0.0255
$LCPILA_t$	-0.3141	0.0390	-8.060	0.0000
$R^2 = 0.96$				
Constant	4.3364	0.4052	10.701	0.0000
LGDPAP	0.0340	0.0849	0.401	0.6931
$LWPIF_t$	-0.0468	0.0693	-0.676	0.5078
TIME	-0.1857	0.0357	-5.201	0.0000
$R^2 = 0.98$				

The upshot of Narain's (1976) results that it is not enough to take into account agricultural performance and time to explain temporal variations in rural poverty; it is equally necessary to consider changes in the normal prices of goods consumed by the poor. He observed that inclusion of price as an independent variable increased the explanation of the variation in rural poverty substantially (R^2 = 0.98) and made regression coefficient of time highly significant. There was also a definite downward trend in the incidence of rural poverty between 1956-57 and 1970-71. Our results after inclusion of price variables show that the explanation power of the independent variables or regressors moved up substantially. These results, after allowance is made for the changes in the incidence of rural poverty associated with other variables, there is definite negative relationship between the incidence of rural poverty and agricultural growth in India. Varied results were obtained after the introduction of Wholesale Price Index. Ahluwalia (1978) indicated that the use of CPIAL to estimate poverty percentages would produce a spurious positive correlation between the price variable and the incidence of rural poverty. Narain (1976) argued that although measurement of poverty line was statistically influenced by CPIAL, its influence on the distribution of household expenditure was casual rather than statistical. If only the distribution of household expenditure remained unchanged over time then the use of CPIAL in estimating poverty percentages will produce a spurious positive correlation. Our results clearly show that such an assumption is not justified on a prior grounds.

V. AGRICULTRUAL INVESTMENT AND AGRICULTURAL PERFORMANCE

It is high time to look into the public investment made in agriculture in the wake of manifestos announced by National Democratic Alliance (NDA) that 60 per cent of plan funds will be allocated to agriculture and rural development to sustain the annual agricultural growth rate of 4 to 5 per cent to push up GDP growth to 7 to 8 per cent. Further, the analysis of demand and supply also indicates the problem of food demand to be faced by the country and the state in the coming years to need food and nutritional security of the population. Nevertheless, there is also evidence that there is a statistically significant inverse relationship between rural poverty and agricultural performance suggesting that agricultural growth by itself tends to reduce the incidence of poverty. Therefore, an attempt was made to find the nature of relationship between the agricultural.

Investment and agricultural performance emphasizing the need for long-term investment in agriculture to reduce of rural poverty.

First to examine the temporal variation in government expenditure on agriculture, the percentage shares of agricultrual government expenditure in total expenditure were estimated for India and summarised in Table 14. Desired emphasis has been given to agricultural sector since the inception of five year plan periods due to the agrarian driven economy; even today agricultural sector fuels GDP growth the contributing over 26 per cent (1998-99). It is evident from the estimates given in table 14 that during the first FYP period more emphasis was given to agriculture since one-third of expenditure was allocate to agriculture. The maximum share of agricultrual government expenditure to total expenditure was 30.60 per cent, which was noticed during the first FYP period. The object seemed to transform rural based agrarian economy and sustain the growth in agriculture. The jump in agricultural growth is mainly due to planned investment made in agriculture through expansion of irrigation facilities and spread of fertilizers and credit outlets with favourable price for agricultural products.

Table 14: Percentage share of government agricultural expenditure in total expenditure - India

Plan period	Total expenditure (Rs. crores)	Govt. agrl. expenditure (Rs. crores)	Percentage shares agrl.govt.expenditure in total expenditure
(1951-52 to 1995-56)	1960.00	60.00	30.60
II (1956-57 to 1960-61)	4600.00	950.00	20.65
III (1961-62 to 1965-66)	8575.50	1750.00	20.40
IV (1969-70 to (1973-74)	15778.80	3300.00	20.90
V (1974-75 to 1978-79)	39426.20	8080.00	20.49
VI (1980-81 to 1984-85)	109645.00	24700.00	22.53
VII (1985-86 to 1989-90)	222169.30	29770.00	13.40
VIII (1992-93 to 1996-97)	434100.00	22467.20	5.18

After making a headway in agriculture starting from first FYP period, emphasis was laid on industrial sector from the second FYP period as it is clear from the share of agricultural government expenditure to total expenditure that the share was nearly stable and approximately stood at 20 per cent. However, the share declined to 13.40 per cent during seventh plan period and further to 5.18 per cent in the eighth plan. The decline has largely been on account of economic reforms initiated in 1991. But the agricultural development in the country heavily rely on government finance due to it's inherent weaknesses such as presence of externalities, high risk and inadequacies in agricultural institutions like rural credit, input supply etc. (FAO, 1987) which discursive investment from private sources. There is a need for improving the agricultural growth to meet the challenges like raising food demand, increase in industrial raw material requirements and providing many gains in employment in agriculture through galvanising potentials of agriculture.

The contribution of government expenditure on agricultural output growth was empirically analysed by employing neo-classical production function of the long-liner type (Hayami and Ruttan, 1970; Antle, 1983; Elias, 1985). The model[1] was estimated by Ordinary Least Aquares (OLS) by incorporating expenditure variable along with other conventional inputs such as land and labour. The results are set out in Tables 15.

---

18. *The function is given by*

$$ln(AGDP)_t = \beta_0 + \beta_1 ln(AGE)_t + \beta_2 ln(GCA)_t + \beta_3 ln(AL)_t + u_t$$

Where, the dependent variable AGDP is agricultural GDP at constant prices expressed in crore rupees. Land and labour, representing resource endowments, were measured by gross cropped area (GCA), which is expressed in million hectares and agricultural labour force (ALF,), which is expressed in million numbers. The agricultural government expenditure at constant prices (AGE) is expressed in crore rupees. ut is the stochastic disturbance term with ut N(0, σ^2*) The time period considered for the analysis is form 1971-72 to 1977-98.* β_1, β_2 *and* β_3 *are the respective elasticity to be estimated. is regression constant.*

The estimated elasticity of the government expenditure on agriculture is 0.3718, which is significant at one per cent level of probability. The elasticity of the government expenditure on agriculture indicates that 10 per cent increase in government expenditure would induce 3.718 per cent increase in agriculture production in India. The results clearly reveal that government expenditure policies are important determinants of the performance of the agricultural sector. The growth of agriculture can be further augmented through adequate investment from public finance. There are obviously potential areas in agriculture sector, which could be adequately tapped through government interventions. Apart from the concerns related to food security and poverty alleviation, government involvement is essential for creating tradable surplus through adequate investment on infrastructure, irrigation, agricultural research and extension as they are expected to have a high pay-off. Such investment almost stimulate private investment in the form of agricultural input markets, agro-based industries, agricultrual processing and product markets.

Table 15: Investment in agriculture and agricultural performance in India -Estimates of log-linear relation (1971 -72 to 1997-98)

Variable	β_1	SE(β_1)	t ratio	Probability level
Constant	2.9257	10.1	0.289	0.7754
AGE_t	0.3718	0.730	5.095	0.0000
GCA_t	-0.3352	2.298	-0.146	0.8853
ALF_t	1 .0332	0.4689	2.204	0.0378

$R^2 = 0.86$, $R^2 = 0.84$, $F = 45.86$

Any uncertainty associated with instability in public expenditure may reduce the level of investment and hence thwart the growth of agricultural sector if risk averse behaviour charcterises the farmers. Lim (1983) observed the agricultural government expenditure instability might affect the development of agricultural sector. Further, instability in government expenditure might also jeopardise the planning ability of the government and parastatal organistions thereby adversely affecting economic growth. In what follows, an attempt was made to analyses the adverse effect of expenditure instability on agricultural growth. The instability index[1] constructed is given in Table 16. The average instability index worked out to 3.38 and it ranged between 1.98 and 6.90 during third and sixth FYP periods, respectively.

To test the effect of fluctuations in government expenditure on agricultural growth, the rate of change of agricultural production is assumed to be explained by the instability of expenditure, after accounting the other relevant explanatory factors such as land and labour. The intensive form of log-linear function[2] was specified and estimated using OLS method. The intensive log-linear function assumes constant returns to scale and reduces problem of multicollinearity and heteroscedasticity. The estimates of intensive log-linear functions are furnished in Table 17. The instability variable has the expected negative sign though not significant. So it is evident from the empirical results production growth. The empirical findings suggest that to attain sustainable growth in agriculture to cope with the future challenges, provision of adequate public finance on a predictable basis in an important stimulus.

---

19. *Instability index for government expenditure on agriculture was estimated from exponential trend equation,*
$AGE_t = \beta_0 \beta_1^t$. The instability was measured by instability index and the instability index is the average absolute percentage deviations from the exponential trend.

$$II = \frac{AGE_t - EAGE_t}{EAGE_1^t} \times 100$$

Where, AGE_t is the agricultural government expenditure at constant prices, which is expressed in crore rupees. FAGE denotes estimated values of agricultural government expenditure from the exponential trend equation.

20. *The intensive form of log-linear function is given as:*
$Ln\ (OPLRC)_t = \alpha_0 + \alpha_1\ ln\ (LPLRC)_t + a_2\ ln\ (IIAGE)_t\ \mu_1$
Where, OPLRC refers to output per labour rate of change (output is agricultural GDP at constant prices), LPLRC referes to land per labour rate of change, IIAGE is instability index of agricultural government expenditure and $\mu_1 N(-0, \sigma^2)$ denotes stochastic disturbance term with classical norma assumption, ie.,. The time period taken for the estimation is from 1971-72 to 1977-98. α_0, α_1 and α_2 are the parameters of the estimable equation.

Table 16: Instability in government expenditure on agriclture during plan period*

Plan period	Instability Index
I	3.62
II	2.14
III	1.98
IV	2.93
V	2.15
VI	6.90
VII	1.98
VIII	5.30
Average	3.38

* - Unweighted average

**- Absolute percentage deviation from an exponential trend.

VI. EMPLOYMENT ELASTICITIES OF AGRICULTURE

Agriculture forms the dominant source of income of rural households and rural household primarily depend on agriculture for their employment. To show how critical is generating employment opportunities in agriculture, which increase purchasing power of the rural population, and income-employment elasticity was worked through regression analysis[1]. The results are presented in Table 18. According to Pabola (1992) the employment elasticity of agriculture in India were 0.64 (1972.73 to 1977-78), 0.49 (1977-78 to 983) and 0.36 (1983 to 1987-88) and show a declining tendency. It is argued that a given rate of growth of national income, a lower growth of employment reflects an increase in labour productivity and should, in fact, be an encouraging rather than a disconcerting phenomenon. The decline in the elasticity is attributed to significant yield and output

21. *The equation is given by*

$$LnGDPA = ln\ \beta_0 + \beta_1\ In\ ALF_t + u_t$$

Where, LnGDPA refers to log of gross domestic product in agriculture and ALF denotes agricultural labour force.

growth supported by green-revolution technologies. The sub-period employment elasticity worked out to 5.19 and -0.38 for period I and II respectively and the overall elasticity was 1.96. Given the decline trend in employment elasticity in India, expansion is employment opportunities, it may be argued, is possible only as a result for faster growth of the economy.

Table 17: Impact of instability in government agricultural expenditure on agricultural output growth in India — Estimates of intensive form of log-linear function

Variable	β_1	SE (β_1)	t ratio	Probability level
Constant	5.5050	0,4273	12.882	0.0000
LPLRC	1 .1 609	0.3589	3.2346	0.0035
IIAGE	-0.0123	0.0936	-0.1314	0.8961

$R^2 = 0.32$, $R^2 = 0.26$, $F = 5.54$

Table 18: Labour employment and income — Log-linear estimates

Variable	β_1	SE (β_1)	t ratio	Probability level
Overall (1971-72 to 1997-98)				
Constant	2.6745	0.0586	45.6399	0.0000
ALF	1.9572	0.0662	29.5650	0.0000
$R^2 = 0.67$				
I. Period (1971-72 to 1984-85)				
Constant				
ALF	-10.1970	0.1675	-60.8776	0.0000
$R^2 = 0.96$	5.1889	0.2752	18.8550	0.0000
II. Period (1985-86 to 1997-98)				
Constant	12.7898	0.0390	327.9436	0.0000
ALF	-0.3767	0.3752	-1 .0040	0.50
$R^2 = 0.06$				

VII. IMPLICATIONS

The rate of growth in domestic output (food grains) should be increased to 2.11 per cent during 2010 from the present level of 1.85 per cent achieved during 1990s. The country has to produce an additional output of 4.72 million tonnes of food grains per year to meet the growing demand in 2010 from the present level of production of 203.04 million tonnes, which was the highest output recorded during 1998-99. Among the food grains, the availability of pulses increased only at the rate of 0.69 per cent per annum, whereas the required of growth was found very high with 6.75 per cent in 2010. The country has to produce an incremental output of pulses at the quantum of 1.37 million tonnes per year to meet the demand in 2010.

Analysis reveals that agricultural investment plays a crucial role for the growth of agriculture. The estimated elasticity proves that any likely changes in agricultural investment, say 10 per cent would induce agricultural output growth more than two per cent. Further, any uncertainty associated with agricultural investment thwart the growth of agricultural sector. In addition, the results indicate that there is a strong negative relationship between incidence of rural poverty and agricultural growth. There is also a decline in employment elasticity. As agriculture forms the dominate source of income of rural households and rural household primarily depend on agriculture for their employment, expansion in employment opportunities is crucial and it may be argued that it is possible only as a result of faster growth of the economy. To make agriculture vibrant and keep the impetus of growth, a sectorial strategy long-term investment is required for galvanizing the potentials of agriculture.

REFERENCES

Ahiuwalia S. Montek (1986), "Rural Povery, Agricultural production and prices: A Reexamination", in Mellor W. John and Desai M. Gunvent (Ed.), *Agricultural change and Rural poverty - Variations on a Theme by Dharm Narain*. (Oxford University Press, New Delhi).

Ahluwalia, MS. (1978), "Rural Poverty and Agricultural Performance in India", *Journal of Development Studies,* Vol 14, No 3, April, pp 298-323.

Antle, J.M. (1983), "Infrastructure and Aggregate Agricultural Productivity: International Evidence', *Economic Development and Cultural Change,* 3, pp. 609-619.

Bardhan K. Pranab (1986), "Poverty and Trickle - Down in Rural India: A Quantitative Analysis", in Mellor W. John and Desai M. Gunvant (Ed.), *Agricultural change and Rural Poverty - Variations on a Theme by Dham Narain.* (Oxford University Press: New Delhi).

Bardhan P.K. (1970), "On the Minimum level of living and the Rural Poor", *Indian Economic Review,* Vol 5. (New series) No 1, April, pp 128-136.

Bardhan, P.K. (1971), "The Incidence of Rural Poverty in the Sixties", *Economic and Political Weekly,* February 1973, reprinted in Bardhan and Srinivasan (eds.).

Bardhan, P.K. (1974), "On the Incidence of Poverty in Rural India in the Sixties", in T.N. Srinivasan and P.K. Bhardhan (Eds.) (1974).

Bhalla, G.S. (1995), "Policy for Food Security in India", in Bhalla G.S. (Ed.) *Economic Liberalisation and Indian Agriculture* (Mcgraw Hill Book Company, New Delhi).

Dandekar, V.M. and Nilakantha Rath (1971), *Poverty in India,* Poona : Indian School of Political Economy, (Originally published in the *Economic and Political Weekly,* Vol 6, Nos 1 and 2, January 2-9, 1971).

Datta Ruddar and Sundharam, K.P.M. (1998), *Indian Economy* (S. Chand and Company Ltd., New Delhi).

Desai M. Gunvant (1986), "Trends in Rural Poverty in India : an Interpretation of Dharm Narain", in Mellor W. John and Desai M. Gunvant (Ed.), *Agricultural Change and Rural Poverty -Variations* on the Theme by Dharm Narain. (Oxford University Press, New Delhi).

Elias, J.V. (1985), *Government Expenditure on Agriculture and Agricultural Growth in Latin America,* Research Report 50, International Food Policy Research Institute, Washington.

Food and Agriculture Organisation of the United Nations (FAO), Conference, Twenty-fourth Session, (1987): Evaluation of the Food Security Assistance Schemes, Rome. c87/8-sup3.

Gaiha Raghav (1985), "Poverty, Technology and Infrastructure in Rural India", *Combridge Journal of Economics,* Vol 9, pp 221-243.

GOI : Agriculture in Brief: Various Issues, New Delhi.

GOI: *Economic Survey,* Various Issues, New Delhi.

GOI : *National Account Statistics,* Various Issues, New Delhi.

Gujarati, D.N. (1995), *Basic Econometrics,* New York: Mc Graw - Hill Book Company.

Hayami, Y and Ruttan, V.M. (1970), "Agricultural Productivity Differences Among Countries", *American Economic Review*, Vol 60, pp 895-911.

Lal, D. (1976), "Agricultural Growth, Real Wages, and the Rural poor in India", *Economic and Political Weekly*, Review of Agriculture, June.

Lim, D. (1983), Government Recurrent Expenditure and Economic Growth in Less Development Countries", *World Development*, Vol. 11, pp 377-380.

Mellor, John, W (1983). *Food Prospects for the Developing Countries*. IPPRI, Reprinted from the *American Economic Review*, Vol. 73, No. 2, May 1983, p. 241.

Minhas, B.S. (1970), "Rural Poverty, Land Redistribution and Development Strategy", *Indian Economic Review*, Vol 5, No 1, April, pp 97-1 28.

Minhas, B.S. (1970), "Rural Poverty, Land Redistribution and Development Strategy", *Indian Economic Review*, 5(1).

Minhas, B.S. (1993), "On Estimating the Inadequacy of Energy Intakes: Revealed Food Consumption Behaviour versus Nutritional Norms (Nutritional Status of Indian People in 1983)", *Journal of Development Studies*, Vol 28, No 1, pp 1-38.

Narain, Dharm (1961), Distribution of the Marketed Surplus of Agriculture produce by Size Level of Holding in India, 1950-57, New Delhi: Asia Publishing House.

Narain, Dhram (1976), "Growth of Productivity in Indian Agriculture", Cornell University. Department of Agricultural Economics, Occasional paper no. 93, published in *Journal of Agricultural Economic* 32 (January-March 1977).

NSSO (50th Round), (1996). Servekshana, October-December.

Papola, T.S. (1992), "The Question of Unemployment", in *The Indian Economy Problems and Prospects* edited by Bimal Jalan, Penguin Books, India.

Planning Commission (1979), *Report of the Expert Group of Estimation of proportion and Number of Poor*. Perspective planning division, Government of India, New Delhi.

Planning Commission (1998), Ninth Five Year Plan (1997-2002).

Radhakrishna, R. (1996), "Food Trends, Public Distribution System and Food Security Concerns," *Indian Journal of Agricultural Economic*, 51 (1 and 2), pp. 168-82.

Radhakrishna, R. and C Ravi (1990). *Food Demand Prolections for India*, Centre for Economic and Social Studies, Hyderabad.

Rao, V.K.R.V. (1977), "Nutritional Norms by Calories Intake and Measurement of Poverty", Bulletin of the International Statistical Institute, Vol 47, Book 4, Contributed papers, pp 553-556.

Rath, Nilakantha (1996), "Poverty in India Revisited", *Indian Journal of Agri cultural Economics,* Vol 51, Nos 1 and 2, January - June, pp 76-108.

Revallion Martin (1998), "Reform, Food Prices and Poverty in India", *Economic and Political Weekly,* January 10, pp 29-36.

Revallion, Martin and Datt Gaurav (1996), "How Important to India's poor is the sectoral Composition of Economic Growth", *The World Bank Economic Review,* Vol. 10, No. 1, pp 1-25.

Roy Sumit (1997), "Globalisation, Structural Change and Poverty—Some Conceptual and Policy Issues, *Economic and Political Weekly,* August 16-23, pp 2117-2135.

Rudra, Ashok (1974), "Minimum Level of Living - A Statistical Examination", in TN. Srinivasan and P.K. Bardhan (Eds.).

Selvaraj, K.N. and Krishnamoorthy, S. (1996), "Changing Structure of Supply of Agricultural Products and Tamil Nadu's Comparative Advantage in Agriculture", report submitted to State Planning Commission, Chennai.

Srinivasan, TN. (1987), "Population and Food", in Gale Johnson, D. and Lee, RD. (Eds.) : *Population and Economic* Development — Issues and Evidence. The University of Wisconson Press, W isconson.

State Planning Commission (1993), 8th Five year plan, 1992-97, Tamil Nadu State Planning Commission, Chennai.

Sukhatme, P.V. (1965), *Feeding India's Growing Millions,* Asia Publishing House, Bombay.

Venkataraman, L.V. (1998), "Population, Poverty, Food Security and Future", *Indian Food Industry,* Vol 17, No 3, pp 145-148.

World Bank (1989), Indian: Poverty, Employment and Social series.

□□□